Cloud-Native Computing

Cloud-Native Computing

How to Design, Develop, and Secure Microservices
and Event-Driven Applications

Pethuru Raj
Reliance Jio Platforms Ltd
Bangalore, India

Skylab Vanga
Hybrid Cloud Architect
Kyndrl Solution Pvt Ltd
Bangalore, India

Akshita Chaudhary
Reliance Jio Platforms Ltd
Mumbai, India

IEEE PRESS

WILEY

Published by John Wiley & Sons, Inc., Hoboken, New Jersey.
Published simultaneously in Canada.

For general information on our other products and services or for technical support, please contact our Customer Care Department within the United States at (800) 762-2974, outside the United States at (317) 572-3993 or fax (317) 572-4002.

Wiley also publishes its books in a variety of electronic formats. Some content that appears in print may not be available in electronic formats. For more information about Wiley products, visit our web site at www.wiley.com.

Library of Congress Cataloging-in-Publication Data
Names: Pethuru Raj, 1968- author. | Skylab Vanga, author. | Akshita Chaudhary, author.
Title: Cloud-native computing: how to design, develop, and secure microservices and event-driven applications / Pethuru Raj Skylab Vanga, Akshita Chaudhary.
Description: Hoboken, New Jersey : Wiley-IEEE Press, [2023] | Includes
    bibliographical references and index.
Identifiers: LCCN 2022017490 (print) | LCCN 2022017491 (ebook) | ISBN
    9781119814764 (cloth) | ISBN 9781119814771 (adobe pdf) | ISBN
    9781119814788 (epub)
Subjects: LCSH: Cloud computing. | Application software–Development.
Classification: LCC QA76.585 .C444 2022 (print) | LCC QA76.585 (ebook) |
    DDC 004.67/82–dc23/eng/20220527
LC record available at https://lccn.loc.gov/2022017490
LC ebook record available at https://lccn.loc.gov/2022017491

Cover Design: Wiley
Cover Image: © da-kuk/Getty

Set in 9.5/12.5pt STIXTwoText by Straive, Pondicherry, India

Contents

About the Authors

Pethuru Raj is a chief architect and vice president at Reliance Jio Platforms Ltd (JPL), Bangalore. Previously, he has worked in IBM Global Cloud Center of Excellence (CoE), Wipro consulting services (WCS), and Robert Bosch Corporate Research (CR). He has more than 22 years of IT industry experience and 8 years of research experience. He has completed his CSIR-sponsored PhD degree at Anna University, Chennai, and has continued with UGC-sponsored postdoctoral research in the Department of Computer Science and Automation, Indian Institute of Science (IISc), Bangalore. Pethuru Raj was granted two international research fellowships (JSPS and JST) to work as a research scientist for three and a half years at two leading Japanese universities.

Pethuru Raj's works focuses on emerging technologies such as the industrial Internet of Things (IoT); artificial intelligence (AI); model optimization techniques; big, fast, and streaming analytics; blockchain; digital twins; cloud-native computing; edge and serverless computing; reliability engineering; microservices architecture (MSA); event-driven architecture (EDA); 5G, among others.

You can see a list of Pethuru Raj's latest books at
https://peterindia.net/MyBooks.html.

Skylab Vanga works as a hybrid cloud architect at Kyndrl Solution Pvt Ltd., Bangalore.

He has had more than 13 years of experience in the IT industry, working on various trending technologies such as Kubernetes, containerization, and big data analytics. Vanga has solid expertise in infrastructure automation for provisioning, compliance, and management of any hyperscale cloud (AWS, Azure, GCP, and IBM Cloud) using Terraform. He has created and published a variety of best practices collaterals and white papers while working at IBM Cloud Center of Excellence, India. Vanga has conducted tutorial sessions on several emerging information technologies and tools for graduate and postgraduate students in engineering colleges in Bangalore. His academic and industry accomplishments are listed on LinkedIn at linkedin.com/in/skylabreddy-vanga-14542018

Akshita Chaudhary has more than four years of experience working in product-based organizations such as Reliance Jio Platforms Ltd. She describes herself as a curious and task-driven software engineering professional, and her education and experience with various innovative projects have taught her the intricacies of the software industry and made her capable of dealing with byzantine problems. Chaudhary's experience includes working with various cloud-native technologies, exploring aspects of machine learning, contributing to microservice-based projects, creating collaterals, and POCs through research-based work. Her creative zeal has helped her develop a penchant toward working with front-end technology. Chaudhary has also made key contributions in the edge-based domain. Her goal is to explore emerging technologies, research, analyze, implement, and spread the word to the world and is glad that she demonstrated the same approach and contributed to this book. Chaudhary looks forward to learning and making a difference in this technological paradigm.

Preface

Undoubtedly the cloud phenomenon is adventuring in the fast track. It all started with server virtualization. Then came a litany of automated tools to simplify and streamline IT environment operations. That is, several complicated tasks such as job/task scheduling, load balancing, workload consolidation, configuration management, capacity planning and provisioning, and resource allocation and monitoring get neatly automated and accelerated through a host of pioneering algorithms, platforms, optimized processes, specialized accelerators, and toolsets. Precisely speaking, the much-touted server virtualization in conjunction with scores of cutting-edge technologies and state-of-the-art tools has laid down a stimulating foundation for the mesmerizing era of cloud computing. The agility, adaptivity, and affordability natively enshrined in cloud environments have led to the grandiose realization of fully virtualized cloud environments. Besides server virtualization, we started to experience storage and network virtualization implementations. This phase is being typically termed as software-defined cloud computing (often referred to as Cloud 2.0). In short, the cloudification concept has resulted in highly optimized and organized IT environments for frequently deploying and efficiently delivering next-generation digital life applications and services. The world is definitely enthralled with a plethora of fresh possibilities and opportunities, which are being instigated by the noteworthy advancements in the cloud IT landscape. The new modernization, migration, hosting, delivery, and operating models articulated and accentuated by the versatile and resilient cloud phenomenon are being pronounced as the way forward for artistically producing and running highly sophisticated digital applications in plenty.

The current buzzword in the IT industry is none other than the paradigm of cloud-native computing, which is all about meticulously leveraging all the distinct capabilities of cloud computing to build and run portable, extensible, available, composable, and reliable applications. Cloud-native technologies and tools have the wherewithal to empower organizations to have scores of service-oriented, event-driven, process-aware, knowledge-filled, cloud-agnostic, and people-centric applications running in modern IT environments such as public, private, hybrid, and edge clouds. Microservices as the agile software design and development technique, containers as an immutable infrastructure and optimal runtime for microservices, container orchestration platforms such as Kubernetes with declarative APIs, API gateways as the aggregator and adaptor in the microservice world, service meshes as resiliency platforms, observability and remediation solutions, and so on greatly exemplify and elevate this new phenomenon of cloud-native computing. Cloud-native architectures and applications are modular (loosely or lightly coupled and cohesive), resilient, robust, observable, and versatile. Combined with a bevy of nimble automation and orchestration tools, the cloud-native concepts allow software engineers to build, operate, and improve highly impactful and inspiring cloud-native systems with minimal toil.

Software applications have become increasingly complicated yet sophisticated with users demanding intimate and orchestrated functionalities and facilities. Numerous third-party applications spread across disparate and distributed cloud environments are being technologically integrated in order to guarantee an integrated and insightful look and feel for users. End users expect rapid responsiveness, intuitive and informative interfaces, innovative features to be consistently incorporated, and zero downtime. Businesses insist for quick accommodation of business and technology changes in software solutions and services. The cloud-native computing paradigm has all in it to empower the software engineering community decisively.

This book is specially planned and prepared to delineate the nitty-gritty of cloud-native computing and how it is to impact the software and hardware engineering precepts in bringing forth connected, composable, and cognitive systems for the ensuing knowledge era.

Chapter 1 – The Dawning of the Digital Era – With the faster maturity and solidity of digitization and digitalization technologies and tools, the dreamt digital era is all set to mesmerize the whole world. There are several path-breaking digitization and edge technologies (sensors, stickers, RFID tags, barcodes, microcontrollers, beacons, LED lights, etc.). These technological innovations and disruptions have solidly and succulently enabled the digitization movement. Thereby today we are being surrounded by so many digital elements, which turn out to be computational, communicative, sensitive, perceptive, vision-enabled, decision-making, responsive, and active. Digital entities have facilitated the mainstream computing in our everyday environments such as homes, hotels, and hospitals. All kinds of physical, mechanical, and electrical systems in our midst are being transitioned into digital assets through the above-mentioned digitization and edge technologies. It is projected that there will be trillions of digital assets in the planet Earth in the years to come. Then came the connectivity technologies. Resultantly digital elements are now being integrated with one another in the neighborhood and with the cloud-hosted software services and databases over the Internet, which is being projected as the world largest communication infrastructure. Such an integration empowers digital assets to gain additional capabilities from remote entities. Digital elements are publicly discoverable and network accessible. Context-aware applications are bound to thrive and will be delivered to humans in an unobtrusive manner. The IoT paradigm typically represents the strategically sound combination of digitization/edge and connectivity technologies.

Chapter 2 – The Cloud-Native Computing Paradigm for the Digital Era – With a series of ground-breaking technologies, the cloud-native computing paradigm is being proclaimed as the futuristic and flexible model for building and deploying highly scalable, available, and reliable applications across cloud environments. The product and tool vendors have come out with a litany of products for elegantly building and releasing cloud-native systems.

Chapter 3 – Kubernetes Architecture, Best Practices, and Patterns – Without an iota of doubt, the Kubernetes (K8s) platform is being touted as the game changer in the IT operations space. The field of software engineering, especially the domain of software deployment, has received a strong boost with the arrival of Kubernetes. The growing IT operational and management complexities are being methodically mitigated through the growing power of Kubernetes. For the increasingly connected and containerized world, Kubernetes is being applauded as the pioneering IT solution that automates and accelerates the application deployment, management, and maintenance of containerized applications. That is, besides auto-scaling, auto-healing of containerized infrastructure modules if anything goes amiss, is being accomplished through Kubernetes. Further on, Kubernetes had laid down an invigorating foundation for visualizing and realizing multi-container composite applications that are process-aware and business-critical. Kubernetes in conjunction with microservices architecture (MSA), containerization, and enterprise DevOps tools has simplified and speeded up the idea of cloud-native computing to flourish across with the nourishment from product and tool vendors.

Chapter 4 – The Observability, Chaos Engineering, and Remediation for Cloud-Native Reliability – Experts reason that cloud-native applications are being designed and developed to be deployed and run in any cloud environment. The widely circulated optimization features of cloud infrastructures are being meticulously used by cloud-native services and application to be distinctive and delightful in their offerings and outputs. As noted in the first chapter, cloud infrastructures have gained some unique characteristics such as elasticity to guarantee workload scalability. Further on, the various DevOps tools built and used for enterprise IT environments are being remedied to achieve the much-wanted continuous integration, delivery, deployment, and improvement in cloud IT environments. Containers have emerged as the most optimal application deployment runtime. There are platform solutions for appropriately managing container life cycle activities. Microservices guarantee agile software design and development. As microservices are the key building-block for cloud-native apps, it is easy to create versatile and resilient cloud-native applications through configuration changes and service composition.

Chapter 5 – Creating Kubernetes Clusters on Private Cloud (VMware vSphere) – This is purely a practical chapter. All the details regarding setting up a Kubernetes cluster on VMware vSphere cloud environment are given in this chapter. This is for explaining how a Kubernetes-managed private cloud environment can be established and sustained.

Chapter 6 – Creating Kubernetes Clusters on Public Cloud (Microsoft Azure) – In this chapter, we are tutoring about creating Kubernetes clusters on a public cloud. Here we have chosen Microsoft Azure Cloud, one of the market leaders in the cloud space.

Chapter 7 – Design, Development, and Deployment of Event-Driven Microservices Practically – This chapter is for articulating the powerful features of the two dominant application architectures: MSA and event-driven architecture (EDA). How these two architectural patterns connect and contribute in constructing cloud-native applications is explained in this chapter. How event-driven microservices can be built and containerized to be deployed, managed, and maintained through a Kubernetes platform is also detailed in this chapter. The code snippets of microservices are being provided in this chapter in order to rekindle the interests of our esteemed readers in cloud-native programming. We have shown a couple of microservices developed using different programming languages and frameworks. The idea here is to showcase how the often repeated vendor lock-in issue gets eliminated through the leverage of MSA best practices. With event-driven microservices, the importance of synchronous and asynchronous communications is described in this chapter for the benefit of our readers.

Chapter 8 – Serverless Computing for the Cloud-Native Era – Cloud computing is all about building, releasing, and running applications through cloud platforms and infrastructures. With the recently ordained serverless capability, application developers need not indulge in server setup and sustenance. Instead server operations and management are being handled by cloud providers through the seamless assistance of a serverless platform solution. This phenomenon describes a next-generation deployment model where software applications, which are typically bundled as a collection of fine-grained functions, are uploaded to a standardized serverless platform. Most of the established public cloud service providers host such a platform to deliver serverless computing services. There are many open-source and commercial-grade serverless-enablement platforms. The serverless platform takes care of everything. That is, functions and applications are automatically called, executed, scaled, and exactly billed in response to users' requests.

Chapter 9 – Installing Knative on a Kubernetes Cluster – We have discussed about the significance of serverless computing for the cloud-native era. This is a practical chapter demonstrating how serverless applications can be quickly built, deployed, and managed in Kubernetes clusters. How the Knative framework comes in handy in accelerating serverless application development and deployment on Kubernetes.

Chapter 10 – Delineating Cloud-Native Edge Computing – With the advent of the 5G and the Internet of Things (IoT) era, the number of connected devices is bound to rapidly grow. This means that the centralized data storage and processing popularized by the traditional cloud computing model can no longer meet the demands of massive amount of multi-structured data getting sourced from heterogeneous IoT sensors, devices, and systems. That is, the conventional cloud model does not guarantee real-time data capture, storage, analytics, decision-making, and actuation. To cope up with this grandiose vision, experts have recommended that the much-celebrated cloud capability must be systematically realized through edge devices and their clusters/clouds to lessen the load on centralized cloud centers. Off course, there are several operational difficulties being associated with edge computing. Device mobility and management, resource and task scheduling, service delivery, resiliency, device operations, integration, orchestration, and security are being touted as the prime challenges of establishing and sustaining edge device clouds. In this chapter, we are to focus on applying the proven and potential cloud-native design principles on edge devices. Edge devices and their clouds are being presented and prescribed as the new service deployment, execution, and delivery platforms.

Chapter 11 – Setting Up a Kubernetes Cluster Using Azure Kubernetes Service – AKS is a managed Kubernetes service that lets you quickly create and manage clusters. With AKS, you can quickly create a production-ready Kubernetes cluster. It enables deploying and managing containerized applications. AKS offers serverless Kubernetes, an integrated continuous integration and continuous delivery (CI/CD) experience, and enterprise-grade security and governance. It also unites development and operations teams on a single platform to rapidly build, deliver, and scale applications with all the confidence. AKS has several features that are attractive for users of Microsoft Azure and provides the ability to easily create, maintain, scale, and monitor AKS cluster. This is a practical chapter illustrating how Microsoft AKS facilitates setting up and sustaining Kubernetes clusters in Azure Cloud environments.

Chapter 12 – Reliable Cloud-Native Applications Through Service Mesh – There is a hugely beneficial convergence between containers and microservices. This distinctive linkage brings forth several strategic advantages for worldwide businesses in accomplishing more with less. Containers are being positioned as the most appropriate packaging and runtime mechanism for microservices and their redundant instances. Subsequently microservices are meticulously containerized, curated, and stocked in publicly available container image repositories. Now with the widespread acceptance of Kubernetes as a promising and potential container clustering and orchestration platform, setting up and sustaining Kubernetes-managed containerized cloud environments are being speeded up across in order to avail all the originally expressed benefits of the idea of containerization. Containers are being deployed, monitored, managed, and empowered through the various automation and acceleration capabilities of the Kubernetes platform. Kubernetes does a lot of things in operationalizing containers. In addition, there are a few DevOps toolsets and techniques emerging and evolving fast to enable frequent and accelerated software deployment in production environments. With containerized services in large numbers even in a reasonably sized cloud environments, service communication must be specially taken care in order to succulently enhance the service resiliency. Service mesh is a framework for ensuring service communication resiliency. In this chapter, we are to focus on how cloud-native applications are adroitly empowered by service mesh to be reliable in their operations, and outputs.

Chapter 13 – Cloud-Native Computing: The Security Challenges and the Solution Approaches – Experts and experienced hands have brought in a series of best practices for ensuring unbreakable and impenetrable security for cloud-native systems. This chapter lists out the security implications and solutions.

Chapter 14 – Microservices Security – This chapter is added in this book in order to tell the significance of producing and maintaining secure microservices in order to ensure secure cloud-native software. The chapter focuses on explaining specific security attacks on microservices and how they can be surmounted through security best practices

Chapter 15 – Setting Up Apache Kafka Clusters in a Cloud Environment and Secure Monitoring – Kubernetes is emerging as the one-stop IT solution for deploying and delivering cloud-native applications. This is a practical chapter explaining how to install, monitor, and secure Apache Kafka on a Kubernetes cluster. As Kafka is being pitched as the most powerful messaging broker for producing message-driven, service-oriented, mission-critical, and cloud-hosted applications, this chapter is relevant to our readers.

Pethuru Raj PhD
Chief Architect and Vice President
Reliance Jio Platforms Ltd.
Bangalore, India

https://www.peterindia.net/Digital.html
https://www.linkedin.com/in/sweetypeter/

Acknowledgments

I (Pethuru Raj Chelliah) express my sincere gratitude to Aileen Storry and Kimberly Monroe-Hill at Wiley for immeasurably helping us from the conceptualization to the completion of this book. I wholeheartedly acknowledge the contributions of my colleagues, Skylab Vanga and Akshita Chaudhary.

I also wish to acknowledge my supervisors, Professor Ponnammal Natarajan, Anna University, Chennai; Professor Priti Shankar (late), Computer Science & Automation (CSA) Department, Indian Institute of Science (IISc), Bangalore; Professor Naohiro Ishii, Department of Intelligence and Computer Science, Nagoya Institute of Technology; and Professor Kazuo Iwama, School of Informatics, Kyoto University, for shaping my research life. I express my heartfelt gratitude to managers, Anish Shah and Kiran Thomas, President, Chief Operating Officer, Reliance Jio Platforms Ltd, India.

I reflect on the selfless sacrifices made by my parents in shaping up me to this level. I would expressly like to thank my wife (Sweetlin Reena) and sons (Darren Samuel and Darresh Bernie) for their perseverance as I have taken the tremendous and tedious challenge of putting this book together. Above all, I give all the glory and honor to my Lord and Savior Jesus Christ for His abundant grace and guidance.

1

The Dawning of the Digital Era

THE OBJECTIVES

This chapter discusses the following:

1) The Trendsetting Technologies and Tools for the Digital Era
2) Why Digitization Is Indispensable
3) The Connectivity and Integration Options
4) About Digitally Transformed Systems, Networks, and Environments
5) The Promising Digital Intelligence Methods
6) The Cloud-Native Principles Are Essential for Producing and Delivering Breakthrough Applications for the Impending Digital Era

---

Demystifying the Digitization Paradigm

With the faster maturity and solidity of digitization and digitalization technologies and tools, the dreamt digital era is all set to mesmerize the whole world. There are several path-breaking digitization and edge technologies (sensors, stickers, RFID tags, barcodes, microcontrollers, beacons, LED lights, etc.). These technological innovations and disruptions have solidly and succulently enabled the digitization movement. Thereby, today we are being surrounded by so many digital elements, which turn out to be computational, communicative, sensitive, perceptive, vision-enabled, decision-making, responsive, and active. Digital entities have facilitated mainstream computing in our everyday environments such as homes, hotels, and hospitals. All kinds of physical, mechanical, and electrical systems in our midst are being transitioned into digital assets through the above-mentioned digitization and edge technologies. It is projected that there will be trillions of digital assets on planet earth in the years to come. Then came the connectivity technologies. Resultantly digital elements are now being integrated with one another in the neighborhood and also with the cloud-hosted software services and databases over the Internet, which is being projected as the world's largest communication infrastructure. Such integration empowers digital assets to gain additional capabilities. Digital elements are publicly discoverable and network-accessible. Further on, remote monitoring, measurement, and management of digital elements are made possible. Multi-device applications, which are process-aware, business-critical, and people-centric will flourish with the proper nourishment. Digital assets become self-, surrounding- and situation-aware. Context-aware applications are bound to thrive and will be delivered to humans in an unobtrusive manner. The IoT paradigm represents the combination of digitization/edge and connectivity technologies.

Cloud-native Computing: How to Design, Develop, and Secure Microservices and Event-Driven Applications, First Edition. Pethuru Raj, Skylab Vanga, and Akshita Chaudhary.
© 2023 The Institute of Electrical and Electronics Engineers, Inc. Published 2023 by John Wiley & Sons, Inc.

Further on, the device ecosystem is growing fast. Today we are bombarded with a dazzling array of slim and sleek, handy and trendy devices, which are increasingly multifaceted and versatile. We have medical instruments, defense equipment, appliances, machineries, kitchen utilities, consumer electronics, personal gadgets and gizmos, handhelds, wearables, implantables, portables, etc., in large quantities. Robots, digital assistants with speech recognition capability, drones, and other edge devices are found in our everyday environments. These devices are also integrated with cloud-based applications. Worldwide market watchers, researchers, and analysts have estimated that there will be billions of connected devices. Interestingly, we have billions of smartphones connected to the Internet. These empowered digital entities and connected devices are being termed the Internet of Things (IoT) sensors and devices, respectively. Typically, IoT sensors are resource-constrained whereas IoT devices are resource-intensive. IoT sensors are for capturing operational aspects of digital assets. In addition, IoT sensors capture environment data in which digital assets are situated. IoT devices have more memory and storage capacities and processing capability, thereby they can participate and contribute to data processing individually and collectively.

IoT devices will naturally interact with human beings also with the emergence of human–machine interfaces (HMIs). Devices will get the power to find and interact with others in the vicinity to accomplish better and bigger things for people. Through digitization and connectivity technologies, every common and casual thing in our personal, professional, and social environments becomes digitized and connected. Ordinary things become extraordinary in providing enhanced services. Dumb things become animated. Precisely speaking, everything becomes smart, every device becomes smarter, and every man becomes the smartest. A variety of automation, augmentation, and acceleration will happen with the skilled usage of the distinct advancements in the IoT space.

Delineating the Digitalization Technologies

We have discussed digitization and edge technologies in the previous section. Also, with the local as well as remote connectivity technologies, how the IoT paradigm is promising a lot for the world is deliberated. It is no exaggeration to state that the human race is to benefit immensely through the hugely potential IoT idea. The IoT phenomenon is to ultimately result in the digital era, which is going to be software-defined. In this section, we are to focus on digitalization technologies and how they are going to shape the digital world. When digitization and digitalization technologies converge seamlessly and spontaneously, there is a possibility for an explosion of hitherto unheard software applications and industry use cases. Newer IT products, solutions and services will emerge and evolve fast to tackle existing and emerging people's problems, societal challenges, and business expectations. Fresh use cases will be unearthed and articulated through technological innovations. The real digital transformation will happen and hence business and people transformations are to see the grandiose reality.

With digitized objects (interchangeably referred to as IoT sensors and devices) abound in our living environments and workplaces, they collaborate, correlate, and corroborate, resulting in a massive amount of multi-structured data. For the digital transformation goals to be realized, the basic tenet is to transition digit data into information and knowledge. Digitalization technologies play a very vital role. There are digitalization technologies and tools for performing data capture, cleansing, preprocessing, storage, processing, analytics, and visualization tasks. That is, the process of transitioning data to information and knowledge is highly optimized. There is a bevy of automated tools fully complying with various digitalization technologies. Thus, the goal of translating data to knowledge gets speeded up and simplified through the adroit usage of digitalization technologies. Here is a list of prominent digitalization technologies:

1) Artificial intelligence (AI) algorithms, frameworks, accelerators, and libraries
2) Big, fast, and streaming data analytics methods and platforms
3) Software-defined cloud infrastructures
4) Digital twins
5) Cybersecurity
6) Cloud-native computing
7) Edge computing
8) Serverless computing
9) Microservices architecture (MSA)
10) Event-driven architecture (EDA)
11) Blockchain technology
12) 5G communication

These technologies come in handy for extracting actionable insights into time out of voluminous data. The knowledge discovered gets disseminated to the concerned systems and people in a time in order to empower them to ponder about the next course of action. This set of cutting-edge technologies is seen as the key contributor and prime method for realizing intelligent business workloads and IT services. Digitized elements and connected devices are also being made intelligent in their actions and reactions through knowledge discovery technologies. Thus, data and learning from data are seen as two crucial enablers for the ensuing intelligent era. Connected assets are bountifully liable for probing and manipulation. With the pervasive Internet communication infrastructure, remote attacks through networks are getting accelerated. Thus, for the digital era to really shine, cyberterrorism activities must be eliminated through competent security technologies and tools. Thus, the field of cybersecurity [1] is gaining prominence these days.

Trendsetting Technologies for the Digital Era

We have discussed both digitization and digitalization technologies. They are together called digital technologies. One of the most visible and value-adding trends in IT is nonetheless the digitization aspect. All kinds of concrete items in our personal, professional, and social environments are being digitized through digitization technologies to be communicative, sensitive, perceptive, and responsive. These days, due to the unprecedented maturity and stability of a host of path-breaking technologies such as miniaturization, sensing, actuation, connectivity, and intermediation technologies, every tangible thing in our environments has grasped the inherent power of finding and binding with one another in its vicinity as well as with remote objects via networks purposefully and on need basis to uninhibitedly share their distinct capabilities toward the goal of providing deeper automation. With such an accumulation of digitized entities in and around us, human beings are all set to become the smartest in their deals, decisions, and deeds. In this section, the most prevalent and pioneering trends and transitions in the IT landscape will be discussed. Especially, the digitization technologies and techniques are given a sufficient push.

As widely reported, there are several delectable transitions in the IT landscape. The consequences are definitely vast and varied. First, it is the incorporation of nimbler and next-generation features and functionalities into the existing IT solutions. Second, the eruption of altogether new IT products and solutions for humanity. These have the intrinsic capabilities to bring forth numerous subtle and succinct transformations for businesses as well as people.

IT Consumerization: There are much-discoursed and deliberated reports detailing the diversity and availability of mobile devices (smartphones, tablets, digital assistants, wearables, drones, robots, etc.) and their management platforms. Today we have millions of mobile apps. This trend is ultimately empowering people in their daily works and walks. The ubiquitous information access is made possible. Further on, the IT infrastructures are being tweaked accordingly in order to gracefully support this strategically sound movement. There are some challenges for IT administrators in fulfilling the device explosion. That is, IT is steadily becoming an inescapable part of consumers directly and indirectly. And the need for robust and resilient device management software with the powerful emergence of "bring your own device (BYOD)" paradigm is being felt and is being insisted across. With smartphones emerging as the most pervasive input and output tools for everyone across the world, there is a myriad of development platforms, cross-compilers, programming and markup languages, enabling frameworks, tools, and lightweight operating systems in the fast-moving mobile space. Precisely speaking, IT is not only for businesses but also for every human being. 5G communication [2] capabilities come in handy in ubiquitous and mobile access to digital applications and services

IT Commoditization: This is another cool trend penetrating the IT industry. Due to the sudden surge of big data analytics (BDA) requirements, there is a demand for large-scale computing and storage. Instead of using expensive hyperconverged infrastructures (HCIs) (alternative referred to as appliances), there is a movement toward leveraging commodity server machines and their clusters. HCIs are basically beset by a high total cost of ownership (TCO) and less return on investment (ROI).

This is in line with the goal of IT optimization. The IT resource utilization has been on the lower side, and there came a series of technologies to bring in highly optimized and organized IT. Such an optimization process is to bring down IT cost sharply. This is the crux of the cloud computing paradigm. This is a new kind of consolidated, centralized, automated, and shared computing model. Virtualization and containerization concepts emerged and evolved fast in order to fulfil the much-touted optimization goal. With these compartmentalization technologies (explained later), the IT resource utilization efficiency is going up steadily. These impactful techniques have penetrated every IT module including networking, security, and storage components.

The intelligence embedded in IT hardware elements is being abstracted and centralized through hypervisor software solutions. Hardware systems are thus software-enabled to be easily manipulated and programmed. With this transition, all the hardware resources in any data center can be easily updated, upgraded, replaced, substituted, and composed for quickly fulfilling different requirements and use cases. Commoditized IT solutions are relatively cheap and hence the IT affordability target is realized along with a number of other advantages. That is, the future IT data centers and server farms are going to be stuffed with a number of commodity servers, storages, and network solutions.

IT Compartmentalization (Virtualization and Containerization): The "divide and conquer" method has been the most versatile and rewarding mantra in the IT field. Abstraction is another powerful and established technique in the IT space. The widely used virtualization, which had laid a stimulating and sustainable foundation for the raging cloud idea, is actually hardware virtualization. The virtualization has penetrated into storage appliances, network components and security solutions. That is, entire data centers are methodically virtualized. There are a few serious drawbacks with virtualization.

Then came the aspect of containerization being represented through the popular Docker platform. Containerization is the operating system (OS)-level virtualization. Containers are lightweight and hence attain the native performance of the physical machines. The real-time horizontal scalability is being facilitated by the concept of containerization. Containerization has surmounted many of the limitations of virtualization. Containerization is enabling the originally expressed goals of cloud computing.

IT Industrialization: The cloud idea has laid down a stellar foundation for IT industrialization. Consolidating, virtualizing, and/or containerizing and centralizing all kinds of IT systems, putting them on-premises and/or off-premises, operating them in a shared and automated fashion, delivering them in an online and on-demand manner, continuously adding newer capabilities by bringing forth fresh technologies and tools, etc., lead toward industrialized IT.

IT Digitization and Distribution: As explained in the beginning, digitization has been an ongoing process and it has quickly generated and garnered a lot of market and mind shares. Digitally enabling everything around us induces a dazzling array of cascading and captivating effects in the form of cognitive and comprehensive transformations for businesses as well as people. With the growing maturity and affordability of scores of edge technologies, every common thing in our personal, social, and professional environments is becoming digitized.

Similarly, the distribution aspect too gains more ground. Due to its significant advantages in crafting and sustaining a variety of large-scale business applications, the distributed computing phenomenon has become popular. Distributed applications, though weighed down by security implications, are good for fulfilling various nonfunctional requirements (NFRs) such as availability, scalability, modifiability, and accessibility. Lately, there is a bevy of software architectures, frameworks, patterns, practices, and platforms for realizing distributed applications. With blockchain grabbing the attention of many, decentralization is picking up for producing decentralized applications.

Why Digitization Is Indispensable

Ultimately, all kinds of perceptible objects in our everyday environments will be empowered to be remotely identifiable, reachable, readable, recognizable, addressable, and controllable. Such profound empowerment will bring forth real transformations for the total human society, especially in establishing and sustaining smarter environments, such as smarter homes, buildings, hospitals, classrooms, offices, and cities. Suppose a man-made or natural disaster occurs. If everything in the disaster area is digitized, then it becomes possible to rapidly determine what exactly has happened, the intensity of the disaster, and the hidden risks in the affected environment. Any worthwhile information extracted provides a way to properly plan and proceed insightfully, reveals the extent of the destruction, and conveys the correct situation of the people therein. The knowledge gained would enable the rescue and emergency team leaders to cognitively contemplate appropriate decisions and plunge into actions straightaway to rescue as much as possible, thereby minimizing damages and losses to properties and people.

In short, digitization will substantially enhance our decision-making capability in our personal as well as professional lives. Digitization also means that the ways we learn and teach are change profoundly, energy usage will become knowledge-driven so that green goals can be met more smoothly, and the security and safety of noble things will go up considerably. As digitization becomes pervasive, our living, relaxing, working, eating, and socializing places will be filled up with a variety of electronics including environment-monitoring sensors, actuators, disappearing controllers, projectors, cameras, appliances, high-definition IP TVs, and robots. In addition, items such as furniture and packages will become empowered by attaching state-of-the-art LEDs, beacons, infinitesimal sensors, specialized electronics, and communication modules. Whenever we walk into such kinds of enlightened environments, the devices we carry and even our e-clothes will enter into a collaboration mode to form wireless and ad hoc networks with the digitized objects in that environment. For example, if someone wants to print a document from his smartphone or tablet, and he enters a room where a printer is installed, the smartphone will automatically begin a conversation with the printer, check its competencies and compatibilities, and send the documents to be printed. The smartphone will then alert the owner about the neat and nice accomplishment.

Digitization will also provide enhanced care, comfort, choice, and convenience. Next-generation healthcare services will demand deeply connected and cognitive solutions. For example, ambient assisted living (AAL) is a new prospective application domain where lonely, aged, diseased, bedridden, and debilitated people living at home will receive a remote diagnosis, care, and management by medical doctors, nurses, and other caregivers who remotely monitor patients' health and physiological parameters.

People can track the progress of their fitness routines. Taking decisions becomes an easy and timely affair with the prevalence and participation of connected solutions that benefit knowledge workers immensely. All the secondary and peripheral needs will be accomplished in an unobtrusive manner so that people nonchalantly focus on their primary activities. However, there are some areas of digitization that need some attention. One is the goal of energy efficiency. Green solutions and practices are being insisted upon everywhere these days, and IT is one of the principal culprits in wasting a lot of precious energy due to the pervasiveness of commoditized IT servers and connected devices. Data centers armed with a large number of server machines, storage appliances, and networking solutions are bound to consume a lot of electricity and dissipate more heat into the fragile environment. So, green IT has become a hot subject for deeper study and research across the globe. Another prime area of interest is remote monitoring, management, and enhancement of empowered devices. With the number of devices in our everyday environments growing at an unprecedented scale, their real-time administration, configuration, activation, monitoring, management, patching, and repair (if any problem arises) can be eased considerably with effective remote connection and correction competencies.

Deeper Connectivity: The connectivity trait has risen dramatically. The network topologies and technologies are consistently expanding and empowering their participants and constituents to be highly productive. There are unified, ambient, and autonomic communication technologies emanating from worldwide research organizations and labs. These transitions draw the attention of executives and decision-makers in a bigger way. All kinds of digitized elements are intrinsically empowered to form ad hoc networks for accomplishing specialized tasks in a simpler and smarter manner. There are a variety of network and security solutions in the form of load balancers, switches, routers, gateways, proxies, firewalls, etc., and these are nowadays available as hardware and software appliances.

Device Middleware or Device Service Bus (DSB) is the latest buzzword enabling seamless and spontaneous connectivity and integration between disparate and distributed devices. That is, device-to-device (in other words, machine-to-machine [M2M]) communication is the talk of the town. The interconnectivity-facilitated interactions among diverse categories of devices precisely portend a litany of supple, smart, and sophisticated applications for people. Due to the multiplicity and heterogeneity of devices, the device complexity is to rise further. Device middleware solutions are being solicited in order to substantially enable devices to talk to one another in the vicinity and with remote ones through appropriate networking.

Software-Defined Networking (SDN) is the latest technological trend captivating professionals to have a renewed focus on this emerging yet compelling concept. With clouds being strengthened as the core, converged and central IT infrastructure, the scenarios for device-to-cloud interactions are fast-materializing. This local, as well as remote connectivity, empowers ordinary articles to become extraordinary objects by distinctively communicative, collaborative, and cognitive.

Another associate topic is **virtual network functions (VNFs)**. With containerization, we are tending toward **cloud-native network functions (CNFs)**. Network capabilities and resources are being shrewdly used to achieve more with less. Network slicing is seen as a paradigm shift. Newer network functionalities are being realized through CNFs. That is, network functions are developed as microservices [3] and they are containerized. With the leverage of container orchestration platform solutions such as Kubernetes, CNFs are portrayed as the way forward for communication service providers to be proactive in offering premium services to their clients and consumers. With such network segmentation/partition, network resource usage productivity goes up significantly. Thus, networks are being readied through versatile technological solutions to be adaptive in order to succulently support smart systems and environments.

Service Enablement: Physical devices at the ground level are being seriously service-enabled in order to uninhibitedly join in the mainstream computing tasks. That is, devices, individually and collectively, could become service providers or publishers, brokers and boosters, and consumers. The prevailing and pulsating idea is that any service-enabled device in a physical environment could interoperate with others in the vicinity as well as with remote devices and applications. Services could abstract and expose only the specific capabilities of devices through service interfaces while service implementations are hidden from user agents. Such a smart separation enables any requesting device to see only the capabilities of target devices, and then connect, access, and leverage those capabilities to achieve business or people services. The service enablement completely eliminates all dependencies so that devices could interact with one another flawlessly and flexibly. Further on, application interoperability gets accomplished through the widely adopted service-enablement facet. Ultimately, the majority of next-generation, enterprise-scale, mission-critical, process-centric, and multi-purpose applications are being assembled out of multiple discrete and complex services.

The Future Internet: As digitization gains more accolades and success, all sorts of everyday objects are being connected with one another as well as with scores of applications running in cloud environments. That is, everything is becoming a data supplier for the next-generation applications, thereby becoming an indispensable ingredient individually as well as collectively in consciously conceptualizing and concretizing smarter applications. There are several promising implementation technologies, standards, platforms, and tools enabling the realization of the IoT vision. The probable outputs of the IoT field are a cornucopia of smarter environments such as smarter offices, homes, hospitals, retail stores, cities, etc. Cyber-physical systems (CPSs), ambient intelligence (AmI), ubiquitous computing (UC), and pervasive and sentient computing are some of the related concepts encompassing the ideals of IoT.

In the upcoming era, computers, communication modules, and multifaceted sensors will be facilitating the right decision-making. Computers of different sizes, looks, capabilities, and interfaces will be fitted, glued, implanted, and inserted everywhere to be coordinative, calculative, consistent, and coherent in their actions. The interpretation and involvement of humans in operationalizing these sophisticated and sentient objects are almost zero. With autonomic IT infrastructures, more intensive and insightful automation and orchestration are bound to happen. Devices collectively will also handle all kinds of everyday needs. Drones will be pervasive and humanized robots extensively will get used in order to fulfil our daily physical chores.

On summarizing, the Internet is fast expanding. Manufacturing machines, medical instruments, defense equipment, home appliances, everyday devices, specialized robots and drones, kitchen utensils, consumer electronics, infinitesimal sensors, etc., will be linked up with the Internet in order to get more people-centric use cases. With the addition of billions of electronic devices and trillions of digitized items, the future Internet is going to be humongous and complex.

Tending Toward the Trillions of IoT Devices: The table below [4] lists the prominent and dominant IoT technologies for realizing IoT devices and applications.

---

1) The realization technologies are maturing (miniaturization, instrumentation, connectivity, remote programmability/service-enablement/APIs, sensing, vision, perception, analysis, knowledge-engineering, decision-enablement, etc.)
2) A flurry of edge technologies (sensors, stickers, specks, smart dust, codes, chips, controllers, LEDs, tags, actuators, etc.)
3) Ultra-high bandwidth communication technologies (wired as well as wireless [4G, 5G, etc.])
4) Low-cost, power, and range communication standards (LoRa, LoRaWAN, NB-IoT, 802.11x Wi-Fi, Bluetooth Smart, ZigBee, Thread, NFC, 6LowPAN, Sigfox, Neul, etc.)
5) Powerful network topologies, Internet gateways, integration and orchestration frameworks, and transport protocols (MQTT, UPnP, CoAP, XMPP, REST, OPC, etc.) for communicating data and event messages
6) A variety of IoT application enablement platforms (AEPs) with application building, deployment and delivery, data and process integration, application performance management, security, orchestration, and messaging capabilities
7) Event processing and streaming engines for event message capture, ingestion, processing, etc.
8) A bevy of IoT data analytics platforms for extracting timely and actionable insights out of IoT data
9) Edge/fog analytics through edge clouds
10) IoT gateways, platforms, middleware solutions, databases, and applications on cloud environments

---

Source: Modified from [4].

Envisioning Millions of Software Services: With the accelerated adoption of MSA and EDA, enterprise-scale applications are being expressed and exposed as a dynamic collection of fine-grained, self-contained, loosely coupled, network-accessible, publicly discoverable, API-enabled, composable, and lightweight services. Not only business applications and IT services but also embedded applications are increasingly built as a collection of microservices. As reported earlier, all kinds of devices express their functionalities as services. Thus, the number of device services is going to grow rapidly. That is, hardware resources are being software-defined in order to incorporate the much-needed flexibility, maneuverability, and extensibility. This arrangement of preparing event-driven microservices and composing them to arrive at relevant applications is all set to lay down a stimulating and sustainable foundation for producing next-generation software applications out of distributed microservices. The emergence of the scintillating concepts such as Docker containers, container orchestration platforms, and DevOps is to lead the realization of cloud-native applications in conjunction with the MSA and EDA [5] patterns.

The disruptions and transformations brought in by the series of delectable advancements are really mesmerizing. IT has touched every small or big entity decisively in order to produce context-aware, service-oriented, event-driven, knowledge-filled, people-centric, and cloud-hosted applications. Data-driven insights and insights-driven enterprises are indisputably the new normal.

Infrastructure Optimization: The entire IT stack has been going for a makeover periodically. Especially on the infrastructure front, due to the closed, inflexible, and monolithic nature of conventional IT infrastructures, there are concerted efforts being undertaken by many in order to untangle them into modular, open, extensible, converged, and programmable infrastructures. Another worrying factor is the underutilization of expensive IT infrastructures (servers, storages, and networking solutions). With IT becoming ubiquitous for automating most of the tasks across industry verticals, the problem of IT sprawl has gone up considerably and they are mostly underutilized and sometimes even unutilized for a long time. Having understood the wastage issue pertaining to IT infrastructures, the concerned have plunged into unveiling versatile and venerable measures for enhanced utilization and infrastructure optimization. Infrastructure rationalization and simplification are related activities. That is, next-generation IT infrastructures are being realized through consolidation, centralization, federation, virtualization, containerization, automation, and sharing. To bring in more flexibility, software-defined infrastructures are being proclaimed and prescribed these days.

With the faster spread of BDA platforms and applications, commodity hardware is being insisted for big data storage and processing. That is, we need low-cost and power infrastructures with supercomputing capability and virtually infinite storage. The answer is that all kinds of underutilized servers are collected and clustered together to form a dynamic and huge pool of server machines to efficiently tackle the increasing and intermittent needs of computation. Precisely speaking, clouds are the highly optimized and organized infrastructures that fully comply with the evolving expectations elegantly and economically. The cloud technology, though not a new one, represents a cool and compact convergence of several proven technologies to create a spellbound impact on both business and IT. Clouds emerge as the one-stop IT solution for all kinds of business modernization requirements. Cloudification represents the virtual IT era. As there is a tighter coupling between the physical and cyber worlds, the distinct contributions of the cloud paradigm are definitely vast and varied.

The tried and tested technique of "divide and conquer" in software engineering is steadily percolating to hardware engineering. Decomposition of physical machines into a collection of sizable and manageable virtual machines/containers for enhanced resource utilization and on the other hand, these segregated virtual machines can be aggregated to create virtual supercomputers. The extreme elasticity, extensibility, scalability, availability, adaptability, and agility of the cloud idea are good signs for the future of IT.

Finally, software-defined cloud centers see the light with the faster maturity and stability of a number of implementation technologies. To attain the originally envisaged goals, researchers are proposing to incorporate software wherever needed in order to bring in the desired separations and sophistication so that a significantly higher utilization level can be reached. When the utilization rate goes up, the cost is bound to come down. In short, the longstanding target of infrastructure programmability can be met with the embedding of intelligent software so that the infrastructure manageability, serviceability, and sustainability tasks become easier and more economical.

Data Analytics: With the amount of digital data getting generated every day projected to be in the range of exabytes, it is important for any corporate to collect, cleanse, and crunch the data in order to be digitally transformed in its strategy-making, planning and execution. We cannot afford to lose any data anymore. All kinds of internal as well as external data have to be meticulously gathered and processed in order to extricate actionable insights out of data heaps. Machine, device, sensor, actuator, business, social, operational, transactional and analytical data have to be consciously gleaned and subjected to a variety of deeper investigations to uncover useful and usable insights out of growing data volumes. Data are predominantly multi-structured. Also, data are categorized as big, fast and streaming data. Batch processing of big data has been the norm thus far. With technological advancements, big data also can be processed and mined quickly. That is, real-time analytics of big data is made possible. Further on, we have fast and streaming data and they are analyzed in time as the timeliness and trustworthiness of data are essential to take correct decisions. Data typically lose their value with time. Thus, real-time analytics becomes dominant and deftly handled.

As we all know, the big data paradigm is opening up a fresh set of opportunities for businesses. The key challenge in front of businesses is how to efficiently and rapidly capture, process, analyze, and extract tactical, operational as well as strategic insights in time to act swiftly and sagaciously with all the confidence and clarity. In the recent past, there are experiments using the emerging concept of in-memory computing. For a faster generation of insights out of a massive amount of multi-structured data, new entrants such as in-memory and in-database analytics are highly reviewed and recommended. The new mechanism insists on putting all incoming data in memory instead of storing it in local or remote databases so that the major barrier of data latency gets eliminated.

Big Data Analytics (BDA): The big data paradigm has become a big topic across nearly every business domain. IDC defines big data computing as a set of new-generation technologies and architectures, designed to economically extract value from very large volumes of a wide variety of data by enabling high-velocity capture, discovery, and/or analysis. There are three core components in big data: the data itself, the analytics of the data captured and consolidated, and the articulation of insights oozing out of data analytics processes. There are robust products and services that can be wrapped around one or all of these big data elements. Thus, there is a direct connectivity and correlation between the digital universe and the big data idea sweeping the entire business scene. The vast majority of new data being generated as a result of digitization is unstructured or semi-structured. This means there is a need arising to somehow characterize or tag such kinds of multi-structured big data to be useful and usable. This empowerment through additional characterization or tagging results in metadata, which is one of the fastest-growing subsegments of the digital universe though metadata itself is a minuscule part of the digital universe. IDC believes that by 2022, a third of the data in the digital universe will have big data value, only if it is tagged and analyzed. There will be routine, repetitive, redundant data and hence not all data is necessarily useful for BDA. However, there are some specific data types that are princely ripe for big analysis such as:

Surveillance Footage: Generic metadata (date, time, location, etc.) is automatically attached to video files. However, as IP cameras continue to proliferate, there is a greater opportunity to embed more intelligence into the camera on the edges so that footage can be captured, analyzed, and tagged in real time. This type of tagging can expedite crime investigations for security insights, enhance retail analytics for consumer traffic patterns and, of course, improve military intelligence as videos from drones across multiple geographies are compared for pattern correlations, crowd emergence, and response or measuring the effectiveness of counterinsurgency.

Embedded and Medical Devices: In future, sensors of all types including those that may be implanted into the body will capture vital and non-vital biometrics, track medicine effectiveness, correlate bodily activity with health, monitor potential outbreaks of viruses, etc., all in real time, thereby realizing automated healthcare with prediction and precaution.

Entertainment and social media: Trends based on crowds or massive groups of individuals can be a great source of big data to help bring to market the "next big thing," help pick winners and losers in the stock market, and even predict the outcome of elections all based on information that users freely publish through social outlets.

Consumer Images: We say a lot about ourselves when we post pictures of ourselves or our families or friends. A picture used to be worth a thousand words but the advent of big data has introduced a significant multiplier. The key will be the introduction of sophisticated tagging algorithms that can analyze images either in real time when pictures are taken or uploaded or en masse after they are aggregated from various websites.

Data empowers Consumers: Besides organizations, digital data helps individuals navigate the maze of modern life. As life becomes increasingly complex and intertwined, digital data will simplify the tasks of decision-making and actuation. The growing uncertainty in the world economy over the last few years has shifted many risk management responsibilities from institutions to individuals. In addition to this increase in personal responsibility, other pertinent issues such as life insurance, healthcare, retirement, etc., are growing evermore intricate increasing the number of difficult decisions we all make very frequently. The data-driven insights come in handy in difficult situations for consumers to wriggle out. Digital data, hence, is the foundation and fountain of the knowledge society.

Power Shifts to the Data-Driven Consumers: Data is an asset for all. Organizations are sagacious and successful in promptly bringing out the premium and people-centric offerings by extracting operational and strategically sound intelligence out of accumulated business, market, social, and people data. There is a gamut of advancements in data analytics in the form of unified platforms and optimized algorithms for efficient data analysis. There are plenty of data virtualization and visualization technologies. These give customers enough confidence and ever-greater access to pricing information, service records and specifics on business behavior and performance. With the new-generation data analytics being performed easily and economically in cloud platforms and transmitted to smartphones, the success of any enterprise or endeavor solely rests with knowledge-empowered consumers.

Consumers Delegate Tasks to Digital Concierges: We have been using a myriad of digital assistants (digital assistants, smartphones, wearables, etc.) for a variety of purposes in our daily life. These electronics are of great help in crafting applications and services. Data-driven smart applications will enable these new-generation digital concierges to be expertly tuned to help us in many things in our daily life.

Source: andrew_rybalko/Adobe Stock.

As articulated above, there are integrated platforms and databases for performing real-time analytics on big data. Timeliness is an important factor for information to be beneficially leveraged. The appliances and HCIs are in general high-performing, thus guaranteeing higher throughput in all they do. Here too, considering the need for real-time emission of insights, several product vendors have taken the route of software as well as hardware appliances for substantially accelerating the speed with which the next-generation BDA get accomplished. A sample of how cloud-based data analytics contributes to establishing and sustaining smarter homes is depicted in the following diagram.

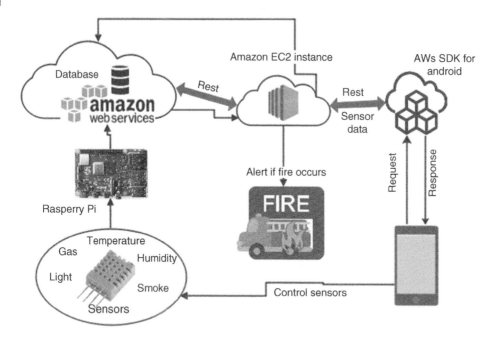

In the business intelligence (BI) domain, apart from realizing real-time insights, analytical processes and platforms are being tuned to bring forth insights that invariably predict something to happen for businesses in the near future. All these advancements enable executives and other stakeholders to proactively and pre-emptively formulate well-defined schemes and action plans, fresh policies, new product offerings, premium services, and viable and value-added solutions based on data-driven insights. Prescriptive analytics, on the other hand, is to assist business executives in prescribing and formulating ways and means of achieving what is predicted.

IBM has introduced a new computing paradigm "stream computing" in order to capture streaming and event data on the fly and to come out with usable and reusable patterns, hidden associations, tips, alerts and notifications, impending opportunities as well as threats, etc., in time for executives and decision-makers to contemplate appropriate countermeasures. The table below clearly tells why cloud centers are efficient and effective for doing IoT data analytics.

- **Agility and Affordability:** No capital investment in large-size infrastructures for analytical workloads. Just use and pay. Quickly provisioned and decommissioned once the need goes down.
- **Data Analytics Platforms in Clouds:** Therefore, leveraging cloud-enabled and ready platforms (generic or specific, open or commercial-grade, etc.) is fast and easy.
- **NoSQL and NewSQL Databases and Data Warehouses in Clouds:** All kinds of database management systems and data warehouses in cloud speed up the process of next-generation data analytics. Database as a service (DaaS), data warehouse as a service (DWaaS), business process as a service (BPaaS) and other advancements lead to the rapid realization of analytics as a service (AaaS).
- **WAN Optimization Technologies:** There are WAN optimization products for quickly transmitting large quantities of data over the Internet infrastructure.
- **Social and Professional Networking Sites** are running in public cloud environments
- **Enterprise-Class Applications in Clouds:** All kinds of customer-facing applications are cloud-enabled and deployed in highly optimized and organized cloud environments.

- **Anytime, Anywhere, Any Network and Any Device Information and Service Access** is being activated through cloud-based deployment and delivery.
- **Cloud Integrators, Brokers, and Orchestrators:** There are products and platforms for seamless interoperability among geographically distributed cloud environments. There are collaborative efforts toward federated clouds and the Intercloud.
- **Sensor/Device-to-Cloud Integration Frameworks** are available to transmit ground-level data to cloud storage and processing.

Artificial Intelligence (AI): There are other noteworthy developments in the enigmatic IT space. We discussed big data comprising both historical and current data. All kinds of deterministic and diagnostic analytics are being realized through big and real-time data analytics platforms. There are techniques and tips galore for extracting useful information out of big data in time.

With machine and deep learning (ML/DL) algorithms (a part of the AI discipline), we are heading toward the era of prognostic, predictive, prescriptive, and personalized insights out of big data. Clustered computers in conjunction with pioneering ML and DL algorithms can pierce through data heaps to bring forth something useful for people. Primarily, prediction and prescription become a new normal. The domain of computer vision gets a strong boost with the general availability of DL algorithms. Similarly, the natural language processing (NLP) discipline is gaining a lot of attention these days due to the path-breaking DL algorithms. With the explosion of IoT data, the various improvisations in the AI space are to come in handy in unambiguously understanding, continuously learning, expertly reasoning out, and proposing new thesis. Thus, building and deploying cognitive systems and services become easier with the convergence of IoT and AI concepts. AI algorithms are capable of doing real-time analytics on all kinds of data emanating from different and distributed sources. The growing maturity of the AI domain and the faster proliferation of connected devices in our everyday places have laid down a sustainable foundation for smarter systems, networks, and environments.

Edge/Fog Computing: As accentuated before, there are plenty of resource-constrained devices in our environments. Similarly, we are being bombarded with resource-intensive devices in our personal, social, and professional locations. The brewing trend is that clustering different resource-intensive devices to form a kind of cloud for acquiring multi-structured data from resource-constrained devices in that environment. Thereafter, processing the collected and cleansed data in order to take quick and correct decisions is becoming the new normal. Here come various valid reasons why data analytics of device data has to be accomplished through edge/fog device clouds:

- **Volume and Velocity:** Ingesting, processing, and storing such huge amounts of data which is gathered in real time.
- **Security:** Devices can be located in sensitive environments, control vital systems or send private data. With the number of devices and the fact they are not humans who can simply type a password, new paradigms, strict authentication, and access control must be implemented.
- **Bandwidth:** If devices constantly send the sensor and video data, it will hog the Internet and cost a fortune. Therefore, edge analytics approaches must be deployed to achieve scale and lower response time.
- **Real-Time Data Capture, Storage, Processing, Analytics, Knowledge Discovery, Decision-making, and Actuation**
- **Less Latency and Faster Response**
- **Context-Awareness Capability**

- **Combining Real-Time Data with Historical State:** There are analytics solutions which handle batches quite well and some tools that can process streams without historical context. It is quite challenging to analyze streams and combine them with historical data in real time.
- **Power Consumption:** Cloud computing is energy-hungry and it is a concern for a low-carbon economy.
- **Data Obesity:** In a traditional cloud approach, a huge amount of untreated data is pumped blindly into the cloud that is supposed to have magical algorithms written by data scientists. This vision is really not the best efficient and it is much wiser to pretreat data at a local level and to limit the cloud processes to a strict minimum.

Thus, edge computing and analytics through edge device clouds are flourishing with burgeoning industrial and people-centric use cases.

There are continuous improvisations and innovations in the technology space. Newer technologies open up fresh possibilities and opportunities for businesses as well as people to embark on deeper and decisive automation. The following diagram pictorially illustrates how devices talking to one another and also with remotely held cloud applications can lead to the realization of numerous sophisticated services.

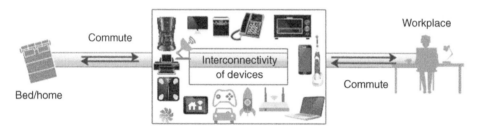

The Connectivity and Integration Options

It is forecast that there will be a dazzling array of devices in large numbers and zillions of digitized objects in the years ahead. They ought to be seamlessly and spontaneously connected and integrated in order to voluntarily share their unique capabilities with others in order to fulfill complex processes. Here is a gist of integration scenarios.

- Multi-Sensor Fusion: Heterogeneous, multifaceted, and distributed sensors talk to one another to create sensor mesh to solve complicated problems.
- Sensor-to-Cloud (S2C) Integration: CPSs will emerge at the intersection of the physical and virtual/cyber worlds.
- Device-to-Device (D2D) Integration: With the device ecosystem on the rise, the D2D integration is important.
- Device-to-Enterprise (D2E) Integration: In order to have remote and real-time monitoring, management, repair, and maintenance, and to enable decision-support and expert systems, ground-level heterogeneous devices have to be synchronized with control-level enterprise packages such as Enterprise Resource Planning (ERP), Supply Chain Management (SCM), Customer Relationship Management (CRM), and Knowledge Management (KM).
- Device-to-Cloud (D2C) Integration: As most of the enterprise systems are moving to clouds, the device-to-cloud (D2C) connectivity is gaining importance.

- Cloud-to-Cloud (C2C) Integration: Disparate, distributed, and decentralized clouds are getting connected to provide better prospects.
- Mobile Edge Computing (MEC) [6], Cloudlets, and Edge Cloud Formation through the clustering of heterogeneous edge/fog devices.

The Big Picture: With the cloud space growing fast as the next-generation environment for application design, development, deployment, integration, management, and delivery, the integration scenario is being visualized as pictorially illustrated in the next diagram.

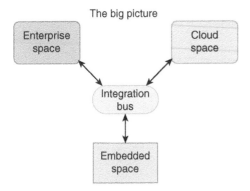

The Promising Digital Intelligence Methods

We are heading toward the era of zettabytes of digital data. Now it becomes mandatory to apply potential intelligence methods to make sense out of the exponentially growing data. There are new databases, file systems, platforms, algorithms, analytics methods, dashboards, other visualization solutions, message queues, event sources, streams, etc., for quickly and easily squeezing out actionable insights. The following list enumerates the key contributors:

1) Analytics methods of digital data (big, fast, and streaming data) for diagnostic and deterministic insights.
2) Machine and deep learning algorithms toward predictive, prescriptive, and personalized insights.
3) There are powerful data storage solutions such as SQL, NoSQL, and NewSQL databases, data warehouses, and lakes for digital data analytics.
4) There are in-memory databases for real-time analytics and actuation.
5) There are data virtualization and knowledge visualization tools, platforms, dashboards, etc.
6) There are data processing and analytics platforms (Spark, Storm, Samza, Flink, etc.) in cloud environments.
7) There are event stores such as Kafka for processing and stocking millions of event messages per second.
8) There are machine and deep learning platforms, frameworks, and libraries for accelerating and automating analytics (cognitive analytics).
9) Fog or edge data analytics is gaining speed with a number of lightweight platform solutions capable of running on fog/edge device clouds.

Here is a macro-level diagram depicting how applications across industry verticals systematically make use of data emanating from multiple sources to be smarter in their actions and reactions. Data analytics platforms and machine learning toolkits on cloud infrastructures contribute enormously to capturing, cleansing, and crunching data to discover and disseminate knowledge. Applications and actuating systems, on getting appropriate insights, exhibit a kind of adaptive and adroit behavior in their delivery. With the process of moving from data to information and knowledge maturing fast along with the implementation technologies, data-driven insights, and insights-driven decisions will become the new normal for every institution, individual, and innovator.

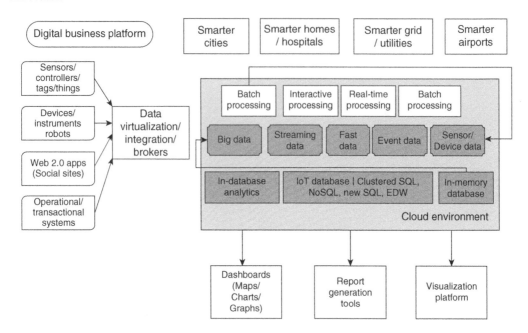

Thus, there are three game changers. Collecting every bit of data, deriving actionable insights out of data volumes, and using the knowledge discovered in a timely and appropriate manner are being touted as the prime factors toward the projected knowledge society.

The Technological Approaches Toward Smarter Environments

Our environments are slowly yet steadily stuffed with IoT devices. Any IoT environment typically comprises scores of networked, resource-constrained as well as intensive and embedded systems. However, IoT artifacts are not individually intelligent. The charter is to make them intelligent individually as well as collectively. Experts have come out with a number of steps to be taken to have intelligent IoT devices. When we have intelligent IoT devices, the environment altogether is bound to be intelligent. All the occupants and owners of the environment will get a variety of people-centric, situation-aware, and knowledge-filled services. People will be hugely assisted by IoT devices in their everyday tasks. Multiple devices gel well in order to bring forth context-aware, insight-driven, and sophisticated services. As digitized entities and connected devices are being continuously empowered by remotely held software packages, data sources, event streams, and knowledge repositories, we can easily anticipate new categories of ground-breaking use cases and applications. In this section, we are to list the prominent and widely accepted ways for empowering our physical, mechanical, electrical, and electronics systems to be cognitive.

1) The **Internet of Agents (IoA)** for empowering each digital object to be adaptive, articulate, reactive, and cognitive through mapping a software agent for each of the participating digital objects.
2) Through realizing **Digital Services** (every digital object and connected device is expressed and exposed as a service) and through service orchestration and choreography, business-critical, process-optimized, and situation-aware digital applications can be crafted instantaneously and enhanced accordingly.
3) The emerging concept of **Digital Twin/Virtual Object Representation** is also maturing and stabilizing fast. Many industrial sectors are keenly evaluating and embracing this new paradigm.
4) With the excellent platform support, the proven and potential **IoT Data Analytics at Edge and Cloud Levels** is the way forward for knowledge discovery and dissemination.
5) The application of **Artificial Intelligence (AI)** technologies (data mining, statistical computing, machine and deep learning algorithms, computer vision, NLP, video processing, etc.) leads to the realization of smarter systems, services, and solutions.
6) The new concepts of **Decentralized Applications** and **Smart Contracts** being popularized through the blockbuster blockchain technology lead to scores of smart and safe applications.

Thus, the connectivity facility being provided by the IoT concept, the cognition capability through the AI algorithms, and the security features being realized through the application of the blockchain technology are being pronounced as the key technological paradigms for the future of IT and the society. With intelligent environments abound around us, we will get a number of noteworthy and trustworthy services. We will tend toward the digital universe, which brings in a growing array of premium and pioneering competencies for everyone.

Briefing the Brewing Idea of Digital Twin

All kinds of devices in our everyday environments are gradually getting integrated with cyber applications deployed in cloud environments to reap distinct benefits. That is, every physical, mechanical, electrical, or electronic system is being accordingly empowered in order to establish and sustain a seamless and spontaneous integration with faraway cloud applications. This technologically inspired linkage brings in a lot of fresh advantages. For example, manufacturing companies tie their machines on the manufacturing floor with one another as well as with enterprise-scale cloud-hosted applications such as SAP, the leading ERP solution, in order to automate several aspects. We call such enabled systems CPSs. This is becoming common nowadays. The phenomena of the IoD and the IoT came around and started to flourish.

Now there is a twist. Increasingly a virtual/logical/digital/cyber version [7] of any physical machine is being created and deposited in cloud environments to be made available online and in an on-demand fashion. The digital version is blessed with all the features and functionalities of the physical machine. With the cloud idea becoming a core technology, its adoption rate has multiplied in the recent past. There are software-defined and even edge clouds being formed with the latest technologies and tools in order to host and manage cyber applications. Due to their affordability, agility, and availability, the digital versions of physical entities are being made and kept in cloud environments. The physical and digital versions are integrated in order to be constantly in touch to communicate the real-time and runtime data of physical machines.

Besides digital versions, all kinds of historical data, enterprise-class applications, integrated data analytics platforms, machine and deep learning algorithms, etc., are being stocked in distributed cloud environments. Thus, comprehensive analytics is easily accomplished. The data flowing from physical machines into their virtual versions enables real-time data analytics. Such a linkage enables architects, product engineers, and original equipment manufacturers (OEMs) in multiple ways. Before producing a machine physically, all its risks and opportunities can be identified and analyzed fully. How the various system components interact, what are the possible implications, etc., can be proactively and pre-emptively understood, and this knowledge helps designers come out with competent solutions. Such a scenario is going to be a game changer for multiple industry verticals.

Envisioning the Digital Universe

The digitization process has gripped the whole world today as never before and its impacts and the associated initiatives are being widely talked about. With an increasing variety of input and output (I/O) devices and newer data sources, the realm of data generation has gone up remarkably. It is forecasted that there will be billions of everyday devices getting connected, capable of generating an enormous amount of data assets, which need to be processed. It is clear that the envisaged digital world is to result in a huge amount of bankable data. This growing data richness, diversity, velocity, viscosity, virtuosity, value, and reach decisively activated business organizations and national governments. Thus, there is a fast spreading of newer terminologies such as digital enterprises and the economy. Now it is fascinating the whole world and this new world order has tellingly woken up worldwide professionals and professors to formulate and firm up flexible and futuristic strategies toward digitally transformed business, hotels, retail stores, healthcare, agriculture, manufacturing, etc. There are product vendors, service organizations, research labs, independent software vendors (ISVs), system integrators, consulting companies, etc., are formulating viable technologies, tools, platforms, and infrastructures to tackle this colossal yet cognitive challenge head-on. Also, cloud service providers are setting up software-defined compute, networking, and storage facilities. Newer types of databases, distributed file systems, data warehouses, data lakes, etc., are being realized to stock up the growing volume of business, personal, machine, people, and online data. These data storage solutions ultimately enable specific types of data processing, mining, and analyzing the data getting collected. This pivotal phenomenon has become a clear reason for envisioning the digital universe.

There will be a litany of hitherto unforeseen applications being built and deployed to empower people to experience the digital universe in which all kinds of data producers, middleware, and preprocessing systems, transactional and operational databases, analytical systems, virtualization and visualization tools, and software applications will be meaningfully connected with one another. Especially, there is a series of renowned and radical transformations in the sensor space. Nanotechnology and other miniaturization technologies have brought legendary changes in sensor design. The nano-sensors can be used to detect vibrations, motion, sound, color, light, humidity, chemical composition and many other characteristics of their deployed environments. These sensors can revolutionize the search for new oil reservoirs, structural integrity for buildings and bridges, merchandise tracking and authentication, food and water safety, energy use and optimization, healthcare monitoring and cost savings, and climate and environmental monitoring. The point to be noted here is the volume of real-time data being emitted by the army of sensors and actuators is exponentially growing and with the help of real-time analytics platforms and algorithms, real-time insights get squeezed out and supplied to actuating devices and people to ponder about and execute right countermeasures in time.

The steady growth of sensor networks increases the need for one million times more storage and processing power by 2020. It is projected that there will be one trillion sensors by 2025 and every single person will be assisted by approximately 150 sensors on this planet. Cisco has predicted that there will be 50 billion connected devices in 2020 and hence the days of the Internet of Everything (IoE) are not too far off. All these scary statistics convey one thing. That is, IT applications, services, platforms, and infrastructures need to be substantially and smartly invigorated to meet up all sorts of business and peoples' needs in the ensuing era of deepened digitization.

Precisely speaking, the data volume is going to be humongous as the digitization prospect is growing deep and wide. The resulting digitization-induced digital universe and economy will, therefore, be at war with the amount of data being collected and analyzed. The data complexity through the data heterogeneity and multiplicity will be a real challenge and concern for enterprise IT teams. That is, as accentuated earlier, the real-time analytics of big data is to lead to a series of disruptions and transformations.

Cloud-Native Applications (CNAs)

Thus far, we have discussed various transformative developments in the IT space, digital data, processes, services, applications, platforms, analytics, and environments [8]. Especially with the surging popularity of MSA, Kubernetes-managed containerized cloud environments, DevOps toolkits, and reliability engineering frameworks, producing and improving highly scalable and continuously available, portable, interoperable, extensible, and easily manageable applications are hugely simplified. Also, with these advancements, the aspect of accelerated software engineering sees the reality. The goal of cloud-agnostic application engineering and execution is also facilitated here. Such futuristic and flexible applications are termed cloud-native applications, which can run on private clouds locally as well as on public clouds remotely. Also, with the widespread focus on setting up edge device clouds, cloud-native services and applications can run on edge devices without any twist or tweak. We have allocated a special chapter on the title "Cloud-native Edge Computing" in this book. Also, a separate chapter for exquisitely explaining the distinct characteristics of cloud-native applications is incorporated in this book in order to clearly convey the nuances and nitty-gritty of cloud-native computing.

Conclusion

Digital transformation is the buzzword these days. It is believed that real digital transformation results in the much-needed business transformation. Customer experience is to go up. There will be fresh avenues to be explored to raise revenues. The enterprise assets' productivity is bound to rise. Premium offerings can be realized and delivered quickly. Business sentiments, technology changes, and users' expectations can be swiftly accommodated. Data-driven insights and insights-driven decisions and actions will become the new normal. Deeper and decisive automation can be accomplished through the participation of digital decisions. Real-time digital life applications can be built and released through edge computing. Digital data acquires special significance in the digital era. There will be a mix and match of digital and physical worlds. Context-aware physical services will be delivered to people in need. Thus, the possibilities and opportunities are literally limitless when digital data gets methodically converted into digital intelligence in association with state-of-the-art digital technologies, platforms, and infrastructures. The emergence of cloud-native computing is seen as a grand stimulator for the ensuing digital era.

References

1 What is cybersecurity? https://www.cisco.com/c/en_in/products/security/what-is-cybersecurity.html.

2 Everything you need to know about 5G. https://www.qualcomm.com/5g/what-is-5g

3 Describing the microservices architecture style. https://docs.microsoft.com/en-us/azure/architecture/guide/architecture-styles/microservices.

4 Top 10 Digital Transformation Technologies for 2021. https://mindsterdx.com/blog/digital-transformation-technologies/

5 What is an event-driven architecture? – Decoupled systems that run in response to events. https://aws.amazon.com/event-driven-architecture/

6 What is edge computing? https://www.redhat.com/en/topics/edge-computing/what-is-edge-computing

7 How does a digital twin work? https://www.ibm.com/topics/what-is-a-digital-twin

8 What is cloud native and what are cloud native applications? https://tanzu.vmware.com/cloud-native.

2

The Cloud-Native Computing Paradigm for the Digital Era

THE OBJECTIVES

This chapter focuses on the following topics:

1) The Maturity of Software-defined Cloud Environments
2) The Significance of Serverless Computing
3) The Hybrid Model of Microservices Architecture (MSA) and Event-driven Architecture (EDA)
4) The Aspect of Containerization
5) The Emergence of Container Lifecycle Management Platforms
6) The Twelve Factors for Cloud-Native Applications
7) Cloud-Native Systems: The Critical Design Considerations
8) Demystifying the Cloud-Native Architecture Style

Introduction

Cloud-native technologies and tools have the wherewithal to empower organizations to build and run highly scalable, extensible, and reliable applications in modern IT environments such as public, private, hybrid, and edge clouds. Microservices, containers as immutable infrastructure, orchestration platforms with declarative APIs, API gateways, service meshes as resiliency platforms, and observability solutions greatly exemplify this new phenomenon of cloud-native computing. These promising and potential technologies enable modular (loosely coupled and cohesive) systems that are resilient, versatile, mission-critical, and observable. Combined with robust automation and orchestration tools, the cloud-native concepts allow software engineers to make highly impactful cloud-native systems with minimal toil.

Software applications have become increasingly complicated yet sophisticated with users demanding more functionalities and facilities. Scores of third-party applications and cloud environments are being integrated in order to guarantee an integrated and insightful look and feel for users. End-users expect rapid responsiveness, intuitive and informative interfaces, innovative features consistently incorporated, and zero downtime. Business and technology changes have to be easily and quickly accommodated in software solutions and services to give a modern look. Cloud-native computing is all about intrinsically achieving agility, adaptivity, and affordability. In this chapter, we are to see how various technological advancements gel well in producing state-of-the-art software solutions.

Cloud-native Computing: How to Design, Develop, and Secure Microservices and Event-Driven Applications, First Edition. Pethuru Raj, Skylab Vanga, and Akshita Chaudhary.
© 2023 The Institute of Electrical and Electronics Engineers, Inc. Published 2023 by John Wiley & Sons, Inc.

The Onset of the Digital Era

There are path-breaking digital technologies and tools emerging to fulfil the digital transformation needs across industry verticals, governments, organizations, and institutions. Every tangible thing in our everyday environments is getting methodically digitized through the application of digitization technologies. And when these digitized entities interact with one another, there is a tremendous amount of digital data gets generated. As widely reported, data has become the new oil or fuel for business transformation. Data is being termed as a strategic asset for any organization to plan ahead. The decision-makers, executives and stakeholders leverage digital data to steer any organization in the right direction to the desired destination. The power of digital technologies comes in handy in transitioning digital data to information and knowledge. We need data capture, integration, virtualization, ingestion, wrangling, masking, pre-processing, storage, analytics, and visualization capabilities. These are being fulfilled through a bevy of digital technologies and tools. We have listed here the prominent digital technologies for the benefit of our esteemed readers.

The Explosion of Digital Technologies: We are being bombarded with digitized entities, connected devices, and microservices. A massive amount of multi-structured digital data gets produced. Now the faster adoption of digital technologies makes sense out of digital data. That is, the process of transitioning raw data into information and into knowledge is being automated through a host of pioneering digital technologies, which we have discussed in the previous chapter.

Thus, the digitization technologies represented by the Internet of Things (IoT) and the earlier mentioned digitalization technologies are destined to establish and sustain a digital living. There are chapters and books explaining the nitty-gritty of each of the digital technologies and how they individually and collectively help in extracting actionable insights out of digital data. That is, the digital intelligence (DI) capability is gaining momentum in order to produce intelligent software systems and services. Business workloads and IT services are being empowered to be adaptively pre-emptive through DI methods. Not only software systems but also our personal and professional devices are being adequately empowered to be cognitive in their actions and reactions. Software-defined cloud infrastructures and platforms are running DI and transformation applications. Thus, cloud infrastructures and platforms in association with other powerful digital technologies and tools contribute to deriving actionable intelligence out of digital data heaps.

The Fructification of Digital Entities: As per the leading market watchers and analysts, there will be trillions of digitized entities, billions of connected devices, and millions of microservices in the years to come. With the faster maturity and stability of path-breaking miniaturization technologies, we have state-of-the-art micro- and nanoelectronics products flourishing everywhere. Further on, there are competent digitization and edge technologies including LED lights, beacons, stickers, tags, codes, chips, controllers, specks, etc. The other important technologies are disappearing sensors and actuators, which are plentifully and purposefully occupying most of our everyday environments these days. Sensors and actuators are also known as "Implantable." By applying these technologies, all kinds of commonly found and cheap things in our living, relaxing, and working spaces are entitled to become smart objects. In other words, ordinary items in our daily places become extraordinary. Any dumb and tangible/concrete object is bound to become animated and sentient material through the smart application of the previously mentioned edge and digitization technologies. In other words, proven and potential edge technologies are being attached or embodied on ordinary and casual items to make them digitized.

Such strategically sound technological paradigms are capable of transforming ordinary things into digitized items. What is the result of all these enablements? All sorts of physical, mechanical, electrical, and electronic systems in our buildings, retail stores, healthcare facilities, war zones, manufacturing floors, entertainment plazas, eating joints, railway stations, air and sea ports, auditoriums, sports stadiums, microgrids, nuclear establishments, shopping malls, etc., are being fruitfully digitized with much care and clarity. It is therefore indisputably correct to state that the digitization movement is at full speed. Our shirts become e-shirts, our doors, cots, windows, chairs, tables, wardrobes, kettles, wares, utilities, utensils, etc., will become smart through the formal attachment of digitization and edge technologies. Especially multifaceted sensors and actuators play a very vital role in shaping up the digital world and living. Everything becomes digitized.

Already all our computers (laptops, tablets, desktops, and server machines) are integrated with the Internet communication infrastructure in order to access web content and services. These days our communicators (smartphones) are web-enabled in order to fulfil anytime, anywhere, any network, any device access of web content and services. Additionally, sensors-attached physical, mechanical, electrical, and electronics are hooked into the Web in order to be remotely empowered. Such empowerment makes our everyday devices and machines to be ready for contributing copiously to the realization of digital societies. Thus, physical devices are set to become digital devices, which are intrinsically revitalized to perform edge computing. Digital elements are called edge devices.

The Proliferation of Connected Devices: We talked about ordinary things getting transformed into digital elements through a few pioneering technologies. Now come to the device world. With the fast-growing device ecosystem, we are being bombarded with a variety of slim and sleek, handy and trendy, resource-constrained and intensive, purpose-specific and agnostic, multimedia, multimodal, and multifaceted devices. There is a growing array of handhelds, mobiles, portables, wearables, nomadic, and fixed devices. Further on, we have consumer electronics, medical instruments, home appliances, communication gateways, robots, drones, cameras, game consoles, machineries, equipment, medical instruments, single board computers (SBCs), programmable logic controllers (PLCs), SCADAs, etc., yearning to be digitized and connected to attain all the originally expressed benefits. It is forecast that there will be billions of such higher-end devices soon. With the surging popularity of the IoT paradigm, every digitized entity and device is solemnly readied to be Web-enabled. Now with the overwhelming adoption of the cloud idea, every device in and around us is ordained to be cloud-enabled. In other words, every electronics is slated to be connected. The number of connected devices is expected to be in billions soon. Device-to-device (D2D) and device-to-cloud (D2C) integration experimentations and scenarios are gaining momentum due to the steady growth of several implementation technologies.

Precisely speaking, digitized entities and connected devices are stuffing and saturating our everyday environments (personal, social, and professional). For enabling context-awareness and multi-device computing applications, the new connected era beckons and dawns upon us. These technologically enabled devices are typically called edge or fog devices because they are at the edge of the network. They are very near to us. We can see, touch, and feel them. For example, the point of sale (PoS) devices in a retail store is an edge device, cameras in our homes, hotels, and hospitals are edge devices, robots in a happening place such as a surgery room inside a hospital is an edge device, the list goes on and on.

Now comes the twist. Edge devices generally generate a lot of data every hour. That is, they collect a lot of useful and usable data about themselves, their environments, owners, users, etc. Edge devices collect operational, log, health condition, performance, and security data. Edge devices are touted as the primary data collectors of the various temporal, special, and behavioral aspects. That is, edge devices plus empowered systems (systems empowered by edge devices) individually and collectively throw a lot of data on their capabilities, capacities, states, change of states, etc. Compared to digital elements, connected devices are computationally powerful. Thus, digital elements are primarily data generators and transmitters. However, connected devices are capable of receiving and processing any amount of digital data in real time.

The Continued Adoption of Cloud Applications, Services, Platforms, Middleware, and Data Sources: We have discussed edge devices and their explosion. At one end, we have zillions of digitized entities being made out of physical elements. The second category in the hierarchy is scores of versatile electronics devices capable of capturing, storing, processing, and mining digital data emitted by exponentially growing digitized entities. Now, at the top of the spectrum is none other than cloud assets and applications. Real-time data analytics is being accomplished through electronics devices. Data collection happens through digitized entities at the lower end. Increasingly, electronics devices (alternatively termed as edge or fog devices) support in-device AI processing. That is, lightweight AI toolkits are deployed on edge devices to subject digital data to a variety of deeper and real-time investigations in order to extract real-time insights that can be looped back to decision-making systems and people to initiate the process of pondering about the next course of actions with all the clarity and confidence.

In cloud environments (private, public, or hybrid), historical and comprehensive data analytics through integrated data analytics platforms and AI frameworks is being done. Thus, the role of cloud infrastructures and platforms in this increasingly data-engulfed world cannot be undermined. Especially, big data analytics through batch processing can be comfortably done in traditional cloud environments.

The Arrival of Edge Clouds: Considering the need for real-time insights and applications for establishing and sustaining intelligent enterprises, industry houses are setting up miniaturized cloud environments in their offices and campuses. Telecommunication service providers are using their base stations to have a small-scale cloud center to ensure a real-time customer experience.

Especially, with edge devices becoming powerful, edge device clusters/clouds are being formed in a dynamic and ad hoc manner to perform specific tasks. With the forecast of billions of connected devices, there will be a bigger focus on forming and using edge device clouds in order to build and release location-specific, context-aware, and real-time applications. Thus, there will be a combination of traditional and modern cloud centers in visualizing and realizing next-generation business and people-proclivity applications in the years ahead. With devices contributing their unique capabilities, the scope and sophistication of software applications will be deeper, deft, and decisive.

Thus, we have discussed all that are together putting a stimulating foundation for the digital era. In the subsequent sections, we are to discuss how the fledgling cloud-native paradigm is going to be the breakthrough phenomenon for creating and running digital life applications.

The Maturity of Software-defined Cloud Environments

The mesmerizing journey of cloud computing is as follows. It all started with the virtualization of physical machines in traditional data centers. Then, besides hypervisors, there came a number of advanced tools for automating a variety of data center operations. Precisely speaking, virtualization has increased resource utilization. That is, virtualization has led to IT optimization. Scores of automated tools have then resulted in the optimal operation of virtualized resources. This combination of technologically enabled IT optimization and organization has led to the grand realization of cloud environments. This is annotated as Cloud 1.0.

In other words, enterprise IT is predominantly turned and tuned into cloud IT. Software-defined cloud infrastructures (Cloud 2.0) are showing a lot of potential and promise in being positioned as the one-stop IT solution for all kinds of personal, social, and professional requirements. Not only server machines but also storage and network solutions too are fully virtualized. There came new terms such as server, storage, and network virtualization. Such a disaggregation has a number of business and technical advantages. Besides extensibility, manageability, and affordability, every hardware and software ingredient of cloud environments is virtualized. That is, every noteworthy module in a cloud center is software-defined.

Software-defined clouds are extremely supple and service-oriented in hosting, running, and delivering highly scalable, reliable, and flexible software systems. Cloud infrastructures support infrastructure elasticity, which, in turn, leads to application scalability. With many cloud centers around cities, countries, and continents, the feature of high availability (HA) of applications is being ensured. Resource redundancy is strengthening the availability aspect. Ubiquitous access to content, information, and services is being facilitated by cloud centers. Clouds are consolidated, centralized or federated, automated, shared, and secured. Because of automation and sharing, clouds fulfil affordability, application agility, and adaptivity. Cloud infrastructures have emerged as the highly optimized and organized IT infrastructure for delivering enterprise-scale microservice-centric applications. With software-defined clouds, all the originally expressed benefits of cloud computing can be obtained with ease.

The Significance of Serverless Computing: The cloud journey is on. A number of improvisations are being unearthed and articulated. Automations in cloud software engineering, deployment, and management are being initiated and implemented. In this section, we dig deeper and describe the distinctions of serverless computing and how it is going to be an enabler of cloud-native computing. Serverless computing is all about delivering backend IT infrastructure services in an on-demand manner with the fine-grained pay-per-usage model. A serverless service provider allows developers to write, deploy, and run code without bothering about setting up and sustaining the underlying IT infrastructure. Based on the user load, automatically additional resources will be allocated to run the code comfortably. Physical and virtual machines (VMs) and containers can be used as the computational resource. The infrastructure provisioning, configuration, scaling, patching, and management are being taken care of by the serverless service provider. The amount of computation accomplished is the basis for accurately calculating the financial obligations. Thus, serverless means all the responsibilities associated with server infrastructure setup, scalability, billing, and management are delegated to serverless providers so that application developers just focus on coding advanced business capabilities.

Entering into Function as a Service (FaaS): Generally, application development is generally split into two realms. The frontend is the part of the application that users see and interact with, such as the visual layout. The backend is the part that the user does not see. This includes the web/application server where the application's files live and the database server where data management logic is persisted. Most serverless providers offer database and storage services to their customers. This is called backend as a service (BaaS).

There is a new cloud service called function as a service (FaaS). This is a type of cloud service that enables executing code in response to events without worrying about setting up the corresponding IT infrastructure. Previously, for microservices applications, enterprise, and cloud IT operations teams have to toil hard to set up appropriate infrastructure to run microservices.

FaaS vs. Serverless: FaaS is actually a subset of serverless. Serverless can be used for any service category: compute, storage, database, messaging, API gateways, etc., where configuration, management, and billing of servers are invisible to the end user. FaaS is focused on the event-driven computing paradigm wherein application code (containers) gets executed in response to events or requests. FaaS is emerging as a valuable tool to efficiently and cost-effectively migrate applications to cloud environments.

With FaaS, it is possible to divide any server-side application into a collection of functions. Functions can be fine-grained and scaled automatically and independently and there is no need to manage any infrastructure. That is, automatically the right and relevant infrastructure modules get sourced and allocated on demand to comfortably run the function. This helps developers focus on the application code. Also, FaaS can dramatically reduce the time that is needed to take a software product to market. With FaaS, you pay only when real action occurs. When the action is done, everything stops. FaaS is efficient for dynamic workloads or scheduled tasks. FaaS also offers a superior total cost of ownership (TCO) for high-load scenarios. There are several best practices that help to use FaaS effectively:

- Make each function perform only one action: As noted earlier, functions are destined to do only one business functionality. Functions respond to events or requests emanating from multiple sources. For complex business processes, multiple functions have to be orchestrated. It is important to make and minimize the scope of the function code. Therefore, functions are usable, reusable, lightweight, and efficient. Thereby, code can be executed quickly. The real value of FaaS lies in having isolated and simple functions. Functions calling other functions for composite functions/microservices will increase the costs and the complexity.
- Use a few libraries in your functions: Leveraging a few libraries to speed up the function execution.

FaaS enables transactions to be isolated and hence functions can be scaled easily. This is extremely good for high-volume and embarrassingly parallel workloads. This contributes handsomely to creating a wide variety of backend systems and/or for requirements such as data processing, format conversion, encoding, or data aggregation. FaaS is also a good tool for web/mobile applications, data/stream processing, or creating online chatbots or backends for IoT devices.

FaaS, PaaS, containers, and VMs all play a critical role in the serverless ecosystem. The provisioning time for FaaS is just a few seconds. For provisioning VMs, it may take a few minutes. Due to the automatic scaling capability, there is no need for capacity planning and management. HA is guaranteed natively in FaaS. Resource utilization is very high. Management and maintenance are being taken care of by serverless service providers. FaaS is the only model that has resource limits on code size, concurrent activations, memory, run length, etc. FaaS has the limited ability to persist connections and the state must be kept in external service/resource. The other models can leverage http, keep an open socket or connection for long periods of time, and can store the state in memory between calls.

Thus, there are a few innovations and disruptions in the cloud space. Much importance is being given to deeper and decisive automation; thereby human instruction, intervention, and involvement become less and less. Software-defined cloud centers and serverless computing bring in intensive optimization. With containers, the world is inching toward contained cloud environments. Through log, operational, performance, reliability, security, and observability data analytics, cognitive cloud environments will emerge and become the new normal.

The Hybrid Model of Microservices Architecture (MSA) and Event-driven Architecture (EDA)

Web-scale application companies such as Netflix, Google, Amazon, and Jio expose systems that compose hundreds of independent and interoperable microservices. The MSA style enables these companies to embed mandated modifications rapidly to rewardingly respond to changing market conditions. It is possible to instantaneously update, patch up, replace, or substitute microservices of a live and complex application without bringing down the entire system. Microservices can be horizontally scaled in order to meet up any spike in user loads and are independently deployable. MSA ensures agile application design and development. With the seamless integration with cloud DevOps tools, frequent and fast deployment of microservice applications is being fulfilled. Microservices are self-contained, easily manageable, observable, composable, publicly discoverable, network accessible, malleable, resilient, etc., and hence microservice applications are flexible, extensible, and dependable. Each microservice runs in its own process and communicates with others using standard communication protocols such as HTTP/HTTPS, WebSockets, or AMQP.

There is a bevy of platform solutions in order to automate many of the manual activities such as microservices development, debugging, delivery, deployment, composition (orchestration and choreography), management, governance, and enhancement. Service meshes are being leveraged in order to closely monitor microservice communication so that any kind of deviation and deficiency can be proactively identified and attended. This is performed in order to guarantee the much-needed resiliency of microservices. When composing resilient microservices, it is possible to have reliable applications. Thus, the MSA pattern with the support of several pioneering platforms, resiliency patterns, enabling products, processes, and practices facilitates the realization of sophisticated applications. We will discuss how MSA comes in handy in fulfilling the goals of accelerated software engineering and also how MSA innately supports distributed computing architecture.

With the surging popularity of microservices, experts write about how microservices applications are supreme, supple, and sustainable when compared to monolithic applications. Figure 2.1 tells all. Monolithic applications are layered or tiered and run in a single process. A backend database is there to support the application. However, as enunciated earlier, the microservice approach disaggregates application functionality into a pool of independent microservices. Each service includes the processing logic and is ably assisted by its own database.

Because microservices are isolated, each microservice has its own sovereign lifecycle and therefore it can evolve in its own way as per changing business sentiments and can be deployed independently. Also, microservices can be deployed frequently in an automated manner by using the enterprise DevOps tools.

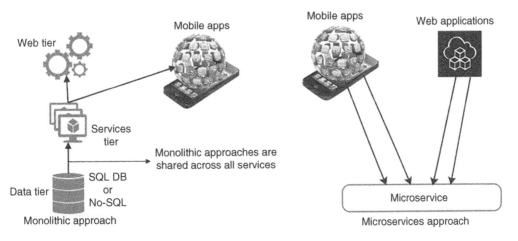

Figure 2.1 Monolithic versus microservices approaches.

The advantage here is that developers need not code the software from scratch. There is no need for packaging the software as a library in the application. MSA encourages a kind of contract-driven development between service providers and consumers. It is all about finding and aggregating different microservices to come out with an application. Software developers across the world develop a variety of microservices and keep them in publicly available service repositories. Through configuration changes and composition, microservices-centric application development gets a boost. This intuitively speeds up software engineering for varied business verticals. There is no dependency among service development teams. The typical dependency-induced limitations are fully avoided in the microservice era. If there is a worthwhile idea, MSA accelerates the logical conclusion of the idea in the form of a versatile product. Therefore, the time to take a minimum viable product (MVP) or a fully finished product to market is sharply reduced. An open environment definitely is a breeding ground for innovations.

Microservices also enable establishing and sustaining clear boundaries between business processes and domains. That is, we can have customer service, order service and inventory service to be developed independently. MSA supports usability and reusability. With containers, we can run multiple instances of a microservice in a distributed manner. Several business applications can then avail the microservices concurrently with heightened performance.

Service mesh solutions bring in additional capabilities like traffic control, service discovery, load balancing, resilience, observability, security, etc. These capabilities are abstracted out of applications and embedded in the service meshes. By separating these commonly used support services, service meshes enable service developers to focus just on core business capabilities. Some service meshes like Istio also support features like chaos injection so that developers can test the resilience and robustness of their applications and microservices. Microservices typically rely on protocols like representational state transfer (REST), Google's open-source remote procedure call (gRPC), and NATS. REST is often used to expose APIs over hypertext transfer protocol (HTTP). For internal communication between microservices, gRPC is often the first choice and performant. NATS enables event sourcing and has publish-subscribe features that facilitate asynchronous communication within the application.

Event-driven architecture (EDA) is another hugely popular architectural pattern for producing event-driven applications. For building and deploying sensitive and responsive (S & R) applications, elegantly capturing and processing events and making sense of them are very vital. There are messaging middleware solutions (message queues and brokers) in order to receive, store, and supply all kinds of events (emitted by business systems, data sources, social websites, IoT devices, mobile, web, and cloud applications). Increasingly the world is event-driven and hence IT systems have to have the right infrastructure, platforms, middleware, databases, etc., in place to glean every decision-enabling event with utmost care and confidence. Microservices are generally synchronous and hence to have asynchronous and non-blocking microservices, there is a need to have an intersection between MSA and EDA. That is, there will be event-driven microservices in plenty in order to realize real-world, real-time and resilient applications. Synchronous microservices interact directly whereas asynchronous microservices need an intermediary to have indirect communication. Asynchronous microservices support "fire and forget" pattern.

The Aspect of Containerization

We have been fiddling with virtualization for long. Physical machines are being logically partitioned into collection VMs. Such compartmentalization brings in a series of technical and business advantages. This disaggregation idea originates from the proven and potential "divide and conquer" concept. Heterogeneous applications can be made to run on a physical machine through VMs. That is, different VMs provisioned and run on the same host can host and run disparate applications. By accommodating multiple applications on a single machine, the much-needed IT resource utilization has gone up with virtualization. Also, there are several platform solutions and toolsets (termed as hypervisors or VM monitors [VMMs]) in order to automate and accelerate the tasks associated with VMs' lifecycle management.

Precisely speaking, IT operations get hugely simplified and speeded up through virtualization. A number of activities such as infrastructure provisioning and configuration, task/job/resource scheduling, IT monitoring (infrastructure modules, applications, middleware, databases, etc.), IT governance and security, performance engineering, and enhancement (PE^2) are getting automated. There is a dazzling array of tools, accelerators, specialized software engines such as cloud orchestration and brokerage solutions, resiliency, and observability platforms. And virtualization-enablement and management platforms flourished with the consistent nourishment from product and tool vendors. Thus, along with the virtualization movement, the steady arrival of a number of enabling tools made all the difference. The faster proliferation of continuous integration (CI), delivery, and deployment tools also speeds up the frequent, faster and risk-free delivery, and deployment of software services.

Now with the steady adoption and adaptation of the containerization paradigm, some of the widely reported weaknesses of virtualization are being surmounted. Containers are typically OS-level and lightweight VMs. Hundreds of containers can be created and used in a single physical machine as containers do not carry their own operating systems. Instead, they leverage the kernel of the host operating system to run their applications. Containers generally host an application and all its dependencies including binaries and files in order to run independently everywhere in a hassle-free manner. The much-expected system portability is easily achieved through containers. The goal of "Write once and run everywhere" has been the motto of software applications. That longstanding goal gets fully vindicated through containers, which turn out to be the best-in-class optimal packaging and runtime option for microservices. The convergence of containers and microservices has turned out to be a huge game changer for the software engineering community. Instances of a microservice can be run on multiple containers. That is, a microservice can be made to run on several containers in order to satisfy the high-availability and location-affinity demands.

Containers are immutable and hence to insert any perceptible change, new containers are being created. Multiple containers comprising different microservices can be programmatically aggregated in order to create composite services (multi-container applications), which are generally process-aware and business-critical. Because of its smaller size, the boot-up time is very less for containerized microservices and hence containers can be provisioned in a few seconds, whereas VMs consume a few minutes because of their bulkiness. In other words, real-time horizontal scalability is being achieved through containerization.

Containerizing microservices is comparatively simple and straightforward. The source code, its dependencies, and runtime are optimally packed into a binary format file. This is called a container image for the microservice. Container images are stored in a registry/repository. Docker Hub is the widely known public repository of Docker container images. Enterprises can maintain their own private container image repository. Established public clouds too have this facility to stock up container images, thereby instantiating microservices and their instances become easy and fast. With just a command, an image can be transformed into an instance that can run everywhere. Figure 2.2 shows three different microservices, each in its own container, running on a single host.

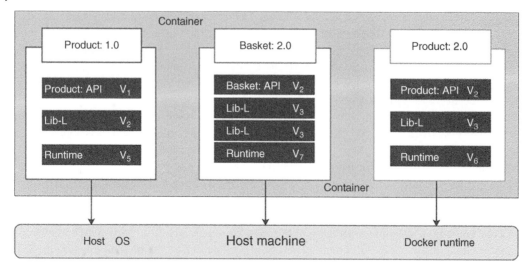

Figure 2.2 Multiple containers running on a container host.

Here, we see different versions of the product microservice running on the same host. Each container shares a slice of the underlying host operating system, memory, and processor. But containers are isolated from one another. As indicated here, containers provide portability and guarantee consistency across environments. By encapsulating everything into a single package, microservices and their dependencies are fully abstracted from the underlying infrastructure. That means containerized microservices can run anywhere. Containerized applications also eliminate the need for installing special frameworks, software libraries, and runtime engines on the host machine. By optimally using the underlying operating system and the host resources, containers deliver with a smaller footprint when compared to VMs.

The close association between microservices and containers, the real-time horizontal scalability of containers, the heightened IT resource efficiency through containerization, the system portability, and the easy manipulation of containers put containerization in a strong and sustainable foundation. However, there are a few limitations related to containerization. With microservices and containerization collectively emerging as the optimal building and runtime ingredients, the number of participating components in any IT environment goes up considerably. That is, there can be thousands of containers in an enterprise or cloud IT environment. The operating challenges in any containerized clouds are greater. To moderate the rising complexity, container orchestration platform solutions have emerged and evolved. Kubernetes is emerging as a hugely popular tool.

The Emergence of Container Lifecycle Management Platforms

We have seen a few unavoidable complexities being associated with containerization. With a higher density of containers, the container management complexity is bound to raise sharply. Therefore, there is a clarion call for appropriate complexity-mitigation approaches. Having considered the prevailing situation, product vendors have come out with container orchestration platform solutions. There are Docker Swarm, Google Kubernetes, and Mesos. These help simplify container management difficulties. A number of technologically advanced automation are being directly provided by these solutions. Especially with a huge adoption of Kubernetes by the IT industry for setting up and sustaining containerized environments, the containerization era is all

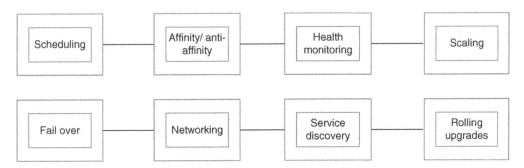

Figure 2.3 What container orchestrators do.

set to bloom. The container tool ecosystem is growing rapidly. With Kubernetes, containerized microservices deployment gets a solid boost. Kubernetes enables multiple microservices to be clubbed together to prop up composite services. Automated horizontal scaling of compute resources (containers), self-healing of containers, ensuring the configured number of container instances at all times, operating stateful applications, allocation of persistent volumes, intelligent resource and task scheduling, extra security, and other requirements are being automated through Kubernetes. Establishing and operating containerized clouds are therefore tremendously simplified and speeded up through orchestration platforms. When operating at scale, container orchestration is essential. Figure 2.3 shows the management tasks that container orchestrators provide.

Most of the factors mentioned hereby are being automated through the combination of containers and container orchestration platforms. As we steadily move from virtualized applications to containerized applications, the role and responsibility of the Kubernetes platform are bound to go up sharply. With the growing maturity and stability of Kubernetes, the era of containerization is all set to flourish. We will have plenty of containerized cloud applications and infrastructures. The application portability, service composability, multi-container applications, automated and real-time scalability, self-healing, resource and task scheduling, etc., will become a new normal.

Tending Toward Cloud-Native Computing

We have deliberated on software-defined cloud computing [1–3]. The cloud journey is definitely on the right path. There are several mesmerizing evolutions and revolutions in the cloud space. Breakthrough techniques, accelerators, advanced algorithms, and automated toolkits have been enviously sustaining the cloud idea. As indicated earlier, some of the difficult-to-implement non-functional requirements (NFRs) such as scalability, availability, accessibility, agility, simplicity, security, affordability, configurability, etc., are being comfortably realized through software-defined cloud centers. Now with containers, microservices and Kubernetes getting adopted fast, next-generation cloud applications are going to be intrinsically sophisticated and sagacious in their offerings, operations, and outputs. This is being pronounced as cloud-native computing.

Cloud-native paradigm (https://tanzu.vmware.com/cloud-native) is an approach to building and running applications that exploits the advantages of the cloud delivery model. When companies build and operate applications using a cloud-native architecture, they bring new ideas and solutions to market faster and respond sooner to customer demands.

Cloud-native computing fulfils the much-needed properties such as extensibility, interoperability, portability, simplicity, malleability, composability, and reliability. The emerging concepts of hybrid and multi-cloud operations are being speeded up through cloud-native computing, which are being astutely enabled by Kubernetes. Cloud federation will become the new normal in the cloud-native era. There are several product, platform, and tool vendors in the cloud-native space to continuously sustain its goals. In this chapter, we are to see why cloud-native computing is going to be a game changer for enterprising businesses across the world.

As inscribed in the first chapter, the digital era is all set to flourish with overwhelming nourishment from different stakeholders. Digitization and digitalization technologies are becoming powerful and pervasive. There will be pioneering digital life applications in order to facilitate digital living. There are digital innovations, disruptions, and intelligence in order to fulfil digital transformations. For the industry, digital technologies are being meticulously leveraged to bring in real business transformations. National governments are strategizing and planning digital movements in order to set up and sustain digitally transformed governance in order to make their constituents and citizens happy. Similarly, our cities are being digitally transformed through a host of digital technologies and tools. This chapter throws light on how cloud-native computing comes in handy in visualizing and realizing next-generation digital transformation applications.

Digging Deeper into Cloud-Native Systems [4–6] – As noted earlier, cloud-native systems take the full advantage of the proven cloud service model. We have cloud infrastructures comprising compute machines, storage appliances and networking solutions. Compute machines vary from bare metal servers to VMs and containers. There are several types of platforms running on cloud infrastructures for facilitating software design, development, debugging, delivery, and deployment. Further on, there are integration, orchestration, security, governance, and management platform solutions installed on cloud infrastructure. For the sake of realizing agile IT, CI, delivery, deployment, and improvement needs are increasingly fulfilled through competent tools on cloud infrastructures. Most of the enterprise-scale and production-ready applications are being run on cloud platforms these days. Massive and monolithic applications are meticulously segmented into a collection of microservices. This is termed legacy modernization. And modernized applications are thereafter migrated to cloud environments in order to avail all the distinct capabilities of cloud environments. That is, legacy applications are being cloud-enabled in order to be modern, flexible, and receptive to newer technologies and tools, etc.

In a traditional data center, we have plenty of physical machines, which are being treated as pets. Each machine is given a meaningful name and is taken care of well. It is possible to add fresh resources in these machines (scale up). If one machine becomes sick, then it is nursed and nourished accordingly to bring it back to its original state. Now any modern data center is comprising a large number of VMs and containers. As explained earlier, one physical machine can be partitioned into a few VMs or tens or even hundreds of containers. This is being denoted as the cattle service model because of the huge number of participants. Herein, horizontal scalability (scale-out) is easy to implement. Any number of containers can be readily created and involved in fulfilling application requirements. Due to the higher density of containers, managing them is quite difficult. Containers are also immutable infrastructure. If one fails or requires an update, then it gets killed and a fresh one gets provisioned in an automated manner. Cloud-native computing has embraced this cattle service model.

As accentuated earlier, cloud-native systems enjoy some special benefits. Fresh and fabulous ideas can be quickly productized through MSA and EDA. Products can be used for creating viable and venerable solutions for business problems. Thus, IT solutions, services and business workloads can be taken to the market quickly and elegantly rendered to the customers and users through the successful cloud delivery model. IT products and solutions can be consistently and continuously updated, upgraded, and deployed in cloud environments through the crowded and crowned DevOps toolkits. Cloud-native applications (CNAs) can run across different and distributed cloud environments without any hitch or hurdle. CNAs are portable, customizable, composable, modern, and modular.

The 12 Factors for Cloud-Native Applications: Experts have formulated 12 factors for constructing CNAs. These factors clearly describe a set of principles and practices that software developers have to follow sincerely while building applications that are optimized for modern cloud environments. Software systems built upon these principles can be easily deployed and scaled horizontally. Bringing in new features in order to reflect business, technology, and user sentiments is comparatively easy. The following table highlights the Twelve-Factor methodology:

	Factor	Explanation
1	Code base	There is a single code base for each microservice and is stored in its own repository. By using version control, a microservice can be deployed in multiple environments such as quality testing, use acceptance testing (staging) and production.
2	Dependencies	Each microservice isolates and packages its own dependencies. In this way, embracing changes is easy and it does not impact the whole system.
3	Configurations	Configuration information is abstracted out of the microservice and separately stored through a configuration management tool. The same deployment happens correctly across environments with the correct configuration applied.
4	Backing up Services	Associated resources such as data stores, caches and message brokers should be exposed via an addressable URL. This separation brings the much-needed decoupling between application and support services, which can be leveraged by other applications as well.
5	Build, release, and run	There has to be a strict separation between build, release and run aspects. Each activity should be tagged with a unique ID. This facilitates easy rollback for an activity.
6	Processes	All the components of monolithic applications run in the same process. But in the case of microservice-centric applications, each contributing microservice has to run on its own process. Further on, it is advised to externalize important state information through a backing service such as a distributed cache or data store.
7	Port binding	As indicated earlier, microservices are self-contained in order to be autonomous in their actions. Every microservice is front-ended by one or more application programming interfaces (APIs) in order to facilitate microservices to find, bind and leverage their unique capabilities. Every microservice functionality is exposed on its own port.
8	Concurrency	Microservices are horizontally scalable. Multiple instances can be made to run via isolated containers to assuage and assure HA.
9	Disposability	Microservices can be decommissioned, updatable, and upgradable. Kubernetes can do all these things on containerized microservices.
10	Dev/prod parity	It is recommended to minimize the difference between different environments such as development, testing, staging and production.
11	Logging	Log analytics brings forth a lot of actionable intelligence. With the easy availability of log analytics platforms and tools, log collection and storage are useful.
12	Admin processes	Run administrative/management tasks as one-off processes. Tasks can include data clean-up and pulling analytics for a report. Tools executing these tasks should be invoked from the production environment.

Three additional factors that reflect today's modern cloud application design are discussed next.

	New Factor	Explanation
13	API first	APIs fulfil the integration requirement. Every microservice has to be stuffed with a well-designed API. Leverage API gateway solution as the first contact for any microservice to find, bind and leverage microservices.
14	Telemetry	It is important to have deeper visibility into our application. But in the case of a third-party public cloud, visibility is less and hence our design has to include the collection of logs, operational, performance, health condition, security, and other specific data. Telemetry data is to be subjected to a variety of investigations to emit actionable insights in time.
15	Authentication/authorization	There are inherent identify and access management (IAM) facilities in public clouds. The recommendation is to use role-based access control (RBAC) features.

Cloud-native Systems: The Critical Design Considerations: The previously mentioned factors enable an appropriate design of CNAs. Further on, there are several critical design decisions we must make when constructing distributed systems.

- Communication: This is an important decision to be taken with a lot of thoughts on several factors. We have client applications on one side and on the other side, we have multiple microservices. Each microservice is backed up by a data store. API gateway solutions are plentifully made available in order to facilitate distributed clients to communicate with correct microservices. The API gateway is a middleware ensuring higher flexibility, control, and security. This is north-to-south communication. The other prominent communication is microservice to microservice. This is denoted as east-to-west communication. We have service mesh solutions to minutely monitor, control, and observe microservices communication. Here is another consideration. It has to be a direct and synchronous communication such as direct HTTP calls. Or, it has to be an indirect and asynchronous communication through a message queue or broker in between microservices. Thus, direct or indirect connectivity decisions are very critical to ensuring desired application performance.
- Distributed Data: As indicated earlier, every microservice sits behind its own interface and there is a separate data storage facility for every microservice. The interface is the principal entry point for any client application or service to query and retrieve data from any microservice. If there is a need for querying multiple data stores for getting an aggregated result, there is a challenge. That is, accomplishing distributed transactions in the microservices world is not that straightforward.
- Identity: Identifying who is accessing what microservice is essential to keep up the sanctity of microservices. Thus, leveraging on-premise or off-premise or both IAM solutions is insisted for the safety of microservices.
- Modularity: This is being achieved through two concepts: The loosely or lightly coupled nature of microservices and the cohesiveness of microservices. Modularity brings in flexibility, visibility, manageability, accessibility, simplicity, isolation, etc. For producing decoupled microservices, MSA and EDA have to be merged.

- Resiliency: When we have cleanly isolated microservices, if there is a problem with one microservice, it does not penetrate or propagate into other services to bring down the whole system. Precisely speaking, the modularity factor enables the resiliency goal. In addition, containers, wherein microservices are being hosted and run, give some isolation. Container orchestration platforms such as Kubernetes bring in a kind of resiliency. Finally, service meshes ensure microservices communication resiliency. It is an overwhelmingly accepted statement that when resilient microservices get composed, the resulting application is reliable.
- Programmability: We hear and read more about infrastructure as code (IaC) and infrastructure as data (IaD) very often these days.

The purpose of IaC is to enable developers or operations teams to automatically provision and manage IT infrastructure (networking, VMs, Kubernetes clusters, load balancers, etc.) rather than manually setting up and configuring them. When one provisions infrastructure in a public or private cloud, he is hitting an API endpoint that talks to the cloud management platforms, which, in turn, provision virtual resources from their available pool of physical resources. There are many cloud management platforms such as OpenStack, Apache CloudStack, Azure Stack, and IBM Cloud Private.

There is one more thing here. For provisioning IT infrastructure, we have to put together a set of specifications or manifest and hand over them to the team, who would fulfil the request. For provisioning cloud IT infrastructure, the specifications are passed to and fulfilled by an API, rather than by a person. We do not bother about how the request is getting fulfilled. So, all we need to do is just describe the resources that we want to create. We describe them using a common format like JSON or YAML. That is, they are just plain text data. This is called IaD, which is a declarative approach to infrastructure. We just say what you want without specifying the precise actions or steps for how to get it.

We have been proficient with software programming. Today we are getting accustomed to hardware programming with the arrival of compartmentalization (virtualization and containerization) technologies. Declarative APIs are turning out to be pivotal and prominent for operation automation. Infrastructure provisioning and management are being increasingly automated through APIs. Network and storage infrastructure modules are also programmed through APIs in the days to come.

- Elasticity: Spinning up VMs and containers is automated. On the basis of varying traffic, additional IT resources could be provisioned and configured quickly. When the traffic goes down, underutilized and unutilized IT resources are closed and added to the pool. Thus, horizontal scalability (scale out) of VMs and containers is being fulfilled through automated tools. That is, when infrastructure modules are natively elastic, the much-expected microservices-centric application scalability feature is truly ensured.

CNAs inherently carry some special capabilities and their design, development, and deployment have to be done by considering a number of technical and business parameters.

A Growing Catalogue of Diversified Support Services: Cloud-native systems rely upon a number of support services and resources such as databases, message queues, brokers, IAM, service registry and repository for discovery, monitoring of applications, their underlying

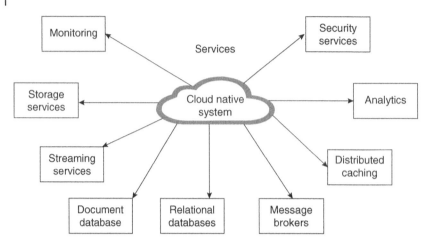

Figure 2.4 A galaxy of support services.

infrastructure modules, etc. Figure 2.4 shows many common services that cloud-native systems invariably consume.

With such support services, it is possible to have stateful applications. Cloud service providers (CSPs) give a number of additional capabilities for their clients and consumers. These services can be incorporated with mainstream applications and IT services on demand. There are search services, monitoring tools, log, operational, and performance analytics platforms, business intelligence (BI) solutions with dashboard facility, vulnerability assessment systems, brokerage services including intermediation, integration, concierge services, etc. Advanced capabilities are being meticulously designed and delivered as remotely invokable and manageable services. Base/atomic/discrete services are composed to bring forth bigger and better services. Thus, the increasing number of commonly and repeatedly applied services is welcome news for the services world. Multiple specialized and core services can acquaint with support services in order to be distinct and deft in their offerings, outputs, and operations.

Deeper Automation: As we all know, newer technologies are capable of solving some of the current limitations and problems. Newer possibilities and opportunities can be envisaged through the smart application of emerging technologies and tools. Precisely speaking, some of the manual activities can be automated through newer technologies. Here too, with the faster adoption of cloud-native computing (microservices, containers, container orchestration platforms, DevOps, observability, etc.), software system design, development, and deployment get real speed and suppleness. Containers and Kubernetes accelerate application deployment and management. Infrastructure provisioning is programmed and templatized, thereby repeatability at a massive scale is being streamlined. With DevOps and site reliability engineering (SRE) practices, the long-pending goals of IT agility and reliability are seeing positive vibes. With declarative APIs and immutable infrastructures, a number of risks are being nipped in the budding stage itself. IT operations, management, and maintenance are being decisively automated through the noteworthy advancements in the cloud space.

The DevOps Process: A developer builds a microservice or adds a new feature to an existing microservice. Or he modifies a feature of a microservice. He runs the updated code, debugs, and pushes it into a code repository. This push triggers a build stage that transforms the code into a binary entity and this is accomplished through a CI tool. It automatically builds, tests, and packages the application. The release stage picks up the binary entity, applies external application and environment configuration information, and produces an immutable release. The release is then deployed to a specified environment. This is being done through the continuous delivery (CD) tool. Each release should be identifiable (this deployment is running the Release 2.1.1 of the application).

Finally, the released feature is run in the target execution environment. With such empowerment, shipping and running software gain real speed. Previously, we heard about software releases every quarter. Today, the release happens on demand. That is, whenever there is an insistence for business-demanded, and technology-inspired changes, these updates and upgrades are being incorporated into application software and released quickly. Such a setup facilitates catching up on any kind of feature deviation and deficiency in the beginning stage itself. It is quite expensive to fix anything at the latter stage. Enterprises are keen on reducing operational expenses through such automation. That is why we would have come across the buzzword "NoOps," which is all about automating cloud operations. That is, there will be less involvement of human operators in ensuring the continuous availability of cloud servers. With containerized cloud infrastructures, we can avail more flexibility, programmability, simplicity, dependability, etc. Thus, cloud-native systems are bound to bring in a bevy of strategically sound impacts on software engineering and IT management.

Demystifying the Cloud-Native Architecture Style

As mentioned earlier, a CNA is an application designed to fully leverage the cloud operating model, which is applauded as a paradigm shift in IT history. CNAs are predictable, decoupled from the infrastructure, resilient from failures, and blessed with right-sized capacity. They also enable a tighter collaboration between development and operations. CNAs are composed of loosely coupled and independently operating microservices. Today most of the web-scale applications are cloud-native and they deal with a large number of transactions per second day in and day out. They are stuffed with several dynamic parts and hence fresh challenges and concerns emerge. The number of participating and contributing microservices in any CNA is literally huge.

The traffic rate for CNAs is incredibly varying, the number of disparate and distributed data sources for CNAs is tremendous, the number of service-accessing input/output devices is exponentially growing, and the response time expected out of CNAs is in milliseconds. CNAs have to be continuously available, adaptively scalable, highly reliable, and configurable. Multimodal interfaces are being attached with CNAs to be used and reused across business domains. Vendor and technology lock-ins are not accepted. Thus, the characteristics of CNAs are steadily expanding. They carry the inherent flexibility of elegantly absorbing all kinds of business and technological changes.

At a high level, cloud-native architecture means adapting to the many new possibilities offered by cloud environments compared to traditional IT environments. This works under a different set of architectural constraints. Functional requirements do not change much but the cloud fulfils NFRs differently. So, architects have to be very careful, otherwise the end result will be inflexible, fragile, expensive, and tough to maintain. A well-architected cloud-native system is self-healing, cost-effective, manageable, and extensible.

Cloud-Native Architecture Principles: In this section, we are to discuss the key principles of cloud-native architecture. Architecting next-generation cloud-native architecture centers around optimizing system architectures by smartly leveraging the unique capabilities of the cloud. We all know that cloudification has brought in some distinct competencies. A lot of right consolidation, centralization, and federation, and in some cases, automation, orchestration, sharing, etc. decorate the irresistible and indispensable cloud computing paradigm. A dazzling array of state-of-the-art automation are brought in to present the cloud as the hugely optimized and organized IT infrastructure. Someone wrote that cloud computing is the marriage between the age-old mainframe and modern computing methods. It is indisputably clear that mainframes guarantee extreme performance. Modern computing ensures hardware programmability, extensibility, configurability, and composability,

Corporates are keenly strategizing and planning to build and run CNAs on cloud infrastructures and platforms. The pay for usage model and cloud delivery model is being seen as a trendsetter for the cloud-native era. Therefore, cloud-native architecture focuses on achieving resilience and scale through horizontal scaling, distributed processing, and automatically replacing failed components and provisioning new components in their place in order to ensure business continuity. With secondary cloud environments, disaster and data recovery are being hugely simplified.

Legacy apps are being methodically modernized and exposed as CNAs. Fresh software applications are being designed and developed in a cloud-native manner from scratch. The cloud-native paradigm enables agile software design, development, and deployment. Application management, observability and enhancement are also seeing a solid improvement. The cloud-native principles and practices innately eliminate all kinds of dependency-induced limitations. Future technologies and tools can be accommodated in the cloud-native world. The much-demanded vendor-neutrality requirement is also achieved here. Rather than developing and deploying the application as a whole through a single codebase, CNAs are composed of distributed microservices. The best-in-class microservices can be chosen and combined to arrive at state-of-the-art applications. The service call happens via a network. Microservices and cloud-native architecture enable multiple cross-functional developer teams to simultaneously work on developing multiple microservices.

Cloud-native computing uses an open-source software stack to develop and deploy applications as microservices, packaging each microservice and its instances into their own containers, and dynamically orchestrating those containers to craft multi-container composite services.

Designed as Distributed Microservices: Microservice architecture (MSA) is the leading application architecture for constructing any application as a dynamic collection of microservices. Each microservice runs in its own process and communicates via lightweight protocols. CNAs are polyglot. Microservices can use a variety of programming languages, runtimes, and frameworks. For example, developers may build a real-time streaming microservice based on WebSockets. Node.js is the development language. For building a machine learning (ML)-based service, developers can choose spring boot for exposing the REST APIs while using Python as the programming language. This technology-agnostic feature is the prime reason for the overwhelming success of the MSA pattern.

Cloud-native services use lightweight APIs that are based on protocols such as REST to expose their functionality. Local services communicate with each other using binary protocols like Thrift, Protobuff, gRPC, etc., for better performance

Automation Using CI/CD Pipelines: DevOps, the amalgamation of "development" and "operations," enables fast and frequent application deployment. There is technology-inspired tighter coordination between development and operations teams to take software solutions to the market quickly. CI and CD is a set of operating principles that enable application development teams to deliver code changes more frequently and reliably. The technical goal of CI is to establish a consistent and automated way to build, package, and test applications. With consistency in the integration process, teams are more likely to commit code changes more frequently, which leads to better collaboration and software quality.

CD picks up where CI ends. CD automates the delivery of applications to selected infrastructure environments. It picks up the package built by CI and deploys it into multiple environments (Dev, QA, and staging). CD runs various tests like integration and performance tests and finally, it deploys the fully verified and validated application into production. CD normally has few manual steps in the pipeline, whereas continuous deployment is a fully automated pipeline, which automates the complete process from code check-in to production deployment.

Design for Automation: With breakthrough technologies, manual and error-prone actions are getting augmented and accelerated. There are several noteworthy automation in software engineering. Even troublesome IT operations are being automated through a variety of tools and methodologies. We often hear the word "infrastructure automation." Automation means less errors and less time for finishing tasks. The widely articulated performance of cloud systems is being enhanced through performance engineering and enhancement (PE^2) methods. Infrastructure elasticity is being achieved through compartmentalization (virtualization and containerization) and this facilitates application scalability. With enterprise and cloud DevOps features, IT agility is being fulfilled and hence there is an insistence on achieving the technology-enabled business agility. Now the IT industry is setting its eye on accomplishing IT reliability, which, in turn, can ensure business reliability. The reliability facet is being tried at service, application and infrastructure levels. A variety of improvements are being explored and experimented with to realize reliable systems. There are resiliency patterns and platform solutions to enhance the reliability of business workloads and IT services.

The cloud-native era consistently unleashes innovations because of isolation at the container level, loose coupling at the microservices level, and composition being facilitated by container orchestration platforms. Automation is peaking. Besides development and deployment, application monitoring, measuring, and managing CNAs are also being accelerated. The operational and management complexities of CNA are being addressed through orchestration solutions.

Monitoring and Automated Recovery: It is essential to continuously monitor cloud-native systems in order to understand whether the system is functioning to its fullest capability or not. If there is any slight deviation or deficiency, then it can be immediately noticed and appropriate measures can be considered and activated. There are monitoring tools for microservices applications, middleware solutions, runtimes such as containers, platforms such as Kubernetes, databases, and infrastructure modules. Log, operational, security, performance, health condition, and other decision-enabling IT data get automatically captured and subjected to a variety of investigations through integrated analytics platforms in order to extract actionable insights.

Further on, with the sharp maturity and stability of artificial intelligence (AI) algorithms, predictive, prescriptive, and prognostic insights can be derived in time in order to battle out any untoward incident proactively and pre-emptively.

State Management: Stateful applications are an important category. The decision on the storing of state information is one of the hardest decisions for architecting cloud-native systems. Stateless services are easy to scale out (horizontal scalability). Also, stateless services are easy to repair and roll back (failed or bad components can be terminated and newer instances can be provisioned immediately). Also, it is simple to balance loads across multiple instances of a microservice. They are easy to recover from any failure. In the case of stateless services and applications, the programming complexity is reduced. Requests are received, processed, and forgotten. There is no need to maintain a state, and often the complexity revolves around maintaining the session state, which typically involves replicating the session state across the cluster. Typically, stateless applications can handle a large volume of requests with ease. They exhibit greater performance by removing server load caused by the retention of session information.

As far as stateless applications are concerned, the meaning is misleading indeed. Applications by their very nature deal with the state of things. Applications create, read, update, and delete stateful items. The typical processing flow of a stateless application is to receive a request, retrieve the state from a persistence store, such as a relational database, make the requested state changes, and store the changed state back into the persistence stores. As application servers do not store state data but persistence store does store state data. This actually leads to the slowdown at the persistence layer. Maintaining the state at the application layer has an associated cost with the potential for increased complexity. However, stateful CNAs carry a few distinct advantages. The well-known benefit is the potential for a reduction in the overhead associated with retrieving the state on every request.

The perception of increased complexity being associated with stateful applications is due to the current approach for maintaining state across a cluster and the relational CRUD-based ways for handling persistence. This can be eliminated through event-based state persistence. This alternative is to persist state changes as a sequence of events. This is termed an event log. Events represent state changes and statements of fact. One of the advantages of persisting data using events is that it is now possible to record all of the interesting events that happened over time that resulted in the current state. Another event log advantage is that the persistence data structure is a simple key and value pair. The event log is also idempotent, events are insert-only, and there are no updates and no deletes. The insert-only approach reduces the load and contention of the persistence layer.

Believe in Defence in Depth: Security is acquiring special significance with the widespread acceptance and adoption of cloud-native computing. We have been banking on perimeter security. However, CNAs are vulnerable to insider attacks. With mobile and web interfaces, cyberattacks are on the rise. Security experts point out the importance of adopting the approach of defence-in-depth by applying authentication between each component, and by minimizing the trust between those components. That is, the new buzzword of zero trust is being recommended for impenetrable and unbreakable CNAs.

Resiliency Comes First: No system is infallible. So, trying to design and develop an error-free system is not a worthy move. Instead, it is paramount and logical to focus on system resiliency. That is, if a system is under attack from internal or external sources, the system has to have the where-withal to understand and wriggle out of the situation toward its original state automatically. The prominent approaches for resilient systems are redundancy, regional deployments/availability zones, and data replication. This helps for data and disaster recovery to ensure business continuity.

In a distributed system, failures are bound to happen. The software can go down. The hardware can fail. The network can have transient failures. Rarely an entire cloud may experience a service disruption. Therefore, resiliency is demanded vociferously. Resiliency is the ability of a system to understand the fault and recover from any failure to ceaselessly continue its ordained function. It is not about avoiding failures but intelligently responding to faults and failures in order to avoid any slowdown and breakdown. That is, a resilient system has the required power to overcome any downtime and data loss. This special feature enables systems to bounce back to their fully functional state and resume their service delivery. The resiliency capability offers the following features:

- High Availability: The systems' availability for transacting their tasks is high. That is, the system fulfils its obligations almost all the time with very minimal disruption.
- Disaster Recovery: Man-made mistakes or a natural disaster can bring down an application or even the entire cloud environment. With resilience in place, the service is made available to its users through a secondary cloud application or environment.

The resiliency requirement is typically achieved through redundancy. That is, multiple containers can be involved in a microservice. Multiple nodes and clusters can be put in place to fulfil resiliency. Even multiple regions and availability zones are recommended to ensure business continuity. Data replication is insisted on for avoiding data loss. Automated monitoring of applications and infrastructure modules is also made mandatory. With AI-backed predictive and prescriptive insights in time, the resiliency aspect gets due importance. There are resiliency patterns and approaches as enumerated hereunder:

- Retry transient failures: Transient failures are not typically permanent or long-lasting. It can be a momentary loss of network connectivity, a dropped database connection or the server may be a bit busy. In such situations, the valid approach is to try again.
- Degrade gracefully: If a service fails and if there is no failover facility, then the application has to degrade gracefully while ensuring an acceptable user experience. Another option is to fail fast.
- Throttle high-volume users: This is called rate limiting. Some users bombard servers with a lot of requests and this cripple the server impacting other users. The solution approach is to throttle high-volume users.
- Use a circuit breaker: This is the widely used resiliency pattern. If a server application is not responding to a client request repeatedly, then the circuit breaker counts the number of recent failures and if that number breaches the threshold value configured, then the circuit breaker responds to any further client request with a failure code immediately without really calling the server.
- Apply compensating transactions: A compensating transaction is actually a transaction to undo a completed transaction. In a cloud-native system, which is a distributed system, it can be very difficult to achieve strong transactional consistency. Therefore, compensating transactions are presented as the way forward to achieve consistency by leveraging a series of smaller and individual transactions that can be undone at each step.
- Testing for resiliency: This is not the usual testing method and this needs a totally different approach for unearthing resiliency-impacting issues. Fault injection is one prominent method to pinpoint what fault lies where. The workload has to be subjected to a variety of tests in order to understand how the workload behaves in failure situations. In the recent past, we often read and hear about chaos engineering. This is a new powerful discipline to enhance system reliability by testing different aspects of the system in production environments. KubeMonkey is a chaos engineering tool for testing containerized workloads running on Kubernetes clusters. Similarly, there is an army of chaos engineering tools for simplifying reliability testing

Thus, architecting cloud-native systems is not a straightforward thing to do. However, there are principles and best practices to simplify and speed up the realization of competent architecture for cloud-native systems. The fluidity, resiliency, and scalability have to be the key outputs of a cloud-native architecture.

The Benefits of Cloud-Native Architecture: The cloud-native architecture is quite inspiring and insightful. This is being portrayed as the next-generation architecture for producing and sustaining sophisticated, enterprise-grade, mission-critical, adaptive, and service-oriented applications. The key motivations include microservices, containers, and orchestration toolkits. Distributed architecture is the key foundation for the massive success and adoption of this architectural style.

- Easy to manage: With the maturity of container lifecycle management platform solutions such as Kubernetes, CNAs are quite easy to deploy and manage. Further on, cloud-native DevOps tools and pipelines come in handy in realizing perceptible improvements iteratively.
- Incremental improvements: Microservices can be improved incrementally, deployed automatically and scaled independently. This allows to continuously incorporate advanced capabilities in

microservices and ultimately in CNAs. As microservices are isolated and hence there is no inter-ruption for application users while bringing forth newer features and functionalities.

- Microservices are technology-agnostic: Microservices can be developed using any framework and coded using any programming language. Any suitable datastore can be attached with a microservice. Every microservice has to expose one or more APIs for the outside world to be found, bound, and used. Microservices can be deployed in any modern IT environment includ-ing edge device cloud.
- Improved resource utilization: Policies play an important role in shaping the resource utiliza-tion efficiency. Pioneering task and resource scheduling algorithms come in handy in the opti-mal selection and usage of resources. Containers are lightweight and hence consume fewer resources. Also, multiple business applications can access and use containerized microservices concurrently.

As indicated earlier, MSA is primed for agile application design and development. With the seamless and spontaneous integration with EDA, asynchronous microservices can be realized and used for sensitive and responsive applications. With enterprise and cloud DevOps toolkits, applica-tion deployment becomes simpler and faster. Thus, cloud-native architecture gets the real speed. Also, through configuration, customization, and composition of already constructed microservices and applications, newer applications are being realized quickly to suit differing business requirements.

The era of starting from scratch is gone forever. All the application-building blocks are already developed using multiple programming languages, thoroughly tested, continuously curated, and stocked in open-source software repositories across the distributed servers. The version control capability is embedded in these repositories. Thus, microservices represent a new way of applica-tion realization. In combination with containers, orchestration platforms and middleware solu-tions such as API gateways and service meshes, the realization of ground-breaking cloud-native systems is going to be the new normal. The difficult-to-implement NFRs such as modifiability, flexibility, extensibility, accessibility, simplicity, scalability, reliability, availability, observability, manageability, and security can be quite easily realized in the cloud-native era.

The Challenges and Concerns: We have seen many powerful advantages of cloud-native systems. By strictly following the described principles and practices, futuristic and flexible cloud-native architectures can be realized. However, despite its many benefits, there are a few critical issues to be taken into consideration while firming up next-generation cloud-native architecture.

1) For cloud-native systems to reliably attain the intended success, an established DevOps pipeline has to be in place to manage distributed workflows and responsibilities related to microservices.
2) Advanced service mesh solutions are needed to continuously monitor microservices communi-cation. Similarly, minutely monitoring containers, which are getting scaled is important to ward off any security risk.
3) Transitioning a legacy application into a microservices-centric application has to be done with all the care and clarity. There is a possibility for complex interdependencies between participat-ing microservices.
4) Microservices, by default, can be deployed across multiple servers and developed to function on any operating system. The one exception is instances where a particular microservices requires certain capabilities like solid-state drives (SSDs) and graphics processing units (GPUs), in which case, it is somewhat dependent on physical capabilities offered by the hardware.

5) Debugging challenges: Spotting a problem or identifying the root cause for a fault or failure in a traditional system architecture means just following a linear plan. But in a cloud-native design, pinpointing a problem is a tough assignment. Firstly, there may be thousands or more of containers connecting and collaborating. Their path may not always be clear because of their dynamic nature.

The surging popularity and faster proliferation of containers in conjunction with the easily manageable microservices make all the difference for cloud-native systems when compared with conventional systems. The combination of microservices and containers brings in a number of disruptions to fulfil real digital transformation. The "divide and conquer" technique has been the a hugely successful facet of software engineering. Now it is being applied to enabling hardware programming. Such a turnaround empowers cloud-native architectures to take full advantage of distributed architecture. The movement from centralized computing to microservices-enabled distributed computing is the key trendsetter for the IT field to continuously shine for not only business IT but also for people IT.

CNAs are being composed of containerized microservices. Containerized applications are ably managed by Kubernetes and hence the much-needed agility, adaptivity, portability, configurability, customizability and composability are being easily accrued out of CNAs. With cloud DevOps, CNAs are being frequently updated, patched, upgraded and deployed to meet up fast-changing market needs. Further on, with service meshes, the reliability of CNAs is being easily delivered. With cloud environments are transitioned to become containerized, IoT, AI, and blockchain applications are being modernized to be cloud-native to enjoy all the originally expressed benefits of cloud computing. Cloud-native applications can be easily moved across.

Distinguishing Cloud-Native Infrastructure

Cloud-native infrastructure has to be adaptive and even invisible. The longstanding goal of infrastructure-aware applications and application-aware infrastructures is seeing the grandiose reality with an overwhelming adoption of the cloud-native phenomenon. That is, applications and underlying infrastructure modules have to be adaptive in order to meet up customers' changing needs with the support of platform solutions. Cloud infrastructure has to insightfully understand and fulfil the nonfunctional aspects of applications. For enabling automation and sharing, cloud environments are majorly virtualized. And now with the solidity of containerization, steadily cloud environments are containerized. Thus, infrastructure programmability, elasticity, and extensibility are guaranteed. OpenStack is the widely used cloud. management platform for virtualized applications whereas Kubernetes is being positioned as the key platform for managing containerized applications. The end result is that CNAs are intelligently aligned with the underlying infrastructure to be right and relevant to their users.

Having fully understood the strategic advantages of cloud infrastructures, business behemoths are methodically modernizing their legacy applications (monolithic) with a single codebase to be cloud-native through microservices and containerization and migrating them to cloud environments. Some mission-critical, high-performance, and security applications are being still kept in their own data centers not to be exposed to the Internet. As there are multiple cloud environments, most of the enterprises are consciously migrating their business applications to different and geographically distributed cloud environments. Some applications reap greater benefits in a particular cloud environment and hence switchover becomes the new normal. Some CSPs are charging less compared to others. Clouds predominantly use commodity servers. Some clouds guarantee high-performance computing through supercomputers. So, there are different reasons and causes for cloud switchovers. This is the main motivation for the multi-cloud strategy to gain prominence and dominance.

Due to the increasing popularity of the multi-cloud ideas, applications ought to be just portable across clouds. This portability facility enables business houses, without bothering about the infrastructure demands of any target environment, to focus on adding next-generation business capabilities. That is, there is a renewed interest in crafting and sustaining invisible infrastructure. In other words, infrastructure does not matter. Applications just run everywhere. Here, the cloud-native concept plays a very valid and vigorous role in producing frictionless infrastructure. All sorts of frictions between infrastructures get eliminated in order to run workloads without any hitch or hurdle.

Cloud-Native Security

The security aspect of cloud-native systems has to be given utmost importance as there are several moving parts. Security experts have indicated that CD means continuous security. As inscribed earlier, there are frequent software deployments. In such situations, security checks must be lightweight, continuous, and embedded into the deployment of toolchains. In traditional environments, enterprise security is all about securing endpoints, segmenting the network and protecting the perimeter. In a cloud-native environment, it is prudent not to rely on fixed routers, gateways, network perimeters, etc. As microservices are running across cloud centers, shifting the focus to secure cloud centers and business workloads is therefore imperative. As we all know, container security has been an important study and research. Thus, the security of containerized microservices and multi-container applications has to be given serious consideration.

As far as microservices are concerned, end-to-end visibility, monitoring, and detection are vital to proactively and pre-emptively pinpoint any security implication. Security data analytics is an important ingredient in predicting security attacks. Cyberattacks will quantitatively and qualitatively become big. Real-time identification of cyberattacks and nullifying them immediately are being demanded for ensuring the intended success of the cloud-native paradigm. If we take security lightly, then the cloud-native performance may degrade and fizzle out eventually. Observability of CNAs is very vital in order to nip any security impact in the budding stage itself.

We read and hear more about chaos engineering these days. It is indispensable to apply proven techniques of chaos engineering in order to detect any security hole/vulnerability before they are getting exploited by evildoers. As microservices are isolated, if there is any error or fault in one microservice, it is easy to identify it and contain it before it gets propagated to other microservices. Thus, real-time security monitoring, analysis, and action are being widely insisted in order to secure cloud-native microservices and their applications.

Also, in order to automate many container lifecycle activities, the industry is veering toward container orchestration platform solutions. There are many such automation platforms. The security pundits and pioneers recommend that there is a need for such tools to get seamlessly and spontaneously integrated with CI/CD toolkits. Thus, securing CNAs, which are composed of distributed microservices, acquires special significance in an open, flexible, and extensible environment. As the container security issue is being attended to vigorously and rigorously, we will have deeper security for CNAs.

With the widespread adoption of the futuristic cloud-native paradigm, there arises a number of newer topics such as cloud-native networking and storage, cloud-native edge computing, etc. All these are very relevant and, hence, we have allocated separate chapters for detailing them in a comprehensive manner.

Cloud-Native Computing Advantages

A cloud-native architecture gives several distinct benefits as listed hereunder:

- Increased Agility and Productivity: Cloud DevOps has speeded up cloud application deployment. With the emergence of GitOps, CNA deployment gets accelerated. Thus, CI, delivery, deployment and improvement processes are creating fully automated CI/CD pipelines to rapidly test and push new code to production in a risk-free manner. Newer algorithms and approaches can be readily accommodated. Businesses can stick to and sustain their brand value by unearthing and incorporating solid innovations and inventions quickly. Premium services can be rewardingly formulated and provided to users in order to retain their loyalty. All these clearly facilitate expediently exploring fresh avenues and revenues can be realized.
- Distributed Microservices: As indicated earlier, microservices are componentized, easily manageable and reusable software modules. Microservices expose discrete functions to applications through APIs. As APIs become pervasive and persuasive, API design, development, testing, versioning, and management are being automated through API-specific platform solutions. APIs solidly promote microservices reusability. That is, heterogeneous applications can leverage microservices and their distributed instances in parallel and get benefited immensely. Generally, microservice APIs are exposed over a RESTful interface and this is a synchronous calling. By leveraging a message queue or broker between applications and services, it is possible to have asynchronous and non-blocking communication. All the unique benefits of highly optimized and organized cloud infrastructure modules prop up microservices to be highly relevant for next-generation business requirements.
- Service Discovery: Service registry/repository is stocking the relevant metadata of microservices. Therefore, discovering appropriate services quickly is being facilitated. The service registry enables multiple services to be dynamically identified and orchestrated into an application.
- Container Lifecycle Management: With the continued nourishment, Kubernetes is all set to shake the IT world. With the growing density of containers in cloud IT environments, container scheduler such as Kubernetes emerges as an important ingredient to insightfully streamline containers and their smart leverage.
- State Separation: There is a clean separation of stateful and stateless services. For example, a service handling a "create session" request implements the logic for creating the session but stores the session information in a separate stateful service, which physically stores the session in memory or disk. Such a separation makes stateless services to be lightweight, easy to upgrade and scale, and autonomous. Also, stateless services are generally high-performing. On the other hand, stateful services have to store their state information in a file system or cloud storage. Thus, service designers ought to consider ways and means for ensuring HA, consistency and portability. This leads to the usage of multiple containers for data replication and the fulfilment of the consistency need.
- Availability and Resiliency: Containers enable horizontal scalability and hence the availability of microservices is guaranteed. Also, with the leverage of service meshes such as Istio, the service resiliency goal is being neatly fulfilled.

- Operational Benefits: As containers are lightweight, the benefits of starting, recovering, and upgrading services are substantially faster.

They have a self-service, agile infrastructure. Cloud platforms abstract application and service operation, providing infrastructure-level speed, safety, and scale. They use API-based collaboration. The architecture defines service-to-service interaction as automatically verifiable contracts, enabling speed and safety through simplified integration work. They exhibit antifragility. The system gets stronger when subjected to stressors, improving robustness to deliver speed and scale. Thus, with cloud-native computing, enterprise IT teams and CSPs are fulfilling the IT agility and reliability needs. Experts are discussing the cloud-native paradigm from several perspectives including technology choice, IT infrastructure optimization, architecture assimilation, process rationalization, and simplification toward process excellence, etc.

Public CSPs started providing online, on-demand, and off-premise IT resources (compute, storage, networking, and security). IT infrastructures become elastic and hence business workloads running on elastic cloud platforms have become scalable. Above all, IT infrastructure services are becoming affordable due to consolidation, centralization, and automation. Also, through the optimal sharing of expensive IT resources, the cloud phenomenon has gained a lot of attention and attraction. In short, the cloud idea has strengthened the path toward IT industrialization. Then the most pertinent question is how to write software applications that intuitively capitalize on the various delightful advantages of the cloud paradigm. Therefore, the concept of cloud-native computing is gaining undiminished popularity. The core technical and business objectives that CNAs have to achieve are given as follows.

- Agility and Productivity: CNAs have to be designed, developed, and deployed in an agile manner. Also, the applications have to guarantee heightened productivity.
- Reliability and Scalability: Producing and composing resilient microservices result in reliable and enterprise-grade applications. With containers as the most optimal runtime for microservices, the infrastructure-inspired elasticity leads to service scalability.
- Optimization and Efficiency: CNAs are portable and hence are optimized to run on any cloud (edge, local, and remote).

The mesmerizing cloud journey is literally a phenomenal one. Today we have software-defined cloud centers. Every single resource is being compartmentalized. That is, most of the cloud resources are virtualized with the ready availability of virtualization-enablement platforms and tools. Now with the faster adoption and adaptation of the containerization paradigm, cloud resources are being containerized and presented as containerized resources. Now we are targeting cloud-native infrastructures, platforms, and applications. The unique capabilities of cloud-native infrastructures are as follows.

- Self-provisioning: It is possible to provision compute, storage, and networking resources instantly.
- Elasticity: All kinds of infrastructure modules can be scaled up and down automatically in an on-demand fashion.
- Auto-recovery: Resources are designed to be fault-tolerant and recoverable if fail. This feature is to sustain business continuity without any involvement of IT professionals. Cloud-native systems are being projected as highly available and reliable.
- Immutable deployment: Containers are immutable infrastructure.
- Declarative provisioning: Server provisioning and configuration toward software deployment are being hugely simplified through declarative methods. There are two ways to deploy into

Kubernetes clusters. In the beginning, it was done imperatively by using many Kubectl commands. Then the declarative methods got introduced. This is done by writing manifests and using Kubectl apply. The declarative provisioning is good for reproducible deployments.

The Kubernetes platform works with any standardized container runtime. Container lifecycle management activities are being elegantly handled by Kubernetes. A number of manual activities in software deployment, scaling, management, and maintenance get automated and accelerated through the smart leverage of the advanced features of Kubernetes. Further on, there are deeper automation including build automation, resiliency through service meshes, pod monitoring, measurement, and management, tracing and tracking for root cause analysis, operational, performance, log and security analytics. Thus, technology-inspired automation, integration, orchestration, and observability capabilities are being facilitated through the Kubernetes platform in conjunction with MSA, containerization, DevOps, and AI paradigms. Further on, with Kubernetes being pitched as the most efficient container orchestration platform, the Kubernetes-centric tool ecosystem surges and hence a variety of noteworthy simplifications are being brought in workload consolidation and placement, resource allocation and efficiency, self-healing, scaling, and provisioning, which are generally touted as the most complicated to implement in any clustered and distributed environment.

Conclusion

Cloud-native computing is being touted as the next-generation model for creating and sustaining digital transformation applications. There will be a deeper and decisive role for software solutions in the ensuing digital era. However, the software will be more integrated, insightful =, orchestrated and sophisticated across industry verticals. The software penetration into every tangible object is simply mesmerizing. The software participation opens up an environment for innovations, inventions, and improvisations. We had been using enterprise servers to automate various business operations within an enterprise. Now with the fast spread of cloud centers across the globe, customer-facing and hugely variable applications are being adequately modernized and migration to cloud environments in order to reap all the originally trumpeted benefits. Thus, we have enterprise, web, and cloud applications.

Now the device ecosystem is growing rapidly to cater to various demands of the society. There are several input/output (I/O) devices these days (handhelds, wearables, implantable, portable, fixed, nomadic, mobile, wireless, etc.) and hence application discovery, access, and usage through these handy and trendy, slim and sleek, resource-constrained as well as intensive devices have to be heavily simplified for all kinds of I/O devices. As per the leading market watchers and analysts, we will have trillions of digitized entities, billions of connected devices, and millions of microservices in the days to unfurl. With the participation of an enormous number of digitized elements and everyday devices (personal and professional), we can aspire to have plentiful context-aware and cognitive applications in the near future. That is, people-centric applications and services will stuff and saturate our everyday environments for unambiguously understanding the special, emotional, information, commercial, and physical needs. With the faster proliferation of the IoT sensors and devices such as robots and drones, physical services will be cogently and competently developed and delivered to the right people at right time at the right place. The long-pending goal of ambient intelligence (AmI) will see the grand reality with the noteworthy advancements in the IoT and AI spaces.

For such a mesmerizing world, how CNAs are doing justice is explained in this chapter. In the forthcoming chapters, we will extensively deal with other important concepts such as cloud-native networking, storage, and security.

References

1 Michael Brenner (2012). Cloud-Native Computing: What It Is and Why Businesses Need It. https://www.nutanix.com/theforecastbynutanix/technology/cloud-native-computing-what-it-is-and-why-businesses-need-it (accessed 16 March 2021)

2 6 Essential Things You Need to Know About Cloud Native Applications. https://www.weave.works/technologies/going-cloud-native-6-essential-things-you-need-to-know/

3 Scott Carey (2021). What is cloud-native? The modern way to develop software. InfoWorld. https://www.infoworld.com/article/3281046/what-is-cloud-native-the-modern-way-to-develop-software.html (accessed 17 August 2021).

4 Cloud native applications: Ship faster, reduce risk, and grow your business. https://tanzu.vmware.com/cloud-native

5 What is Cloud-Native? Is It Hype or The Future of Software Development? https://stackify.com/cloud-native/

6 What is Cloud Native? https://docs.microsoft.com/en-us/dotnet/architecture/cloud-native/definition

3

Kubernetes Architecture, Best Practices, and Patterns

THE OBJECTIVES

This chapter discusses the following aspects:

1) The Emergence of Containerized Applications for IT Portability
2) Microservices Architecture (MSA) Applications for IT Agility and Adaptivity
3) The Onset of Containerized Cloud Environments
4) The Need for Container Orchestration Platform Solutions
5) The Significance of Kubernetes for Cloud-Native Systems
6) Kubernetes for Edge Cloud Environments
7) Kubernetes for Multi-cloud Implementations
8) Delineating the Kubernetes' Master–Slave Architecture

The faster maturity and stability of the Kubernetes platform has heralded the faster proliferation of cloud-native applications and services across cloud environments such as public, private, and edge clouds.

Introduction

Without an iota of doubt, the Kubernetes (K8s) platform is being touted as the game changer in the IT operations space. The field of software engineering, especially the domain of software deployment, has received a strong boost with the arrival of Kubernetes. The growing IT operational and management complexities are being meticulously mitigated through the growing power of Kubernetes. For the increasingly connected and containerized world, Kubernetes is being appreciated and applauded as the flexible and futuristic IT solution that automates the application deployment, management, and maintenance of containerized applications. Further on, Kubernetes had laid down a stimulating foundation for visualizing and realizing multi-container applications that are process aware, business critical, composite, and service oriented. Further on, Kubernetes in conjunction with microservices architecture (MSA), containerization, and enterprise DevOps tools has accentuated and accelerated the idea of cloud-native computing to flourish.

Typically, implementing non-functional requirements (NFRs) such as scalability, availability, manageability, extensibility, accessibility, and security in a distributed computing setup is beset with a lot of challenges and concerns. But Kubernetes through a host of advanced techniques simplifies and streamlines the inclusion of aforementioned NFRs. The aspect of cluster computing, operations, management, networking, governance, resource efficiency, workload consolidation, and deployment gets greatly simplified through Kubernetes. Through a well-defined abstraction layer, there is a clear-cut separation between Kubernetes workloads and the underlying

Cloud-native Computing: How to Design, Develop, and Secure Microservices and Event-Driven Applications,
First Edition. Pethuru Raj, Skylab Vanga, and Akshita Chaudhary.
© 2023 The Institute of Electrical and Electronics Engineers, Inc. Published 2023 by John Wiley & Sons, Inc.

infrastructure modules. Thereby the workloads can run anywhere without any twist and tweak. The much-talked system portability gets facilitated through K8s. Increasingly, for the container world, the faster maturity and stability of the K8s platform is being seen as an inspiring and intelligent IT solution.

The Emergence of Containerized Applications for IT Portability

The concept of containerization is being widely accepted and adopted by IT service organizations, independent software vendors (ISVs), product and tool vendors, communication service providers, enterprise and cloud IT teams, and many more groups. Containers are being positioned as the optimized application hosting and runtime environment. Containers carry a number of special features and facilities and hence are fast proliferating. Containers are lightweight virtual machines (VMs) and consume less memory footprint. The enterprise DevOps concept got hugely strengthened with the arrival of containers, which are fast maturing and stabilizing. Containers inherently simplify and streamline packaging, sharing, storing, deploying, managing, and maintaining software applications. Containers maintain a cool convergence with MSA in optimally hosting and running enterprise-grade business workloads. All kinds of information and communication technologies (ICT) services are being containerized, deployed, and maintained. A variety of deeper and decisive automations in the struggling field of software engineering are being accomplished through the power of containerization. Containers are being seen as a huge boost for the software-defined world. Containers fulfil the long-pending promise of application portability. That is, containerized applications run everywhere without any tweaking and twisting.

With the emergence of edge, private, public, and hybrid cloud environments, the role and responsibility of containers have gone up significantly. That is, in the midst of rapidly growing heterogeneous IT infrastructures, platforms, frameworks, programming languages, and libraries, the software complexity is bound to rise. That is, the multiplicity plus heterogeneity adds complexity. With containers emerging as the key complexity-mitigation tool, the larger focus on software-defined devices, systems, networks, and environments is being simplified and sped up. With containers, it becomes easier and quicker for software engineers and developers to pick and package an application and its dependencies together.

Microservices Architecture (MSA) Applications for IT Agility and Adaptivity

MSA is being presented as the next-generation service-oriented architecture (SoA) pattern for composing business-critical, process-aware, and enterprise-scale applications. Microservices are small-scale services fulfilling a business functionality. This complies to the single responsibility principle. Microservices are horizontally scalable, independently deployable, interoperable, composable, publicly discoverable, network accessible, easily manageable, and highly available. With additional tools, microservices can be made resilient. Microservices enable agile software design, development, and deployment. Microservices are being containerized and stored as container images so that they can be found and used in an automated manner. MSA is open, extensible, and has opened up a series of innovations and disruptions. MSA is also being pronounced as the significant factor toward visualizing and realizing real digital transformations. The high availability need is being easily fulfilled by having multiple instances of microservices. Through a close and beneficial association with containers, composite microservices are being built dynamically and delivered to support complex tasks. Multi-container applications became the new normal with the surging popularity of containers.

Another noteworthy point here is the faster evolution of event-driven architecture (EDA). Events are everywhere. There are personal, social, and business events in plenty. Organizations are empowering themselves to capture all kinds of internal as well as external event messages in order to be adaptive, accommodative, and adjustive in their operations, offerings, and outputs. Event-driven applications and services are gaining prominence considering the prevailing trend. In order to cope with the brewing trend, event-driven microservices are being built and released for capturing and crunching event data to make sense out of it. Thus, the hybrid architecture of MSA and EDA is all set to penetrate and participate in a pervasive and persuasive manner.

The Onset of Containerized Cloud Environments

Even in a small-scale IT environment, there may be hundreds of containers in the microservices world. As we know, enterprise applications are being segmented into a dynamic collection of microservices. On the reverse side, complicated problems are subdivided into easily manageable modules, which are then implemented as microservices, which are generally front-ended by Application Programming Interfaces (APIs). Now, by composing microservices in parallel or in sequence, bigger and better service-oriented applications can be constructed.

There are microservices and their instances everywhere. IT services, Internet of Things (IoT) devices, cyber-physical systems (CPSs), storage appliances, networking and security solutions, business workloads, and network-embedded systems are being meticulously expressed and exposed as API-driven microservices. Each microservice and its multiple instances are being accommodated in different containers. For a suitable example, let us consider a large-scale B2C e-commerce application such as amazon.in or flipkart.com. This monolithic and massive application is being rewritten as a collection of resilient and versatile microservices. Suppose the full e-commerce application is represented through 1000 microservices. For the sake of high availability, there can be multiple instances for every microservice. As containers are termed and touted as the most efficient runtime for microservices, such large-scale and enterprise-grade applications get dismantled and deployed through tens or even hundreds of thousands of containers.

The Need for Container Orchestration Platform Solutions

These transitions and trends insist for highly sophisticated container lifecycle management platform solutions. That is, container orchestration capability has to be technologically accelerated and automated. This is the key motivation for the unprecedented adoption and success of the Kubernetes platform. Market watchers and analysts say that Kubernetes has captured more than 85% market among the container orchestration platform solutions.

There are requirements to run multiple containers across multiple machines. There is a need to figure out the right containers at right time. Containerized applications have to be deployed on compute clusters. They have to be scaled up and out automatically. If there is any issue, it has to be auto-healed. The required resources are made available all the time for successfully running containerized application. There are a number of other operations to be fulfilled in an automated manner. Kubernetes solves the orchestration needs of the containerized application.

Thus, Kubernetes (K8s) is fast maturing, stabilizing, and converging. The K8s ecosystem is rapidly growing with the contributions of so many product and tool vendors across the globe. A variety of limitations, loopholes, and lacunae are being identified and addressed through additional tools. Newer possibilities and opportunities are being unearthed and accomplished through the inherent power of Kubernetes. Data science applications and artificial intelligence (AI) models are being deployed in Kubernetes clusters through MLOps and ModelOps platforms. For example, Kubeflow is a popular and open-source MLOps platform for swiftly deploying machine learning models in Kubernetes clusters. Knative is another interesting open-source project for enabling next-generation serverless applications on Kubernetes clusters. Similarly, there are platforms for facilitating blockchain applications on Kubernetes systems. Thus the scope and application domains of the Kubernetes platform are expanding steadily. Kubernetes-managed, -containerized, and microservices-centric applications are the future and are being termed as cloud-native applications.

The Significance of Kubernetes for Cloud-Native Systems

This is an increasingly connected world with the phenomenon of distributed computing gaining dominant prominence. Compute machines, storage appliances and arrays, and networking gears in conjunction with cybersecurity solutions are being centralized to form cloud environments. Such cloud centers are being established and sustained across the globe in order to comfortably meet the needs of growing business and people. Now, the much-celebrated centralization is tending toward distribution and decentralization. That is, there are private clouds in plenty especially built and maintained by large enterprises. On the other side, companies are still keeping their traditional data centers to continue their services without any hitch or hurdle. Thus, with public, private, and traditional IT environments, there are choices and facilitates for enterprises to host and run their mission-critical applications in many locations.

Critical, customer, corporate, and confidential data are being still kept in private cloud environments in order to ensure their tightest security. Further on, enterprises are keenly working on hybrid and multi-cloud strategies to keep up their operations, offerings, and outputs. Now with the surging popularity of the edge/fog computing paradigm, the aspect of distributed computing has really dawned and rekindled for the cloud era. In short, to visualize and realize premium and path-breaking services, organizations are keenly working on various cloud advancements (hybrid and edge) to bring in real digital transformations. Precisely speaking, the flourishing distributed computing idea has laid down a stimulating and scintillating foundation for world businesses to bring forth a galaxy of sophisticated products, solutions, and services.

The cloud concept, which is enabling the setting up of highly optimized and organized IT infrastructures for hosting and running next-generation business applications and IT services, is meticulously sustained through a host of pioneering digital technologies and tools. With such advanced IT infrastructures in place, a bevy of innovations and disruptions are bound to flourish. Especially, the non-functional needs of business workloads are to be fully guaranteed with ease. The prominent NFRs of cloud applications include high availability, scalability, reliability, manageability, simplicity, accessibility, portability, sustainability, extensibility, and security. In this section, how the arrival of Kubernetes is being seen as a victory for building and running highly scalable, available, reliable, portable, and manageable applications is discussed.

As discussed in the earlier chapters, MSA cogently assists agile design of services and applications. Software architects and engineers create a number of small-scale, discrete, self-contained, observable, and resilient services that can communicate through well-defined REpresentational State Transfer (REST) APIs. This is a network call rather than a function call. Enterprise-scale applications can be composed of such technology-agnostic microservices. In short, microservices emerge as the solid and stimulating building block for next-generation business and IT applications. On the other side, massive and monolithic applications get methodically decomposed into a dynamic set of microservices to have flexible and futuristic applications. This successful mantra of "divide and conquer" has been once again reinforced through the MSA pattern. Containerization steps in to simplify and speed up application integration and delivery. Containers bring in a standardized application packaging format, and there are standardized container runtimes in order to ensure application and runtime portability for containerized applications. From there, Kubernetes accelerates and automates the deployment of containerized services and applications.

The much-needed agility and automation in software engineering for the increasingly software-defined world are being elegantly achieved through the distinct combination of MSA pattern, containerization, and orchestration platforms. Microservices empower service design agility; containerization fulfils the long-standing goal of application building, integration, and delivery; and Kubernetes enables automated formation and deployment of multi-container applications, takes care of horizontal scalability, performs auto-healing, and ensures unbreakable security for applications and data. That is, much of the application complexity and composition get transferred to orchestration platforms such as Kubernetes. The much-published enterprise DevOps capabilities are being greatly augmented and automated through this strategically sound combination. Cloud-native systems are being quickly and easily realized and deployed through microservices, containers, and orchestration platforms.

Kubernetes for Edge Cloud Environments

It is projected that there will be billions of IoT edge/fog devices on the planet earth in the years to come. Increasingly edge devices are being stuffed with bigger resources (memory, storage, and processing power). This strategically sound transition enables edge devices to join in the mainstream computing. Besides proximate data processing, edge devices are instrumented to find, connect, and interact with nearby devices in the vicinity as well as with remotely held software services, applications, and databases seamlessly and spontaneously. This inherent connectivity enables edge devices to connect, collaborate, and correlate to gather context details and environment information to envisage and release sophisticated context-aware applications. Further on, edge devices can be clubbed together to form dynamic, ad hoc, purpose-specific, and optimal edge clusters/clouds to perform real-time data capture, storage, processing, analyzing, knowledge discovery and dissemination, decision-making, and actuation. For real-time applications and enterprises, the fledgling domain of edge computing has to surge ahead in the years ahead

With the increased participation of edge devices in any IoT edge environment, there is a need for lightweight versions of the enterprise-grade Kubernetes platform for managing edge devices, which are acquiring the capacity and capability to run containerized services. For performing edge analytics to extract real-time insights out of edge device data, Kubernetes-managed analytics processes at the edge can do wonders. Kubernetes powers clusters of edge devices that host and run service and application containers. The Kubernetes ecosystem grows dramatically so that there is a growing ecosystem of tools to better deploy, maintain, monitor, and govern those clusters [1].

The considerations for choosing a platform for edge environments are as follows.

- **Infrastructure Abstraction:** As indicated above, the device heterogeneity and multiplicity are steadily increasing and hence the edge platform has to work with heterogeneous devices by bringing an abstraction layer
- **Ability to Leverage Distributed Compute Elements:** The number of edge devices in any environment is exponentially growing. The edge platform has to be able to harness different and distributed edge devices to intrinsically support application scalability.
- **Extensibility:** Technologies are constantly changing, and business sentiments are also varying. So, the choice of any competent edge platform depends on these factors and facets. Any transition in technology and business has to be easily accommodated by the platform.
- **Community and Ecosystem:** There is no doubt on this. There has to be a strong community to support the addition of advanced features into the platform. Similarly, the platform ecosystem has to continuously grow to support a variety of integration, orchestration, automation, augmentation, etc.

There are a few Kubernetes-centric platforms for managing edge environments.

- **K3s [2]:** This is a really lightweight Kubernetes distribution. K3s is fast and has got a small footprint, and it is easy to install. K3s is highly available and designed for production-grade workloads in IoT edge devices. K3s is packaged as a single <40MB binary that clearly reduces the dependencies. And also, there are a smaller number of steps to install, run, and auto-update a Kubernetes cluster. K3s works great from something as small as a Raspberry Pi to an Amazon Web Services (AWS) a1.4xlarge server. This is a low-ops and minimal production Kubernetes version for tackling edge device clusters.
- **KubeEdge [3]:** This extends the enterprise k8s to the edge. That is, it creates remote worker nodes on edge devices.
- **MicroK8s [4]:** This automatically chooses the best nodes for the Kubernetes data store. When you lose a cluster database node, another node gets promoted. MicroK8s is small, with sensible defaults that "just work." A quick install, easy upgrades, and great security make it perfect for micro clouds.

Kubernetes for Multi-Cloud Implementations

There are public cloud environments being set up in plenty across the globe. The renowned public cloud service providers (CSPs) include AWS, Microsoft Azure, Google Cloud, IBM Cloud, Alibaba Cloud, etc. On the other side, large-scale enterprises keep up their own cloud environments. On-premise private clouds are famous for ensuring the tightest security for confidential, customer, and corporate data. Further on, deeper visibility and controllability are being provided by private clouds. On the other shore, we have public clouds famed for affordability, elasticity, availability, scalability, configurability, etc. Thus, the concept of hybrid clouds came up and are capable of gaining the distinct advantages of both private and public clouds. There are several scenarios for such hybrid clouds.

Now there is a twist. Forming multiple cloud environments incorporating public and private clouds is gaining prominence in the recent past. Enterprises are increasingly preferring to host their business-critical applications in different and distributed cloud environments in order to reap the originally expressed benefits of cloud computing. However, there are technical challenges in formulating and firming multi-cloud implementations. As we have discussed above, there are enabling technologies in surmounting the limitations. Kubernetes is being pronounced as the one for overcoming the challenges and concerns in setting up and sustaining multi-cloud environments.

Kubernetes offers a uniform way to deploy and manage applications on any infrastructure. There is no need for any twist and tweak to be performed on the applications to run on the infrastructure. Kubernetes could do this by abstracting the underlying infrastructure from the application environment. That is, application portability is achieved through containers and Kubernetes, which is the widely used container orchestration platform. Kubernetes guarantees a consistent deployment and management experience across any compatible IT environment. The following things are getting simplified and streamlined through the expert usage of Kubernetes.

Provisioning Multi-Cloud Resources for Business Workloads: If your workloads are running in a Kubernetes cluster successfully, then the workloads can comfortably run on any Kubernetes cluster, which is being built on any cloud infrastructure (on-premise and off-premise). This uniformity across cloud environments is realized through the proven and potential templatization method. Kubernetes defines its configurations as code. With such an arrangement, provisioning resources out of disparate cloud infrastructures to set up Kubernetes clusters is standardized.

Monitoring Multi-Cloud Environments: Kubernetes supplies a rich set of metrics that can be used to track workload availability and health. There are also automated tools to observe Kubernetes applications minutely, and if there is any deviation in the functional as well as non-functional aspects of applications, then appropriate countermeasures can be proactively initiated and implemented to ensure the desired application performance, throughput, reliability, security, etc.

Securing Multi-Cloud Applications and Data: Cloud security has been a talking point for many years now. With the participation of several clouds, there is a greater possibility for deeper and broader cyberattacks. That is, the attack surface goes up significantly instigating hackers to exhibit their special skills. Kubernetes comes handy in simplifying security configurations and reducing the attack surface. There are security policies, role-based access control methods, best practices, and a host of security-enablement tools to ward of any external and internal attacks on Kubernetes applications and data.

> **D2iQ Kommander** [5] simplifies this process with a single control plane for managing multiple clusters. Each cluster can run a different distribution of the Kubernetes platform. This comes with a rich set of features for centralized monitoring, lifecycle automation, security, governance, and cost management.

Delineating the Kubernetes' Master–Slave Architecture

Container-enablement platforms such as Docker have brought in a paradigm shift in software packaging and portability. Continuous and consistent integration, delivery, and deployment are being accelerated through containers. Therefore, with containers thriving everywhere, container management software solutions are articulated and accentuated as a vital ingredient for intelligent management of containers. Thus, Kubernetes (K8s), as an open-source project, has metamorphized into a critical component for the container world. Precisely speaking, K8s automates the process of deploying and managing multi-container applications at scale.

Kubernetes is a container management software and has become an essential tool for containerized IT environments. Especially, large-scale enterprises skilfully leverage the distinguished features and functionalities of Kubernetes in attaining hitherto unheard automations in running, managing, and maintaining IT environment operations in an agile and adaptive fashion. The Kubernetes tool ecosystem is steadily growing in order to bring in decisive and deeper automation in IT operations and service management.

Kubernetes is a leading container orchestration platform exclusively designed for elegantly running distributed applications and services at scale. Kubernetes is a set of processes running on several machines (cluster) to bring in a flurry of distinct automations. It involves a cluster of compute nodes, which gets presented as master and worker nodes. The worker nodes host the pods and control plane manages the worker nodes. Each node is a physical or VM. Each node runs pods, which are made up of containers. This diagram shows the macro-level Kubernetes architecture.

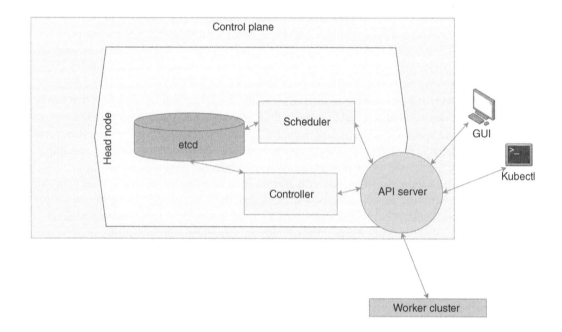

Kubernetes Master Node Components: This is the primary control unit that manages workloads in the downstream and also takes care of the communication across the entire system. There are several components running in the master node. All these can run on a single machine or on a cluster of machines. The cluster is being recommended to ensure the highest availability of Kubernetes master's components. Its components are as follows:

1) **Etcd Storage** (https://etcd.io/): This is a distributed and highly available key-value data store used by Kubernetes to store all of its cluster data (configuration data, state, and metadata). Kubernetes is a distributed system and hence needs a distributed data store. Etcd lets any of the nodes in the Kubernetes cluster read and write data. Etcd has the following properties:

    - **Fully Replicated:** This data store is available on every node in the cluster.
    - **Highly Available:** Etcd is designed to avoid single points of failure in case any hardware or network issue crops up.
    - **Consistent:** Every read returns the most recent write across multiple hosts.
    - **Simple:** This includes a well-defined and user-facing API (Google Remote Procedure Call [gRPC]).
    - **Secure:** This implements automatic transport layer security (TLS) with optional client certificate authentication.
    - **Fast:** This can achieve 10000 writes per second.
    - **Reliable:** The store is distributed using the **Raft** algorithm.

How Does Etcd Work? To gain a deeper understanding of how etcd works, we need to understand three key concepts: leaders, elections, and terms. In a Raft-based system, the cluster holds an election to choose a leader for a given term.

Leaders: Reads, which could be processed by any node in the cluster, do not need any consensus. But there are requests that need cluster consensus. Leaders are typically responsible for accepting new changes, replicating the same to all the follower nodes, and then committing the changes once the followers verify the receipt. Each cluster can only have one leader at any point of time. If a leader dies, the rest of the nodes has to initiate a new **election** after a predetermined timeout to select a new leader. Each node has to wait certain time before calling for a new election and selecting itself as a potential leader. It also asks for votes from the other nodes. Each node votes for the first candidate that requested its vote. If a candidate receives a vote from the majority of the nodes in the cluster, it becomes the new leader. Since the election timeout differs on each node, the first candidate often becomes the new leader.

As indicated earlier, any change has to be directed to the leader node to decide appropriately. Rather than accepting and committing the change immediately, etcd uses the Raft algorithm to ensure that the majority of nodes agree on the change. The leader sends the proposed new value to each node in the cluster. The nodes then send a message confirming receipt of the new value. Then, the leader commits the new value and messages each node that the value is committed to the log. This means that each change requires a quorum from the cluster nodes in order to be committed. The important deployment method is made known through the following architecture diagram [6]. You can find more information on this in this page ().

> **etcd** is a strongly consistent, distributed key-value store that provides a reliable way to store data that needs to be accessed by a distributed system or cluster of machines. It gracefully handles leader elections during network partitions and can tolerate machine failure, even in the leader node.

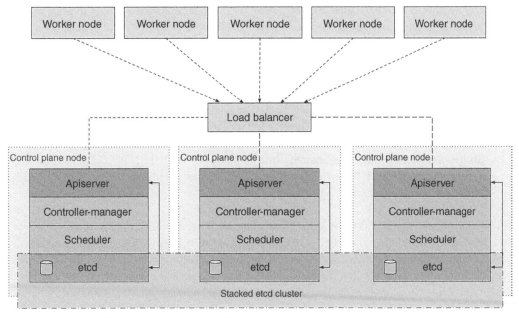

Source: Ref. [6] / The Kubernetes Authors / Public Domain.

Etcd is a unique data store for shared configuration, service discovery, and scheduler coordination of distributed systems or clusters of machines. Etcd helps to facilitate safer automatic updates, coordinates work being scheduled to hosts, and assists in the setup of overlay networking for containers.

2) **Kube-Apiserver:** This is the front end of Kubernetes. It exposes all the APIs and handles all kinds of internal and external requests. This module can be scaled horizontally. It is possible to access the API server through REST calls, the kubectl command-line interface, or other command-line tools such as kubeadm. The API server is the central management entity. This communicates with etcd database cluster. This makes sure that the data is stored in etcd. The API server brokers the interaction between the control plane, the worker nodes, and the administrators as they apply configuration changes.

3) **Kube-Scheduler:** This module checks whether the cluster is healthy, whether new containers are needed to cope with sudden spikes, and where they have to be deployed. These are all some of the prominent tasks of the Kubernetes scheduler. The scheduler carefully considers the resource needs of a pod, such as CPU or memory, along with the health of the cluster before scheduling the pod to an appropriate worker node.

The Kubernetes scheduler is a policy-rich, topology-aware, workload-specific function that significantly impacts availability, performance, and capacity. The scheduler needs to take into account individual and collective resource requirements, quality of service requirements, hardware/software/policy constraints, affinity and anti-affinity specifications, data locality, interworkload interference, deadlines, and so on. Workload-specific requirements will be exposed through the API as necessary [7]. The scheduler gives the information regarding the resources available for configuring the service to run.

In short, this is a main module that assigns nodes to newly created pods. Through policies and configuration details, the scheduler continuously watches pods and ensures that pods run on appropriate worker nodes.

4) **Kube-Controller-Manager:** It runs a number of distinct controller processes in the background to regulate the shared state of the cluster and perform a routine task. One controller consults the scheduler and makes sure the correct number of pods is running. If a pod goes down, another controller notices and responds. A controller connects services to pods to take requests to the right endpoints. And there are controllers for creating accounts and API access tokens. When there is any change in the service, the controller spots the change and starts working toward the new desired state. Logically, each controller is a separate process. In order to reduce complexity, they are all compiled into a single binary and run in a single process. Some types of these controllers are:

- **Node Controller:** This is responsible for noticing and responding when nodes go down.
- **Job Controller:** This actually watches for Job objects that represent one-off tasks, and then creates Pods to run those tasks to completion.
- **Endpoints Controller:** This populates the Endpoints object (that is, joins Services and Pods).
- **Service Account and Token Controllers:** This creates default accounts and API access tokens for new namespaces.

The controller component is responsible for keeping the cluster in the desired state as configured, and moving it toward that state when it drifts away from it. In Kubernetes, you create an object, which is a persistent entity logged within etcd. The object is a record for how things should be. The controller then acts to ensure that the object has the desired specs or properties. As an example, a ReplicaSet defines how many pods should be running based on usage criteria. The ReplicaSet is the object, and the specified pod count is the spec. The actual state of the cluster with respect to that

ReplicaSet is the status. The controller receives consistent reports from the cluster as to this status, and takes action to bring the status into agreement with the specs by creating or destroying pods.

The control plane's components make global decisions about the cluster. They also detect and respond to various cluster events. Application pods are not run on the nodes where control plane is installed.

Kubernetes' Worker Nodes: A worker node can be a physical or virtual server. Node components run on every worker node. These components execute and maintain runtime for all pods based on instructions received from control plane. The worker node components are vividly illustrated in this figure.

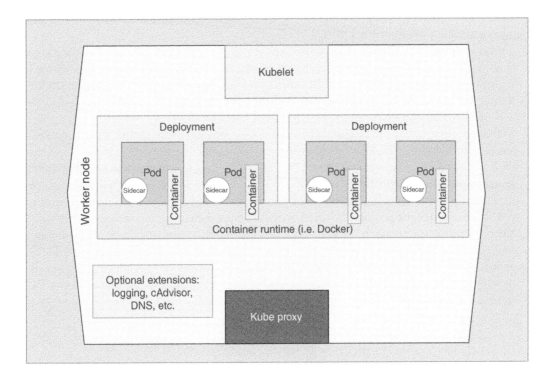

1) **Nodes:** A Kubernetes (K8s) cluster needs at least one compute node. For a production environment, a cluster has to have many nodes. Pods are scheduled and orchestrated to run on multiple nodes.

2) **Pods** – A pod is the smallest unit in the Kubernetes concept. It typically represents a single instance of an application. Each pod is made up of one or more tightly coupled containers. Pods also can be connected to persistent storage to run stateful applications. Pods provide a way to logically group and isolate containers that run together. Pods can communicate with one another on the same node/machine. The relationship between containers and pods is controlled by Kubernetes deployment descriptors. Pods are an extra level of abstraction above containers. Containers are not enough for Kubernetes to manage business workloads. Pods allow you to incorporate additional details such as restart policies and probes to continuously monitor the health of containers. Pods also allow you to involve heterogeneous containerization-enablement platforms including Docker. That is, you can deal with pods regardless of the underlying container runtime.

3) **Container:** This is an optimal runtime for hosting and running microservices. Multiple containers are being used to run microservices-centric applications. This is placed inside the pod and needs an external IP address to view the outside process.

4) **Container Runtime Engine:** You need to install a container runtime into each node in the cluster so that Pods can run there. There are several common container runtimes with Kubernetes, on Linux:

   - containerd
   - CRI-O
   - Docker

   Docker is one prominent example. This essentially pulls a Docker image and runs the containers. Any runtime software, which is implemented using Kubernetes container runtime interface (CRI), can be used in a cluster.

5) **Container Images Registry:** This registry/repository exists outside the cluster and is accessed by administrators and the control plane to download and use the container images of software applications, platforms, middleware, databases, etc. Registries can be private or public. Docker Hub is the leading public registry serving the whole world. Large-scale enterprises and CSPs offer managed repositories.

6) **Kubelet:** Each worker node contains a kubelet, a tiny application that enables the communication with the control plane. The kubelet makes sure containers are running in a pod. When the control plane needs something to happen in a node, the kubelet executes the action. Kubelet continuously monitors the state of a pod. If pod is not in the desired state or if a node fails, then a replication controller instance observes this change and launches pods on another healthy pod. It simply takes the pod specifications and makes sure containers run according to that.

7) **Kube-Proxy:** Each worker node also contains kube-proxy, a network proxy for facilitating Kubernetes networking services. The kube-proxy handles network communications inside or outside of the cluster. This relies either on the operating system's packet filtering layer or on forwarding the traffic itself. It also acts as a load balancer. This forwards the request to the correct pods across isolated networks in a cluster. This maintains network rules on nodes and takes care of network communications to pods.

Other components being attached with Kubernetes are given next.

cAdvisor: This acts as an assistant who is responsible for monitoring and gathering data about resource usage and performance metrics on each node.

Persistent Storage: Kubernetes can persist and manage the application data attached to a cluster. Kubernetes allows users to request storage resources without having to know the details of the underlying storage infrastructure. Persistent volumes are specific to a cluster, rather than a pod, and thus can outlive the life of a pod.

Service: This is an abstract mechanism to expose an application running on a group of pods in a node. This is considered as a network service. A service defines a policy by which to access the set of pods. With Kubernetes, there is no need to modify an application to use an unfamiliar service discovery mechanism. Kubernetes gives Pods their own IP addresses and a single Domain Name System (DNS) name for a set of pods and can load balance across them. Kubernetes pods are created and destroyed to match the state of the cluster. Pods are temporary resources. If you use a deployment to run your application, it can create and destroy pods dynamically. If some set of Pods (call them as "backend Pods") provides functionality to other Pods (call them as "frontend Pods") inside your cluster, the question is how the frontend pods find out and keep track of the IP address of each of the backend pods to use the application. For example, consider a stateless image processing backend application running with three replicas, which are fungible. The frontend pods do not care which backend pod has to be used. The service abstraction enables this decoupling.

A service in Kubernetes is a REST object like a pod. Like all of the REST objects, you can POST a service definition to the API server to create a new instance. The name of a service object must be a valid DNS label name. Kubernetes pods can run different types of workloads. In short, due to the constantly moving nature of pods, the IP addresses also are bound to change. This creates the networking problem. The service abstraction solves this problem.

With service, there is no need to bother about whether any of those Pods are restarting or IPs are changing. We just need to communicate with the Kubernetes service, which will route our requests to the pods just like a local balancer. Kubernetes assigns an IP address and DNS name to a service, and this never changes though the pool of pods behind the service may change due to various reasons. It is also possible to add some policies to this service such as what ports can be accessed. For example, port mapping between service and pod can be specified. That is, service is listening on 443 for Hypertext Transfer Protocol Secure (HTTPS) traffic that routes to 8443 on the pods.

In Kubernetes, the service component is used to provide a static URL through which a client can consume. The service component is for enabling Kubernetes to handle more than one connectivity scenario. A Kubernetes service works by dynamically tracking the endpoints that were created for the matching pods. For example, when you configure the service resource to track pods labeled app=web, then any healthy pod with that label is likely to receive traffic from the service.

A service can have more than one IP endpoint. So, if there is an external service exposing more than one IP address for high availability, then the service abstraction can load balance among them. The external application/component can change its IP address or go out of service. The service concept comes handy in making the changes only in the service. There is no need of making any change in clients' pod configuration.

Inter-App Communication: For hosting a modular application, there are more than one pods cooperating with one another. For example, one pod hosts the authentication module of the application. There are other modules to be connected and integrated to realize the full application.

Connecting to an Outside Resource: Sometimes there may be a situation demanding one or more pods to connect with an external resource. There is a third-party API service running on a different machine. The service abstraction takes care of the correct integration.

Accepting Outside Connections: If you are hosting a web application, people across the globe can access the web application through the Internet, which is the world's largest communication infrastructure. There are two methods through which the web clients can consume your service.

NodePort: In this, you can use the external IP address of any of the cluster nodes combined with a specific port. Any traffic that arrives at one of the nodes on the assigned port gets automatically routed by the service to the appropriate pod.

LoadBalancer: Herein, the service automatically starts and configures a load balancer that distributes traffic among the nodes.

The Headless Service: A headless service is a service with a service IP. This service, instead of load balancing, will return the IPs of our associated pods. This allows us to interact directly with the pods instead of a proxy. It is as simple as specifying none for .spec.clusterIP.

In stateful applications, the client is interested in contacting a specific pod. This is accomplished through StatefulSets. Here the service should not load balance across the pods. That is, a service does not distribute traffic. Still, we need a service to update the list of endpoints of the pods it matches. A service of that type is called "headless service." When the DNS name of the service is queried, the service does not return an IP. Instead, it returns a list of the pod endpoints that it manages. It is the client's responsibility to select the pod that it needs to connect to.

The Ingress Controller: If your application needs only one entry point for your clients to start using the application, the way forward is load balancer. However, many applications expose more than one endpoint. For example, we may have www.example.com. This supplies a lot of details. But we may also have api.example.com. This is the API version for programmers to access. Similarly, app.example.com is the GUI version of the application. Further on, blog.example.com is the community portal of the application. Inside the Kubernetes cluster, each of these (the web, API, app, and blog versions) is being run on a number of pods. Instead of using a load balancer, a better solution is to have one main gateway for all your backend application services (web, API, app, and blog). The ingress controller/gateway knows which URL request should be routed to which backend service.

Storing Configuration and Secret Data: It is possible to store config and secret data in Kubernetes for any running workloads and pods. And resources are accordingly assigned to the pods and typical persistent storage.

- **ConfigMaps:** A ConfigMap allows us to store non-confidential data in key-value pairs. Pods can consume ConfigMaps as environment variables, command-line arguments, or as configuration files in a volume. A ConfigMap allows you to decouple environment-specific configuration from your container images so that your applications are easily portable.
- **Secrets:** Kubernetes secrets lets to store confidential data in an encrypted format. This is secure than storing in ConfigMaps or pod definitions.

The Kubernetes platform can run on bare metal (BM) servers and VMs in private, public, and hybrid cloud environments. The Kubernetes architecture is a bit complicated as it involves many unique components, which have to connect, communicate, and collaborate to finish different operations. Kubernetes comes with a number of enabling tools to orchestrate complex container-ized application. Still there are several decisions to be considered and finalized by us. We need to choose the operating system, container runtime, continuous integration/continuous delivery (CI/CD) tooling, application services, storage, etc. There is also the work of managing roles, access control, multitenancy, and secure default settings.

The Special Features of the Kubernetes Platform

Kubernetes offers several scalability features:

- **Horizontal Infrastructure Scaling:** Newer infrastructure resources can be added or removed easily in order to maintain desired performance levels.
- **Auto-scaling:** Based on the CPU resource usage and/or application metrics, Kubernetes can add or remove containers.
- **Manual Scaling:** Through command line interface, it is possible to add fresh containers.
- **Replication Controller:** The replication controller primarily is to ensure that any cluster is running a specified number of equivalent pods in a healthy condition. That is, replication con-troller can add or remove extra pods.

Kubernetes can handle the availability requirements of both applications and infrastructure.

- **Health Checks:** Kubernetes continuously and consistently check the health condition of nodes, pods, and containers. Thereby the high availability of applications is being guaranteed. Kubernetes offers self-healing capability and does auto-replacement if a pod goes down due to an error.

- **Traffic Routing and Load Balancing:** Kubernetes load balancer distributes the load across multiple pods. This feature is to balance the resources quickly during incidental traffic or batch processing.

Designed for Adaptive Deployment: Kubernetes has some automated deployment of containerized applications. As we know, containerization has simplified and speeded up software building, testing, and release.

- **Automated Rollouts and Rollbacks:** Kubernetes deploys updated and upgraded applications without any downtime. It continuously monitors the application health during its rollout. If there is any failure or deviation, then it rollbacks the application to its older and functioning version.
- **Canary Deployments:** Kubernetes tests the new and the old version in production concurrently. If everything goes smoothly, then the new deployment can be scaled up or out whereas the old version can be scaled down or in.

Kubernetes provides DNS management, resource monitoring, logging, and storage orchestration. It gives much importance to the security aspect. It makes sure that information such as passwords or ssh keys are stored securely in Kubernetes secrets. Without Kubernetes, software development teams have to write scripts to do software deployment. Further on, automatic scaling and healing are not possible without Kubernetes. Kubernetes brings forth advanced automation in conjunction with containers to speed up software deployment, management, and security. Workflow optimization and automation see a grand reality with the leverage of Kubernetes. Precisely speaking, the domain of software engineering gets a huge boost with the steady and sagacious participation of the Kubernetes platform.

Modernizing and moving from traditional data centers to cloudified and containerized environments are being enabled through the power of Kubernetes. Further on, as worldwide enterprises contemplate the futuristic and flexible multi-cloud approach, the role and responsibility of Kubernetes is bound to go up significantly. Kubernetes brings a kind of abstraction in order to decouple applications from their underlying infrastructures. Thus, the long-pending goal of application and platform portability is being realized through containerization and orchestration platforms.

Kubernetes and Stateful Containers: Kubernetes StatefulSets provides resources like volumes, stable network ids, and ordinal indexes from 0 to N to deal with stateful containers. Volume is one such key feature that enables to run the stateful application. Two main types of volumes supported are:

- **Ephermal Storage Volume:** Data is stored across the container and hence if pods go down, then the volume is removed.
- **Persistent Storage:** Here the data gets stored in one or more remote nodes, and hence if pods go down, then the application data is made available.

Kubernetes can Accommodate Different Workloads: Pods in Kubernetes can host and run different sorts of applications as articulated next.

- **Deployment:** This is for running stateless applications. Herein any pod in the deployment is interchangeable and can be replaced without any impact.
- **Cronjob:** This is for running activities based on a schedule. As per definition, pods will be created, they will run the job, and then they will stop.
- **DaemonSet:** These are pods that run on every node of a Kubernetes cluster and provide node-local services. So, if you have a product or a service, which needs to run on every node, using DaemonSet will make sense.
- **StatefulSet:** This is generally used for running stateful applications. Generally, it uses a persistent storage volume to store data that is needed by every pod of a defined StatefulSet.

Best Practices for Efficient and Effective Kubernetes

Experts have aggregated and articulated several best practices for skilfully and smartly using the various capabilities of the Kubernetes platform in establishing and operating containerized IT environments for hosting and running cloud-native applications.

Use a Non-root User Inside the Container: When packages are updated inside your container as root, you have to change the user to a non-root user. In Kubernetes, you can enforce this by setting the security context runAsNonRoot: true. This will make it a policy-wide setting for the entire cluster.

Make the File System Read-Only: This is another best practice that can be enforced by setting the option readOnlyFileSystem: true.

Stick to the Policy of One Process per Container: It is recommended to run only one service/application/process per container. Kubernetes monitors and manages containers based on whether a process running inside a container is healthy or not. If we run more than one process in a container, then Kubernetes cannot pinpoint which process is healthy and which is not. Typically, the same instance of a microservice can be run in multiple containers in order to ensure service availability.

Understand That Error Code is Essential: Kubernetes restarts failed containers for you. Containers have to crash cleanly with an error code. This helps Kubernetes to restart the failed ones with all the clarity and confidence.

Use the "Record" Option for Easier Rollbacks: When applying a yaml, use the --record flag kubectl apply -f deployment.yaml –record. With this option, every time there is an update, it gets saved to the history of those deployments and this gives the information to rollback a change.

Use Sidecars for Proxies: As mentioned earlier, different services ought to run in different containers. Related services (highly cohesive) can run in a pod. Services have to connect, communicate, and collaborate to produce process-aware, business-critical, and composite services.

Service communication has to happen securely and reliably in order to create resilient microservices. Therefore, in the recent past, the industry is leaning toward service mesh implementations. Service meshes recommend using a sidecar proxy so that every service request has to be routed through this proxy. Such a proxy handles a number of common activities, which are actually abstracted from participating microservices. For example, there are multiple services depending on a database. Now it is not necessary to hardcode the database credentials into each container. Instead, the proxy securely stores and uses to facilitate services to interact with their databases.

Use Readiness and Liveness Probes: Kubernetes uses various probes to check whether nodes are functioning in a healthy manner or not. If found unhealthy, Kubernetes avoids sending any request to any failing node. Now it is possible to add additional logic into it to expand its functionality. Liveness probes allow Kubernetes to determine whether an application within a container is alive and actively running. Kubernetes can periodically run commands within the container to check the basic application behavior. Kubernetes also can send Hypertext Transfer Protocol (HTTP) or Transmission Control Protocol (TCP) network requests to determine if the process is available and able to respond. If a liveness probe fails, Kubernetes restarts the container to give the same functionality within the pod.

Readiness probes are for checking whether a pod is ready to serve traffic. Applications within a container may need to perform initialization procedures before they are ready to accept client requests, or they may have to reload if they are notified of a new configuration. When a readiness probe fails, instead of restarting the container, Kubernetes stops sending requests to the pod temporarily. This allows the pod to complete its initialization or maintenance routines without impacting the health of the group as a whole.

Map External Services to Internal Ones: There are some services that work outside the cluster. Now if you need such an external service, you can call it by its name with the type ExternalName. Then, the Kubernetes manager passes your request to it as if it is a part of the cluster.

Use Helm Charts: Helm is basically a repository for packaged Kubernetes configurations. If you want to deploy a MongoDB, there is a preconfigured Helm chart for it with all of its dependencies. This simplifies its deployment into the cluster greatly. There are many Helm charts for widely used software packages. Such a set up hugely reduces time and efforts.

Leverage Service Meshes for Reliability: As mentioned earlier, the adoption of service mesh implementations is on the rise with the faster proliferation of containerized microservices-centric applications. We have written the unique features and facilities of service meshes in the next chapter. With the faster maturity and stability of DevOps tools and processes, the business agility is being achieved easily and quickly. Now the worldwide business houses are demanding reliability. It is indisputably clear that IT reliability leads to business reliability. Service meshes enable the much-needed reliability in the increasingly containerized cloud environments.

Stick to the 12 Factor Application Philosophy: Twelve factor app principles [8] have been the keystone for cloud application design, development, and deployment. These 12 principles (you can get them from the website) hold good for applications that are to run in clustered environments. By adhering to the guidelines laid down, you can produce applications that can run efficiently in Kubernetes clusters. Applications have to be aware of their underlying infrastructure modules. On the other side, infrastructures have to be aware of the applications running on them in order to be adaptive and adroit. These principles come handy for expertly architecting applications that can run predictably in Kubernetes clusters.

Containerize Applications: Containers are being positioned as the most optimal runtime for microservices-centric applications. Containers provide a transparent isolation between the application environment and the underlying infrastructure. This is predominantly for ensuring application portability. Containers leverage the proven service-oriented method for enabling inter-application communication. Containers gain prominence as they intrinsically facilitate the DevOps activities (continuous integration, delivery, deployment, monitoring, operational analytics, and improvement). Containers are lightweight and hence assist real-time horizontal scalability, which is termed as the much-needed feature for hugely varying and unpredictable applications. This containerization-inspired abstraction is giving a kind of standardization for application packaging and execution. Microservices, business workloads, IT platforms, databases, middleware solutions, and other renowned software packages are formally containerized, curated, and deposited in container image registries/repositories to be searched, matched, instantiated, and run anywhere. These characteristics make containerized applications to be fetched and deployed by Kubernetes in various IT environments.

Optimize Containers: As discussed earlier, encapsulating an application inside a container opens up a series of hitherto unheard possibilities and opportunities. It is therefore important to create and store an optimal image for each of the applications to kickstart the phenomenon of containerization. Image building has to be done in an optimal manner. Experts suggest that image sizes have to be kept small. The layering approach for image building brings the aspect of composability to the forefront. Small-sized images can remarkably reduce the time and resources required to start up a new container on a cluster. The reusability of existing layers for quick image updates and upgrades and to produce altogether newer images is also suggested by pioneers and pundits. When creating container images, the best practice is to separate your build steps from the final image that will be run in production. This is done by using Docker multistage builds [9].

One of the challenges while building container images is to keep the image size on the lesser side. As we know, each instruction in the Dockerfile adds a layer to the image, and we need to clean up any artifacts that we do not need before moving on to the next layer. To arrive at an efficient Dockerfile, we ought to employ shell tricks and other logic to keep the layers as small as possible and it has to be ensured that each layer has the artifacts it needs from the previous layer. It was actually very common to have one Dockerfile to use for development (which contained everything needed to build your application) and a slimmed-down one to use for production, which only contained your application and exactly what was needed to run it.

Decide the Scope for Containers and Pods: As indicated earlier, pods are the smallest unit of abstraction and a pod generally consists of one or more containers. Kubernetes can manage pods directly but not containers individually. Containers in a pod share a lifecycle and are managed together as a single unit. The containers are always scheduled on the same node and are started or stopped together. Containers share resources like filesystems and IP space of the node.

At first, it can be difficult to discover the best way to divide your applications into containers and pods. This makes it important to understand how Kubernetes handles these components and what each layer of abstraction provides for your systems. A few considerations can help you identify some natural points of encapsulation for your application with each of these abstractions. A pod with many containers hosts an application and its components. The idea of high cohesiveness gets fulfilled through such a setup. It is prudent to bundle items that have to scale together in a single pod. For example, web server and application servers have to be run in different pods. That is, the web server can be separately scaled up and out without impacting the application server. However, disaggregating a web server and a database adaptor is not a wise move because the web server and the Database (DB) adaptor have to be tightly coupled to fulfil certain tasks quickly.

Enhance Pod Functionality by Bundling Support Containers: Generally, a primary container is responsible for fulfilling the core functions of the pod, but there are additional containers to support the core container. For instance, in a web server pod, a Nginx container might listen for requests and serve content while an associated container updates static files when a repository changes. There are certain benefits of running the web server container and the repository puller container separately. Both of them can be independently updated and upgraded.

Extract Configuration into ConfigMaps and Secrets: We have written about these two storage mechanisms available with Kubernetes. It is possible to bake configuration details into container images. But it is better to empower components to be configurable at runtime to support deployment in different environments. To manage runtime configuration parameters, Kubernetes offers two objects called **ConfigMaps** and **Secrets**.

ConfigMaps store data that can be exposed to pods and other objects at runtime. Data stored within ConfigMaps are presented as environment variables or mounted as files in the pod. By designing your applications to read from these locations, it is possible to inject the configuration details at runtime. This helps to modify the behavior of your components at runtime. This also eliminates the need to rebuild the container image to reflect different needs.

Secrets securely store sensitive data and selectively allow pods and other components to access them on need basis. Secrets enable granting confidential and crucial data to applications in secure manner. In short, ConfigMaps and Secrets help you not to put configuration details directly in Kubernetes object definitions. You can map the configuration key instead of the value. This allows you to update configuration on the fly by modifying the ConfigMap or Secret.

Use Deployments to Manage Scale and Availability: Deployments are the compound objects that build on other Kubernetes primitives to bring forth additional capabilities. They add lifecycle management capabilities to intermediary objects (**replicasets**). The key capabilities include the ability to perform rolling updates, rollback to earlier versions, and transition between states. The replicasets allow to define pod templates to spin up and manage many copies of a single pod design. This helps to scale out your infrastructure, manage availability requirements, and automatically restart pods in the case of any failure. The much-talked self-healing of pods gets fulfilled through these additional features. As explained earlier, pods run the workloads. But you need not bother about provisioning and managing pods. Deployments are the higher-level objects that come handy in provisioning, monitoring, and managing pods to ensure workload availability and serviceability.

Create Services and Ingress Rules to Manage Access to Application Layers: Pods host and run workloads, but the challenge is how to route traffic to the provisioned pods. Pods are replaced, restarted, or moved out due to various activities such as workload rollouts, rollbacks, failures, and upgrades. These changes severely affect the network addresses previously associated with pods. Kubernetes **services** are another abstraction brought in to mitigate this complexity. A service is an abstraction that defines a logical set of pods and a policy by which to access them. This is done by maintaining routing information for dynamic pools of pods and controlling access to various layers of the infrastructure.

Services play an important role in traffic routing and management. It forwards traffic from external clients and manages connections between several internal components. Services help you to decide how traffic should flow. Kubernetes continuously updates and maintains all the information needed to forward connections to the relevant pods. In short, in dynamic environments such as Kubernetes, the role of services is vital.

Access Services Internally: As mentioned earlier, Kubernetes services allow external connection to the internal cluster pods and also manage internal communication among the pods within the cluster via different service **types.** The **ClusterIP** service type is one type allowing you to connect to a set of pods using a stable IP address that is only routable from within the cluster.

In any given cluster node, there can be multiple types of pods such as:

- Frontend pods
- Backend pods
- Redis pods
- Database MySQL pods

Each of these types of **pods** lying within an internal cluster will have a different internal network IP, which is liable to change. To facilitate the pods to talk to other pods, there is the requirement for a more reliable and efficient mechanism, and **ClusterIP** is the one [10].

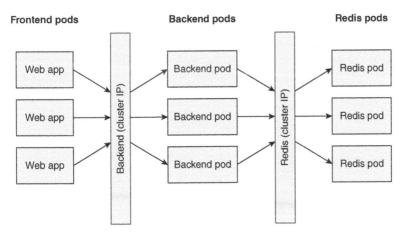

Whenever a frontend pod wants to talk to backend pods, it has to simply communicate to a ClusterIP service named **backend**. This is a single endpoint service enabling the communication with all of its backend pods. Similarly, if backend pods need to access the Redis cache service, they have to make a service call to cluster IP service named **Redis**. This then allows the backend pods to interact with the respective Redis pods.

Expose Services for Public Consumption: For public access, the **load balancer** service type is recommended. Load balancer has been a basic necessity for ensuring high availability. This facilitates routing external requests to the pods in your service in the internal cluster. Since the load balancer service type creates a load balancer for every service, it turns out to be an expensive affair.

As an affordable solution, Kubernetes **ingress** objects can be used to describe how to route different types of requests to different services based on a predetermined set of rules. For instance, requests for "peterindia.net" might go to service A, while requests for "news18.com" might be routed to service B.

Ingress rules must be interpreted by an **ingress controller** such as Nginx, which is deployed as a pod within the cluster. This controller implements the ingress rules and forwards traffic to Kubernetes services accordingly. Ingress is to load-balance multiple services through a single endpoint. Ingress works only if you are using HTTP. This will not work for TCP and User Datagram Protocol (UDP)-based applications.

Use Declarative Syntax to Manage Kubernetes State: Kubernetes is quite flexible in defining and controlling the resources deployed to its clusters. Using tools like kubectl, it is possible to imperatively define ad hoc objects to deploy various resources to your cluster. However, this does not leave any record of the changes you have brought into your cluster. This makes it difficult to track all the operational changes performed on the cluster. Also, in this case, the prospect or possibility for automated recovery is also remote.

Having understood this limitation, the Kubernetes platform is incorporated with the declarative syntax that allows you to fully define resources within text files and then use kubectl to apply the configuration or any change. Storing these configuration files in a version control repository greatly simplifies monitoring any change. File-based management adapts existing patterns to new resources by only copying and editing existing definitions. Storing Kubernetes object definitions in versioned directories is to take a snapshot of the desired cluster state at each point in time. This helps to do recovery operations and migrations. Further on, it helps to pinpoint the root cause of unintended changes introduced to your system.

In summary, Kubernetes is a complex environment due to the participation of several dynamic components. With multiplicity and heterogeneity, the complexity is bound to go up considerably. There are several complexity-mitigation technologies and tools. Further on, automation through technologically advanced solutions is being given the thrust. Thus, optimization, automation, and orchestration technologies are gaining a lot of attention these days in the increasingly complicated IT environment. As IT is being presented as the direct enabler of business operations, IT experts, exponents, and evangelists play a very delicate and decisive role in shaping up to meet changing business sentiments.

Kubernetes Patterns

Cloud-native applications are designed and deployed to be inherently scalable, portable, available, reliable, and predictable. A cloud-native application is a collection of objects like Pods, Deployments, Services, or ConfigMaps that need to be connected individually. However, there are several CSPs employing heterogeneous technologies and specific APIs. For example, an application's state can be stored in an external and cloud-based database or a message broker. But the cloud specifies its own APIs to enable fruitful interactions. Different cloud providers go for different APIs. Thus, the much-published portability feature suffers here. Precisely speaking, we need to fill the gap between the application's business logic and interaction with third-party services. The way forward for this predicament is to adopt Kubernetes-native environments, which ensure true portability for the hybrid cloud.

Kubernetes native's single object nature considerably reduces the complexity of managing its connectivity. With Kubernetes-native applications, it is possible to escape from vendor lock-ins. For Kubernetes-native applications, Kubernetes patterns [11–13] are essential. Kubernetes patterns depend on microservice applications designed and implemented with microservice patterns in mind.

The popular pattern [14] is none other than the sidecar pattern. The world is inching toward multi-container systems due to the faster stability and maturity of Kubernetes. The sidecar pattern uses a helper container to assist a primary container. The well-known examples include logging agents that collect logs and ship them to a central log analytics system. The main container is sufficiently is also good empowered through a sidecar proxy container. Such a separation brings forth a lot of advantages. If the helper container goes down, it does not affect the primary container. Another example is a file sync sidecar. The primary container in the pod is the web server container. The sidecar is a content puller. The content puller syncs with an external content management system to get the latest files for the web server to serve. This pattern has become popular with the adoption of service meshes for ensuring resilient service communication. Herein, the secondary container extends and enhances the primary container's core functionality. Some common and utility-like functions are being accomplished through such separated containers. For example, a container minutely watches for updated configuration values and can considerably augment the pod capability.

The second pattern is the ambassador pattern. The ambassador pattern uses a container to proxy communicate to and from a primary container. The primary container connects directly to the ambassador container, which, in turn, connects and gets to know pools of potentially complex external resources, like a distributed Redis cluster. The primary container need not bother about the growing third-party services. Instead, the primary container is fully supported by ambassador containers.

In production environments, the ambassador can implement logic to work with sharded databases, but the application in the primary container only needs to consider a single logical database, accessible over localhost. The ambassador may also be used by multiple applications written in different languages.

Here is a web application that uses a database for persistence. The primary container is the web application, and the ambassador is a database proxy container. The web application handles requests from clients and when the data needs to be updated, the web application sends a request over local host, where it is received by the database proxy. This proxy then forwards the request to the correct database backend. The database could have a single endpoint. Or the database could be shared across multiple database instances. In that case, the ambassador can encapsulate the logic for sharding the requests.

Another renowned pattern is the adaptor pattern. The adaptor pattern uses a container to present a standardized interface across multiple pods. Predominantly, the adaptor pattern is used to translate the primary container's data, protocols, or interfaces in order to facilitate the interactions with third-party services and data sources. The adaptor pattern is the opposite of the ambassador pattern. The ambassador presents a simplified view to the primary container, while the adaptor pattern presents a simplified view of the application to the outside world.

Conclusion

The world is increasingly software defined. Someone said that software eats the world. Software has permeated into every tangible thing in and around us to bring forth not only sophisticated business use cases but also for people-centric applications. Software has thus become pervasive and persuasive too. Every concrete thing, which we can see, touch, and experience, is being meticulously enabled through software. All kinds of physical, mechanical, electrical, and electronics systems in our personal, social, and professional places are being appropriately software-enabled so that they could exhibit a kind of adaptive and adroit behavior. Especially for creating and using context-aware applications, every common and cheap thing in our everyday environments (homes, buildings, offices, hospitals, retail stores, manufacturing floors, etc.) gets empowered through software modules. Thus, the number, variety, usage, scope, and complexity of software applications getting designed, developed, deployed, managed, and decommissioned are steadily increasing.

For fulfilling the long-pending goal of mitigating software engineering and management complexities, several pioneering technologies and tools have been unearthed and being leveraged with all the care and clarity. Cloud-native computing is a concerted effort gaining prominence as a way forward to easily and quickly build and run highly available, scalable, portable, composable, and reliable applications. Microservices-centric applications are containerized, deployed, and managed through the power of Kubernetes. Kubernetes is highly configurable and flexible enough to deal with the wide range of container-based application scenarios.

References

1 Kubernetes at the Edge. https://www.weave.works/blog/kubernetes-at-the-edge-part-1
2 **https://k3s.io/**
3 **KubeEdge** – A Kubernetes Native Edge Computing Framework. https://kubeedge.io/en/
4 https://microk8s.io/
5 https://d2iq.com/products/kommander
6 How Etcd database contributes for Kubernetes? https://superuser.openstack.org/articles/a-guide-to-kubernetes-etcd-all-you-need-to-know-to-set-up-etcd-clusters/
7 How Kubernetes Scheduler works? https://jamesdefabia.github.io/docs/admin/kube-scheduler/
8 The twelve-factor application principles. https://12factor.net/
9 **Use** multi-stage builds. https://docs.docker.com/develop/develop-images/multistage-build/
10 Web Links for Kubernetes Knowledge bases. https://www.peterindia.net/Kubernetes.html
11 Discovery and Interaction Patterns. https://www.magalix.com/blog/kubernetes-patterns-the-service-discovery-pattern
12 A Blog on Kubernetes Patterns by BMC. https://www.bmc.com/blogs/kubernetes-patterns/
13 Kubernetes Patterns (Basic and Advanced). https://github.com/k8spatterns/examples
14 Kubernetes Multi-Container Patterns. https://cloudacademy.com/course/kubernetes-patterns-for-application-developers/multi-container-patterns/

4

The Observability, Chaos Engineering, and Remediation for Cloud-Native Reliability

> **THE OBJECTIVES**
>
> This chapter conveys the significance of observability, chaos engineering, and remediation to ensure the reliability of cloud-native systems. This chapter focuses on the following topics:
>
> 1) Cloud-Native Observability
> 2) Cloud-Native Chaos Engineering
> 3) AIOps for Real-Time Predictive and Prescriptive Insights
> 4) Remediation
> 5) Cloud-Native Resilience

Introduction

Experts reason that cloud-native applications (CNAs) are being designed and developed to be deployed and run in any cloud environment (private, pubic, hybrid, and edge). The on-demand and elastic nature of cloud infrastructures have enabled the much-needed cloud application scalability. The high availability and easy accessibility of cloud applications have rekindled worldwide enterprises to embrace the enigmatic cloud paradigm. The remote monitoring, management, and maintenance of cloud applications and infrastructure modules have accelerated the cloud adoption. There are a suite of automated tools simplifying and streamlining various development, deployment, and operational aspects and activities of cloud environments. There are powerful algorithms for cloud task and resource scheduling, load balancing, resource provisioning, configuration and activation, workload consolidation, etc. Thus, the long-pending goal of IT optimization and industrialization through the cloudification process has gained immense traction these days. In nutshell, a comity of path-breaking algorithms, powerful products, optimized processes and procedures, integrated platforms, programmable infrastructures, design patterns, best practices, etc. have made worldwide institutions, individuals, and innovators to leverage the flourishing cloud paradigm in a big way. Such a cloud-enabled IT has laid down a stimulating foundation for enterprising businesses and national governments to visualize and realize sophisticated software solutions and services. Precisely speaking, the cloud IT has led to the realization of hardware programming through the highly matured and stabilized concept of compartmentalization (virtualization and containerization).

There is another concept getting a lot of attention these days. It is none other than agile software engineering. Agile and accelerated software design and development see the grand reality these

Cloud-native Computing: How to Design, Develop, and Secure Microservices and Event-Driven Applications,
First Edition. Pethuru Raj, Skylab Vanga, and Akshita Chaudhary.
© 2023 The Institute of Electrical and Electronics Engineers, Inc. Published 2023 by John Wiley & Sons, Inc.

days through the smart leverage of microservices architecture (MSA) and event-driven architecture (EDA) styles. Further on, enterprise and cloud DevOps tools and procedures help to achieve continuous integration, delivery, deployment, feedback, and improvement. Eventually, the ability to automate multiple stages of the continuous integration (CI)/continuous deployment (CD) pipeline results in reliable, quicker, and higher-quality software as well as application deployments. Thus, the end-to-end software engineering activities are being made supple and sustainable. In nutshell, the long-pending phenomenon of IT agility is being fulfilled through a host of technological advancements. The next logical target is to guarantee IT reliability.

Due to its unique positions and propositions, cloud environments provide the much-needed reliability to some extent. With the emergence of platform solutions such as Kubernetes, fulfilling the reliability requirement is becoming quite easy. There are additional technological solutions, such as service meshes like Istio and Linkerd, to guarantee the much-needed service resiliency. There are several reliability-enablement patterns such as circuit breaker, retry, timeout, bulkhead, and throttling/rate limiting. Reliability engineering experts and evangelists have come out with best practices and knowledge guides for embodying reliability in IT services and business workloads.

The Emergence of Cloud-Native Observability

The observability feature can be accomplished through two ways. One is through control theory, which explains how observability helps in understanding the state of a system through the inference of its external outputs. Another approach is by building various capabilities into the system to gauge all kinds of uncertainties and unknowns. Observability helps to understand the property of a system or an application. As enterprises move their business workloads to cloud environments, the aspect of observability is very vital. The observability is needed for cloud systems to ensure less downtime and faster velocity of application updates.

Experts say that business-critical applications that are getting modernized and migrated to cloud environments have to be tested for their stability, reliability, availability, and resilience. Stability ensures that the business workloads and IT services have to be highly stable. They should not collapse or crash often. Availability means that IT systems' uptime have to be on the higher side. This is achieved by distributing applications across different locations. Cloud infrastructures are famous for elasticity, which, in turn, guarantees workload scalability, which ultimately contributes for availability. Reliability means that cloud IT systems are efficiently functioning and continuously available. Resilience is a bit different. That is, cloud systems have to tackle unforeseen problems successfully. They have to have the inherent intelligence to foresee any issue and to circumvent the issue to continuously deliver their services to the fullest satisfaction of their end users. Resilience testing is therefore important.

Resilience accepts the fact that anything can go wrong at any point of time for cloud systems and hence through appropriate testing, additional capabilities ought to be identified and incorporated into cloud systems to empower them to wriggle out of any limiting factor. Thus problem anticipation and correct identification along with immediate resolution are mandated for any cloud system to be resilient. Bringing forth the system resilience is neither simple nor straightforward. Complex systems are majorly liable for faults and failures. It is therefore indispensable to work progressively to ponder and take steps to counter errors. Continuous testing is recommended to unearth any kind of hidden loopholes and bugs. Chaos testing is one of the proven testing procedure to uncover any runtime error. Observability, which is continuous and deep monitoring of various symptoms and signals, is therefore touted as the way forward to ensure system resilience.

In the past, the IT industry was relying on monitoring tools for ensuring the mandated application performance. In the recent past, with the surge in the number of cloud-native services and applications, there are observability tools and platforms made available to closely and deeply monitor cloud-native services and applications. Further on, these platforms come in with real-time analytics capability in order to emit out actionable insights in time. That is, all the observed data gets subjected to a variety of investigations in order to extract useful and usable information to avoid any kind of IT slowdown or breakdown. Based on the collected insights, the process of automated remediation gets initiated so that cloud applications can come back to its original and preferred state even if it gets subdued through internal or external attacks. Thus the concept of remediation through observability gains prominence and dominance to achieve resilient and intelligent cloud environments.

The Key Motivations for Cloud-Native Applications

The CNA architecture has garnered the attention of IT professionals as it has the influence, suppleness, versatility, and robustness to surmount the common bottlenecks of monolithic applications. Monolithic applications are typically closed, inflexible, and expensive to add new features and functionalities. That is, management and maintenance of legacy applications are definitely tedious and time-consuming. A small fault in one component/service of an application could penetrate into every other functionalities because application components are tightly coupled. Further on, monolithic applications are not suitable for the mobile and web world. It is not an exaggeration to state that the world is steadily tending toward scores of web-scale applications. For example, social media and e-commerce apps are drawing a tremendous number of consumers across the globe. Bringing in a slight advancement into monolithic applications involves a lot of talent, time, and treasure. Deploying a massive application is beset with a number of operational challenges and concerns. Handling a single codebase is a tricky affair. If there is a fault in a monolithic application, then the implications are really bad. The whole system may be brought down affecting the business continuity. Patching, updating, and upgrading a legacy app involves enormous amount of work from multiple teams.

Having understood the significance of legacy modernization, experts and exponents have come out with a list of ways and means of building sophisticated CNAs, which are modern, portable, reliable, available, scalable, and easily manageable. MSA, EDA, containerization, DevOps, container orchestration, 12-factor application principles, and health checkup and telemetry data collection and crunching are being pronounced as the essential ingredient toward CNAs. For the software-driven and defined world, the contributions of CNAs to automating, accelerating, and augmenting personal, social, and professional requirements are invariably immense. CNAs are being viewed as the bright and brilliant future for the digital world. In the subsequent sections, we throw more light on these topics.

Cloud-Native Applications: The Realization Technologies

We are at the cusp of harmonization of multiple technologies. This synchronization goes a long way in overcoming a litany of business and IT challenges and concerns. Above all, this transition has enabled the realization of the strategically sound paradigm of cloud-native computing.

Cloud-Native Applications Are Microservices-Centric: As indicated earlier, multiple technologies converge to simplify developing, deploying, and operating CNAs. Microservices are independently deployable, publicly discoverable, network-accessible, modular (loosely or lightly coupled and highly cohesive), composable, horizontally scalable, and highly available through containerization and resilient through service meshes. In addition, the aspects of automated deployment, management, and self-healing of containerized microservices are being achieved through Kubernetes-like container orchestration platforms. Monitoring and observability platforms come in handy in enhancing service resiliency. Finding, leveraging, integrating, and orchestrating microservices are fulfilled through APIs. With the smart usage of the EDA pattern, event-driven microservices are seeing the light. That is, microservices are acquiring the capability of receiving and handling event data and messages. Non-blocking microservices will be pervasive and persuasive too. Thus, the faster maturity and stability of MSA and EDA have resulted in realizing event-driven, service-oriented, modular, and modern applications. The combination of EDA and MSA patterns has laid down an exciting foundation for implementing CNAs.

The fine-grained and autonomous features of microservices come in handy in empowering service reusability across industry verticals. Microservices are technology-agnostic. Any development technology can be used to build findable, portable, configurable, usable, and interoperable microservices. Today there are several programming languages, application frameworks, integrated development environments (IDEs), rapid application development (RAD) tools, and other enablers to quickly build high-quality microservices. The simplicity, agility, and adaptability facilitated by the MSA pattern go a long way in fulfilling the originally expressed benefits of cloud-native computing. Further on, the decoupling nature of EDA pattern comes in handy in strengthening the autonomy of microservices. All kinds of dependency-induced limitations and loopholes get eliminated through the EDA adoption. Both synchronous and asynchronous communication capabilities are being provided through the smooth harmonization of MSA and EDA styles.

Highly cohesive and lightly coupled microservices are built around a well-defined business context. Any technical, technological, and business changes can be easily accommodated in microservices, and typically any microservice implements only one business functionality. This tenet has its own benefits. Updating and upgrading microservices are quite simple and swift. Through configuration and composition of microservices, preparing and pampering newer or specific applications are easy. In association with other relevant technologies and tools, microservices-centric application development gets quickened and the subsequent deployment in production environments is also eased.

Fresh enterprise-grade applications are being created using MSA. Legacy and monolithic applications are dismantled and developed as a collection of microservices as a part of digital transformation strategy. Thus, application modernization is being facilitated through the MSA pattern. Subsequently migrating MSA-centric applications to cloud servers is accelerated through a host of automated tools and migration services being offered by hyperscale cloud service providers.

Segregating IT and business problems into smaller and easily manageable pieces is always a good technique. That is, an application gets divided into multiple pieces. However, this sharply increases the number of participating and contributing components. Thereby the operational and management complexities of microservices-centric applications turn out to be on the higher side. It is not straightforward to have a tighter grip on each of the microservices and how they interact with one another in order to accomplish different business tasks. Microservices are dynamic and hence establishing microservice resiliency, security, and observability is being claimed as troublesome and tedious tasks. Thus came a few platform solutions to moderate the rising complexity of microservices-centric applications.

From Monolith to Microservices: Enterprises across the world still have many old-fashioned monolithic applications to automate their business operations. With a deeper understanding and awareness of the drawbacks of legacy applications, enterprises are working on different schemes to move over from monolithic to microservices. But this transformation journey is neither simple nor straightforward. As articulated earlier, there are several benefits being associated with microservices-centric applications. Advanced functionalities and features can be incorporated in microservices applications quickly and easily. Separate teams can work on formulating and bringing forth newer microservices with fresh business capabilities. The pace of change in the MSA world is quite speedier. The business value goes up significantly with microservices-centric applications. Hence there is a strong and sustained urge to slaying the monolith architecture into microservices. Business houses are keenly strategizing and planning the journey of monolithic to microservices in an affordable, controlled, and risk-free manner. This is touted as an epic journey because it has to go through multiple thought-provoking iterations.

Enterprise-grade legacy applications comprise several tightly knit layers/tiers (multitiered applications). Identifying unique and business-specific functionalities from that single codebase mandates a considerable time and thought. The business context is one prime aspect to pinpoint the functionalities that can be expressed and exposed as API-attached microservices to the outside world. The expectation is that without disturbing the legacy system, new microservices with modern capabilities should be developed outside the system. Such services allow scalability and facilitate speedy delivery.

Another way to choose the business functionality that has to be decomposed into microservices is to go for parts of the legacy code that are frequently changed or the code segment that needs to be scaled very often to meet up traffic spikes. The next step is to select the one, which is fairly loosely coupled. With such selection procedures, the detrimental effect will be heavily minimized. The selected component has to be separately deployable along with the monolith app, and it has to have a separate CI/CD pipeline toward its frequent deployment. The selection of functionalities is not an easy task as there are several problematic interdependencies in a monolithic application. Thus, the modernization and migration are an iterative and incremental process. The pros and cons have to be analyzed deeply before embarking on the modernization journey.

It is widely accepted that legacy modernization brings forth a number of advantages to businesses and users. Potential and promising technology stacks can be used while building and deploying microservices. Advanced algorithms can be used in newly created microservices. For example, the "Go" language has become a popular programming language choice while coding microservices because the Go language has the innate ability to handle heavy loads, provide better speed, and support for concurrency.

The **Strangler pattern** is an important pattern toward legacy modernization. Business functionality that gets extracted from the monolith application is in the form of services that interact with the monolith application via Remote Procedure Call (RPC) or REpresentational State Transfe (REST) or via messaging-based events. In due course of time, once the functionality and the associated code within the monolith is ready to be retired, the new microservices strangle the existing codebase in the monolith. Thus, gradually newer microservices get implemented and used without affecting the system functioning. Microservices are then containerized and the corresponding container images have to be deposited in local or remote registries/repositories. The infrastructure and operations team have to be synchronized to set up a continuous integration and delivery pipeline. The next step is to have infrastructure as code (IaC)-enabled automated infrastructure provisioning.

Once microservices are running in production-grade environments with all the required performance parameters, they have to be minutely monitored in order to capture and capitalize on their operational, performance, latency, scalability, health condition, and logging data. There are microservices monitoring and observability platforms. A microservices API gateway can be set up for transparently routing service requests to their corresponding back-end services. This gateway acts as a proxy engine, which can also help in protocol translation. For example, the new microservice supports a different protocol (say, gRPC), while the monolithic application supports something different (SOAP), then there is a need for protocol translation to enable their fluent interactions.

Similarly, if there is a need for translation of service requests and response, the proxy engine performs them. Another approach is to come out with a new microservice to do such intermediary tasks so that the proxy engine is not stressed with additional needs.

Even proxy engine is being developed as a collection of microservices and hence newer and specific microservices can interact with the proxy engine through a service call. Just embracing MSA does not solve application architecture and design issues. As noted earlier, decoupled microservices fight against system failure. If one microservice of an application is affected or attacked, due to the inherent decoupling nature, the fault does not percolate into other microservices of the application. This prevents and prohibits the going down of the whole system. Many microservices connect, communicate, and collaborate through network calls. However, if one particular microservice is receiving so many requests at a time, then there is a possibility for the downstream and upstream microservices to be eventually impacted. That is, the system performance is bound to go down. Thus, direct and indirect communication between microservices have to be planned accordingly. That is, architects must arrive at a general rule as to how many microservices should be called in a sequence following an asynchronous communication protocol. There are synchronous and asynchronous communications. MSA supports typically the request and response model. The EDA empowers microservices performing their designated functions through event data and messages. The hybrid model of MSA and EDA styles is highly recommended for producing next-generation microservices-centric applications.

Decomposing the Database: There are several best practices for designing microservices applications. As per the ideals of the MSA pattern, every microservice has to have its own database. Such a setup fulfils the decoupling characteristic, which enables flexibility. That is, microservices are self-contained to be autonomic in their operations. With dedicated databases, microservices have the complete control over their data. Today we have a variety of database types such as SQL, NoSQL, and distributed SQL databases besides file systems to stock and retrieve microservice data. However, legacy systems have their data spread across multiple tables in a single database schema. The SQL queries usually involve performing join operations to fetch the required information from multiple tables linked through foreign keys. As we all know, shared database has the performance issue. Also, when we move over to microservices, there is no clarity on what part of schema has to be changed safely. Also, the issue of data inconsistency across microservices crops up.

Therefore, the best approach is to split the database apart. While splitting, the architect has to consider issues of data synchronization, transaction integrity, joint operations, etc. If more than one business functionality shares information, then the splitting becomes a difficult proposition. In that case, the shared data can be together taken out and can be wrapped around a service. Each co-dependent microservice can call the wrapper service to change/view the data in synchronous or asynchronous mode.

Thus, such peculiar limitations are being proactively identified and addressed through technological solutions. Such a pre-emptive approach catapults the MSA style to be the architectural pattern for digital life applications. Thus, in the recent past, the transition from monolithic to microservices has picked up the speed with the steady maturity of technologies, integrated platforms, automated tools, best practices, patterns, and processes. As monolithic applications are becoming complicated, not conducive for scalability and troubleshooting, the modernization process takes over with all the clarity and alacrity.

In summary, MSA is emerging as an architecture style to simplify and speed up software development. MSA goes hand-in-hand with the cloud-native trend by using containers as a vehicle for building, packaging, and running software components. The world is zeroing down on the indisputable truth that instead of creating an application as a single entity from the ground up, it is futuristic and fertile to develop applications as a collection of already developed, verified and curated, independently deployable, and easily manageable services that communicate with each other to fulfil business functionalities. This fresh and fertile approach is beneficial in many ways. Each microservice, which is a distinct and decisive component of an application, can be attended separately for fulfilling the sustainability, simplicity, accessibility, scalability, availability, reliability, and security demands.

Cloud-Native Applications Are Containerized: The Docker official site says that a container packages up an application source code and all its dependencies so the application runs quickly and reliably across computing environments without any hitch and hurdle. A Docker container image is a lightweight, standalone, and executable package of the application that includes the application code, runtime, system tools, libraries, and settings. Docker images become containers when they are run in Docker Engine. The beauty is that containers isolate software from its underlying environment to smoothly run applications everywhere. Application portability is being achieved through containerization.

The idea of containerization has brought in a delectable transformation in application deployment. Containers are being positioned as the best-in-class microservice hosting and runtime environment. Containers are being increasingly run inside bare metal (BM) servers or virtual machines (VMs). That is, containers are apt to be run in commodity servers, which are inexpensive but fallible. Therefore, containers are typically ephemeral and hence container instances ought to be easily created or restarted on the same server machine or in other servers in the cluster. There is a close association between microservices and containers. The affinity between them is definitely creating waves of interests among application developers and architects in envisaging portable business-critical applications. Microservices are containerized and stocked in public or private container image registries/repositories. The publicly available images can be the source for making multifaceted microservices-centric applications. There are management platforms for accurately and artistically managing microservices-enabled applications. Containers offer several advantages as indicated in the following text:

- **Containers Provide a Unique Application Packaging Mechanism:** With containers, all the runtime dependencies for an application are bundled together. If there is a need for a specific version of Windows, Linux or Java, those dependencies can be packaged in the container. This means a developer's application will work in cloud as it works in his or her laptop. The optimal representation of application modules is enabled through containerization.
- **Stateless and Immutable:** Containers are designed to perform a specific task and they do not persist after executing their task. Containers are immutable and hence the information within the container cannot be changed. If there is any deliberate attempt to manipulate containers, then they collapse.
- **Self-Contained and Isolated:** Each application component lives within its own container. For example, you could have a database application running in Container A and a web application running in Container B on the same server. That is, containers are isolated and hence containerization intrinsically ensures greater security.
- **Patching:** Instead of updating the files and folders inside a container to support a new version of an application, the way forward is to create a new container with an updated image.
- **Portability:** It is easy to move application containers across cloud environments (local or remote), and also new containers can be spun up quickly because they are lightweight. Thereby the real-time scalability is being facilitated. The portability is fulfilled since all the dependencies of any application are included in the container. Containers can be deployed to multiple different operating systems (OSs) and hardware platforms.
- **Less Overhead:** Containers are lightweight and hence consume less boot time. Containers allow applications to be more rapidly deployed, patched, or scaled.

The containerization aspect has brought in a few important use cases.

- It is possible to lift and shift existing applications into cloud environments. Currently running applications can be containerized and migrated to clouds.
- Existing applications can be decomposed into a collection of microservices and then each microservice gets containerized. Such a refactoring enjoys the full benefits of a container environment.
- It is also recommended to develop new container-native applications. This approach unlocks the full benefits of containerization.
- Containers take care of the infrastructure requirements of microservices. Besides running microservices, containers also help microservices to be scaled out, quickly deployed, and easily isolated. Microservices support distributed application architecture. Containers here play a vital role in empowering distributed applications made out of microservices.
- Containers play a facilitating role in continuous integration and deployment. That is, containers contribute immensely to accelerated software engineering. Containers support streamlined build, test, and deployment from the same container images.

Containers contribute as a highly optimized software infrastructure to hosting and running CNAs. The elasticity of containers comes in handy toward the scalability of cloud-native apps. Further on, the portability of CNAs is fulfilled through the concept of containerization. In short, containerization play an indispensable role in propelling CNAs.

DevOps for Cloud-Native Applications (CNAs)

CNAs are famous for their native resiliency, agility, operability, and observability. The agility part comes from the shrewd usage of the popular DevOps tools. Now the security aspect is being incorporated to bring forth the newer concept of DevSecOps. DevOps is the widely used method of automating the complicated processes between software development and IT operations. For fulfilling the agile characteristic of CNAs, DevOps is being touted as the way forward. Since CNAs have to be taken to the market rapidly, DevOps turns out to be an essential ingredient. DevOps achieves faster, frequent, and flexible end-to-end software engineering workflow.

Two important themes (containerization and orchestration) have brought in a bevy of automations in the activities that are part and parcel of the DevOps workflow. The continuous integration, delivery, deployment, and feedback tasks get accelerated and augmented with containers and container orchestration platforms. The IT continuity, agility, and consistency are being provided through a host of DevOps technologies and tools, and this has an influencing impact on businesses.

GitOps-Enabled Application Deployments (https://www.gitops.tech/):The cloud-native computing does well with GitOps-style deployments. GitOps unifies deployment, monitoring, and management of CNAs. The goal of GitOps enables development teams to make changes and updates safely and securely to complex applications running in Kubernetes clusters. In short, GitOps is emerging as a new way of fulfilling CD for CNAs.

The central idea of GitOps is having a Git repository that contains declarative descriptions of the infrastructure currently desired in the production environment. Further on, there is an automated process to make the production environment matching up with the described state in the repository. If there is a need to deploy a new application or update an existing one, just updating the repository is sufficient. Subsequently everything else happens automatically. The unique thing about GitOps is that there is no need to switch tools for deploying CNAs. Everything happens in the version control system that are in use for developing the application. With GitOps, we gain the complete history of how our environment changed over time. This makes recovering from any error an easy thing by issuing a git revert.

GitOps allows managing deployments completely from inside our environment. For that, the environment only needs access to the code repository and image registry. There is no need to give developers the direct access to the environment. With GitOps, every change to any environment must happen through the repository. It is to just check out the master branch to get a complete description of what is deployed where. Plus the complete history of every change ever made to the system is also made available.

GitOps is the best thing since configuration as code. Git changed how we collaborate. But declarative configuration is the key to dealing with infrastructure at scale and its configuration changes. GitOps organizes the deployment process around code repositories as the central element. There are at least two repositories: the application repository and the environment configuration repository. The application repository contains the source code of the application and the deployment manifests to deploy the application. The environment configuration repository contains all deployment manifests of the currently desired infrastructure of an deployment environment. It describes what applications and infrastructural services (message broker, service mesh, monitoring tool, etc.) should run with what configuration and version in the deployment environment. There are two ways to implement the deployment strategy for GitOps: Push-based and Pull-based deployments.

Push-Based Deployments: This strategy is implemented by popular CI/CD tools such as Jenkins, CircleCI, or Travis CI. The source code of the application lives inside the application repository along with the Kubernetes Yet Another Markup Language (YAMLs) needed to deploy the application. Whenever the application code gets updated, the build pipeline is triggered, which builds the container images, and finally the environment configuration repository is updated with new deployment descriptors. This is vividly illustrated in the diagram below.

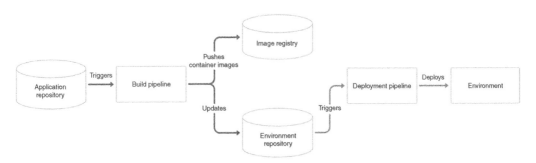

Push-based software deployment.

Any change to the environment configuration repository triggers the deployment pipeline. This pipeline is responsible for applying all manifests in the environment configuration repository to the infrastructure. With this approach, it is indispensable to provide credentials to the deployment environment. In some use cases, a push-based deployment is inevitable when running an automated provisioning of cloud infrastructure. In such cases, it is strongly recommended to utilize the fine-granular configurable authorization system of the cloud provider for more restrictive deployment permissions.

The deployment pipeline is only triggered when the environment repository changes. It cannot automatically notice any deviations of the environment and its desired state. Therefore, there is a need for a monitoring system so that one can intervene if the environment does not match what is described in the environment repository.

Pull-Based Deployments: This strategy uses the same concepts as the push-based deployments. The difference lies in how the deployment pipeline works. Traditional CI/CD pipelines are triggered by an external event. For example, when a new code is pushed to an application repository, there is a trigger. With the pull-based deployment approach, the operator is introduced. It takes over the role of the pipeline by continuously comparing the desired state in the environment repository with the actual state in the deployed infrastructure. Whenever there is a difference, the operator updates the infrastructure to match the environment repository. The image registry can be monitored to find new versions of images to deploy. This is depicted in the following diagram.

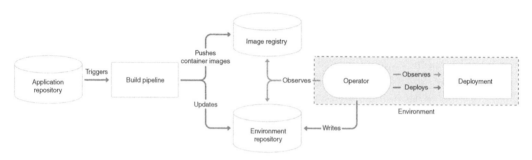

Pull-based software deployment.

Just like the push-based deployment, this model updates the environment whenever there is a change in the environment repository. However, with the operator, changes can also be noticed in the other direction. Whenever the deployed infrastructure changes in any way not described in the environment repository, these changes are reverted. This ensures that all changes are made traceable in the Git log, by making all direct changes to the cluster impossible.

This change in direction solves the problem of push-based deployments, where the environment is only updated when the environment repository is updated. This does not remove any monitoring completely. Operators support sending mails or Slack notifications if it cannot bring the environment to the desired state for any reason. For example, if it cannot pull a container image, operators send an email or a notification. This mandates setting up a monitoring mechanism for the operator itself, as there is no automated deployment process getting initiated without it.

The operator should always live in the same environment or cluster as the application to deploy. When the actual deploying instance lives inside the very same environment, no credentials need to be known by external services. The authorization mechanism of the deployment platform in use can be utilized to restrict the permissions on performing deployments. This has a huge impact in terms of security. When using Kubernetes, Role-based Access Control (RBAC) configurations and service accounts can be utilized.

Working with Multiple Applications and Environments: Working with just one application repository and only one environment is not realistic for most applications. If an application is made of microservices, then each service has to keep its own repository. GitOps can also handle such a use case. It is possible to set up multiple build pipelines that update the environment repository. From there on, the regular automated GitOps workflow kicks in and deploys all parts of your application.

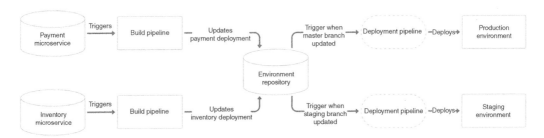

Multiple applications deployment.

Managing multiple environments with GitOps can be done by just using separate branches in the environment repository. You can set up the operator or the deployment pipeline to react to changes on one branch by deploying to the production environment and another to deploy to staging.

Container Orchestration Platforms

The container density is bound to go up considerably in any IT environment. As articulated in the following text, for running a dozen microservices, there is a need to involve hundreds of containers. This transition results in aggregated operational and management complexities. Therefore, there is a clarion call for breakthrough technologies and tools for minimizing this rising complexity. Thus came container life cycle management platform solutions. Especially Kubernetes has garnered huge market and mind shares. We have allocated a few dedicated chapters to tell all about the humble beginning and the rapid growth attained by Kubernetes. The solidity of Kubernetes is seen as the trend-setting phenomenon for the cloud-native paradigm to start and shine. A variety of automations have been harvested by containerized applications through Kubernetes. As containerized microservices are made to run on clusters, we need a competent cluster management system to tackle clusters of nodes. Kubernetes has filled up this demand beautifully. Self-scaling and self-healing of containerized microservices and maintaining the preferred number of container pods in order to guarantee non-disruption of services are natively accomplished by Kubernetes. It started with stateless applications, and the latest versions of Kubernetes have specified the ways and means of running stateful applications with options for persistent storage.

Kubernetes clusters can span hosts across local as well as remote clouds. With this feature, Kubernetes turns out to be an ideal platform for hosting CNAs, which are typically distributed across multiple cloud environments. Kubernetes gives you the platform to schedule and run containers on clusters of BM servers or VMs. Kubernetes helps you fully implement and rely on a container-based infrastructure in production environments.

- **Orchestration and Deployment:** It orchestrates containers across multiple cloud environments and deploys a specified number of containers to a specified host and keep them running in a desired state.
- **Resource Utilization Efficiency:** In conjunction with containers, Kubernetes helps to optimize resource utilization. That is, Kubernetes contributes for the mantra of achieving more with less.
- **Rollouts:** Kubernetes lets you initiate, pause, resume, or roll back rollouts.

- **Storage Provisioning:** It mounts persistent local or cloud storage for your containers as needed to run stateful applications.
- **Declarative Model:** Declaratively it does infrastructure provisioning, server configuration, and application management.
- **Health Checks and Self-heals:** Kubernetes can do these things to your applications with auto-placement, auto-restart, auto-replication, and autoscaling.
- **Service Discovery:** Kubernetes can automatically expose a container to the internet or to other containers using a Domain Name System (DNS) name or IP address.
- Kubernetes **load balancing** can distribute the workload across the network to maintain performance and stability.
- **Autoscaling:** When traffic spikes, Kubernetes autoscaling can spin up new clusters as needed to handle the additional workload.
- **Self-healing for High Availability:** When a container fails, Kubernetes can restart or replace it automatically to prevent downtime. It can also take down containers that do not meet the health-check requirements.

On concluding, Kubernetes is a container orchestration platform for scheduling and automating the deployment, management, and scaling of containerized applications.

The Cloud-Native Application Challenges [1, 2]

Legacy modernization is a buzzword in the IT industry and is a vital component of digital transformation. Businesses have accepted the fact that digital transformation through a host of digital technologies and tools leads to real business transformation. Creating and running CNAs is termed as the prime digital transformation activity. CNAs, which are modern, open, extensible, versatile, portable, and modular, have the power to bring in desired business transformations. Fresh software applications are being built directly using the proven and promising ideals of cloud-native computing. However, currently running monolithic applications have to be dismantled to be cloud-native in their operations and outputs. The division of a legacy application into multiple interactive microservices remains a huge challenge for software architects and engineers. There are experts' guidance and knowledge guides for aptly finalizing various microservices based on various considerations including the business functionality and context. Besides fulfilling all the business functionalities, there are other parameters such as non-functional requirements (NFRs)/ the quality of service (QoS) attributes to be taken into consideration while arriving at the application's microservices. Thus, creating, registering, discovering, and keep tracking microservices for perfecting cloud-native apps development is beset with a few critical challenges and concerns. More number of microservices in an IT environment always complicates the matter.

The next challenge is service resiliency and observability. In the beginning sections, we have discussed the ways and means of fulfilling these requirements. Due to the participation of heterogeneous and multiple microservices, the system complexity is to rise further. Complexity mitigation is the need of the hour to make the cloud-native paradigm popular and pervasive. Application failure is being subsidized through MSA. Because of lightly coupled and sometimes decoupled nature, failure of one service can be stopped not to cascade into other services. Containerized microservices give additional isolation. All these are OK but if there are more number of microservices collaborating and correlating with one another, there is a possibility for partial failure turns out to be the system failure. Thus, MSA and design have to be handled with utmost care. Otherwise, the application availability is in serious danger. The security of containerized microservices and data is also widely expressed as a serious threat for CNAs.

Cloud-Native Resiliency

To some extent, the resiliency requirement of CNAs is being delivered through the resiliency capabilities of the Kubernetes platform. Due to a series of breakthrough automations, Kubernetes ensures resilient CNAs. Still there are some gaps. As enunciated in Chapter 12, the emerging concept of service mesh is guaranteeing the much-needed microservices communication resiliency. Thus, the isolation provided by containers, the seamless addition of security verification and validation through DevSecOps, self-healing and self-scaling features guaranteed by Kubernetes, resilient service communication by service meshes, and a host of security solutions and tools for CNAs ensure the new requirement of cloud-native resiliency.

1) **Cloud-Native Observability**
2) **Cloud-Native Chaos Engineering**
3) **Cloud-Native Remediation**

In the subsequent sections, we are to detail each of them.

Cloud-Native Chaos Engineering

Experienced people strongly pitch for systematic and chaos testing of cloud systems to achieve cloud resilience. With the faster and increased adoption and adaption of the cloud paradigm and potency, the resilience of cloud applications and infrastructures is being insisted as an important ingredient for the cloud idea to flourish. If there is a downtime, this can create serious implications such as business loss along with a decline in the brand value. Thus, as cloud is being proclaimed as the one-stop IT solution for business requirements, cloud resilience acquires special significance. Observability, chaos testing, and remediation solutions are being presented as the viable solution approach for cloud resilience.

Chaos testing comes in handy in embedding appropriate resilience into cloud systems. In this section, we are to look into what exactly chaos testing and why it is portrayed as the way forward for making cloud resilient. Also, cloud performance can be substantially improved through chaos engineering. All kinds of performance bottlenecks and barriers can be proactively identified and addressed to increase performance radically.

Due to the COVID-19 pandemic, work from home (WFH) has become the new normal across the world. Cloud has become the core and central platform for hosting, delivering, and managing mission-critical applications. Cloud-based service delivery has picked up considerably. Cloud systems still have to have the wherewithal to tolerate any kind of traffic spike and to provide the required services without any loss of quality. The system has to find alternate ways and means to fulfil the functionality. Even cloud systems can resort to the proven technique of pooling resources in case additional resources are not granted for meeting up fluctuating user traffic.

The pandemic has highlighted the need for resilient cloud systems, which will be able to manage unpredictable and hugely varying traffic in a secure, smart, and stable way. In order to detect the unknowns, the field of chaos engineering is prescribed as the first and foremost solution approach.

It is very true that CNA design alone is not enough to achieve the much-needed resiliency. In the cloud-native era, enterprise-scale applications are being designed and developed as a dynamic collection of microservices. Thus, the MSA and EDA patterns definitely simplify the assimilation of resilience facilities. However, application resiliency through chaos testing, observability, and remediation is critical for attaining the cloud success. With the resurgence of hybrid and multi-cloud options, the resiliency need has to be inducted into software applications. Application resilience is the most vital aspect for ensuring cloud resilience. By following an architecture-driven testing approach, organizations can ensure application resiliency. Also the remediation activities for application performance can also be initiated and then the application can go live. But still the application has to be tested for any hidden security and performance-affecting holes. Continuous and chaos testing unravels any unknown failure point with cloud architectures are becoming distributed and decentralized.

Chaos testing is an approach that intentionally induces stress, defects, and anomalies into the cloud system to systematically and sagaciously pinpoint any system lacunae. The knowledge discovered goes a long way in establishing and sustaining the resilience of the system.

Chaos engineering is to methodically gauge errors through engineering chaos in mission-critical systems. With clouds getting positioned as the highly optimized and organized IT environment for hosting and delivering web, mobile, blockchain, IoT, AI, microservices-centric, operational, transactional, and analytical applications, chaos engineering is gaining prominence and dominance to ensure the cloud resilience. By introducing deviations, distortions, and degradations to the system, IT operators in conjunction with application developers, testers, DevOps professionals, and site reliability engineers (SREs) can see what happens and how it reacts. This unique testing methodology helps the concerned to gain a deeper understanding of the widening gaps between observability and resilience of the system. What is observed and what has to be observed to guarantee the resilience can be known through this chaos testing, which easily brings to light the prevailing inefficiencies. This empowers the development team all the expertise necessary to accurately and artistically change, measure, and improve resilience. Further on, system designers and application architects can better understand what needs to be freshly added to enhance resilience.

In nutshell, constant, systematic, and chaotic testing increases the resilience of cloud infrastructure, which, in turn, effectively enhances the applications' resilience and ultimately boosts the confidence of enterprise IT teams as well as end users. Besides reliability engineering techniques, chaos engineering and observability collectively contribute to cloud resilience.

How Chaos Engineering Works? The process of chaos engineering starts with a deeper understanding of the software's functionalities.

1) **Hypothesis:** Forming a hypothesis is the first and foremost task. Engineers have the knowledge what should happen if they change a variable. If they take away one or more services at random, they assume that the service still has to deliver its functionality. The question and the assumption form a hypothesis.
2) **Testing**: For testing the hypothesis, chaos engineers orchestrate simulated uncertainty along with load testing and watch for signs of any upheaval in the services, infrastructure, networks, and devices. Any failures in the stack break the hypothesis.
3) **Blast Radius**: By isolating and studying failures, engineers can understand what happens under unstable cloud conditions. Any damage or influence caused by the test is known as the "blast radius." Chaos engineers have to minimize the blast radius by controlling the tests.
4) **Insights**: The knowledge obtained can be conveyed to software development and deployment teams to plan and execute the right things

To reduce any perceptible damage to production environments, chaos engineers do not straightaway start their tests in production environment. Instead they start in a non-production environment and from there, they slowly move to production environments. Once everything goes smoothly, then chaos engineering techniques become a risk-free and rewarding affair.

The Benefits of Chaos Testing The insights that are being accrued through chaos testing help to understand the limits of our applications. With a well-intended and managed chaos engineering team, business **houses benefit in the form of heightened application reliability. Chaos**

testing clearly articulates how an application performs or provides its functionality under stress. The insights derived through chaos testing can be funneled back to development team to incorporate all the techniques while designing, developing, and deploying applications. Business reliability is the prime benefit of chaos engineering.

Cloud-Native Observability [3–5]

Let us start with monitoring, which refers to instrumenting an application to carefully collect, aggregate, and analyze logs and metrics to improve the understanding of its behavior under different conditions and circumstances. While logs describe specific events, metrics are a measurement of a system at a given point in time. Both combine well to present the full picture of a system's health. Monitoring includes everything from watching memory consumption, CPU usage, and others on individual nodes. Sometimes synthetic transactions are recommended to see if an application is responding correctly and in a timely manner. Monitoring allows you to know if an application is working correctly, securely, and cost-effectively, and is accessed only by authorized users. Monitoring allows operators to respond quickly and automatically if when an emergency occurs. It provides insights into the current health of a system and watches for changes. Logz.io (https://logz.io/) is an end-to-end cloud monitoring platform built for scale enabling unified log, metric, and trace analytics.

Observability is an advanced form of monitoring necessitated due to the movement toward cloud-native environments. The subsequent sections talk about observability and how it contributes to CNA engineering. The observability factor provides deeper visibility into modern distributed applications for automating the problem identification and resolution. The observability capability is illustrated as the extent to which we can understand the internal state or condition of a complex system based only on knowledge of its external outputs. Experts prescribe that the more observable a system is, the more quickly and accurately it is possible to navigate from an identified performance problem to its root cause without any additional coding. There are observability platforms and tools for aggregating, slicing, correlating, corroborating, and analyzing performance data of a distributed application and the hardware it runs on. This is to help in minutely monitoring, pinpointing bottlenecks and their locations, and debugging the identified loopholes in order to meet service-level agreements (SLAs) and operation-level agreements. This is also fulfilling the customer experience expectations.

Till recent past, enterprise and cloud IT teams have relied primarily on application performance management (APM) software to monitor and troubleshoot distributed applications, which are naturally complex. APM periodically samples and aggregates application and system data (this is called telemetry data). This is to get the clue of performance problem areas and to address them comprehensively. There are key performance indicators (KPIs) to compare.

APM is good for traditional applications. But for the CNAs, it is found to be insufficient. The frequent and fast deployment of applications and services are being seen as a huge challenge to APM solutions. Another noteworthy factor is the growing adoption of serverless computing for automating application operation and management activities. Containers are being spun up in a matter of seconds. Serverless goes to the level of deploying function and event code in seconds. The APM's once-a-minute data sampling cannot keep pace. Enter observability. Observability platforms discover and collect performance telemetry continuously by integrating with existing instrumentation built into application and infrastructure components. Observability focuses on four main telemetry data types.

Logs: These are granular, timestamped, and immutable records of application events. Logs can be used to create a high-fidelity, millisecond-by-millisecond record of every event. Logs come out with the surrounding context. These can be played back by developers toward troubleshooting and debugging tasks. Applications emit a steady stream of log messages describing what they are doing at any given time. These log messages capture various events happening in the system such as failed or successful actions, audit information, or health events. There are logging tools collect, store, and analyze these messages meticulously to track error messages.

Log analytics has been a primary activity for confidently troubleshooting applications. However, with the emergence of CNAs, log data handling has gone for a drastic change. The traditional approaches to logging did a commendable job for applications running on virtual and physical machines. For example, writing logs to a file is OK in VMs. But those approaches are ill-suited to containerized applications, where the file system does not outlast an application. For CNAs, log collection tools like Fluentd (https://www.fluentd.org/), run alongside application containers and collect messages directly from the applications. Messages are then forwarded on to a central log store to be aggregated and analyzed in a comprehensive manner. There are powerful log analytics tools and platforms. AI algorithms are luxuriously leveraged in performing log analytics. Sophie is an Artificial Intelligence for IT Operations (AIOps)-powered log analytics solution (https://www.loomsystems.com/product-overview) capable of preventing IT incidents before customers are affected, and providing resolutions in plain English.

- **Logs for Cloud-Native Applications:** Logging plays a very vital role in enhancing application reliability and performance. However, collecting, managing, and analyzing log data need to change to keep pace with the unique demands of cloud-native environments. As reported earlier, logging has worked wonders for application performance engineering and enhancement in the past. That is, in the era of virtual and physical machines, application development teams just focused on collecting and analyzing application and OS logs, which got deposited in persistent storage. Logs were comparatively simple in structure. Different applications produced different types of log data, and they are sometimes structured in different ways. Yet it was easy to transform log data in order to aggregate data from different and distributed sources. For log analytics, differently structured log data has to be transitioned into a consistent format.

  But in the case of CNAs, the log data structure varies hugely, the number of log repositories to be kept is rising, and the log data size is growing rapidly. CNAs are being made of distributed microservices. There are multiple versions and instances for each microservice. Each of them gets hosted and executed in containers. For the sake of high availability, redundant containers are incorporated. Holistically speaking, there are hundreds of containers for running dozens of microservices. Each microservice could produce its own log. Such a rapid rise has resulted in a large number of logs to manage and maintain. Containerized cloud environments are being managed by container/cloud orchestration platform solutions such as Kubernetes, which is a complicated system comprising several components. Each component produces its own logs. Any decent Kubernetes system comprises one or two master nodes and many worker nodes. Each node throws its own log. Precisely speaking, with disaggregation, there arises many sources of logs.

- **Ephemeral Log Storage:** Containers typically write logs to their internal file systems, and those logs will disappear when container goes down. This ephemeral nature of log storage in cloud-native environments mandates log data has to be collected and deposited in a persistent storage.

- **Diversity of Logs:** There are several coordinating components in a cloud-native environment. There are microservices-centric applications, container pods, container orchestration platforms, nodes, and clusters continuously emitting out a wider variety of log data. Cloud-native applications are typically distributed and hence log data has to be collected from distributed components.

In short, cloud-native logging is so much more complex than traditional logging and hence the other data sources turn out to be essential for achieving true observability. That is why distributed traces, metrics, and any other information emanating from cloud-native services and applications should be garnered, integrated, and correlated with the insights you derive from logs. Such integration results in clear and comprehensive context information, which has the inherent strength to gain a deeper and decisive understanding of what is happening in your environment.

Metrics: These are for measuring application health over a period of time. The measurements include how much memory and CPU are used, how many requests came, how many got the response, and what is the latency experienced by the application during traffic spikes.

Traces: These record the end-to-end flow of every user request from the front end to the back end of the application and on the reverse side. In a microservices-centric application, several services have to interact in a pre-defined sequence to accomplish specific business tasks. A complex job normally involves a number of distributed microservices and a well-defined workflow. In such a complicated scenario, understanding how a microservice application behaves at any point of time is definitely a challenging task. Fortunately, tracing solves this tricky problem by adding a unique identifier to each message sent by the application services. That unique identifier allows you to trace individual transactions as messages plough through the participating application services. This extracted detail helps to understand the health condition of the application and to debug faulty microservices.

Tracing is an important debugging tool facilitating troubleshooting and fine-tuning the behavior of a distributed application. Application code has to be modified accordingly to emit tracing data and any spans ought to be propagated by infrastructure components. In the recent past, we started to leverage service mesh implementations to have this tracing capability. Jaeger and Open Tracing are the popular tools for distributed tracing.

Dependencies: These are to reveal how each application service is dependent on other services, applications, and IT resources. These details are captured and subjected to a variety of investigations by an observability platform instantaneously. The knowledge extracted in time gives the full contextual information (what, why, where, and how of any event). This empowers the concerned with all the right and relevant information to address any performance problem. Many observability platforms have the wherewithal to automatically discover new sources of telemetry data. There may be a new API call to another service.

Cloud-Native Observability: The Benefits

The following figure vividly illustrates how cloud-native observability functions.

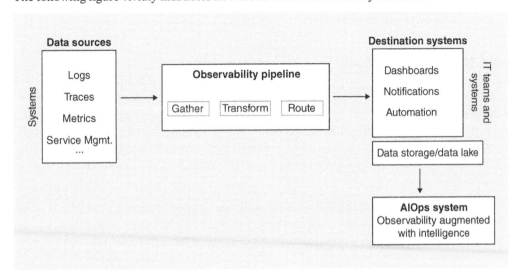

Cloud-native observability pipeline.

Experts have articulated that the aspect of cloud-native observability is capable of producing the following advantages:

- **DevOps Acceleration:** DevOps accelerates application delivery, deployment, and improvement. Now with the observability feature, DevOps becomes efficient. Using automated observability, it is possible to find and correct errors holistically. It allows in identifying and rectifying issues occurring between different projects and containers before they happen.
- **AI and Automated Detection:** By integrating AI into cloud-native logging and monitoring tools, potential problems can be learned before they occur.

Precisely speaking, observability, chaos engineering, and real-time data analytics combine well to emit out all the details including the context information to empower decision-makers to plunge into the counter measures in time.

The quality and quantity of innovations have clearly laid down a stimulating and sparkling foundation for visualizing and realizing CNAs. These applications are not only for enterprise and cloud IT environments but also for edge device clouds. Thus, the cloud-native paradigm is being seen as the core and central aspect for the future IT. CNAs are also empowered through the serverless methods. Such a convergence sharply reduces the operational and management complexities. Multi-cloud environments can be swiftly established and sustained through cloud-native computing.

Thus, various renowned features and facilities of cloud infrastructures are being meticulously used by software solutions and services to be distinctive and delightful in their offerings. As noted earlier, cloud infrastructures have gained some unique characteristics to produce and sustain agile and reliable software engineering. Further on, various DevOps tools built and used in enterprise IT environments are now readied and remedied to achieve the much-wanted continuous integration, delivery, deployment, and improvement in cloud IT environments. Containers have emerged as the most optimal building block for enterprise-grade applications, middleware, and databases. Containers are being positioned as the efficient application runtime environment. There are platform solutions for managing container life cycle activities. Microservices guarantee agile software design and development. As microservices are the key building blocks for cloud-native apps, it is easy to create versatile and resilient CNAs through configuration changes and service composition. Thus, with the seamless and spontaneous convergence of several powerful technologies, the prospects for constructing cloud-native software have gone up drastically these days. In this chapter, we are to dig deeper and dwell at length to deal with the extempore of CNAs.

Cloud-Native Observability for Chaos Engineering

End-to-end observability and monitoring into the system is essential for chaos engineering to get the desired success. The deeper visibility into the system helps chaos engineers to formulate a good hypothesis. All kinds of critical and non-critical dependencies are unwrapped through the observability factor. Thus, chaos engineering goes hand-in-hand with observability in order to considerably enhance system resilience. The steps to be taken to ensure a successful chaos testing are given as follows:

1) **Identify:** This is to pinpoint key weaknesses within your system and create a hypothesis based on that knowledge acquired along with an expected outcome. Then engineers have to analyze and identify what kind of failures ought to be injected within the formulated hypothesis framework to squeeze out system vulnerabilities, problematic areas, and failure points.

2) **Simulate:** This is to inject anomalies into the system running in production environment. Anomalies ought to be chosen in such a way that they closely reflect real-life events. This ensures that you include situations that may happen within your systems. This could entail an application failure, network disruption, container, VM, or BM server breakdown, etc.

3) **Automate:** It is important to automate the varied fault-injection experiments. Based on the business and technical requirements and the critical nature of the application, this experiment for finding any sickening loophole can be repeated every hour/day/week, etc.

4) **Continuous Feedback and Refinement:** With these fault-injection methods, the system may fail or withstand. This helps architects and operators to ponder about the best course of actions quickly with all the clarity and confidence. The results of those experimentations reveal a lot about which way to proceed.

The prominent faults being injected into a system under verification are as follows:

1) Taking away of containers, VMs, and even physical machines
2) Disconnecting system(s) from the cluster
3) Bombarding microservices with more user or data load
4) Adding network latency

The steps such as ethical hacking, fault injection, and misconfiguration are being recommended to deeply understand the internal structure and functioning of cloud systems. As there are many dynamic components in modern systems such as CNAs, there are more possibilities for them to misbehave and deviate from the prescribed action under certain situations. Proactively and pre-emptively cloud systems, which are generally distributed, have to be tested to make them fault-tolerant. They must be able to bounce back to its original and preferred state if they are attacked from internal or external sources. The system design has to start with the conjecture that complex systems are failure-prone. In short, we need brilliant minds to create chaos to understand where and why the system falters, fumbles, and fails.

As indicated elsewhere, it is vital to ensure the resilience for cloud applications. Resilience has become one of the KPIs. Continuous and systematic testing is insisted to delightfully guarantee the SLAs. By preventing lengthy outages, businesses can save significant costs and enhance their good-will and brand value sharply. Thus, chaos engineering turns out to be an important phenomenon for cloud resilience.

Chaos engineering refers to the unique practice of intentionally introducing faults into a system in order to pinpoint risks and security holes that in turn sets in a stimulating foundation for visualizing and realizing resilient applications. A chaos engineering tool will provide a controlled way to introduce faults and run specific experiments against a particular instance of an application. As it is going to be software-defined world, software systems are becoming complex. As enterprise applications tend to be extremely connected and integrated, enterprise software solutions are becoming complicated gradually. Complex systems tend to fail often. Pinpointing the source of errors, faults, and failures is a tough assignment. Also, if enterprise systems fail, the damage is simply unfathomable and irreparable resulting in heavy financial losses for business houses. The brand value slowly will fade away. Considering all these challenges and concerns, business houses are keenly strategizing and planning to have the in-house chaos engineering capability. Chaos engineering is therefore embraced by organizations to proactively and pre-emptively find and eliminate hidden loopholes. Chaos engineering has the wherewithal to ensure software reliability. Traditionally the reliability is being tried through a couple of metrics such as mean time to repair (MTTR) and mean time between failures (MTBF). This is the reactive approach. But the chaos engineering is the preferred proactive and pre-emptive approach.

CNAs have to adapt to varying realities and failures quickly in order to be relevant to their users. Cloud-native systems are expected to intelligently identify incoming failures and to adjust accordingly. They have to be fault-tolerant to ensure there is no service disruption. Disaster and data recovery in order to ensure business continuity are touted as the hallmark of CNAs. When something goes wrong, it does not penetrate or cascade into other components of the application. This is to ensure that one small fault in a component should not bring down the whole system. Chaos engineering tools are gaining critical momentum as they help experimenting software solutions in production. Imaginations and innovations are bound to thrive on this space in order to deliver continuously available and highly reliable software solutions across industry verticals. There are automated tools and platforms to facilitate chaos engineering processes and practices. Chaos Mesh and Litmus Chaos are popular. Chaos engineering offers a lot of benefits.

If chaos engineering processes are performed with all the care and clarity, application reliability is bound to go up sharply. Chaos engineering helps developers to pinpoint common failure scenarios that ultimately result in any unwanted system failure. This acquired knowledge helps developers to strengthen software systems accordingly against known failures. Further on, tools-assisted and advanced chaos engineering practices help to identify hidden errors and vulnerabilities too. All these equip software engineers to embolden software solutions against well-known as well as buried faults. This leads to an improved system resilience. That is, the system will experience fewer downtime. With less service disruption, the revenue collection goes up. The customer experience is bound to go up significantly.

Precisely speaking, chaos engineering enables system reliability. All kinds of possible failures can be proactively found and used to enhance system reliability. The system will be strengthened to fight against any internal and external errors. The brand value will rise. The traditional software testing only tests the code's functional requirements and NFRs. This process assumes that all other infrastructural components are always in good shape and hence it cannot predict all possible failure modes. But chaos engineering tests the underlying software and hardware infrastructure modules including the network component. Such a comprehensive testing in production environment ensures the system resiliency.

Because of the need for continuous integration, delivery and deployment of CNAs, the DevOps principles and products are being leveraged skillfully. Now to fulfil the system resiliency requirement, chaos engineering precepts are being incorporated with the DevOps pipeline. Thus, the aspect of cloud-native resiliency is being attended through a host of proven techniques and tips.

AIOps-Enabled Cloud-Native Observability

Monitoring highly distributed CNAs does not bring out all the necessary details to ensure application availability and reliability. Keeping up the performance levels of CNAs does mandate for observability techniques and tools. The traditional application performance monitoring and management (APM) platforms are found to be inadequate to ensure the required performance for CNAs.

AIOps has proved to be a solution for enhancing cloud-native observability. With AIOps, the advanced cloud-native observability can be fulfilled. AIOps gels well with observability platforms to bring in the necessary insights in time to empower SREs and operators to plunge into appropriate measures.

By combining AIOps with cloud-native observability, it is easy to significantly decrease the metric value of mean time to detect (MTTD). That is, you can quickly find the source of an issue within the cloud environment. As with the sharp reduction of the MTTD value, the mean time to resolve (MMTR) value also will see a decrease. Cloud-native observability with AIOps can help you in making the best use of user, system, and business data. The insights generated goes a long way in easily and quickly resolving the incidents. All AIOps initiatives should address four stages of this data journey.

- **Acquire:** AIOps platforms are being stuffed with a variety of connectors, adaptors, and drivers to acquire data coming from various sources and at scale. The primary data includes metrics, logs, and traces.
- **Aggregate:** Data has to be cleansed, transformed, and stocked in order to facilitate data analytics. AIOps platforms typically automate most of the activities at this stage and this, in turn, can accelerate the time to get value.
- **Analyze:** This is the prime activity of AIOps platforms. There are machine learning (ML) algorithms helping to filter out noise, pinpoint hidden patterns, and derive insights in time. Thus predictive and prescriptive insights are being supplied by AIOps platforms.
- **Act:** The knowledge discovered goes a long way in assisting and automating the root cause analysis, exposing the problems and embarking on remediation. AIOps ultimately facilitates deep visibility into the cloud system.

Thus, all the advancements in artificial intelligence (AI) come in handy in purposefully analyzing observed data in order to unravel and reveal actionable insights.

In a nutshell, lately AI algorithms are used to separate the signals of real problems from noise data. AI processing is done on operational data to emit out actionable insights in time as operational data size is growing rapidly. AIOps is a recent phenomenon gaining the trust of IT professionals toward operational insights. The observed data and aggregated context details can be crunched through an AIOps tool to bring forth intelligence. Thus, it is not only collecting value-adding and relevant data but also embarking on purpose-specific analysis to make sense out of data is crucial. The combination of AIOps and observability platform is going to be a trendsetter for producing sophisticated and smarter applications.

In short, an observable system is easier to understand and monitor, safer to update with new code, and simpler to repair. Ultimately, observability comes in handy in delivering high-quality software faster. It is essential to continuously observe and analyze every aspect of the application so that any kind of outliers/anomalies can be caught hold of and rectified immediately. The observation process is being performed on every layer in the software stack. This is for ensuring that there is no service disruption. The observation platform is stuffed with several automated tools for logging, monitoring, tracing, etc.

Building System Resilience Through AIOps

As explained earlier, the role and responsibility of AIOps platforms are increasingly felt across. As business workloads and IT services become more distributed and complicated, dynamic, and composable, AIOps is bound to take more responsibility in driving business value and empowering teams to create flexible and secure software faster. Product vendors are empowering their AIOps solutions to build operational resiliency and automate remediation. SREs are to benefit immensely with the contributions of AIOps in ensuring system resilience. The unique automation capabilities of AIOps facilitate continuous resiliency, availability, and system health.

By integrating your AIOps solution with the system, it is possible to garner and feed critical contextual information around configuration and deployment changes directly into the system. Experts point out that the following benefits will be accrued by the system:

- This integration pinpoints the root causes of any abnormal behavior in your system quickly and precisely.
- It alerts the relevant teams if an ongoing load test in production is to affect the system health.
- This integration also alert application teams if the rollout for a new version of a critical micros-ervice is inadvertently creating a high failure rate for that service.
- This arrangement provides a detailed rundown of both the root cause and its impact on users.

The ultimate goal of AIOps is to predict any deviations and to automate notification features. It can also prescribe and automate right remediation steps in time. AIOps supplies detailed information on root causes and their impacts on the system. All these come in handy for SREs to explore and experiment ways and means of achieving the much-needed system resilience. The insights extracted by AIOps empower operators to ponder about appropriate counter measures to keep the system running.

AIOps can quickly crunch system monitoring and observability data to emit out actionable insights, which can enable building resilient services and applications. That improves MTTR, reducing downtime and alerting the relevant teams about when an issue has occurred and when it was resolved. More details can be found at https://thenewstack.io/aiops-done-right-automating-remediation-and-resiliency/

Cloud-Native Remediation

The cloud paradigm is journeying fast with numerous technological advancements in the cloud space. Today we are reading extensively about setting up and sustaining multi-cloud environments for tackling varying business sentiments. Mission-critical business workloads are being hosted and run on different cloud environments. Application services are deployed across geographically dis-tributed and disparate cloud environments to reap some unique benefits. However, such an arrangement adds an unwanted complexity. The visibility goes down with diminishing controlla-bility. To have a 360-degree view of application components and their underlying platforms, infra-structures along with any middleware, databases, and customer viewpoints are being seen as a viable challenge for application owners and cloud service providers. Observability tools will pin-point blind spots and cut down the complexity of running business workloads in multiple clouds. AIOps coupled with observability tools provide actionable insights. But experts insist for remedia-tion tools to simplify and streamline the risk-mitigation process.

Monitoring has been doing good with monolithic applications. But for cloud-native systems, there is a need for leveraging observability tools to pinpoint the root cause for any error. It helps in identifying latency issue, anomalies, performance bottlenecks, etc. Observability and remediation tools can feed your software team with a lot of decision-enabling metrics across the technology stack (OS, applications, network, and third-party services). This combination provides insights and context details toward application resilience.

In multi-cloud environments, fulfilling SLAs remains a huge challenge. The gap between risk detection and remediation has to be lesser side. That means any security attack has to be observed and stopped quickly. Thus, the value for remediation tools and services goes up significantly with the faster adoption of the cloud idea across industry verticals. Automating remediation process goes a long way in preventing exploitation of any misconfiguration in multi-cloud environments. AI-enabled observability and remediation tools provide holistic visibility into multi-cloud environments.

Remediation tools continuously monitor access privileges across multi-cloud environments to check for any control violations. When it comes across anything, then it can inform the concerned with all the details to initiate appropriate remediation actions such as setting time limits and rejections. The remediation tool can automatically terminate any risky communication. Thus, intelligence-based remediation tools are indispensable to ensure distributed applications running continuously and delivering their obligations without fail. In a nutshell, remediation tools in conjunction with observability products are the need of the hour in ensuring cloud resilience. Various cloud operations are being identified and getting automated through technologically advanced tools. For cloud reliability, continuous availability through various measures is being insisted. Even if there are internal or external threats, observability tools identify them in time and remediation tools come forward to mitigate them well before any nasty incident happens. CloudMatos (https://www.cloudmatos.com/) has a remediation tool to establish self-healing cloud infrastructure.

Conclusion

Cloud-native services and applications play a very vital role in shaping up digital transformation. That is, digitally transformed enterprises can be realized and sustained through the leverage of cloud-native principles in a shrewd manner. CNAs carry a few unique and futuristic characteristics and benefits. Enterprises across industry verticals are therefore confidently embracing the cloud-native paradigm in order to be ahead of their competitors. All kinds of technology, business, and user sentiment changes can be easily and early accommodated in software solutions through the leverage of the cloud-native phenomenon. Through configuration and composition, sophisticated and smarter applications can be visualized and realized fast out of cloud-native services. CNAs are modern and modular, versatile, nimbler, robust, and resilient. The future of software-defined world is very safe and secure with the faster maturity and stability of CNAs. The mesmerizing domain of cloud-native paradigm has laid down a stimulating foundation for several other native applications such as Kubernetes-native and edge-native applications.

References

1 What is Cloud Native Observability and Why is it so Important? https://www.mantisnet.com/blog/what-is-cloud-native-observability-v-visibility
2 Cloud-native Observability and Analysis, https://thenewstack.io/the-cloud-native-landscape-observability-and-analysis/
3 What is Cloud Native Observability? https://newrelic.com/blog/best-practices/what-is-cloud-native-observability
4 What is observability? https://www.ibm.com/cloud/learn/observability
5 An E-book – Gaining Observability in Cloud-Native Applications. https://www.instana.com/resources/monitoring-and-observability-of-cloud-native-applications/monitoring-and-observability-of-cloud-native-applications/

5

Creating Kubernetes Clusters on Private Cloud (VMware vSphere)

THE OBJECTIVES
Traditional and local data centers are methodically modernized to be cloud-enabled through a host of proven modernization and migration techniques. Due to certain reasons, on-premise data centers are being continued by businesses, governments, financial services providers, and establishments across the world. Now to empower local data centers to be modern to seamlessly join in the mainstream cloud arena, transitioning them to be Kubernetes-enabled is the most logical thing to do for enterprises. Predominantly, on-premise data centers are being activated through VMware technologies and tools. There are other options too. OpenStack is another cloud operating system software for both public and private clouds. However, VMware vSphere is the highly visible technology stack to support and sustain complex cloud operations. The purpose of this chapter is to provide the reader with step-by-step instructions on how to deploy Kubernetes on vSphere infrastructure.

Introduction

The best Kubernetes architecture for any organization depends on its needs and goals. As inscribed in the previous chapters, Kubernetes has become a dominant container orchestration platform solution. The reasons are obvious. Kubernetes has a number of advanced features to considerably reduce the complexities associated with cloud-native application deployment and management. Kubernetes in conjunction with container abstraction assists in fulfilling the long-pending goal of application portability. A kind of Kubernetes cluster is being formed as software infrastructure, which is abstracted away from the underlying infrastructure. Such a separation goes a long way in eliminating all kinds of dependency-induced infirmities. Thus, any application can run on a Kubernetes environment in a risk-free and rewarding manner. Kubernetes is imposing a kind of standardization for ensuring software portability. Thus, the interest in the bewildering idea of Kubernetes.

Public cloud service providers have incorporated a new service offering "Kubernetes as a Service." For setting up containerized cloud environments locally, private clouds are also strengthened accordingly with the Kubernetes platform solution.

However, in hyperscale clouds, there are automated tools to simplify the setup of Kubernetes clusters. That is not the case with private clouds. That is, running Kubernetes in on-premise clouds involves setting up and managing different enablers such as etcd datastore, load balancing,

Cloud-native Computing: How to Design, Develop, and Secure Microservices and Event-Driven Applications, First Edition. Pethuru Raj, Skylab Vanga, and Akshita Chaudhary.
© 2023 The Institute of Electrical and Electronics Engineers, Inc. Published 2023 by John Wiley & Sons, Inc.

auto-scaling, roll-back in case of faulty deployments, etc. Besides networking and persistent storage, there are security, governance, management, and observability requirements. There are other important tasks such as configuration settings to be performed manually. As enterprises are keen to bring in deeper automation in IT operations, they are planning to modernize their data centers/private clouds through the inherent and insightful power of Kubernetes. There is widespread approval that cloud-native is the future for IT. Kubernetes is being seen as a game-changing tool for business behemoths to be intrinsically cloud-native. Here is a list of best practices published by Kubernetes experts.

- There is a need for one or two master server nodes and a few worker nodes. In the master node (control plane), Kube-apiserver, Kube-scheduler, Kube-controller-manager, and etcd database. In the worker nodes, along with Kube-proxy, Kubelet is a tool running on each worker node. This is for ensuring that all containers are running and meeting network regulations.
- Kubernetes has the wherewithal to recover from any failure without any data loss. This is through a system of leaders, elections, and policies. All of these are termed Quorum. This mandates good-quality hardware in place to ensure high availability and recoverability.
- An SSD is a high-performance module. It is recommended for etcd, which writes to disk. Any delay here affects the system performance.
- You also want to run Kubeadm on the master. Kubeadm is an installation tool that uses kubeadm init and kubeadm join as the best practices to create clusters.
- For production environments, you would need a dedicated HAProxy load balancer node, as well as a client machine to run automation.
- Modern Kubernetes servers typically feature two CPUs with 32 cores each, 2 TBs of error-correcting RAM and at least four SSDs, eight SATA SSDs, and a couple of 10G network cards.
- It is recommended to run your clusters in a multi-master fashion in production to ensure high availability and resiliency of the master components themselves. This means you need at least 3 Master nodes (an odd number, to ensure quorum). It is imperative to continuously monitor the master(s) and to fix any issues in case if any replica is down.
- **HA edcd:** etcd is an open-source distributed key-value store, and the persistent storage for Kubernetes. Kubernetes uses etcd to store all cluster-related data. This includes all the information that exists on your pods, nodes, and cluster. Accounting for this store is mission-critical, to say the least since it is the last line of defense in case of cluster failure. Managing highly available, secured etcd clusters for large-scale production deployments is one of the key operational complexities. This is quite tough to handle when managing Kubernetes on your own infrastructure. For production use, where availability and redundancy are important factors, running etcd as a cluster is important. Ensuring a secure etcd cluster is difficult as it involves downloading the right binaries, writing the initial cluster configuration on each etcd node, setting and bringing up etcd. This is in addition to configuring the certificate authority and certificates for secure connections. For an easier way to run etcd cluster in on-premise infrastructures, the open-source etcd adm tool is recommended.

Kubernetes in production needs more than just infrastructure. Once you are done with accounting for Kubernetes-specific dependencies, which are Docker, kubeadm, kubelet, and kubctl (CLI tool to communicate with the cluster), it is time to look at the additional services used to deploy applications. In case you are deploying offline or in an air-gapped environment, you will need to have your own repositories in place for Docker, Kubernetes, and any other open-source tools you may be using. This includes helm chart repositories for Kubernetes manifests, as well as binary repositories.

You also definitely want to install the Kubernetes dashboard, which is one of the most useful and popular add-ons. To do this, you will need to log in, select the token, get the list of dashboard secrets, and then describe them to gain full access. Experienced professionals recommend checking logs. That is, when something goes wrong, it is possible to pinpoint the fault by intently looking at syslog files. Weaveworks and Flannel are both great networking tools, while Istio and Linkerd are popular service mesh options. Grafana and Prometheus help with monitoring and there are a number of tools to automate CI/CD like Jenkins, Bamboo, and JenkinsX. Security is a major concern. Every open-source component needs to be thoroughly scanned for hidden threats and vulnerabilities. Additionally, keeping track of version updates and patches and then managing their introduction can be labor-intensive, especially if you have a lot of additional services running.

In conclusion, Kubernetes helps on-premise data centers benefit from cloud-native applications and infrastructure. Data centers could be on Openstack, KVM, VMware vSphere, or even bare metal and still reap the cloud-native benefits that come from integrating with Kubernetes. A complete Kubernetes infrastructure on-premise needs proper DNS, load balancing, Ingress, and K8's role-based access control (RBAC), alongside a slew of additional components that then makes the deployment process quite daunting for IT teams. Once Kubernetes is deployed, then comes the addition of monitoring, tracing, logging, and all the associated operations for troubleshooting – such as when running out of capacity, ensuring HA, backups, and more production use.

Purpose

The purpose of this chapter is to install OpenShift Container Platform (OCP 4.5) on VMware vSphere instance by using the installer-provisioned infrastructure.

Red Hat OpenShift Container Platform and VMware vSphere 6 and 7 are a great combination for running an enterprise container platform on a virtual infrastructure. Enterprises are increasingly deploying the proven OpenShift on VMware for their production-ready applications.

- This guide will explain how to install OCP with the installer-provisioned infrastructure (IPI) method on vSphere
- Communicate a conceptual understanding of the "OpenShift Container Platform"
- Provide a high-level vision of the architecture and scope of the proposed OCP Platform
- Enable early recognition and validation of the implications of the architectural approach
- Facilitate effective communication between different communities of stakeholders and developers

Scope

- Single Site, Single-tenant Standard with OpenShift Container Platform v4.5 installed IPI method on VMware vSphere
- Build of OpenShift installer-provisioned infrastructure method standard architecture to build on Private Cloud (vSphere)
- Application monitoring using Prometheus, Alert manager, and Grafana
- Application log management and visualization using Elasticsearch, Fluentd, and Kibana

Deployment Pre-requirements

OpenShift installation on VMware vCenter with installer-provisioned infrastructure procedure.

Prerequisites

vCenter Requirements

To install an OCP in a vCenter, the required details are as follows:

1) Required vCenter hostname and administration access details
2) Administration access details required to get the datacenter, network details, etc.

Cluster Resources

While deploying an OCP with installer-provisioned infrastructure, the following resources create several resources in your vCenter instance:

1) 1 Folder
2) 1 Tag category
3) 1 Tag
4) Virtual machines:
   - 1 template
   - 1 temporary bootstrap node
   - 3 control plane nodes
   - 3 compute machines
5) 900 GB storage is required

Note: If you deploy more compute machines, the OpenShift Container Platform cluster will use more storage.

Required IP Addresses

Installer-provisioned vSphere installation requires two static IP addresses:

- The API address is used to access the cluster API.
- The Ingress address is used for cluster ingress traffic.

Note: Provide these IP addresses to the installation program when you install the OpenShift Container Platform cluster.

DNS Records

Create DNS records for two static IP addresses (Section "Required IP Addresses") in the appropriate DNS server for the vCenter instance that hosts your OpenShift Container Platform cluster. In each record, <cluster_name> is the cluster name and <base_domain> is the cluster base domain that you specify when you install the cluster.

A complete DNS record takes the form: <component>.<cluster_name>.<base_domain>.

Component	Record	Description
API VIP	api.<cluster_name>.<base_domain>.	This DNS A/AAAA or CNAME record must point to the load balancer for the control plane machines. This record must be resolvable by both clients external to the cluster and from all the nodes within the cluster.
Ingress VIP	*.apps.<cluster_name>.<base_domain>.	A wildcard DNS A/AAAA or CNAME record that points to the load balancer that targets the machines that run the Ingress router pods, which are the worker nodes by default. This record must be resolvable by both clients external to the cluster and from all the nodes within the cluster.

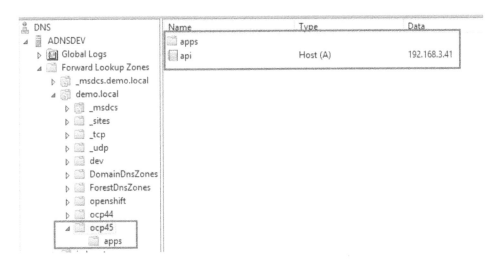

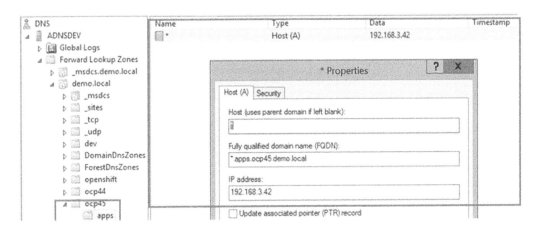

Create Local Linux Installer VM on VMware vSphere

1) Create RHEL VM with 2 vCPU, 4 Gb RAM, and 100 GB HDD.
2) SSH to RHEL VM and create installer directory.
   mkdir -P /var/www/html/<directoryname>
   e.g.: mkdir -P /var/www/html/ocp45

Generating an SSH Private Key and Adding it to the Agent

To perform installation and debugging on your cluster, you must provide an SSH key to both your ssh-agent and to the installation program.

Note: You can use this key to SSH into the master nodes as the user core. When you deploy the cluster, the key is added to the core user's ~/.ssh/authorized_keys list.

Procedure

1) SSH to local Linux Installer VM
2) If you do not have an SSH key that is configured for password-less authentication on your computer, create one. For example, on a computer that uses a Linux operating system, run the following command.

```
# ssh-keygen -t rsa -b 4096 -N " \
   -f <path>/<file_name>
E.g.: ssh-keygen -t rsa -b 4096 -N " \
   -f ~/.ssh/id_rsa
```

3) Start the ssh-agent process as a background tool.
   ```
   # eval "$(ssh-agent -s)"
   Agent pid 31874
   ```

4) Add your SSH private key to the ssh-agent.
   ```
   # ssh-add <path>/<file_name>
   E.g.: # ssh-add ~/.ssh/id_rsa
   ```

Note: When you install OpenShift Container Platform, provide the SSH public key to the installation program.

Create DHCP Server

1) SSH to local Linux Installer VM
2) Install DHCP server on local VM
3) Update below content in "dhcpd.conf"

```
subnet 192.168.3.0 netmask 255.255.255.0 {
        option domain-name-servers x.x.x.x;
       option domain-name "demo.local";
       option subnet-mask x.x.x.x;
       option routers x.x.x.x;
       option broadcast-address x.x.x.x;
      default-lease-time 86400;
     range x.x.x.x x.x.x.x;
}

Eg:
subnet 192.168.3.0 netmask 255.255.255.0 {
        option domain-name-servers 10.162.43.144;
        option domain-name "demo.local";
        option subnet-mask 255.255.255.0;
      option routers 192.168.3.1;
      option broadcast-address 192.168.3.255;
      default-lease-time 86400;
      range 192.168.3.50 192.168.3.100;
}
```

4) Restart the DHCP server
   ```
   # systemctl restart dhcpd
   ```

Download OpenShift Installation for vSphere

Before you install the OpenShift Container Platform, download the installation file on a local Linux Installer VM.

Procedure

1) Access the Infrastructure Provider page "https://cloud.redhat.com/openshift/" on the Red Hat OpenShift Cluster Manager site. If you have a Red Hat account, log in with your credentials. If you do not, create an account.
2) Click on "Create Cluster."
3) Select "Red Hat OpenShift Container Platform" and select VMware vSphere.
4) Select OS and download OpenShift Installer.
5) Extract the installation program. For example, on a computer that uses a Linux operating system, run the following command.
   # tar xvf <installation_program>.tar.gz
   E.g.: tar xvf openshift-install-linux.tar.gz

```
[root@bastion ocp45]# ls
openshift-install-linux.tar.gz
[root@bastion ocp45]# tar xvf openshift-install-linux.tar.gz
README.md
openshift-install
[root@bastion ocp45]# ls
openshift-install  openshift-install-linux.tar.gz  README.md
[root@bastion ocp45]#
```

Adding vCenter Root CA Certificates to your Installer VM

OCP installation program requires access to your vCenter's API, add vCenter's trusted root CA certificates to Installer VM (Bastion VM) trust before instaling an OpenShift Container Platform cluster.

1) From the vCenter home page, download the vCenter's root CA certificates. Click Download trusted root CA certificates in the vSphere Web Services SDK section. The <vCenter>/certs/download.zip file downloads.

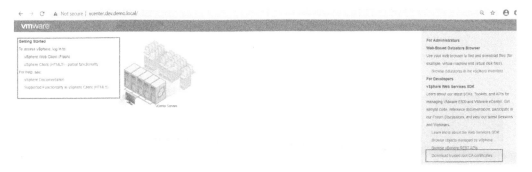

2) Extract the compressed file that contains the vCenter root CA certificates. The contents of the compressed file resemble the following file structure.

```
[root@bastion /]# unzip download.zip
Archive:  download.zip
  inflating: certs/lin/cef35441.0
  inflating: certs/mac/cef35441.0
  inflating: certs/win/cef35441.0.crt
  inflating: certs/lin/cef35441.r1
  inflating: certs/mac/cef35441.r1
  inflating: certs/win/cef35441.r1.crl
[root@bastion /]# ls
bin  boot  certs  dev  download.zip  etc  home  lib
[root@bastion /]# certs
-bash: certs: command not found
[root@bastion /]# cd certs
[root@bastion certs]# ll
total 0
drwxr-xr-x. 2 root root 43 Aug  3 01:31 lin
drwxr-xr-x. 2 root root 43 Aug  3 01:31 mac
drwxr-xr-x. 2 root root 51 Aug  3 01:31 win
[root@bastion certs]#
```

3) Add the files for your operating system to the system trust. For example, on a Fedora operating system, run the following command.

   # cp certs/lin/* /etc/pki/ca-trust/source/anchors

```
[root@bastion /]# cp certs/lin/* /etc/pki/ca-trust/source/anchors
[root@bastion /]#
```

4) Update your system trust. For example, on a Fedora operating system, run the following command.
   # update-ca-trust extract

```
[root@bastion /]# update-ca-trust extract
[root@bastion /]#
```

Deploying the OCP Cluster on VMware vSphere

Install OpenShift Container Platform on a VMware vCenter platform.

1) SSH to local linux Installer VM
2) Switch to installer directory
    cd /var/www/html/ocp45
3) Run the installation program
    # ./openshift-install create cluster --dir=. --log-level=debug

```
[root@bastion ocp45]# ./openshift-install create cluster --dir=. --log-level=debug
DEBUG OpenShift Installer 4.5.4
DEBUG Built from commit 01f5643a02f154246fab0923f8828aa9ae3b76fb
DEBUG Fetching Metadata...
DEBUG Loading Metadata...
DEBUG   Loading Cluster ID...
DEBUG     Loading Install Config...
DEBUG       Loading SSH Key...
DEBUG       Loading Base Domain...
DEBUG         Loading Platform...
DEBUG       Loading Cluster Name...
DEBUG         Loading Base Domain...
DEBUG         Loading Platform...
DEBUG       Loading Pull Secret...
DEBUG         Loading Platform...
DEBUG   Loading Install Config...
DEBUG   Fetching Cluster ID...
DEBUG     Fetching Install Config...
DEBUG       Fetching SSH Key...
DEBUG       Generating SSH Key...
? SSH Public Key  [Use arrows to move, enter to select, type to filter, ? for more help]
    /root/.ssh/id_rsa.pub
> <none>
```

4) Select SSH public key path that you created in earlier steps. Use up arrow to select pub key.

```
DEBUG     Fetching Install Config...
DEBUG       Fetching SSH Key...
DEBUG       Generating SSH Key...
? SSH Public Key  [Use arrows to move, enter to select, type to filter, ? for more help]
> /root/.ssh/id_rsa.pub
    <none>
```

5) Select platform of installation **vSphere** as the platform to target and click enter key.

```
DEBUG         Generating Platform...
? Platform  [Use arrows to move, enter to select, type to filter, ? for more help]
    aws
    azure
    gcp
    openstack
    ovirt
> vsphere
```

6) Enter vCenter details like vCenter hostname, username and password

```
DEBUG              Generating Platform...
? Platform vsphere
? vCenter vcenter.dev.demo.loca
? Username Administrator@vsphere.loca
? Password [? for help] *******█
```

7) Select "Default Datastore" (Use arrows to move, enter to select, type to filter, ? for more help)

```
INFO Defaulting to only available cluster: cluster1
? Default Datastore  [Use arrows to move, enter to select, type to filter, ? for more help]
  datastore1
  datastore1 (1)
  datastore1 (2)
  management-share
> workload_share_CFTou
  workload_share_TUpgM
  workload_share_cAhah
```

8) Select "Network" which nic is used to provision the IPs for VM (Use arrows to move, enter to select, type to filter, ? for more help)

```
? Network  [Use arrows to move, ente
  vxw-dvs-19-virtualwire-2-sid-6001-
  vxw-dvs-19-virtualwire-3-sid-6002-
  vxw-dvs-19-virtualwire-4-sid-6003-
  vxw-dvs-19-virtualwire-5-sid-6004-
  vxw-dvs-19-virtualwire-6-sid-6005-
> vxw-dvs-19-virtualwire-7-sid-6006-
  vxw-vmknicPg-dvs-19-0-8aea1998-6b2
```

9) Select "Virtual IP Address for API" and "Virtual IP Address for Ingress" what we created in AD.

```
? Virtual IP Address for API 192.168.3.41
? Virtual IP Address for Ingress [? for help] 192.168.3.42█
```

10) Enter "Base Domain" of cluster

```
? Base Domain demo.local
DEBUG          Fetching Cluster Name...
DEBUG          Fetching Base Domain...
DEBUG          Reusing previously-fetched Base Domain
DEBUG          Fetching Platform...
DEBUG          Reusing previously-fetched Platform
DEBUG          Generating Cluster Name...
```

11) Enter "Cluster Name"

```
DEBUG          Generating Cluster Name...
? Cluster Name ocp45
DEBUG          Fetching Pull Secret...
DEBUG          Generating Pull Secret...
```

12) Enter "Pull Secret" of cluster from "https://cloud.redhat.com/openshift/"

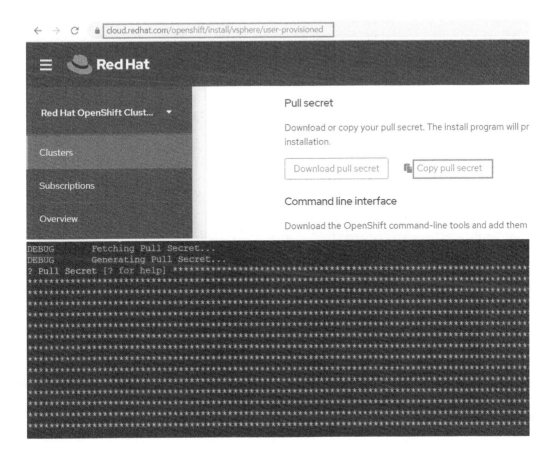

13) It will start creating the cluster

```
DEBUG module.master.vsphere_virtual_machine.vm[0]: Creating...
DEBUG module.master.vsphere_virtual_machine.vm[2]: Creating...
DEBUG module.master.vsphere virtual machine.vm[1]: Creating...
DEBUG module.bootstrap.vsphere_virtual_machine.vm: Creating...
DEBUG module.master.vsphere_virtual_machine.vm[0]: Still creating... [10s elapsed]
DEBUG module.master.vsphere_virtual_machine.vm[2]: Still creating... [10s elapsed]
DEBUG module.master.vsphere_virtual_machine.vm[1]: Still creating... [10s elapsed]
DEBUG module.bootstrap.vsphere_virtual_machine.vm: Still creating... [10s elapsed]
DEBUG module.master.vsphere_virtual_machine.vm[0]: Still creating... [20s elapsed]
DEBUG module.master.vsphere_virtual_machine.vm[2]: Still creating... [20s elapsed]
DEBUG module.master.vsphere_virtual_machine.vm[1]: Still creating... [20s elapsed]
DEBUG module.bootstrap.vsphere_virtual_machine.vm: Still creating... [20s elapsed]
```

```
DEBUG module.master.vsphere_virtual_machine.vm[2]: Creation complete after 1m28s [id
DEBUG
DEBUG Apply complete! Resources: 8 added, 0 changed, 0 destroyed.
DEBUG OpenShift Installer 4.5.4
DEBUG Built from commit 01f5643a02f154246fab0923f8828aa9ae3b76fb
INFO Waiting up to 20m0s for the Kubernetes API at https://api.ocp45.demo.local:6443
DEBUG Still waiting for the Kubernetes API: Get https://api.ocp45.demo.local:6443/ve
DEBUG Still waiting for the Kubernetes API: Get https://api.ocp45.demo.local:6443/ve
DEBUG Still waiting for the Kubernetes API: Get https://api.ocp45.demo.local:6443/ve
DEBUG Still waiting for the Kubernetes API: Get https://api.ocp45.demo.local:6443/ve
DEBUG Still waiting for the Kubernetes API: Get https://api.ocp45.demo.local:6443/ve
INFO API v1.18.3+012b3ec up
INFO Waiting up to 40m0s for bootstrapping to complete...
```

```
DEBUG Still waiting for the cluster to initialize: Working towards 4.5.4: 88% complete
DEBUG Cluster is initialized
INFO Waiting up to 10m0s for the openshift-console route to be created...
DEBUG Route found in openshift-console namespace: console
DEBUG Route found in openshift-console namespace: downloads
DEBUG OpenShift console route is created
INFO Install complete!
INFO To access the cluster as the system:admin user when using 'oc', run 'export KUBECONFIG=/var/www/html/ocp45/auth/kubeconfig'
INFO Access the OpenShift web-console here: https://console-openshift-console.apps.ocp45.demo.local
INFO Login to the console with user: "kubeadmin", and password: "Z7yNU-MGspT-YjPnv-poNNr"
DEBUG Time elapsed per stage:
DEBUG     Infrastructure: 2m4s
DEBUG Bootstrap Complete: 11m34s
DEBUG             API: 3m11s
DEBUG  Bootstrap Destroy: 21s
DEBUG  Cluster Operators: 23m46s
INFO Time elapsed: 51m19s
[root@bastion ocp45]#
```

INFO To access the cluster as the system:admin user when using "oc," run "export KUBECONFIG=/var/www/html/ocp45/auth/kubeconfig"

INFO Access the OpenShift web-console here: https://console-openshift-console.apps.ocp45.demo.local

INFO Login to the console with user: "kubeadmin," and password: "xxxxxxxxx"Access above URl from browser and validate the OpenShift Console

https://console-openshift-console.apps.ocp45.demo.local

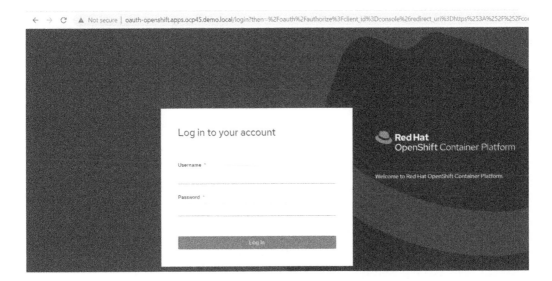

14) Try to login in with the above username and password

Installing the CLI on Linux

You can install the OpenShift CLI (oc) binary on Linux by using the following procedure.
  Procedure

1) Navigate to the Infrastructure Provider page on the Red Hat OpenShift Cluster Manager site "https://cloud.redhat.com/openshift/."
2) Select your infrastructure provider, and, if applicable, your installation type.
3) In the **Command-line interface** section, select **Linux** from the drop-down menu and click **Download command-line tools**.
4) Unpack the archive with "tar xvzf <filename>"

E.g.: tar xvzf openshift-install-linux.tar.gz

```
[root@bastion ocp44aws]# ls
auth       metadata.json   openshift-client-linux.tar.gz   openshift-install-linux.tar.gz
kubectl  oc               openshift-install               pull-secreat
[root@bastion ocp44aws]#
```

5) Place the oc binary in a directory that is on your PATH.
   cp kubectl oc /usr/local/bin/

```
[root@bastion ocp44aws]# oc --help
OpenShift Client

This client helps you develop, build, deploy, and run your applications on any
OpenShift or Kubernetes cluster. It also includes the administrative
commands for managing a cluster under the 'adm' subcommand.

Usage:
  oc [flags]

Basic Commands:
  login         Log in to a server
  new-project   Request a new project
  new-app       Create a new application
  status        Show an overview of the current project
  project       Switch to another project
  projects      Display existing projects
  explain       Documentation of resources
```

Uninstall OpenShift Cluster

1) Go to install directory run below command
   # ./openshift-install destroy cluster --dir=. --log-level=debug

```
[root@bastion ocp45]# ./openshift-install destroy cluster --dir=. --log-level=debug
DEBUG OpenShift Installer 4.5.2
DEBUG Built from commit 6336a4b3d696dd898eed192e4188edbac99e8c27
DEBUG find attached objects on tag
DEBUG find VirtualMachine objects
DEBUG delete VirtualMachines
INFO Destroyed                              VirtualMachine=ocp45-shrss-rhcos
DEBUG Powered off                           VirtualMachine=ocp45-shrss-master-1
INFO Destroyed                              VirtualMachine=ocp45-shrss-master-1
DEBUG Powered off                           VirtualMachine=ocp45-shrss-master-2
INFO Destroyed                              VirtualMachine=ocp45-shrss-master-2
DEBUG Powered off                           VirtualMachine=ocp45-shrss-master-0
INFO Destroyed                              VirtualMachine=ocp45-shrss-master-0
DEBUG Powered off                           VirtualMachine=ocp45-shrss-worker-hx5cz
INFO Destroyed                              VirtualMachine=ocp45-shrss-worker-hx5cz
DEBUG Powered off                           VirtualMachine=ocp45-shrss-worker-2wxhr
INFO Destroyed                              VirtualMachine=ocp45-shrss-worker-2wxhr
DEBUG Powered off                           VirtualMachine=ocp45-shrss-worker-vd6tk
```

Considerations When you Delete OpenShift for VMware (https://cloud.ibm.com/ docs/vmwaresolutions)

- Before you delete OpenShift for VMware, you must remove any additional VMs that you created in the ocp directory on VMware. The VMware Solutions automation removes only the items that were deployed during the initial installation of OpenShift (VMs, storage, and NSX). Any node that is deployed after the installation is not cleaned up.

- The VXLAN, DLR, and the Edge Gateway that were created during the initial deployment of OpenShift for VMware are deleted. The VMs that you deployed on VXLAN will lose connectivity after the removal of OpenShift for VMware starts.
- If you are using a vSAN datastore, it is recommended to delete any persistent volumes that you no longer need before you uninstall OpenShift. Any volumes that are not deleted will remain in the vSAN storage after the OpenShift uninstallation.
- If your cluster uses NFS storage, deleting OpenShift deletes the NFS datastore that was added during installation.
- Before you delete the service, you must remove any personal VMs from storage that are deployed with this service. OpenShift only orders personal VMs if it's not vSAN.

Conclusion

Red Hat OpenShift is powerful enough to offer automated installation, upgrades, and lifecycle management throughout the container stack (the operating system, Kubernetes and cluster services, and applications on any cloud). OpenShift helps teams build with speed, agility, confidence, and choice. The manageability of operating an OpenShift environment with virtualized infrastructure can be improved over the management of traditional IT infrastructure on bare metal. Since the demand for resources can fluctuate with business needs, operating an OpenShift environment with virtualized infrastructure is quite beneficial. Virtual infrastructure is flexible, scalable, and secure to handle the ever-changing demands of OpenShift. This chapter is to vividly illustrate how to install and make use of OpenShift on VMware virtual infrastructure.

Further Reading

1 OpenShift Container Platform IPI Installation on VMware vSphere. https://docs.openshift.com/container-platform/4.5/installing/installing_vsphere/installing-vsphere-installer-provisioned.html
2 How VMware vCenter will work? https://docs.vmware.com/en/VMware-vSphere/index.html

6

Creating Kubernetes Clusters on Public Cloud (Microsoft Azure)

THE OBJECTIVES

Kubernetes is emerging as a mainstream technology guaranteeing a fulsome implementation of the cloud-native paradigm. As containerization is being touted as the way forward for achieving resource utilization efficiency and for ensuring the elegance of infrastructure elasticity, containerized platforms, and applications are flourishing these days to simplify a variety of container operations. Bare metal and virtualized servers are therefore transitioned to have tens or even hundreds of application containers. Thus, traditional cloud centers are becoming containerized. This is being touted as a game-changing phenomenon in the IT industry. Business establishments are also enjoying this transformation. The originally portrayed vision of digital transformation is being accelerated through containerization. Fortunately, there are a host of automated tools to take care of and tackle containerized cloud environments. The leverage of Kubernetes for managing and maintaining containerized clouds is gaining the attention of many. Hyperscale cloud environments provide managed Kubernetes services to simplify the setup and use of Kubernetes clusters. In this chapter, we illustrate how to create Kubernetes clusters on an established public cloud.

Introduction

In the containerization era, there is the surging popularity of the Kubernetes platform for managing containerized workloads and services. Kubernetes natively support both declarative configuration and automation. The advantage lies with the truth that the core Kubernetes platform solution is being ably supported through a host of automated tools to greatly simplify and streamline container lifecycle management activities.

Early on, the enterprise IT teams ran software applications on physical servers. There are a few noteworthy issues. If multiple applications run on a physical server, then there were instances wherein one application would take up most of the resources as there is no isolation layer between applications. This resulted in the underperformance of other applications. If a separate physical server is allocated for running an application, then it would lead to resource underutilization. Also, managing a large number of physical servers becomes a tough and time-consuming affair.

Virtualization came as a viable solution for this problem and predicament. This allows for a few heterogeneous applications on a physical server. That is, multiple virtual machines (VMs) can be carved out of a single physical server and in each VM, an application can be run. Virtualization brings in a kind of isolation between VMs and this acts allows applications to be isolated between VMs and provides a level of security for virtualized applications. Virtualization enhances resource

Cloud-native Computing: How to Design, Develop, and Secure Microservices and Event-Driven Applications,
First Edition. Pethuru Raj, Skylab Vanga, and Akshita Chaudhary.
© 2023 The Institute of Electrical and Electronics Engineers, Inc. Published 2023 by John Wiley & Sons, Inc.

utilization efficiency. With better utilization, the IT costs (capital and operational) come down. Managing VMs and their applications is getting automated through a host of tools. However, there are a few drawbacks. Each VM comprises the full operating system. If there are five VMs in a physical machine, then there are five guests and one host operating system running on a single physical machine. This wastes a lot of memory and storage. Due to the bulkiness/verbosity of VMs, VM provisioning consumes several minutes.

Then came the much-applauded containerization era. Containers are similar to VMs, but they share the host OS among the applications. Therefore, containers are lightweight. It takes very less time to boot up. Similar to a VM, a container has its own filesystem, the share of CPU, memory, process space, etc. Containers are isolated and decoupled from the underlying infrastructure. Such an arrangement supports application portability. Containers surmount many of the VM issues and provide several benefits as enumerated hereunder.

- As indicated earlier, container creation is fast due to its lightweight nature. The agile and accelerated software engineering, deployment, management, and improvement requirements are being facilitated through containers.
- The much-needed faster and more frequent software deployment is enabled by containers. Containers maintain a close relationship with DevOps concepts and toolkits. Also, quick and efficient rollbacks of deployed software are simplified due to the trait of container mage immutability.
- Application container images get created at the build and release time. During the deployment phase, images get instantiated. Thus, there is a separation between build and deployment. Thus, applications are decoupled from their underlying infrastructure. Containers fulfill the paradigm of write once and run everywhere. They run on our personal laptops and also on private, public, and edge clouds. Further on, they maintain consistency across different and distributed environments ranging from development, testing, staging, and production.
- There are container-centric observability platforms in order to monitor, measure, collect, and crunch OS-level metrics and also application health.
- Resource utilization is high, and density is also bound to raise.
- Containers are being positioned as the optimal hosting and runtime environment for microservices. As enterprise-class applications are being dismantled and presented as a collection of easily manageable microservices. Thus, the role and responsibility of containers are steadily growing.

Containers bring forth an efficient way to bundle and run software applications. Due to their lightweight nature, containers can be created quickly and hence the goal of real-time scalability gets fulfilled. The continuous availability, horizontal scalability, and easy and end-to-end manageability of applications are being guaranteed through the inherent power of containers. However, with the rising density of containers in an IT environment, they have to be managed. Here comes the need for container orchestration platform solutions. Kubernetes provides all that are needed to run distributed applications in a deterministic and resilient manner. It takes care of auto-scaling, self-healing, and automated software deployment in containerized environments. The recent versions of the Kubernetes platform enable software deployment in VMs.

Kubernetes provides several deployment patterns. Kubernetes can easily manage a canary deployment for your system. Kubernetes can expose a container using the DNS name or using their own IP address. If traffic to a container is high, Kubernetes is able to load balance and distribute the network traffic so that the deployment is stable. Kubernetes allows you to automatically mount a storage system such as local storage and remote cloud providers.

It is possible to describe the desired state for your deployed containers using Kubernetes. It can change the actual state to the desired state at a controlled rate. For example, you can ask Kubernetes to create new containers for your deployment by removing existing containers. And it allocates all its resources to the new containers.

Kubernetes is an excellent cluster management solution. You can tell Kubernetes how much CPU and memory (RAM) each container needs. Kubernetes can fit containers onto the cluster nodes to make the best use of node resources. Kubernetes lets you store and manage sensitive information, such as passwords, OAuth tokens, and SSH keys. You can deploy and update secrets and application configurations without rebuilding your container images. In this chapter, we are tutoring about creating Kubernetes clusters on a public cloud. Here we have chosen Microsoft Azure Cloud, one of the market leaders in the cloud space.

Prerequisites

Configuring a Public DNS Zone in Azure

1) Identify your domain, or subdomain, and registrar. You can transfer an existing domain and registrar or obtain a new one through Azure or another source.
2) For more information about purchasing domains through Azure, see Buy a custom domain name for Azure App Service in the Azure documentation.
   1) Buy an App Service domain
   2) Open the Azure Portal and sign in with your Azure account.
   3) In the search bar, search for and select **App Service Domains**.

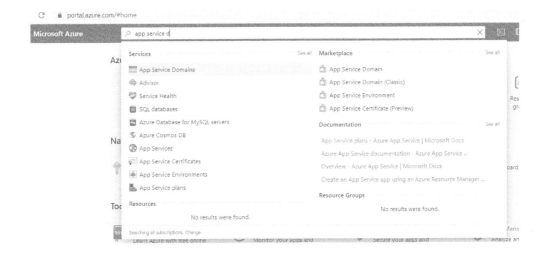

4) In the **App Service Domains** view, click **Add**.

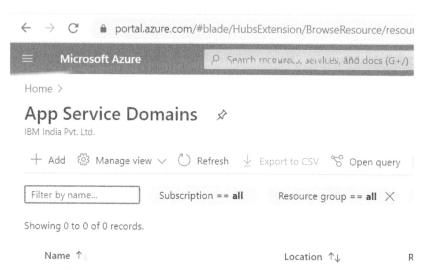

5) Select **Click to try the newer version of the App Service Domains create experience**.

Home > App Service Domains >

Create App Service Domains

🛈 Looking for the App Service Domains classic create experience? →

Find and purchase a domain, and use Azure Domain Name System to manage your domains, all within Azure. Azure DNS also gives you a range of secure, reliable domain hosting options.

Note: Available top level domains are: com, net, co.uk, org, nl, in, biz, org.uk, and co.in. Learn more ☑

Project Details

Select a subscription to manage deployed resources and costs. Use resource groups like folders to organize and manage all your resources.

Subscription * 🛈   Azure

Resource Group * 🛈
Create new

Domain Details

Enter a domain name and select it from the list. If you don't see the domain you entered, it's not available. All domains shown here are available for $11.99 USD each.

Domain *

✅ This domain is available.

Review + create   < Previous   Next : Contact information >

6) Click on Review and Create

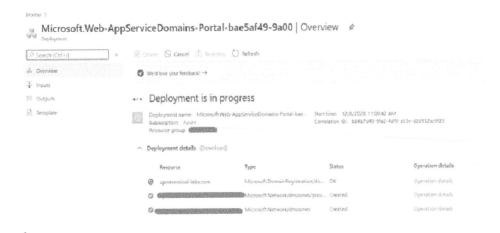

7) Wait till deployment is completed message

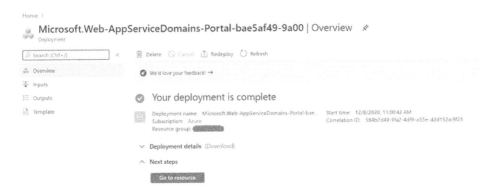

DNS Creation

Prerequisites

You must have a domain name available to test with that you can host in Azure DNS. You must have full control of this domain. Full control includes the ability to set the name server (NS) records for the domain.

Create a DNS Zone

1) Go to the Azure portal to create a DNS zone. Search for and select **DNS zones**.

2) Select **Create DNS zone**.
3) On the **Create DNS zone** page, enter the following values, and then select **Create**: for example, contoso.net
4) Click on Add

Home > DNS zones >

Create DNS zone

Basics   Tags   Review + create

A DNS zone is used to host the DNS records for a particular domain. For example, the domain 'contoso.com' may contain a number of DNS records such as 'mail.contoso.com' (for a mail server) and 'www.contoso.com' (for a web site). Azure DNS allows you to host your DNS zone and manage your DNS records, and provides name servers that will respond to DNS queries from end users with the DNS records that you create. Learn more.

Project details

Subscription *	Azure
Resource group *	

Create new

Instance details

☑ This zone is a child of an existing zone already hosted in Azure DNS ⓘ

Parent zone subscription * ⓘ	Azure
Parent zone * ⓘ	
Name *	azcloudlab

.apmterminal-labs.com

Resource group location ⓘ	West US

Review + create   Previous   Next : Tags >   Download a template for automation

5) Click on Next: Tags

6) Specify the Tags and click on Review + Create

7) Click on Create

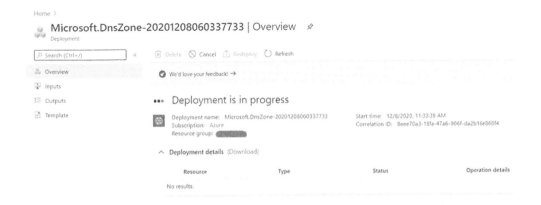

8) Wait till deployment is complete

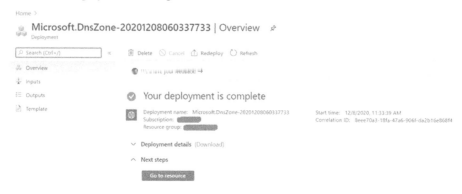

Required Azure Roles

Your Microsoft Azure account must have the following roles for the subscription that you use:
• User Access Administrator

Creating a Service Principal

Because OpenShift Container Platform and its installation program must create Microsoft Azure resources through Azure Resource Manager, you must create a service principal to represent it.

Azure CLI Setup

1) sudo rpm --import https://packages.microsoft.com/keys/microsoft.asc

```
[root@bastion azcloudlab]# sudo rpm --import https://packages.microsoft.com/keys/microsoft.asc
[root@bastion azcloudlab]#
```

2)

```
echo -e "[azure-cli]
name=Azure CLI
baseurl=https://packages.microsoft.com/yumrepos/azure-cli
enabled=1
gpgcheck=1
gpgkey=https://packages.microsoft.com/keys/microsoft.asc" | sudo tee
/etc/yum.repos.d/azure-cli.repo
```

```
[root@bastion azcloudlab]# echo -e "[azure-cli]
> name=Azure CLI
> baseurl=https://packages.microsoft.com/yumrepos/azure-cli
> enabled=1
> gpgcheck=1
> gpgkey=https://packages.microsoft.com/keys/microsoft.asc" | sudo tee /etc/yum.repos.d/azure-cli.repo
[azure-cli]
name=Azure CLI
baseurl=https://packages.microsoft.com/yumrepos/azure-cli
enabled=1
gpgcheck=1
gpgkey=https://packages.microsoft.com/keys/microsoft.asc
[root@bastion azcloudlab]#
```

3) Install with the yum install command.
   # sudo yum install azure-cli

```
[root@bastion azcloudlab]# sudo yum install azure-cli
Loaded plugins: product-id, search-disabled-repos, subscription-manager
azure-cli
rhel-7-server-ansible-2.9-rpms
rhel-7-server-extras-rpms
rhel-7-server-rpms
(1/9): rhel-7-server-ansible-2.9-rpms/x86_64/group
(2/9): azure-cli/primary_db
(3/9): rhel-7-server-ansible-2.9-rpms/x86_64/updateinfo
(4/9): rhel-7-server-ansible-2.9-rpms/x86_64/primary_db
(5/9): rhel-7-server-extras-rpms/x86_64/updateinfo
(6/9): rhel-7-server-extras-rpms/x86_64/primary_db
(7/9): rhel-7-server-rpms/7Server/x86_64/updateinfo
(8/9): rhel-7-server-rpms/7Server/x86_64/group
(9/9): rhel-7-server-rpms/7Server/x86_64/primary_db
```

4) Run the Azure CLI with the az command. To sign in, use az login command.
5) Run the login command.
   # az login

```
[root@bastion azcloudlab]# az login
To sign in, use a web browser to open the page https://microsoft.com/devicelogin and enter the code R7BTCUBAT to authenticate.
```

https://microsoft.com/devicelogin

6) Enter Azure Code from CLI command

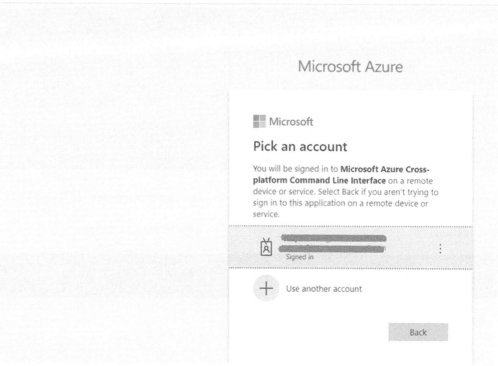

7) Click on User

[root@bastion azcloudlab]# az login
To sign in, use a web browser to open the page https://microsoft.com/devicelogin and enter the code R6Q86CUPU to authenticate.

```
[
  {
    "cloudName": "AzureCloud",
    "homeTenantId": "xxxxxxxxxxxxxxxxxxxxxxxxx",
    "id": "xxxxxxxxxxxxxxxxxxxxxxxxxxxxxxx",
```

```
      "isDefault": true,
      "managedByTenants": [],
      "name": "Azure",
      "state": "Enabled",
      "tenantId": "xxxxxxxxxxxxxxxxxxxxxxx",
      "user": {
        "name": "xxxxxx.onmicrosoft.com",
        "type": "user"
      }
    }
  ]
  [root@bastion azcloudlab]#
```

8) View your active account details and confirm that the tenantId matches the subscription you want to use:

   # az account show

```
[root@bastion azcloudlab]# az account show
{
  "environmentName": "AzureCloud",
  "homeTenantId": "xxxxxxxxxxxxxxxxxxxxxxxxxxxx",
  "id": "xxxxxxxxxxxxxxxxxxxxxxxxxxxxxxxxxxxxx",
  "isDefault": true,
  "managedByTenants": [],
  "name": "Azure",
  "state": "Enabled",
  "tenantId": "xxxxxxxxxxxxxxxxxxxxxxxxxxxxxxxxxxxx",
  "user": {
    "name": "xxxxxxxxxxxxxxxxxxxxxxxxxxxxxxxxxx",
    "type": "user"
  }
}
[root@bastion azcloudlab]#
```

9) Record the values of the tenantId and id parameters from the previous output. You need these values during OpenShift Container Platform installation.

10) Create the service principal for your account:
    # az ad sp create-for-rbac --role Contributor --name <service_principal>
    E.g.: az ad sp create-for-rbac --role Contributor --name demo

```
[root@bastion azcloudlab]# az ad sp create-for-rbac --role
Contributor --name demo
Changing "demo" to a valid URI of "http://demo", which is the
required format used for service principal names
Creating a role assignment under the scope of "/subscriptions/
xxxxxxxxxxxxxxxxxx"
{
  "appId": "xxxxxxxxxxxxxxxxxxxxxxxxxxxx",
  "displayName": "demo",
  "name": "http://demo",
  "password": "xxxxxxxxxxxxxxxxxxxxxxxxxxxxxxxxxx",
  "tenant": "xxxxxxxxxxxxxxxxxxxxxxxxxxxxxxxxxx"
}
[root@bastion azcloudlab]#
```

11) Record the values of the appId and password parameters from the previous output. You need these values during OpenShift Container Platform installation.
12) Grant additional permissions to the service principal.

- You must always add the Contributor and User Access Administrator roles to the app registration service principal so the cluster can assign credentials for its components.
- To operate the Cloud Credential Operator (CCO) in mint mode, the app registration service principal also requires the Azure Active Directory Graph/Application.ReadWrite.OwnedBy API permission.
- To operate the CCO in passthrough mode, the app registration service principal does not require additional API permissions.

For more information about CCO modes, see the **Cloud Credential Operator** entry in the **Red Hat Operators reference** content.

a) To assign the User Access Administrator role, run the following command:
   # az role assignment create --role "User Access Administrator" \

```
--assignee-object-id $(az ad sp list --filter "appId eq '<appId>'" \
  | jq '.[0].objectId' -r)
```

Note: Replace <appId> with the appId parameter value for your service principal.

E.g.: # az role assignment create --role "User Access Administrator" \

```
--assignee-object-id $(az ad sp list --filter "appId eq
'xxxxxxxxxxxxxxxxxxxx'" \
  | jq '.[0].objectId' -r)
```

b) To assign the Azure Active Directory Graph permission, run the following command:
   # az ad app permission add --id <appId> \

```
--api 00000002-0000-0000-c000-000000000000 \
--api-permissions 824c81eb-e3f8-4ee6-8f6d-de7f50d565b7=Role
```

Note: **Replace <appId> with the appId parameter value for your service principal.**

E.g.: # az ad app permission add --id 9c7a256f-8626-4f42-a1fa-09f14fd69189 --api 00000002-0000-0000-c000-000000000000 --api-permissions 824c81eb-e3f8-4ee6-8f6d-de7f50d565b7=Role

Invoking "az ad app permission grant --id xxxxxxxxxxxxxxxxxxxxxxxxxxxxxx --api 00000002-0000-0000-c000-000000000000" is needed to make the change effective

---

c) Approve the permissions request. If your account does not have the Azure Active Directory tenant administrator role, follow the guidelines for your organization to request that the tenant administrator approve your permissions request.
   # az ad app permission grant --id <appId> \
   ```
   --api 00000002-0000-0000-c000-000000000000
   ```
   E.g.: az ad app permission grant --id xxxxxxxxxxxxxxxxxxxxxxxxxxxxxxxxxxx \
   ```
   --api 00000002-0000-0000-c000-000000000000
   ```

```
[root@bastion azcloudlab]# az ad app permission grant
--id xxxxxxxxxxxxxxxxxxx --api 00000002-0000-0000-c000-000000000000
{
  "clientId": "xxxxxxxxxxxxxxxxxxxxxxxxxxxxxxxxxxxxxx",
  "consentType": "AllPrincipals",
  "expiryTime": "2021-12-08T07:01:37.637907",
  "objectId": "xxxxxxxxxxxxxxxxxxxxxxxxxxxxxxxxxxxxxx",
  "odata.metadata":
  "https://graph.windows.net/xxxxxxxxxxxxxxxxxxxxxxxxxxxxxx/$metadata
  #oauth2PermissionGrants/@Element",
  "odatatype": null,
  "principalId": null,
  "resourceId": "xxxxxxxxxxxxxxxxxxxxxxxxxxxxxxx",
  "scope": "user_impersonation",
  "startTime": "2020-12-08T07:01:37.637907"
}
[root@bastion azcloudlab]#
```

Manually Create IAM

The CCO can be put into manual mode prior to installation in environments where the cloud identity and access management (IAM) APIs are not reachable, or the administrator prefers not to store an administrator-level credential secret in the cluster kube-system namespace.

1) Run the OpenShift Container Platform installer to generate manifests:
   # openshift-install create manifests --dir=<installation_directory>

```
[root@bastion azcloudlab]# openshift-install create manifests --dir=.
INFO Credentials loaded from file "/root/.azure/osServicePrincipal.json"
INFO Consuming Install Config from target directory
INFO Manifests created in: manifests and openshift
[root@bastion azcloudlab]#
```

2) Insert a config map into the manifest's directory so that the CCO is placed in manual mode:

```
cat <<EOF > mycluster/manifests/cco-configmap.yaml
apiVersion: v1
kind: ConfigMap
metadata:
  name: cloud-credential-operator-config
  namespace: openshift-cloud-credential-operator
  annotations:
    release.openshift.io/create-only: "true"
data:
  disabled: "true"
EOF
```

```
[root@bastion azcloudlab]# cat <<EOF > manifests/cco-configmap.yaml
> apiVersion: v1
> kind: ConfigMap
> metadata:
>   name: cloud-credential-operator-config
>   namespace: openshift-cloud-credential-operator
>   annotations:
>     release.openshift.io/create-only: "true"
> data:
>   disabled: "true"
> EOF
[root@bastion azcloudlab]#
```

3) Remove the admin credential secret created using your local cloud credentials. This removal prevents your admin credential from being stored in the cluster:
   # rm mycluster/openshift/99_cloud-creds-secret.yaml

```
[root@bastion azcloudlab]# rm openshift/99_cloud-creds-secret.yaml
rm: remove regular file 'openshift/99_cloud-creds-secret.yaml'? yes
[root@bastion azcloudlab]#
```

4) Obtain the OpenShift Container Platform release image your openshift-install binary is built to use:

openshift-install version

```
[root@bastion azcloudlab]# openshift-install version
openshift-install 4.6.6
built from commit db0f93089a64c5fd459d226fc224a2584e8cfb7e
release image quay.io/openshift-release-dev/ocp-release@sha256:c7e8f18e8116356701bd23ae3a23fb989
[root@bastion azcloudlab]#
```

5) Locate all CredentialsRequest objects in this release image that target the cloud you are deploying on:

oc adm release extract quay.io/openshift-release-dev/ocp-release:4.y.z-x86_64 --credentials-requests --cloud=azure

Example

oc adm release extract quay.io/openshift-release-dev/ocp-release@sha256:c7e8f18e811635670 1bd23ae3a23fb9892dd5ea66c8300662ef30563d7104f39 --credentials-requests --cloud=azure

This displays the details for each request.

oc adm release extract quay.io/openshift-release-dev/ocp-release@sha256:c7e8f18e811635670 1bd23ae3a23fb9892dd5ea66c8300662ef30563d7104f39 --credentials-requests --cloud=azure

```
[root@bastion azcloudlab]# oc adm release extract quay.io/openshift-release-dev/ocp-release@sha256:c7e8f18e8116356701bd23ae3a23fb9892dd5ea66c8300662ef30563d7104f39
cloud=azure
---
apiVersion: cloudcredential.openshift.io/v1
kind: CredentialsRequest
metadata:
  labels:
    controller-tools.k8s.io: "1.0"
  name: openshift-image-registry-azure
  namespace: openshift-cloud-credential-operator
spec:
  providerSpec:
    apiVersion: cloudcredential.openshift.io/v1
    kind: AzureProviderSpec
    roleBindings:
    - role: Contributor
  secretRef:
    name: installer-cloud-credentials
    namespace: openshift-image-registry
apiVersion: cloudcredential.openshift.io/v1
kind: CredentialsRequest
metadata:
  labels:
    controller-tools.k8s.io: "1.0"
  name: openshift-ingress-azure
```

6) Create YAML files for secrets in the openshift-install manifests directory that you generated previously. The secrets must be stored using the namespace and secret name defined in the spec.secretRef for each credentialsRequest. The format for the secret data varies for each cloud provider.

Start Installation of OCP

./openshift-install create install-config --dir= <installation directory>

```
[root@bastion azcloudlab]# ./openshift-install create install-config --dir=.
? SSH Public Key  [Use arrows to move, enter to select, type to filter, ? for more help]
> /root/.ssh/id_rsa.pub
  <none>
```

Select the SSH Public Key and enter

```
? Platform  [Use arrows to move, enter to select, type to filter, ? for more help]
  aws
> azure
  gcp
  openstack
  ovirt
  vsphere
```

Select Platform Azure and hit on enter key

```
? SSH Public Key /root/.ssh/id_rsa.pub
? Platform azure
? azure subscription id [? for help] ▮
```

Enter the Azure subscription id and click on enter key

```
? azure subscription id ▬▬▬▬▬▬▬▬▬▬▬▬▬▬▬▬▬▬▬▬▬▬▬
? azure tenant id [? for help] ▮
```

Enter the tenant id and click on enter key

```
? azure subscription id ▬▬▬▬▬▬▬▬▬▬▬▬▬▬▬▬▬▬▬
? azure tenant id ▬▬▬▬▬▬▬▬▬▬▬▬▬▬▬▬▬
? azure service principal client id [? for help] ▮
```

Enter the client id

```
? azure tenant id ▬▬▬▬▬▬▬▬▬▬▬▬▬▬▬▬▬▬
? azure service principal client id ▬▬▬▬▬▬▬▬▬▬▬▬▬▬▬▬▬▬
? azure service principal client secret [? for help] ▮
```

Enter the client secret id

```
? azure service principal client secret [? for help] **********************************
INFO Saving user credentials to "/root/.azure/osServicePrincipal.json"
INFO Credentials loaded from file "/root/.azure/osServicePrincipal.json"
? Region [Use arrows to move, enter to select, type to filter, ? for more help]
  centralindia (Central India)
  centralus (Central US)
  eastasia (East Asia)
> eastus (East US)
  eastus2 (East US 2)
  francecentral (France Central)
  germanywestcentral (Germany West Central)
```

Select deployment zone

```
INFO Credentials loaded from file "/root/.azure/osServicePrincipal.json"
? Region eastus
? Base Domain  [Use arrows to move, enter to select, type to filter, ? for more help]

> azcloudlab
```

Select the domain

```
INFO Saving user credentials to "/root/.azure/osServicePrincipal.json"
INFO Credentials loaded from file "/root/.azure/osServicePrincipal.json"
? Region eastus
? Base Domain
? Cluster Name az
? Pull Secret [? for help]
```

```
? Cluster Name az
? Pull Secret [? for help] ***********************************************

INFO Install-Config created in:
[root@bastion azcloudlab]#
```

3) Modify the install-config.yaml file. You can find more information about the available parameters in the **Installation configuration parameters** section.

```
[root@bastion azcloudlab]# openshift-install create cluster --dir=
INFO Credentials loaded from file "/root/.azure/osServicePrincipal.json"
INFO Consuming Master Machines from target directory
INFO Consuming OpenShift Install (Manifests) from target directory
INFO Consuming Common Manifests from target directory
INFO Consuming OpenShift Manifests from target directory
INFO Consuming Worker Machines from target directory
INFO Creating infrastructure resources...
```

```
[root@bastion azcloudlab]# ./openshift-install create cluster --dir= --log-level=info
INFO Credentials loaded from file "/root/.azure/osServicePrincipal.json"
INFO Creating infrastructure resources...
INFO Waiting up to 20m0s for the Kubernetes API at https://api.az.                6443...
INFO API v1.19.0+43983cd up
INFO Waiting up to 30m0s for bootstrapping to complete...
INFO Destroying the bootstrap resources...
INFO Waiting up to 40m0s for the cluster at https://api.az.azcloudlab               to initialize...
INFO Waiting up to 10m0s for the openshift-console route to be created...
INFO Install complete!
INFO To access the cluster as the system:admin user when using 'oc', run 'export KUBECONFIG=/var/www/html/azcloudlab/auth/kubeconfig'
INFO Access the OpenShift web-console here: https://console-openshift-console.apps.az.              labs.com
INFO Login to the console with user: "kubeadmin", and password: "RI5dF-KJGXe-ojgP6-tLBSy"
INFO Time elapsed: 44m21s
[root@bastion azcloudlab]#
```

Enter the console URL in Brower to check the UI
https://console-openshift-console.xxxxxxxx.com

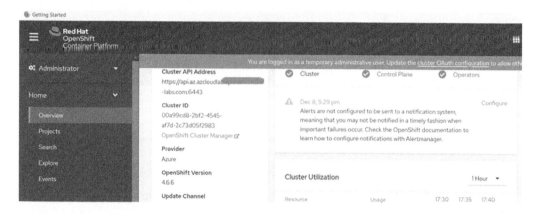

Uninstall Cluster

./openshift-install destroy cluster –dir=. –log-level=info

```
[root@bastion azcloudlab]# ./openshift-install destroy cluster --dir=. --log-level=info
INFO Credentials loaded from file "/root/.azure/osServicePrincipal.json"
INFO deleted                                    record=api.az
INFO deleted                                    record="*.apps.az"
INFO deleted                                    resource group=az-jkdh5-rg
INFO Time elapsed: 11m41s
[root@bastion azcloudlab]# █
```

Conclusion

To fulfill the nuances and nitty-gritty of the cloud-native computing phenomenon, there is a greater role for Kubernetes. In this chapter, we have shown how to create Kubernetes clusters in a Microsoft Azure cloud environment. With a cluster in place, it is quite straightforward to deploy and manage containerized applications without any hitch or hurdle.

Further Reading

1 OpenShift Container Platform IPI Installation on Azure Cloud. https://docs.openshift.com/ container-platform/4.6/installing/installing_azure/installing-azure-default.html
2 OpenShift with Azure Cloud: https://docs.microsoft.com/en-us/azure/virtual-machines/linux/ openshift-get-started

7

Design, Development, and Deployment of Event-Driven Microservices Practically

---

THE OBJECTIVES

Microservices are being presented and proclaimed as the best-in-class software-building block for build-ing and deploying enterprise-grade and web-scale applications. The microservices architecture (MSA) pattern is being positioned as the forward-looking mechanism for agile software design and develop-ment. With business and technology changes happening frequently, software deployment has to happen fast and frequent. MSA enables accelerated application building. Now with the association of event-driven architecture (EDA) style, asynchronous microservices are being readily and rewardingly constructed and composed to create and release event-driven microservices applications, which bring forth additional automation in order to make software engineering appropriate for the ensuing digital era. In this chapter, we want to showcase how to develop and deploy microservices in a cloud environment to be publicly discovered and accessed.

Introduction

Hello Readers! Or this could be a subtle reminder that yes! it is the right time and the right chapter to get your hands dirty.

The principles of microservice can be elusive to sustain in mind unless carved practically. To make your understanding credible and ceaseless, let us commence the roller coaster journey of implementing microservices and deploying them with a hassle-free approach. This chapter pro-vides you with insights into creating a microservice more simply. Hence, put on your seat belts and get ready to develop a sample microservice.

The intent is to develop and deliver a highly scalable application by making it viable in every aspect. This can be achieved in two ways:

1) Design the desired application **development** architecture
2) Decide the correct **deployment** methodology

The best practice that is widely used by major enterprises while building a large-scale applica-tion is to adopt a **microservice-based architecture** and deploying the same in a **cloud-native environment using a DevOps methodology**.

Understanding the business use case and other niche complexities can help us decide whether to adopt the microservice-based architecture pattern. Today we are going to talk about the BEST in-town strategies to implement a highly scalable, resilient, lightweight, and cost-effective micros-ervice application.

Cloud-native Computing: How to Design, Develop, and Secure Microservices and Event-Driven Applications,
First Edition. Pethuru Raj, Skylab Vanga, and Akshita Chaudhary.
© 2023 The Institute of Electrical and Electronics Engineers, Inc. Published 2023 by John Wiley & Sons, Inc.

Let us have a quick look over the paramount differences depicted as follows:

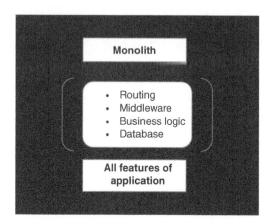
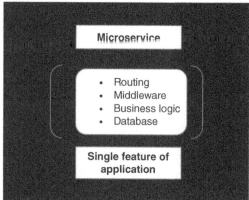

Before hopping onto the journey toward building a sample microservice application, it is significant to highlight the prominent issues faced while building microservices. There are many design patterns available when it comes to microservices. Let us discuss and break down the primary issues associated with microservice-based architecture and the resolution revolving around it. This approach shall unveil and enable us to analyze the microservice architecture design patterns.

- **Database Per Service Architectural Pattern**
  This architectural pattern allows each service to run, scale, and deploy independently of another service. This enables loose coupling in services. Also, unexpected changes in the database schema of one service will not let other services get hampered in any way. Each service will have the ability to incorporate different databases too. This pattern provides varied options to plug different databases into service as per the feasibility and the requirements.

  One can encounter issues when dealing with this design pattern. Imagine having a service that will only function if it can access data from other service's databases. Let us consider the example of an eCommerce application wherein there is a product service, a user service, and an order service, each comprising its database. Now, comes one more service that will display all the products ordered by a particular user. This will automatically create some dependency as this service will require communication with other service's databases and managing the data will now be the primary issue. To resolve this issue of data access and management, we must figure out ways to understand the communication mechanism between services.

- **Communication Between Services**
  1) Synchronous
     When services communicate with each other using direct HTTP requests, it is referred to as a Synch Approach. These are our normal REST requests or the APIs that we build to access the information. There are some downsides to this communication approach. It introduces a dependency element between services which we would like to avoid in the first place. If any interservice request fails, the overall request fails. Hence, it is not the best solution from an engineering standpoint.
  2) Asynchronous or an Event-Driven Approach
     When services communicate with each other using events, this is referred to as an Async approach. This is a broker-based communication approach wherein the event broker receives notifications from the different services when any notable change is introduced. These

notifications are further distributed to other services that are interested in utilizing that information. This makes our services run faster and eliminates the dependency on other services. This makes the overall architecture more reliable.

The promising approach to designing a microservice architecture is to opt for an Async Approach wherein event-driven communication takes place between microservices.

Now we are aware of the prerequisites, let us dive in to develop the same.

Technology Stack to Build Microservices

There are some popular open-source frameworks available in the market to build microservices with ease. The most widely used ones are as follows:

- JavaScript-Based Microservices: ExpressJs
- Java-Based Microservices: Spring Boot
- Python-Based Microservices: Django, Flask

The wait is over, and it is time to analyze and build some microservices. In this chapter, we will explore the JavaScript-based framework used to develop the microservices.

Express Framework

The motive is to initiate with the simplest use case and discover the concepts of microservices as discussed earlier. We will begin with the basic approach and further make our app powerful with an event-driven architectural pattern.

Use case: Blog Post microservice-based react web application.

This application involves two microservices, which have the following specific features:

1) Blog Post Microservice
   - Create a new blog post
   - List all blog posts
2) Comment Microservice
   - Create a comment
   - List all the Comments

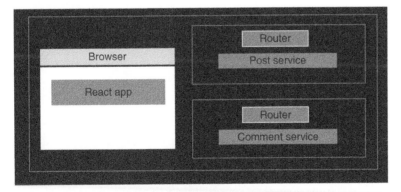

Note: Comment service has a dependency over post service and vice versa as each comment shall be tagged to a specific post.

Steps to Set Up Your Project

1) Client
   - Produce a New React Application using Create-React-App.
   - Open a terminal, create a new folder, and write the following command to create a new react app. Here, the name of the web application folder is "client" as our react app will act as a client.

```
C:\Users\akshita.chaudhary\Desktop\Blog_React_App>npx create-react-app client
```

2) Blog Post MicroService
   - Create an Express-based project for the post microservice.
   - It is time to create a service now. Hence create a new folder named "posts." Navigate to that folder and run the following command which will generate a package.json

```
C:\Users\akshita.chaudhary\Desktop\Blog_React_App\posts>npm init -y
```

   - The following four packages are used in this sample React-based application:
     1) Express: Open source flexible web framework that provides an interface to develop the application.
     2) Cors: Acts as a reverse proxy that bypasses the security protocol of the API.
     3) Axios: HTTP client to send asynchronous web requests.
     4) Nodemon: Restarts the node application when any change is detected in the directory.

```
C:\Users\akshita.chaudhary\Desktop\Blog_React_App\posts>npm install express axios cors nodemon
```

3) Comment MicroService
   Create an Express-based project for the comments service and follow similar steps to build the comment microservice.

Blog Post Microservice

1) As discussed earlier, the posts service will have the following two REST requests:
   - To create a blog post
     Method: POST
     Request Body: { "blogTitle": string}
   - To fetch all the blog posts
     Method: GET

2) Navigate to the "posts" folder in any code editor of your choice. Initiate by creating a javascript file. The process of setting up different project folders emits the vibe of a microservice. Each new feature acts as a separate application. Also, each microservice can be built using a different technology stack. Here, we are using node-js for constructing both microservices.

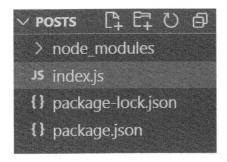

3) Create the desired request template with the express framework. The blog post microservice skeleton can be designed based on the features of the service.

```
const express = require('express');

const app = express();

app.post('/posts/create', (req, res) => {

});

app.get('/posts', (req, res) => {

});

app.listen(4000, () => {
    console.log("Post Service running on Port 4000")
});
```

4) This sample application does not have an explicit database; we will use the in-memory database. Hence, we can create an empty object named posts to store the data.

```
const posts={};
```

5) The creation of a blog post requires two entities, i.e. ID and BLOG TITLE. ID can be generated randomly in this case. The title creation activity is performed by the user who is sending the request.

```
app.post('/posts/create', (req, res) => {

    //Generate a random id
    const id= randomBytes(2).toString('hex');

    //Pass blogTitle through request body
    const {blogTitle}= req.body;

    //Create the post
    posts[id]={id, blogTitle};

    //On Successful post creation, send the same response
    res.status(201).send(posts[id]);
});
```

6) Service is triggered by the start script command tag in the package.json file. The Nodemon package enables the automatic restart of the service if any change is produced in the file without shutting off the service.

```
"scripts": {
    "start": "nodemon index.js"
},
```

7) The Post Request can be tested using the API Testing Software named "Postman" wherein the request body is passed as a JSON and the desired response is received on a successful request.

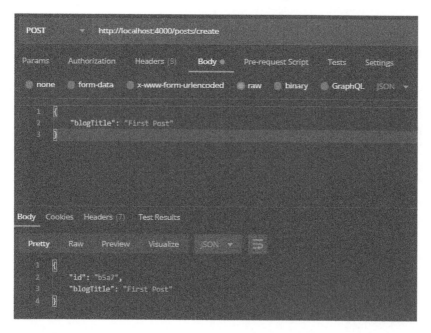

8) The GET request to fetch all the created blog post is far simpler than creating one.

```
app.get('/posts', (req, res) => {
//Fetch all the available posts as response
res.send(posts);
});
```

Comments Microservice

1) As discussed earlier, the comments service will have two REST requests:
   - To create a comment associated with a given blogPost ID.
     Method: POST
     Path: posts/:id/comments
     Request Body: {"content": String}

- Retrieve all comments associated with the given blogpost ID.
  Method: GET
  Path: posts/:id/comments

2) Create the desired request template with the express framework, which includes the two REST requests.

```
const express = require("express");
const bodyParser = require("body-parser");

const app = express();
app.use(express.json());

app.get("/posts/:id/comments", (req, res) => {});

app.post("/posts/:id/comments", (req, res) => {});

app.listen(4001, () => {
  console.log("Comment Service running on Port 4001");
});
```

3) Now, we will store our comments in an in-memory database exactly as we did for the blog post microservice.

```
//DB for comments
const commentByPostId= {};
```

4) On every request to create a comment, a specific post id is passed as a request parameter, which will enable the comment to be tagged with that post id. This code snippet is a basic demo approach to designing the comment ByPostId array.

```
app.post("/posts/:id/comments", (req, res) => {

  //Generate random comment ID
  const commentId= randomBytes(4).toString('hex');

  //Pass the content parameter in the request body
  const {content}= req.body;

  //Lookup to check if comments are returned with a specific ID
  const comments= commentByPostId[req.params.id] || [];

  //Push the created comment into the array
  comments.push({id: commentId, content});
  commentByPostId[req.params.id]=comments;

  res.status(201).send(comments)
});
```

```
app.get("/posts/:id/comments", (req, res) => {

    //Fetch the response from the DB that includes comment tagged to a post
    res.send(commentByPostId  [req.params.id]) || [];
});
```

5) Time to test the created post request. The comment is created with a comment id and also tagged to a presumed post id. Currently, we are passing a random post id as a request parameter because we have not implemented the communication between the post service and comment service.

The list of all the created comments will be displayed on the GET request call.

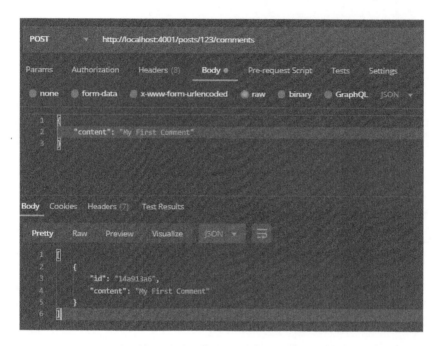

We have successfully kickstarted the journey of building a basic yet useful microservice. But it remains incomplete without a client. The requests were placed through POSTMAN, the prominent API testing tool. It is time to trigger the same from our web interface. Build a react web application by navigating to the client project folder that we created in the initial stage of setting up the project. The intent is to focus on microservices rather than creating an impressive frontend application. Hence, we will not look into the intricate details of building a react application.

We must build a frontend React-based app in a way that triggers all the services efficiently. Create a basic app to depict the desired features. The react application must allow the creation of blog post service, retrieval of all the blog posts, creation of comments, and fetching all the comments tagged to each post. We are making use of all the APIs that we have built through Express Framework.

The objective is to design and implement the event-based approach rather than a synchronous one. Currently, there is a dependency on service communication. We need to redesign the code that we have created so far, as we want to follow the event-based approach.

Implementation of Event-Driven Model

The design of an event-driven model involves the event bus implementation.

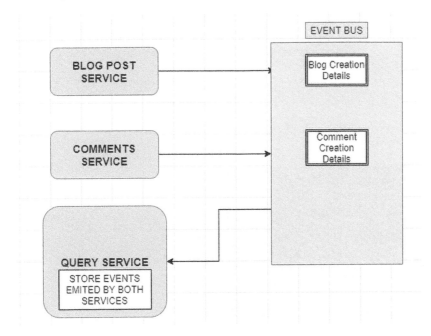

- Select an event bus that streams the events/messages from one point to another.
  There are many such event streaming platforms or message brokers like Apache Kafka, Rabit MQ, and NATS. The widely used one is Apache Kafka, which we will explore in detail in another chapter. In this existing sample app, we will use an easier event bus implementation, which is not powerful in terms of features but will help us understand the working of the event-driven model.

- Now, we are going to create one more folder named "event-bus," another express-based service. Repeat the same steps as done for other services

```
C:\Users\akshita.chaudhary\Desktop\Blog_React_App\event-bus>npm init -y
```

- Install the necessary packages

```
C:\Users\akshita.chaudhary\Desktop\Blog_React_App\event-bus>npm install express nodemon axios
```

Event Bus

- The goal of an event bus implementation is to receive an event from any service and distribute those event details across all the other services.

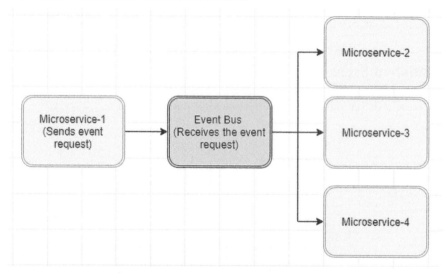

```
app.post('/events',(request,response)=>{

    //Recieve an event
    const event= request.body;

    //Send the event to all the micro services

    //Blog Post Service
    axios.post('http://localhost:4000/events',event);
    //Comments Service
    axios.post('http://localhost:4001/events',event);
    //Query Service
    axios.post('http://localhost:4002/events',event);

    //Response
    response.send({status: 'Successful!!'})

    app.listen(4005,()=>{
        console.log("Event Bus running on Port 4005")
```

- We have implemented the event bus mechanism. Now, we need to edit all the microservices to add the mechanism of sending an event request to the event bus on any notable change.
- Blog Post Microservice: On a post creation, an async event is emitted to the event bus.

```javascript
app.post('/posts/create', async (req, res) => {
  //Generate a random id
  const id= randomBytes(2).toString('hex');
  //Pass blogTitle through request body
  const {blogTitle}= req.body;
  //Create the post
  posts[id]={id, blogTitle};

  //On creation of a new post, send the event request to event bus
  await axios.post('http://localhost:4005/events',{
     type: "blogPostCreated",
     data: {
         id, blogTitle
     }
  })
  //On Successful post creation, send the same response
  res.status(201).send(posts[id]);
});
```

- Let us validate whether the event is being generated by the blog post service. Add the following to the blog post service:

```javascript
app.post('/events', (req,res)=>{

     console.log("Event Recieved")

     res.send({});
})
```

- When a new blog post is created, an event is generated by the blog post service.

Create Post

Title

Submit

Posts

My First Blog Post

Comment

Submit

```
[nodemon] watching extensions: js,mjs,json
[nodemon] starting `node index.js`
Post Service running on Port 4000
Event Recieved
```

- Create a new microservice named "query" that will receive events from the event bus on the creation of a new blog post and comment. This service is being created to provide information based on both blog posts and comment services. It will run on port 4002 as mentioned in the event bus implementation.
- Query microservice will work independently based on the received events. This is the GET request to fetch all the posts.

```
posts={}



app.get('/posts', (req,res)=>{


    res.send(posts);
})
```

- This code snippet depicts the request to handle all the received events.

```
//Event Handling
app.post('/events', (req,res)=>{
const {type, data}= req.body;

//If a new blog post is created, array of comments are tagged to it
if (type==='blogPostCreated'){
const {id, blogTitle} =data;

posts[id]= {id, blogTitle, comments: []}
}
//If any comment is created, a postId is tagged to the comment
if (type==='CommentCreated'){
    const {id, content, postId}= data;

    const post= posts[postId]
    post.comments.push({id, content});
}
console.log(posts);
res.send({});
})
```

- Now make sure that the client web application directly makes requests to the query service to fetch the data from the post or comment service. Therefore, a single request solves the purpose of retrieving all the posts and comments associated with it.
- On the creation of a new blog post, the query service fetches the "blogPostCreated" event from the event bus.

```
Query Service running on Port 4002
{ '2ca4': { id: '2ca4', blogTitle: 'Fourth Blog Post', comments: [] } }
```

- Even when the post or the comment service crashes, the query service will work as is and will show the posts and comments if any.

We have discovered an event-driven implementation more simply. Loose coupling, easy scaling, and recovery support provided by the event-driven approach have an advantage over REST or synchronous approach. The selection of a message queue in the event-driven design holds a paramount position as event notification is a paragon functionality.

Deployment Strategies

Our application is now in a pretty complete state. So, we are going to start to think about how we could take this app and deploy it online. All our services are running on some very specific ports and each of them can reach directly out to the other services and send requests. The communication is direct and elementary between each of our different services.

So, how can we somehow take the same kind of structure, make as few changes as possible, and deploy it online? Well, an easy way would be to go out to Digital Ocean or RWC, or Microsoft, or rent a virtual machine.

So, this would work, without a doubt, but as we start to think through this scenario and think about how we would grow our application in the future, well, it starts to get a little bit more challenging.

Let us imagine we have a tremendous number of users coming into our application and trying to create comments. At some point in time, we might decide that we need to create a second or third instance of this common server to handle this additional demand. An easy way to do that would be to say whenever someone tries to create a comment, we can then load the balance between these three different services. Now, there are a couple of challenges with this approach. First, these additional copies of the Comment Service would have to be allocated some new port on this machine. That is relevant because remember, our event bus needs to know the exact IP address and port of all the different services that it is going to send events to. So, in other words, as soon as we create these additional copies of the Common Service over here, we would have to open up our event bus code. If we ever decide to increase or decrease the number of comment service servers running at any given time, we are going to have to make a change or event bus code and deploy that change as well and as you can imagine, that would not be a good solution. This whole scenario gets even more complicated if we see that the common services right here that we added on are overburdening the one virtual machine we have.

Finally, let us imagine one more scenario here very quickly. Let us imagine that our website is very popular at just certain times of the day. So, maybe at 10 a.m., a lot of people visit our website and they start to create comments and so, at 10 a.m., we would want to have these additional copies of the Comment Service running. But then maybe at 1:00 a.m., like at the dead of night, nobody is visiting our application and so to save money on our hosting fees, we might decide at 1:00 a.m. to temporarily shut down this second virtual machine and just say, hey, no one is coming to our website. We do not need those additional copies of the Comment Service and now, in this scenario, once again, the event just needs to know that that second virtual machine is now dead and it should not attempt to send any events over there. Well, to handle that, we would have to come back over to our event bus and maybe add in some code.

Everything we are discussing gets complicated in every aspect. We need a better solution. We need something that is going to keep track of all the different services that are running inside of our application. Something that can maybe create new copies of the service on the fly.

That something is none other than Docker, a containerization platform. Docker is the optimal solution to resolve these deployment issues. It involves a container that creates a feasible environment to run a microservice application. The container runs as a single program. Docker can run multiple copies of these containers based on the scaling requirements.

The need for scalability enables the creation of multiple containers. To handle the containers' management process, there is a prominent container orchestration platform called Kubernetes, which manages all the containers, thus making our application highly scalable and fault-tolerant.

Kubernetes has features of achieving horizontal scaling and load balancing. It has self-healing capabilities as it can reschedule, replace, and restart containers that get faulty or die.

Conclusion

MSA and event-driven architecture EDA are being presented as the next-generation architectural patterns. Together they contribute immensely to producing and deploying event-driven microservices-centric applications, which are the foundation for visualizing and realizing cloud-native applications. Therefore, MSA in association with EDA is being pitched as the optimal framework for realizing futuristic and flexible cloud-native systems, which are natively portable, scalable, available, reliable, and secure. In this chapter, we have showcased how to design, develop, deploy, and manage event-driven microservices. When related microservices get clubbed together, composite microservices, which are process-aware and business-critical, get realized to smoothen the road toward the goal of regal and real digital transformation.

8

Serverless Computing for the Cloud-Native Era

THE OBJECTIVES

Cloud-native applications are to immensely benefit from all the distinct advancements happening in the serverless domain. This chapter is to discuss the following in detail.

1) The Key Motivations for Serverless Computing
2) The Serverless Implications
3) The Evolution of Serverless Computing
4) Serverless Application Patterns
5) Containers as the Function Runtime
6) Serverless Computing Components
7) Top Benefits of Serverless Computing
8) Overcoming Serverless Obstacles

It is clear that the evolving phenomenon of serverless computing is to be a crucial contributor to the envisioned and expected success of cloud-native computing.

Introduction

Serverless computing refers to the bewildering idea of building and running applications that do not require explicit server operations and management. This phenomenon describes a next-generation deployment model where software applications, which are typically bundled as a collection of fine-grained functions, are uploaded to a standardized serverless platform. Most of the established public cloud service providers host such a platform to deliver serverless computing services. There are many open-source and commercial-grade serverless-enablement platforms. The serverless platform takes care of everything. That is, functions and applications are automatically called, executed, scaled, and exactly billed in response to users' requests.

Without an iota of doubt, serverless computing represents the next destination for the IT industry. Cloud-native applications are to immensely benefit from all the distinct advancements happening in the serverless domain. Cloud-native application developers and operators will be too excited to embrace the serverless model. In this chapter, we would like to throw more light on serverless computing and how it is simplifying and speeding up cloud-native application development, deployment, and delivery. The cool convergence of serverless and cloud-native computing models is to result in a series of development, and operational and management advantages for worldwide businesses. Cloud-native applications will be produced and provided to serverless

Cloud-native Computing: How to Design, Develop, and Secure Microservices and Event-Driven Applications,
First Edition. Pethuru Raj, Skylab Vanga, and Akshita Chaudhary.
© 2023 The Institute of Electrical and Electronics Engineers, Inc. Published 2023 by John Wiley & Sons, Inc.

platforms to take care of subsequent activities so that the time being taken to take software solutions and services to the market will be hugely reduced.

The Key Motivations for Serverless Computing [1, 2]

There are a number of noteworthy technological innovations. These have laid down a stimulating foundation for the cloud-native era to flourish. The wider adoption of microservices architecture (MSA) for building and deploying enterprise-scale, service-oriented, and event-driven applications has clearly invigorated the movement toward cloud-native computing. Microservices have brought in a paradigm shift in software engineering. Microservices are typically network accessible, publicly discoverable, independently deployable, horizontally scalable, highly available and extensible, and composable (through orchestration and choreography methods). The promise of increased agility, resilience, scalability, versatility, and developer productivity and a desire for a clear separation of concerns have fueled an indomitable interest in the huge adoption of the microservice architecture pattern for software development and integration.

Software developers and architects visualize microservices as small and autonomous services built around a particular business capability or purpose. Microservices facilitate building mission-critical and enterprise-grade software applications using the promising and potential distributed architecture style. Enterprise-grade applications are being constructed as a collection of microservices. That is, different and distributed microservices have to be identified and composed to form software applications. Further on, microservices can be built by multiple teams independently in different time zones. Microservices-centric applications are loosely or lightly coupled. All kinds of dependency-initiated issues get eliminated here.

The maturity of DevOps concepts and toolsets has also accelerated building, delivery, and deployment of microservices-centric applications. There is surging popularity of containers (a powerful DevOps toolkit) as the most optimal runtime for software applications especially for hosting, running, and managing microservices. Containers are lightweight runtime environment for hosting application components/microservices. Containers combine source code with all the operating system (OS) libraries and dependencies required to run the code in any environment.

This has come as a key motivation for the struggling field of software engineering. The cool convergence between microservices and containers has opened up fresh possibilities and opportunities. Due to the increased density of containerized microservices and their instances through additional containers in any IT environment, the operating and management complexities of containerized environments go up and hence the arrival of Kubernetes, the leading container orchestration platform solution, is being seen as a positive and progressive step in bringing forth a number of automation and acceleration in hosting microservices-centric applications in containers and running them in any IT infrastructure. Kubernetes facilitates multi-container applications, which are generally process-aware and business-critical.

A well-built MSA application may scale better than a tightly coupled monolith. However, distributed systems have their own set of concerns and challenges such as complex error handling. Also, it is the network that calls for microservices to interact, whereas, in the case of massive monolithic applications, it is an in-process call. Another challenge is the significant overhead in infrastructure provisioning and management. Server resources need to be provisioned. Containers or VMs have to be prepared and deployed, the software has to be deployed and patched, and the system stress level has to be tested to make sure that it can withstand and scale under a heavy load. Thus, the IT side of having microservices-centric applications is becoming complicated.

Adopting microservices and running more servers to accommodate microservices and their instances across multiple cloud environments (private, public, hybrid, and edge) are not easy tasks. To ensure high availability and reliability, more instances of microservices are being run and hence the number of nodes to be monitored, measured, and managed is steadily climbing. Servers might be busy handling multiple requests or sitting idle. That is, whether they are fully utilized or under-utilized, the infrastructure cost remains the same. What exacerbates this problem is that the unit of scale for compute resources is not granular enough. Additional compute resources can be provisioned automatically but that is not commensurate with what is needed to handle a sudden spike in user traffic. Here is a necessity for clinical automation for adding and removing IT resources in time to cater to varying user and data loads.

The question is – can we go build scalable, efficient, and high-performance systems without the overhead of IT infrastructure management? Similarly, is it possible to pay exactly for IT resources and their usage? Such automation ultimately helps software engineers focus on their core tasks rather than getting bogged down with the botheration of infrastructure planning, setup, and management. For executing microservice applications, infrastructure management is a tedious and troublesome activity. In a production environment, there can be several microservices teaming up for an application and the number of instances for each of the microservices is bound to go up rapidly. For continuous availability, one instance can be made to run in multiple containers. So, there is rising system complexity. These are some of the brewing challenges of software engineering and IT operations. Even with microservices, setting up and scheduling appropriate infrastructure resources to run microservices consume a lot of time and involve toil.

Hence, the serverless computing paradigm is getting a lot of attention these days. Developers need not bother about putting infrastructure modules in place in order to run and showcase their applications. Cloud service providers with the help of a serverless platform can automate the process of providing resources clinically to run application components dynamically. In short, it is all about bringing in deeper and decisive automation in IT operations. The goal of NoOps is to see the reality sooner than later.

Briefing Serverless Computing

Serverless refers to the concept that developers of serverless applications no longer need to spend time and resources on server provisioning, maintenance, updates, scaling, and capacity planning. Instead, all of these requirements are automatically handled by a serverless platform hosted in on-premise or off-premise IT environment. As a result, developers could completely focus on writing their applications' business logic. IT operations engineers are able to elevate their focus on business-critical tasks. Precisely speaking, developers write code and immensely benefit from a serverless platform. Cloud service providers have to deploy a serverless platform and maintain it consistently. In short, the much-celebrated automation is penetrating IT operations. A variety of IT administration, operation, management, and maintenance tasks are being technologically automated and abstracted away from IT developers and operators. A serverless computing platform may provide one or both of the following modules.

1) **Function-as-a-Service (FaaS):** Functions are typically triggered by events or HTTP requests. Developers deploy small units of code to the FaaS platform. When triggered, a function gets a container to run. Thus, functions get executed immediately after any request. Functions can be scaled if there are spikes in requests. Scaling out containers is faster and easier. Monolithic

applications and even microservices are being segmented into a number of small-scale and purpose-specific functions. Such a segmentation brings in the much-needed dynamism and automation. The distinct advantage here is that any function can be quickly resourced and run to deliver its designated functionality to its requester. Serverless functions/tasks get elegantly mapped with containers and hence allocating containers for hosting and running functions is swift and beneficial.

Through the AWS Lambda offering, developers can run code on-demand or on-schedule. AWS Lambda is a serverless compute service that lets anyone run code without

- provisioning or managing servers,
- creating workload-aware cluster scaling logic
- maintaining event integrations,
- managing runtimes.

With Lambda, it is possible to run code for virtually any type of application or back-end service with zero administration. Just upload your code as a ZIP file or container image, and Lambda automatically and precisely allocates compute execution power and runs your code based on the incoming request or event, for any scale of traffic. You can write Lambda functions in your favorite language (Node.js, Python, Go, Java, and more) and use both serverless and container tools, such as AWS SAM or Docker CLI, to build, test, and deploy your functions.

2) **Back end-as-a-Service (BaaS):** This allows developers to focus on the front end of their applications and leverage back-end services without building or maintaining them. BaaS vendors provide pre-written software for activities that take place on servers such as user authentication, database management, remote updating, and push notifications for mobile applications, as well as cloud storage and hosting.

BaaS includes applications that use third-party services to manage server-side logic. With FaaS, you can upload front-end code to a service like AWS Lambda or Google Cloud Functions and the cloud provider takes care of back-end functions such as provisioning, managing processes, etc.

Function-as-a-Service (FaaS) is an event-driven computing execution model where developers write logic that is deployed in containers fully managed by a serverless platform and then executed on demand. In contrast to BaaS, FaaS affords a greater degree of control to the developers, who create custom applications rather than relying on a collection of prewritten services. Specifically, the containers are:

- Stateless: This makes data integration easy.
- Ephemeral: That is, containers run for a very short time.
- Event-triggered: Containers get created and run when required and go away when not needed.

The FaaS platform comes with an API gateway module to handle function requests. For serverless applications, the tasks associated with infrastructure provisioning, scaling, and management are automated through a competent serverless platform. This abstraction-facilitated automation enables developers to increase their focus on producing advanced business logic and deliver more value to the core of the business. In short, serverless computing helps software and IT teams increase their productivity substantially and bring products to market faster. Further on, resource utilization and efficiency are being easily achieved through the serverless mechanism. The obstacles of cloud-native computing get eliminated. This speeds up and strengthens the cloud-native era. This serverless-inspired automation is being seen as a huge breakthrough in the field of software engineering, which is being deemed and described as the most vital factor for the expected success of the knowledge era.

Once deployed, serverless applications respond to users' requests. Also, on the basis of varying user loads, serverless applications are given appropriate resources in an automated manner. That is, through infrastructure elasticity, application scalability is being intrinsically guaranteed. A serverless platform solution brings in the necessary augmentation. Additionally, containers can be provisioned and incorporated quickly in order to meet up any spike in user activity. There are serverless offerings from established public cloud service providers. AWS Lambda (AWS Lambda is an event-driven serverless computing platform that executes your code in response to events. It manages the underlying infrastructure scaling it up or down to meet the event rate. You are only charged for the time your code is executed. AWS Lambda currently supports Java, Python, and Node.js language runtimes.), Azure Functions, Google Cloud Functions, IBM Cloud Functions, etc., are to execute serverless function code by leveraging third-party services and APIs in a more thoughtful way. Also, these natively apply serverless architectures and patterns.

By taking a serverless compute service and making use of various powerful single-purpose APIs and microservices, developers can build loosely coupled, scalable, and efficient application architectures quickly. In this way, developers can move away from servers and infrastructure concerns and focus primarily on code. The serverless services are usually metered through an event-driven execution model. As a result, when a serverless function is not transacting anything for a user, he or she is not charged. The overall flow is given hereunder:

- An event (e.g. an online order at a retailer) is received by an API Manager of the serverless platform.
- The Manager creates an HTTP request that results in a particular function being launched.
- The function gets instantiated in a container. The container has all the configuration the function needs to run, including its dependencies.
- The function processes the request and delivers the result to the requester.
- The container is then automatically destroyed.
- The user only pays for the resources consumed (RAM, CPU, Disk, etc.) during the time the function ran.

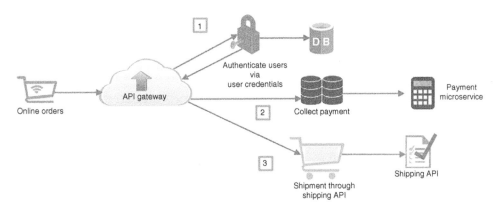

Serverless application architecture.

A serverless compute service, such as AWS Lambda, can execute code in response to events in a massively parallel way. It can respond to HTTP requests (using the AWS API Gateway), events raised by other AWS services, or it can be invoked directly using an API.

The Serverless Implications

This paradigm shift has brought in a series of noteworthy implications as stated hereunder:

Serverless IT vs. Traditional IT: Serverless differs from traditional cloud computing models in a few crucial aspects. In the traditional setup, software developers decide and purchase IT (compute, storage, and networking) resources from cloud service providers. Capacity planning and management actually rest with software producers. That is, software developers have to approach one or more cloud providers to allocate a certain quantity of IT resources to smoothly run their software applications. The performance key indicators (PKIs) for an application are being fulfilled through the smart selection of cloud resources. The scalability need also has to be fulfilled manually by the software developer. Provisioning additional bare metal (BM) servers, virtual machines (VMs), and containers for meeting up higher user activity and deprovisioning them when the user activity goes down noticeably are the responsibility of the software developer. The cloud infrastructure provisioned to run an application is still active even when the application is not being used by the software developer and his users. This ultimately costs for software developers.

On the other hand, serverless applications as a collection of functions are generally deployed in containers and they start the execution automatically when appropriately invoked. With serverless architecture, applications are launched only when needed. When an event triggers application code to run, cloud infrastructure resources are allocated for that code to be run. The user stops paying when the code finishes executing. In addition to the cost and efficiency benefits, serverless frees developers from routine and menial tasks associated with application scaling and server provisioning. With serverless, routine tasks such as managing OSs and file systems, applying security patches, load balancing, capacity management, scaling, logging, and monitoring are all delegated to cloud service providers. Cloud service providers actually automate these tasks by leveraging a powerful serverless platform. It is also possible to build an entirely serverless application or an application composed of partially serverless and partially traditional microservices components. Precisely speaking, serverless platforms deeply automate most of the infrastructure lifecycle management tasks.

There are platform solutions and services to automate several things associated with IT operations. For example, take the hugely popular Kubernetes platform solution. Still, infrastructure operations are mandatory. The serverless platform solution solves this prickling challenge. Such empowerment relieves software developers from worrying about the software deployment aspect. With serverless, the containers running workloads are neither provisioned nor monitored by the developers. Applications are accordingly and appropriately resourced and run to deliver their designated functionalities.

Serverless Computing for IT Transformation: IT transformation is very vital for accomplishing the much-needed business transformation. IT is the greatest enabler of businesses. Cloud-native computing is one such technological domain inspiring strategically sound transformations in the IT field. With the greater awareness of the unique accomplishments of the serverless computing model, the cool convergence of cloud-native and serverless computing models had led to a series of real IT transformations. Definitely serverless is to serve as a harbinger for a bevy of innovations and disruptions in the IT space.

Serverless is to contribute immensely to both greenfield and brownfield projects. Greenfield projects, where an application is built from scratch, get most of the attention these days. A greenfield project is equivalent to building a new house with new materials and no legacy considerations. There could be even broader and bigger opportunities for serverless with brownfield projects. Greenfield projects start with microservices, containers, Kubernetes, Istio, etc. This is pureplay serverless. On the other hand, brownfield projects are often suited for augmentation through the addition of serverless functions. Thus, legacy applications can steadily move to be categorized as cloud-native applications. DevOps teams can modernize APIs of old applications. Also, they can express and expose extract, transform, and load (ETL) tasks as serverless functions. Thus, legacy modernization and migration can be accomplished in a cloud-native way and using serverless functions.

Serverless Will Further Extend to Online Services from Offline Services: Serverless technologies, such as FaaS, were initially a bit slow to respond to users' requests due to various reasons. Now with the additional capabilities and options being extended by major cloud providers such as AWS and Azure cloud, the response time issue gets solved. Therefore, the fast-emerging and evolving serverless paradigm facilitates the move from offline applications to online applications.

Serverless computing is typically a cloud-based service where server management rests with a cloud provider, who also dynamically allots other infrastructure resources as needed to execute application code. A serverless-enablement platform comes in handy for cloud service providers to automate the server allocation, monitoring, and management tasks. With serverless computing, the service provider takes care of all the infrastructure modules. Therefore, software developers can just focus on writing code.

Thus, the automation scenario in the IT operations space is definitely mesmerizing. A number of IT provisioning, configuration, scaling, and management activities are meticulously automated through a host of path-breaking technological innovations. There came a number of cutting-edge technologies and state-of-the-art tools to accelerate and automate the tricky and time-consuming tasks associated with software delivery and deployment. Especially, the aspect of containerization in sync up with container orchestration platforms is being seen as an enabler in empowering the operation side of software products, solutions, and services across multiple and heterogeneous cloud environments. Serverless computing is an amalgamation of proven and potential technologies to speed up IT operations with less human instruction and intervention. Precisely speaking, the serverless paradigm has laid down a strong and sustainable foundation toward the NoOps vision. Serverless has gone from cutting-edge to the mainstream as software developers started to discover the ease and cost-effectiveness of adopting serverless computing in their day-to-day activities.

The Evolution of Serverless Computing [3, 4]

The concepts of serverless architecture and FaaS have grown hand-in-hand with the popularity of containers and on-demand cloud offerings. The "1.0" phase of serverless came with limitations that made it less than ideal for general computing. Serverless 1.0 is characterized by:

- HTTP and a few other sources
- Functions only
- Limited execution time (5–10 minutes)
- No orchestration
- Limited local development experience

The advent of Kubernetes ushered in the "Serverless 1.5" era where many serverless frameworks started to auto-scale containers. Serverless 1.5 is characterized by:

- Knative
- Kubernetes-based auto-scaling
- Microservices and functions

- Easy to debug and test locally
- Polyglot and portable

Today, the "Serverless 2.0" era is emerging with the addition of integration and state. Providers have started adding the missing parts to make serverless suitable for general-purpose business workloads. Serverless 2.0 is characterized by:

- Basic state handling
- Use of enterprise integration patterns
- Advanced messaging capabilities
- Blended with the enterprise PaaS
- Enterprise-ready event sources
- State and integration

Serverless Application Patterns

Front-end and back-end services are fully managed by the cloud provider, who handles scaling, security, and compliance requirements. Developers build serverless functions and applications using a variety of application patterns to meet specific requirements and business needs.

- **Serverless Functions:** Event-driven programming accelerates the development of serverless functions. Events from local or remote sources trigger serverless functions to execute the designated function code immediately. That is, serverless functions receive and respond to events from multiple and distributed sources. There are bindings to seamlessly integrate additional and third-party services. That is, serverless functions can do bigger and better things through such integrations. Containers host serverless functions and hence provisioning and instantiating serverless functions is quite easy and fast. This is a pay-per-execution model with sub-second billing charges only for the time and resources it takes to execute the code.
- **Serverless Kubernetes:** As explained elsewhere, Kubernetes-orchestrated clusters can automatically provision additional containers and deprovision the added containers to precisely cater to varying traffic levels. Thus, the declarative scaling of infrastructure modules through Kubernetes comes in handy in empowering the unique ideals of serverless computing. The serverless idea is to march ahead with the substantial contributions of the Kubernetes platform.
- **Serverless Workflows:** Serverless workflows are becoming popular because they take a low-code/no-code approach to simplify service orchestration. Developers can easily find and integrate local and remote services instantaneously without much difficulty. The serverless platform helps developers do such integration and interaction without any coding. There is no need for involving any glue code or a middleware solution toward such integration.
- **Serverless API Gateway:** A serverless API gateway is a centralized and fully managed entity, which is the entry point for serverless services (front-end as well as back-end). The API gateway enables developers to publish, manage, secure, and analyze APIs at a global scale.

The serverless paradigm surges ahead because of the worthwhile contributions of serverless platforms. The serverless approach offers developers, teams, and organizations a level of abstraction that enables them to minimize the time and resources needed for managing the underlying infrastructure modules. Applications, middleware solutions, databases, etc., can go the serverless way. All kinds of analytical and operational applications can be made to express and expose as serverless applications. By leveraging a comprehensive serverless platform, serverless service providers, software developers, and serverless service consumers benefit greatly. There are a number of business, technical, and user advantages through a host of powerful serverless technologies and tools. Serverless is a powerful phenomenon and a number of laudable improvisations are to propel the serverless concept to the next level.

Containers as the Function Runtime

We have been fiddling with BM servers and VMs for long. Compared to these popular compute machines, the arrival and spread of containers are being applauded widely and wisely too. Containers carry certain unique characteristics. Further on, the concept of containerization has rekindled a number of commendable innovations in the software engineering domain. Containers allow software developers to realize highly configurable, composable, and customizable applications quickly in a declarative fashion. The layered approach proposed and propelled by the containerization idea has accelerated the speed with which software applications are being constructed and deployed. Software portability is being achieved through containerization. Now with the synchronization with the flourishing serverless idea, the future beckons for the realization of highly scalable and versatile applications. There is a cool convergence between containers and microservices. That is, containers emerge as the most optimal runtime for microservices. Microservices get containerized and deposited to be found and used. With the emergence of serverless functions, containers are revisited and repurposed to host functions. Through such an arrangement, a number of operational benefits are being accrued. Real-time horizontal scalability of functions gets fulfilled as containers can be generated and deployed in a matter of seconds. Thus, the intersection of containers and functions is to bring forth a dazzling array of newer possibilities and opportunities for providers as well as consumers.

Serverless Computing Components [5, 6]

We know that serverless computing has started its long and fruitful innings as a function-as-a-service (FaaS). Then came the back end-as-a-service (BaaS). In this section, we are to discuss the other prominent components to enlighten our esteemed readers.

Queue Buffer: Queuing services hold data when it is moved from one application to another. This is through the leverage of asynchronous communication. Amazon Simple Queue Service (SQS) is a fully managed message queuing service. SQS cleanly decouples and scales distributed microservices and applications, and serverless applications. SQS eliminates the need for operationalizing messaging middleware (brokers and queues). This empowers software developers to focus on their expertise.

A useful AWS serverless microservice pattern is to distribute an event to one or more SQS queues using a simple notification system (SNS). This gives us the ability to use multiple SQS queues to "buffer" events. This eventually helps to throttle queue processing to alleviate pressure on downstream resources. For example, if we have an event that needs to write information to a relational database AND trigger another process that needs to call a third-party API, this pattern would be a great fit.

Stream Processing: Data getting generated and streamed from multiple sources have to be subjected to a variety of investigations in time to extract real-time insights. Amazon Kinesis is a suite of managed services that can help you collect, process, and analyze streaming data in near-real time. Processing streaming data enables an application to react accordingly and adaptively as new data arrives. That is, this real-time processing of streaming data in conjunction with new data brings forth newer functionality for applications. For example, payment processors can analyze payments in real time to detect fraudulent transactions. Ecommerce websites can use streams of clickstream activity to determine site engagement metrics in near-real time. Kinesis integration with AWS Lambda goes a long way for serverless applications. Using Lambda as a stream consumer can also help minimize the amount of operational overhead for managing streaming applications.

Event Bus: Event-driven architecture (EDA) is a popular architectural style for producing event-driven applications. That is, these applications receive and respond to events. Event-driven applications are loosely coupled and distributed. Such isolation considerably improves developer agility. Event-driven applications are also resilient. The event bus is an intermediary for receiving messages from different sources and delivering them to distributed and different recipients. The event bus resembles a queue buffer. An event bus can process multiple topics. It is possible to incorporate custom rules for delivering event messages to different subscribers. AWS EventBridge (\https://aws.amazon.com/eventbridge/) is a cloud-based event bus with additional support and security.

As articulated and accentuated several times in this chapter, for serverless applications to grow and glow, events are the key communication mechanism. There are disparate and distributed sources such as API Gateways, databases, or data streams for emitting out events while serverless functions react to them astutely in order to accomplish a business task. Not only as a communication module but events also enable application integration. Thus, there are enablers to receive and use them to simplify the integration outlooks of distributed applications. All these clearly insist that there is a need for ways and means of generating and injecting a variety of events into the system. Thereby, the usage of Webhooks has gone up in the recent past to connect external event sources with the cloud. Webhooks are the HTTP endpoints which consume HTTP requests. This translates the incoming request data into an event which is then forwarded to the respective cloud service.

However, there are a couple of challenges being associated with Webhooks. Webhooks require additional infrastructure such as API Gateways to be created and maintained. The API endpoint has to be scalable and always available to ensure successfully delivering events. The need for marshaling and unmarshaling of requests and responses introduces additional overheads. Scaling the event delivery gets tricky if there is a need to dispatch events to multiple recipients based on rules. Precisely speaking, such management and maintenance-heavy method is not suitable for the ensuing serverless era.

Events and serverless applications are inseparable. Therefore, there have to be competent tools and techniques to easily and elegantly create, ingest, and react to events emanating from multiple sources. The AWS EventBridge helps software developers build next-generation event-driven applications. EventBridge is a serverless pub-/sub-service, enabling and establishing seamless and spontaneous connectivity between growing event sources and a variety of AWS cloud services via event buses. As noted down, event producers can be business applications, datastores, SaaS applications, AWS services, etc. On the other side, event consumers may be AWS compute instances, serverless functions, etc. Event buses act as the intermediary in voluntarily linking up different systems. Thus, serverless application development and deployment are being distinctly spruced and speeded up.

Serverless Databases: Predominantly, serverless computing is event-driven. Originally it does not have a persistent state. Local variables' values do not persist across instantiations. This is seen as a potential drawback for developing and running stateful applications. Serverless databases help overcome this limitation by enabling application development with a data storage facility. Serverless databases function the same as other serverless architecture. The key difference is serverless databases store data in a persistent manner. The job of maintaining and provisioning a database is also taken care of by a serverless service provider. Software developers have to pay only for the usage. There are many serverless databases (https://dashbird.io/blog/what-is-serverless-database/).

Advantages of Using a Serverless Database

- **Cost Efficiency:** Buying a predefined number of cloud servers generally leads to resource underutilization and this turns out to be expensive for software developers. Thus, going for the serverless database is definitely cost-effective because infrastructure allocation and management are fine-grained and automated. There is no OS cost, which, in turn, aggregates the licensing, installations, maintenance, support, and patching costs. The recently popularized "pay-as-you-go" paradigm is really fulfilled through serverless databases.
- **Operations, Scalability, and Productivity:** With serverless computing being sufficiently enabled through serverless platform solutions, developers just focus on creating business logic while the load on operations gets considerably reduced. Automated and fine-grained scaling is being accomplished. The IT productivity goes up remarkably.

Disadvantages of Using Serverless Databases

- **Slow Response:** The cloud provider spins down a serverless database entirely if it is not used. This means that it would take more time to start up a serverless database instance for attending to users' requests. Therefore, online applications and high-performance workloads get slowed down a bit. As written earlier, leading cloud service providers such as AWS and Azure cloud are giving multiple options so that the time-critical and low-latency applications could get a faster response.
- **Monitoring and Debugging:** It is important to continuously monitor, measure, and manage business workloads. The key performance indicators (KPIs) metrics are critical for the continued success of mission-critical applications. The health condition is very vital. Therefore, application performance management (APM) software products are widely used. However, performance monitoring and debugging of serverless applications are not straightforward. Fortunately, there are some serverless monitoring tools to ensure the continuous availability of serverless apps.
- **Security:** As the installation and control of serverless databases are with cloud service and database providers, there are valid concerns regarding serverless security.

Manually managing database capacity can waste a lot of valuable time and can lead to inefficient use of database resources. With Aurora Serverless (https://aws.amazon.com/rds/aurora/serverless/), you simply create a database endpoint, optionally specify the desired database capacity range, and connect your applications. You pay on a per-second basis for the database capacity you use when the database is active, and migrate between standard and serverless configurations with a few clicks in the Amazon RDS Management Console.

Amazon Aurora Serverless scales instantly from hundreds to hundreds of thousands of transactions in a fraction of a second. As it scales, it adjusts capacity in fine-grained increments to provide just the right amount of database resources that the application needs. There is no database capacity for you to manage, you pay only for the capacity your application consumes, and you can save up to 90% of your database cost compared to the cost of provisioning capacity for peak load.

Fauna (https://fauna.com/) is a unique indexed document system that supports relations, documents, and graphs for unmatched modeling flexibility. Its query interface features complex joins and custom business logic as well as support for real-time streaming and GraphQL. Fauna is connectionless, and accessible directly from the browser or mobile clients. Fauna provides serverless, multiregional, and transactional database instances that are accessible via a cloud API. This is easy to adopt and highly productive to use. Fauna gives you the data safety and reliability you need, without the operational pain typically inflicted by databases.

Akka Serverless (https://www.lightbend.com/akka-serverless) provides the building blocks that make it quick and simple for every developer to build highly scalable, low-latency stateful APIs and services.

Serverless Framework (https://www.serverless.com/) facilitates zero-friction serverless development. It easily builds applications that auto-scale on low-cost and next-generation cloud infrastructure.

API Development by Serverless: APIs are a crucial part of any web application and there are different techniques for API development and design. The most common models for API implementation are REST and Graph. REST allows two systems to communicate with the help of HTTP methods. It requires knowing the endpoints, parameters, and filters in advance. For REST architecture, there is an AWS API Gateway (This is a service allowing developers to create and manage HTTP endpoints, map them to particular AWS resources, and configure custom domains, authorizing mechanisms, caching and other features). Graph API allows combining filters, selecting which data points to return, aggregating information before retrieval, etc. For Graph, there is the AWS AppSync service.

Serverless is one powerful approach gaining popularity because of its productivity, affordability, scalability, and simplicity. API Gateway is the fundamental part of serverless API because it is responsible for the connection between a defined API and the function handling requests to that API. There is a tutorial explaining how to build a REST API following the Serverless approach using AWS Lambda, API Gateway, DynamoDB, and he Serverless Framework (https://www.serverless.com/blog/node-rest-api-with-serverless-lambda-and-dynamodb).

Authentication Management: A serverless user management system allows apps to authenticate, authorize, and manage users by applying high-level security standards. AWS Cognito provides a level of security that can be replicated by an extended app development team only.

Offerings like AWS Lambda, Fauna, Google Firebase, and AWS Step Functions provide the incredible capability.

Top Benefits of Serverless Computing

Holistically speaking, the serverless phenomenon is a huge step toward deeper automation on the IT operations side. The solidity of containerization has facilitated this paradigm shift. There are a few noteworthy advantages of serverless computing as accentuated later. The first key benefit is that the infrastructure management gets delegated to cloud providers. And serverless platform solutions adequately empower cloud providers to achieve more with less. Software developers benefit the most here.

Secondly, here is a widely reported advantage. The infrastructure modules scale out and in dynamically. Any variation in user traffic is well-accounted for and tackled through horizontal autoscaling. Serverless computing increases development teams' agility and hence more functionality gets developed and delivered in less time. Thus, taking software products and solutions to the market is faster compared to traditional programming and deployment. Writing code for serverless functions is relatively easier and quicker. The new code is uploaded and changes are initiated through an API call.

Shifting to the serverless concept helps organizations reduce the total cost of ownership (TCO) and enhance return on investment (RoI). This is due to the automated allocation of resources to accelerate the pace of innovation. Serverless architecture includes BaaS building blocks for common functionalities. That is, there are ready-made solutions available for databases, file storage, API, etc. All these come in handy in swiftly integrating any software application with the necessary back-end services.

The pricing model (pay per usage) drastically reduces the software operational costs. The execution lasts for a few milliseconds and the charge is made only for that short duration. The application scalability is automated. As the infrastructure allocation (compute, storage, networking, database, etc.) is facilitated through a competent serverless platform solution, developers easily deploy their applications. As infrastructure allocation and management activities are fully taken care of by cloud servers, developers need not bother about provisioning infrastructure resources. Continuous availability and fault-tolerance rest with cloud service providers.

Serverless resources can be availed from multiple cloud locations and hence users do get their services delivered quickly from a nearby cloud environment. Thus, the serverless idea is picking fast to bring in the much-needed affordability, adaptability, and agility.

Overcoming Serverless Obstacles

Traditionally, applications have been developed and deployed with persistent data stores. Even microservices are stateless and ephemeral by definition. Microservices, these days, evolve to produce stateful applications. Microservices are always made to run in "always-on" VMs or containers. In the serverless world, functions are even more ephemeral. They get executed individually or in parallel. Once the task is over, the infrastructure module is taken away. Functions are activated by events and they are stateless. Stateful applications remember preceding events or user interactions. Since serverless functions are ephemeral, the state from one invocation of a function is not available to another invocation of the same function. To build a serverless application that requires state data, the state data must be stored in an external database or cache. Solutions such as Microsoft Azure Durable Functions help write stateful functions in a serverless environment.

Similarly, there are a few important barriers that need to be technologically surmounted in order to make the fledgling serverless idea flourish.

Event-driven Programming: EDA has been a prominent architectural style for creating and running decoupled applications in the enterprise IT space. Application components/services are fully isolated and hence all kinds of dependency problems get eliminated at the source itself. Application services can be independently deployed and scaled out. As it turns out, EDA is more appropriate for the serverless world as the event-driven design of serverless functions guarantees a number of benefits. The aspect of versioning can be accomplished by bringing up a new service.

Thus, event-driven programming is being seen as a positive thing for building next-generation serverless applications.

Observability: This is an important requirement for large-scale applications. Enterprise-grade applications have to be observable. Monitoring, measuring, and managing mission-critical applications are important for continuous availability and business continuity. However, imposing the observability feature on serverless applications is not a straightforward thing. As noted down earlier, serverless functions are invoked on an event and shutdown or scale to zero upon completion of the requested task. Therefore, serverless system state and health conditions are being inferred through the properties of a system over time. Especially log data throws some light on the performance of serverless systems.

Security: The cloud service provider takes care of the infrastructure (compute, storage, and network) security. And hence there is a reduced role for application developers. Still, there are valid reasons for software developers to have a reasonable worry on the security front. New attack vectors emerge continuously to target server applications and their underlying infrastructure modules.

Stateless vs. Stateful Functions: Perhaps the biggest difference with serverless development is that functions are stateless, whereas most applications are stateful. The serverless idea will progress further to take care of stateful applications with ease.

The Future of Serverless Computing

The identified drawbacks of the serverless idea will be overcome through competent technological solutions. Some widely reported serverless challenges are long-running jobs, heavy computing jobs, or processes that require control over the execution environment. As Kubernetes is being pitched and positioned as the one-stop IT solution for all the ills affecting IT operations, we can easily visualize that there will be closer cooperation between Kubernetes and the serverless phenomenon to pursue greater automation. The aspect of cloud-native computing will penetrate further through tighter integration with serverless computing. Further on, as the edge computing phenomenon is gaining prominence these days, the unique capabilities of serverless computing will be a huge value addition for edge computing to shine. Fulfilling the serverless function orchestration and producing stateful serverless applications will get greater attention in the days to unfurl. By skillfully using the blooming serverless idea, sophisticated yet complicated applications such as business-to-consumer (B2C) e-commerce application development, deployment, management, and improvement can be speeded up.

A WebAssembly (WASM)-based FaaS Solution to Emerge: Although WASM is widely considered a browser technology, it provides excellent security isolation, an extremely fast start-up speed, and support for more than 20 languages. These technical features make WASM to suit the needs of FaaS.

Software is eating the world. However, software development and deployment are becoming complex with the multiplicity of heterogeneous technologies. Thereby the time being taken to make software products, solutions, and services is going up. Therefore, business houses and IT organizations are betting on path-breaking technologies toward accelerated software building. Software delivery and operation have to be radically simplified in order to guarantee the speed with which software applications get realized and released. Cloud environments exhibit automated scaling of their resources. Cloud resources are charged based on their usage. When scaling, capacity planning, and cost management are getting automated, application development and maintenance (ADM) becomes cheaper. This is what the Serverless architecture offers – it is built on next-generation public cloud services that auto-scale and charge only when used. When scale, capacity planning, and cost management are automated, the result is software that is easier to build, maintain, and often up to 99% cheaper.

Conclusion

The serverless computing model:

- provisions appropriate amount of computing resources on demand, scales transparently based on varying request sizes and scales down to zero when requests are no longer there;
- offloads all the infrastructure management tasks such as scheduling, patching, provisioning, scaling, etc., to the cloud provider. This transition enables application developers to focus on research and development;
- lessens the workload of cloud administrators and operators through a competent serverless platform solution;
- enables serverless application customers and users to pay only for resources being used. They need not pay for unutilized resources;
- leads to the destination of NoOps vision.

Serverless computing is well positioned to play a critical role in the enterprise. The serverless approach is being explored across all kinds of applications, databases, middleware solutions, and platforms. Especially with cloud-native applications becoming mainstream, the power of serverless computing comes in handy in accelerating and augmenting cloud-native software deployment and management for the ensuing cloud-native era. Further on, edge-native applications are also being tried to be benefited from all the improvisations happening in the serverless space. Some of the major limitations of serverless computing are being faithfully addressed by cloud service providers and serverless platform providers. Especially with Kubernetes emerging as the best-in-class platform solution for deploying and managing microservices-centric applications, the serverless phenomenon is to further accelerate and automate setting up Kubernetes clusters to run enterprise-grade and production-ready applications.

Appendix

Knative for Serverless Computing

As deliberated at the beginning of this chapter, automation technologies are acquiring special significance in the IT field. Because any advancement in the IT space has a direct impact on business operations. As told in previous chapters, the faster maturity and stability of Kubernetes is being seen as a positive thing for the betterment of the IT field. Kubernetes in conjunction with containers has brought a series of improvisations in effectively and efficiently tackling the IT operations. Kubernetes is gaining surging popularity as it is enabling the automated deployment and management of software applications, especially containerized applications. Other noteworthy contributions include resource and task scheduling, load balancing, health monitoring, and infrastructure elasticity toward application scalability. Container lifecycle management is being fully taken over by Kubernetes. As we all know, containers are being positioned as the most optimal runtime for software applications, especially microservices.

Containers allow application components/microservices to share the resources of a single instance of an OS. Containers have become the de facto compute units of cloud-native applications. Companies using containers gain other benefits including real-time horizontal scalability, less memory footprint, greater levels of innovation, etc. As there is faster adoption of cloud-native principles and processes, containerized microservices-centric applications are abounding everywhere. Kubernetes' container orchestration capabilities make this proliferation faster, deeper, and easier. However, Kubernetes is a complex tool. That means developers have to do a lot of things to set things right. For example, pulling application source code from software repositories, building and provisioning a container image from the source code, configuring network connections, and incorporating Kubernetes-managed containers into an automated continuous integration/continuous delivery (CI/CD) pipeline requires special tools and custom coding.

To simplify the usage of the Kubernetes platform penetrative and pervasive, there are hundreds of enabling tools from a number of product and tool vendors (https://www.peterindia.net/Kubernetes.html). With serverless applications gaining prominence, building and running serverless applications on Kubernetes clusters have to be accelerated. And hence the Knative framework is very popular among Kubernetes enthusiasts. On its own, Kubernetes cannot run serverless applications without specialized software that integrates Kubernetes with a specific cloud provider's serverless platform. Knative enables any container to run as a serverless workload on any Kubernetes cluster – whether the container is built around a serverless function, or other application code (e.g. microservices) – by abstracting away the code and handling the network routing, event triggers, and autoscaling.

Knative eliminates this complexity with a slew of automated tools. Knative creates the container and performs the network programming to set up a route, ingress, load balancing, and others. Knative also offers a command-line interface, Knative CLI. This allows developers to access Knative features without editing YAML files. Knative achieves all of these by adding three main components – build, serving, and eventing.

Build: This automates the process of turning source code into a container. This process typically involves multiple steps:

- Pulling source code from a code repository such as GitHub
- Installing the underlying dependencies such as environment variables and software libraries, which the code needs to run as per the expectation
- Building container images
- Putting container images into a registry where Kubernetes (and other developers) can find them.

Knative uses Kubernetes APIs and other tools for the Build process. A developer can create a single manifest (typically a YAML file) that specifies all the variables – location of the source code, required dependencies, etc., and Knative uses the manifest to automate the container build.

Serving: This is for deploying and running containers as scalable Knative services. Serving provides the following important capabilities:

- **Configuration** defines and maintains the state of a service. It also provides version control and management. Each modification to the configuration creates a new version of the service and the previous versions get saved.
- **Intelligent service routing** lets developers route traffic to different versions of the service. For example, a small set of users can be allowed to access the new version. This is a prominent feature of Istio, an open-source service mesh implementation.
- **Autoscaling:** Knative can scale services up into thousands of instances. It can also scale them down to zero.

Eventing: This enables different events to trigger their container-based services and functions. Knative queues and delivers those events to the appropriate containers. This module eliminates the need for writing scripts or any middleware functionality. Knative also handles the message broker/queue/bus to deliver events to containers. It also enables developers to set up feeds, which connect an event to an action for their containers to perform.

The Contributions of Knative for the Serverless Era: Knative contributes immensely to taking and running serverless applications on Kubernetes clusters to reap all the originally expressed benefits of Kubernetes. Software developers can directly leverage the Kubernetes capabilities through Knative, which eliminates repetitive build and configuration tasks.

Secondly, Knative accelerates the journey toward serverless. Setting up and sustaining serverless environments on Kubernetes clusters is not an easy assignment. Knative declaratively builds and runs applications and services inside containers. Instantiating containers get automated by Knative. In short, the arrival of Knative is seen as an enabler for enterprise and cloud IT teams to quickly set up serverless workloads.

Knative Inherently Supports Agile and DevOps Lifecycles: Knative makes it speedier and easier to deploy containerized applications. Knative integrates application components and services into automated CI/CD pipelines without mandating any special software or custom programming.

Knative Smoothens New Feature Rollouts: Knative through its configuration and routing feature lets developers expose new container revisions to a subset of the user base.

Thus, there is a slew of powerful technologies such as MSA, EDA, containerization, Kubernetes, DevOps toolkits, and serverless computing. These gel well to simplify and speed up the cloud-native computing paradigm to flourish.

Kumologica: This is the first low-code development solution that runs your integration and automation services serverlessly on any cloud. Kumologica provides a drag-and-drop visual designer and low-code approach to ensure the greatest speed and flexibility to support a wide range of integrations compatible with most of the platforms and cloud providers.

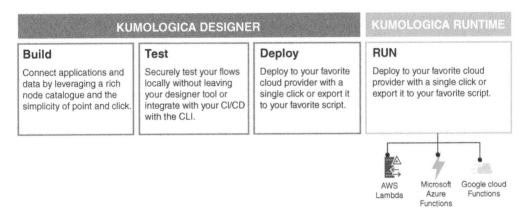

Kumologica consists of two parts:

- **Kumologica Designer** has been designed to maximize IT productivity. It allows developers to automate business processes, to create customer APIs, and in data integrations using point and click and not coding. Using fields and choices, teams can customize their deployments and generate automatically Serverless or AWS CloudFormation scripts that can integrate with existing CI/CD solutions.
- **Kumologica Runtime:** A library which is responsible to run integration flows on top of your FaaS in a scalable, high-performing, and cost-efficient manner.

A Use Case: A plant supervisor is sending the asset information to an asset management application as well as to a data lake for reporting purposes. The supervisor is using a mobile client App, which is invoking a serverless integration (Kumologica) application that runs on AWS Lambda. The integration application will then publish the message into a broker topic (Solace PubSub+), which will be subscribed by the Asset management application and data lake.

The implementation details are found on this page: https://kumologica.medium.com/?p= 45bfbb2a6f6c

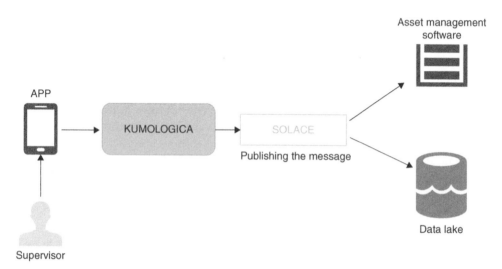

A serverless computing use case.

Source: Modified from Kumologica [7].

Benefits: In addition to all the benefits aforementioned of using FaaS, there are two main benefits when using Kumologica:

- **Cloud Portability:** You have one tool and one way to describe and run your integration flows, and thanks to the different cloud bindings, there is no headache anymore in porting those flows to other cloud providers. This reduces the risk of cloud vendor lock-in.
- **Quick Development Feedback-Loop:** Develop with zero or almost zero code, test your flows locally (without any Docker dependencies) and deploy into the cloud in a secure and quick manner, and all within your designer. There is no need to jump into the terminal to run other scripts or go to web consoles to configure security roles/triggers, etc. Kumologica Designer will take care of these tasks.

References

1 Understanding cloud-native application. https://www.redhat.com/en/topics/cloud-native-apps
2 About Serverless architecture. https://www.ibm.com/cloud/learn/serverless
3 Serverless Through Cloud Native Architecture. https://www.ijert.org/serverless-through-cloud-native-architecture

4 How Cloud Native, Serverless Can Breathe New Life into Legacy Apps. https://thenewstack.io/how-cloud-native-serverless-can-breath-new-life-into-legacy-apps/

5 Serverless Computing Resources. https://www.peterindia.net/Serverless.html

6 AWS Serverless Computing, Benefits, Architecture and Use-cases. https://www.xenonstack.com/blog/aws-serverless-computing/

7 Kumologica (n.d.). Serverless integration with Solace PubSub+ cloud using Kumologica. https://kumologica.medium.com/serverless-integration-with-solace-pubsub-cloud-using-kumologica-45bfbb2a6f6c

9

Instaling Knative on a Kubernetes Cluster

THE OBJECTIVES

Knative delivers a bevy of enabling components to build and run serverless applications on Kubernetes clusters. Knative offers some of the advanced features like autoscaling, in-cluster builds, and an eventing framework for cloud-native applications on Kubernetes. Knative codifies the best practices shared by enterprise Kubernetes solutions. Knative enables developers to focus on writing code without bothering about setting up and sustaining cloud infrastructure to run their applications. In this chapter, we would like to articulate how Knative can be installed on a Kubernetes cluster to our esteemed readers.

Introduction

Knative is an open-source project which adds components for deploying, running, and managing serverless, cloud-native applications to Kubernetes. The serverless cloud computing model can lead to increased developer productivity and reduced operational costs. Knative eliminates the tasks of provisioning and managing servers. This lets developers focus on their code without having to worry about setting up complex infrastructure. This benefit is extended even further if entire application components are incorporated from a third party through Backend-as-a-Service (BaaS), rather than being written in-house.

The Knative serverless environment lets you deploy code to a Kubernetes platform. With Knative, you create a service by packaging your code as a container image and handing it to the system. Your code only runs when it needs to, with Knative starting and stopping instances automatically. Resources are not consumed unless your code needs to do something. Operations costs can be reduced – you can pay for cloud-based compute time as it is needed instead of running and managing your own servers all the time.

Knative Simplifies Container Development and Orchestration: Developers generally write code for software applications and containerize the applications. But the act of containerizing application source code is not an easy job. This container image creation requires lots of repetitive steps. Further on, we have a few proven container orchestration platforms. Kubernetes stands tall and occupies the top slot for container orchestration. Even with Kubernetes, orchestrating containers requires lots of configuration and scripting such as generating configuration files, installing dependencies, managing logging and tracing, and writing continuous

Cloud-native Computing: How to Design, Develop, and Secure Microservices and Event-Driven Applications, First Edition. Pethuru Raj, Skylab Vanga, and Akshita Chaudhary.
© 2023 The Institute of Electrical and Electronics Engineers, Inc. Published 2023 by John Wiley & Sons, Inc.

integration/continuous deployment (CI/CD) scripts. Knative makes these tasks easier by auto-mating them through three important components:

- **Build:** This component automatically transforms application source code into a cloud-native container or function. The Build component pulls the source code from the repository, installs the required dependencies, builds the container image, and puts it in a container registry to be found and used by other developers. Developers have to specify the location of these software components so Knative can find them. Then Knative plunges into real action to automate the build process.
- **Serve:** This component runs containers as scalable services. That is, it can spin up thousands of container instances and scale down to none instantaneously. The Serve component has two important features: configuration and service routing.
  - **Configuration:** This saves the versions of a container (called snapshots) every time a container is pushed into production. This feature helps in running those versions concurrently.
  - **Service routing:** This feature is for directing different amounts of traffic to these versions. This comes in handy to gradually phase a container rollout or to stage a canary test of a con-tainerized application before putting it into production.
- **Event:** This enables specified events to trigger container-based services or functions. Serverless functions get triggered and plunge into action when an event hits them. This component allows development teams to express an interest in types of events, and then it automatically connects to the event producer and routs the events to the container. There is no need to code these connections.

As cloud-native development becomes a mainstream activity and containers proliferate in enter-prise and cloud IT environments, Kubernetes' container orchestration capabilities (specifically scheduling, load balancing, health monitoring, etc.) make that container proliferation a lot easier to manage.

As indicated here, Kubernetes is a complex platform requiring developers to perform or template many repetitive tasks. Kubernetes has to pull application source code from software repositories. Then, it builds and provisions a container image around the code. It also has to configure network connections within and outside. These tasks are being performed through a growing array of tools. There are several DevOps tools to put containers into an automated CI/DC pipeline. Thus, Kubernetes-inspired container management mandates different toolsets. Additional coding is necessary to activate all these.

Knative eliminates this complexity with tools that automate these tasks. A developer just defines the container's contents and configuration in a single YAML manifest file, and Knative does the rest, creating the container and performing the network programming to set up a route, ingress, load balancing, and more.

Knative delivers a set of important components to build and run serverless applications on Kubernetes clusters. Knative offers features like scale-to-zero, autoscaling, in-cluster builds, and an eventing framework for cloud-native applications on Kubernetes. Whether in private or public cloud environments, Knative codifies the best practices shared by successful real-world Kubernetes-based frameworks. Most importantly, Knative enables developers to focus on writing code without the need to worry about the parts of building, deploying, and managing their application.

Knative offers a set of reusable components that simplify workflows like building applications from source code to container images, routing and managing traffic during deployment, auto-scaling your workloads, or binding running services to the growing ecosystem of event sources. Knative recognizes container images as the deployment unit. Therefore, developers can use any language, framework, or idiom they are familiar with.

Knative is designed to plug easily into an existing build and CI/CD toolchains. By focusing on open-source-first technologies that run anywhere, on any cloud, on any infrastructure supported by Kubernetes, enterprises are free to move their workloads wherever they run best. This offers the flexibility and control customers need to adapt the system to their own unique requirements.

Knative provides an open API and runtime environment that enables you to run your serverless workloads anywhere. By using Knative as the underlying platform, you can move your workloads freely across platforms, while significantly reducing the switching costs. In short, Knative enables serverless workloads to run on Kubernetes clusters and makes building and orchestrating containers with Kubernetes faster and easier. In this chapter, we are to discuss how to install Knative Serving using YAML files.

Knative Serving builds on Kubernetes to support deploying and serving of serverless applications and functions. Serving is easy to get started with and scales to support advanced scenarios.

The Knative Serving project provides middleware components that enable:

- Rapid deployment of serverless containers.
- Autoscaling including scaling pods down to zero.
- Support for multiple networking layers such as Ambassador, Contour, Kourier, Gloo, and Istio for integration into existing environments.
- Point-in-time snapshots of deployed code and configurations.

Knative Serving Resources

Knative Serving defines a set of objects as Kubernetes Custom Resource Definitions (CRDs). These objects are used to define and control how your serverless workload behaves on the cluster:

- **Service:** The service.serving.knative.dev resource automatically manages the whole lifecycle of your workload. It controls the creation of other objects to ensure that your app has a route, a configuration, and a new revision for each update of the service. Service can be defined to always route traffic to the latest revision or to a pinned revision.
- **Route:** The route.serving.knative.dev resource maps a network endpoint to one or more revisions. You can manage the traffic in several ways, including fractional traffic and named routes.
- **Configuration:** The configuration.serving.knative.dev resource maintains the desired state for your deployment. It provides a clean separation between code and configuration and follows the Twelve-Factor App methodology. Modifying a configuration creates a new revision.
- **Revision:** The revision.serving.knative.dev resource is a point-in-time snapshot of the code and configuration for each modification made to the workload. Revisions are immutable objects and can be retained for as long as useful. Knative Serving Revisions can be automatically scaled up and down according to incoming traffic. See Configuring the Autoscaler for more information.

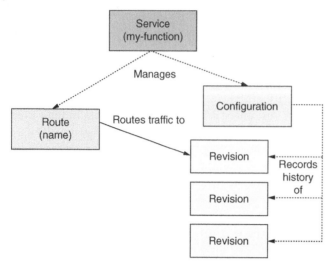

Knative serving architecture.

Knative Serving supports deploying and managing cloud-native applications by providing a set of objects as Kubernetes CRDs that define and control the behavior of serverless workloads.

There are tutorials and guides to enable Knative developers and architects to install Knative on Kubernetes clusters. The following page has the required details to accelerate installing Knative and its key components.

https://knative.dev/docs/install/

1) **Prerequisites**
   1) System Requirements
      For prototyping purposes, Knative will work on most local deployments of Kubernetes. For example, you can use a local, one-node cluster that has 2 CPUs and 4 GB of memory.
      For production purposes, it is recommended that:
      - If you have only one node in your cluster, you will need at least 6 CPUs, 6 GB of memory, and 30 GB of disk storage.
      - If you have multiple nodes in your cluster, for each node, you will need at least 2 CPUs, 4 GB of memory, and 20 GB of disk storage.

      Before installation, you must meet the following prerequisites:
      - You have a cluster that uses Kubernetes v1.18 or newer.
      - You have installed the `kubectl` CLI.
      - Your Kubernetes cluster must have access to the Internet, since Kubernetes needs to be able to fetch images.

2) **Install the Serving Component**
   To install the serving component:
   1) Install the required custom resources:
      # kubectl apply -f https://github.com/knative/serving/releases/download/v0.22.0/serving-crds.yaml

Knative serving component installation.

2) Install the core components of Serving:
   # kubectl apply -f https://github.com/knative/serving/releases/download/v0.22.0/serving-core.yaml

The core components of Serving Installation.

3) **Install a Networking Layer**

   With following commands, install Kourier and enable its Knative integration.

   1) Install the Knative Kourier controller:
      # kubectl apply -f https://github.com/knative/net-kourier/releases/download/v0.22.0/kourier.yaml

Networking layer Installation.

2) To configure Knative Serving to use Kourier by default:

```
kubectl patch configmap/config-network \
  --namespace knative-serving \
  --type merge \
  --patch '{"data":{"ingress.class":"kourier.ingress networking.
knative.dev"}}'
```

The Installation snapshot.

3) Fetch the External IP or CNAME:

kubectl --namespace kourier-system get service courier

Fetching the external IP.

4) **Verify the Installation**

Monitor the Knative components until all of the components show a STATUS of Running or Completed:

kubectl get pods --namespace knative-serving

Verifying the Installation.

5) **Configure DNS**

You can configure DNS to prevent the need to run curl commands with a host header.

6) **Install kn using a Binary**

You can install kn by downloading the executable binary for your system and placing it in the system path.

1) **Install kn using Go**

Check out the `kn` client repository:

git clone https://github.com/knative/client.git

```
[root@bastion8 skylab]# git clone https://github.com/knative/client.git
Cloning into 'client'...
remote: Enumerating objects: 731, done.
remote: Counting objects: 100% (731/731), done.
remote: Compressing objects: 100% (623/623), done.
remote: Total 26562 (delta 173), reused 297 (delta 77), pack-reused 25831
Receiving objects: 100% (26562/26562), 19.29 MiB | 20.90 MiB/s, done.
Resolving deltas: 100% (16346/16346), done.
[root@bastion8 skylab]#
```

Kn Installation.

2) Build an executable binary:

./build.sh –f

```
[root@bastion8 go_projects]# cd /usr/skylab/client/hack/
[root@bastion8 hack]# ./build.sh -f
⊨  Compile
[root@bastion8 hack]#
```

Building an executable binary.

3) Move kn into your system path and verify that kn commands are working properly. For example:

mv kn /usr/local/bin

```
[root@bastion8 client]# cp kn /usr/local/bin
[root@bastion8 client]# kn version
Version:      v20210409-local-33deb82a
Build Date:   2021-04-09 12:26:38
Git Revision: 33deb82a
Supported APIs:
* Serving
  - serving.knative.dev/v1 (knative-serving v0.22.0)
* Eventing
  - sources.knative.dev/v1alpha2 (knative-eventing v0.22.0)
  - eventing.knative.dev/v1 (knative-eventing v0.22.0)
[root@bastion8 client]#
```

Moving Kn into the system path.

7) **Sample Application**

1) **Creating your Deployment with the Knative CLI**

To create a Service directly at the cluster, use:

kn service create helloworld-go --image gcr.io/knative-samples/helloworld-go --env TARGET="Go Sample v1"

Creating your deployment with the knative CLI.

2) **Interacting with Your App**

To see if your app has been deployed successfully, you need the URL created by Knative.

1) To find the URL for your service, use either `kn` or `kubectl`

kn service describe helloworld-go

Further Reading

1 Knative documentation. https://knative.dev/docs/install/
2 Knative developers guide. https://knative.dev/docs/getting-started/
3 Knative Cluster Administrator Guide. https://knative.dev/docs/install/
4 About the Knative Framework. https://cloud.google.com/knative
5 What is Knative? https://www.redhat.com/en/topics/microservices/what-is-knative

10

Delineating Cloud-Native Edge Computing

THE OBJECTIVES

There is a continued accumulation of Internet of things (IoT) edge devices (resource-constrained and intensive) in mission-critical environments such as homes, hotels, hospitals, manufacturing floors, retail stores, warehouses, and research labs. Cloud computing, which is typically a centralized and consolidated computing, has been tackling the heavy load of big data storage and analytics. Now to lessen the increasing workload, edge devices and their clusters/clouds are being explored and experimented to do local computing. Such proximate data processing leads to real-time insights, which, in turn, facilitate building and releasing real-time services and applications.

Resource-constrained IoT devices such as sensors are primarily used for collecting data from the various occupants such as assets, devices, and people. But resource-intensive IoT devices are primely focused on receiving, aggregating, filtering, funneling, and processing of all kinds environment data. Thus, there originated several niche concepts such as edge computing, analytics, clouds, and artificial intelligence (AI). This chapter also pitches the following.

1) Cloud-native Technologies for Edge Computing
2) Kubernetes for Edge Computing
3) Benefits of Bringing the Cloud-Native Principles to the Edge
4) The Deployment Scenarios at the Edge
5) Kubernetes Deployment Options for Edge Computing
6) Cloud-Native at the Edge: The Use Cases
7) Navigating Heterogeneous Environments at the Edge
8) Monitoring Kubernetes-enabled Edge Environments
9) Edge Analytics for Real-time Video Surveillance
10) Describing Edge AI

Introduction

With the advent of the 5G and the Internet of things (IoT) era, the number of connected devices is bound to rapidly grow. This means that the centralized data storage and processing popularized by the traditional cloud computing model can no longer meet the demands of massive amount of multi-structured data getting created by IoT sensors, devices, and systems. That is, the conventional cloud model does not guarantee real-time data capture, storage, analytics, decision-making, and actuation. To cope up with this grandiose vision, experts have recommended that the much-celebrated cloud computing capability has to be systematically realized through edge devices and clouds in order to lessen the load on centralized cloud centers.

Off course, there are several practical and operational difficulties being associated with edge computing. Device mobility and management, resource and task scheduling, service delivery, resiliency, device operations, integration, orchestration, and security are being touted as the prime challenges of establishing and sustaining edge device clouds. In this chapter, we focus on applying the proven and potential cloud-native design principles on edge devices. Edge devices and their clusters/clouds are being presented and prescribed as the new service deployment, execution, and delivery platforms.

Briefing Cloud-Native Computing

As articulated in the first chapter of this book, cloud-native is the modern way to develop highly scalable, extensible, flexible, portable, available, and reliable software applications across industry verticals. Cloud-native applications are designed to run on any cloud infrastructure (private, public, hybrid, and edge clouds). A cloud-native application takes advantage of various cloud competencies to ensure IT agility, adaptability, affordability, and accessibility. A cloud-native application is a distributed system. Cloud-native systems are being designed to embrace rapid change, large scale, and resilience to meet business goals. Cloud-native technologies can help organizations increase productivity, accelerate time to market, deliver superior experiences for their customers, and gain operational efficiency. Cloud-native is all for overcoming the distributed computing challenges and to bring forth secure, performant, robust, and versatile software systems.

Typically, cloud-native applications are developed as a group of loosely coupled microservices, which follow the single functionality principle. The key characteristics of microservices are that they are publicly discoverable, network accessible, self-defined, interoperable, application programming interface (API)-driven, and composable (through orchestration and choreography). Because of their autonomous nature, all kinds of dependency-induced problems get eliminated. Smaller teams can independently focus on microservices design, development, debugging, delivery, and deployment. Microservices architecture (MSA) is hugely popular because it strictly follows the proven design mantra of divide and conquer. For fulfilling the much-needed portability goal, microservices are being containerized and are deposited in container image repositories (local as well as remote). The containerized microservices facilitate easier and faster customization and configuration as per the business requirements. There are version control systems assisting container image repositories.

Containers are aptly and adroitly managed through container orchestration platforms. Especially Kubernetes has occupied the top slot in intelligently managing containerized services and applications. Multi-container applications can be realized through Kubernetes. The end-to-end life cycle management of containers is being accomplished through the Kubernetes platform solution. The management console of Kubernetes has a firm grip on containers and their performance and health condition. Scalability, availability, and reliability requirements are guaranteed through the Kubernetes platform. Additional capabilities are being provided for operationalizing container clusters through a host of Kubernetes-centric tools. In short, with the continued surge in strengthening the Kubernetes platform through a slew of additional techniques and tools, the long-standing goals of application-aware infrastructure modules and infrastructure-aware applications are to be fully met soon.

Cloud-native technologies empower engineering microservices-centric applications and modernize the underlying infrastructure modules appropriately. That is, organizations build and run highly available and scalable applications in dynamic environments. There are a number of enabling advancements: microservices as the agile design technique for producing enterprise-grade applications, containers as the most optimal runtime for microservices, service meshes for enabling resilient microservice-to-microservice communication, the arrival of immutable infrastructure modules, and the accumulation of declarative APIs. All these combine well to produce service-oriented, process-centric, and sophisticated software products, solutions, and services, which are configurable, customizable, and composable. In other words, these breakthrough techniques collectively facilitate the visualization and realization of modern and modular systems that are intrinsically resilient, versatile, and observable. When combined with the robust automation provided by DevOps tools, it is easy and fast to bring in required updates and upgrades in cloud-native applications. Software delivery and deployment also get succulently accelerated. Cloud-native technologies ultimately can help worldwide business houses to pursue and achieve the goals of increasing productivity, reaching market quickly, enhancing customer satisfaction, complying to all kinds of business and technology changes, and gaining operational efficiency.

Cloud-native computing is definitely a futuristic and flexible approach for the field of software engineering and IT world. The cornerstone principles of cloud native [1, 2] are

- **Microservices-Centric:** Applications are made as a collection of microservices, which are modular, malleable, modern, and manageable. Microservices are being developed as12-factor applications. Microservices are containerized to be portable and easily maneuverable. The container images can be easily found and instantiated. Multiple instances can be formed out for a microservice. Multiple versions of a microservice are also widely used to suit business requirements. Microservices are being composed to form process-aware and business-critical applications. Each microservice can be deployed, upgraded, scaled, and restarted independently of other services. Microservices are greatly enriched through the aspect of containerization. Multi-container microservices applications can be easily built and released.
- **Containerized:** Microservices are methodically containerized. There are container orchestration tools providing complete container life cycle management including scheduling, placement, start/stop/re-start, and observability. As we all know, containers accomplish operating system (OS)-level virtualization. A single OS instance is dynamically divided among one or more isolated containers. Each container is blessed with a unique writable file system and resource quota. Containers can be deployed in bare metal (BM) servers as well as virtual machines (VMs). Although microservices are commonly deployed in separate containers, multiple microservices may be deployed in a container toward incremented resource utilization. The advantages include the colocation of microservices logically simplifies the design or when microservices fulfil several processes in a container.
- **Dynamically Managed:** Containerized applications are being managed by Kubernetes, which brings in a variety of automation and acceleration capabilities.
- **DevOps:** Increasingly lean, agile, and accelerated techniques are being leveraged for software design, development, delivery, deployment, and operations. DevOps enables organizations to build, test, and release software more rapidly and iteratively. DevOps enables the automation of deploying and validating a new software feature in an isolated production environment. The idea is to avoid any last minute hiccup. If there is any issue, then it can be taken out and subjected to a fresh check to pinpoint any prickling problem. Then it gets moved into production environment. Precisely speaking, DevOps tools enable continuous application deployment. Newer technologies, algorithms, features, business changes, and other noteworthy requirements get quickly and easily incorporated in software applications in production environments.

Containers and Kubernetes in association with other DevOps tools greatly simplifies, streamlines, and speeds up continuous integration/delivery/deployment/feedback/improvement tasks. Ultimately software engineering gets a strong and sustainable boost in reaching the digital living vision soon.

The other key components and considerations are as follows:

Service Discovery: Microservices are being developed by worldwide developers. Enterprises are also investing their talent, time, and treasure in building high-end microservices. IT organizations are also producing microservices for catering business and IT needs. Microservices are technology-agnostic and hence any programming language can be used for constructing microservices. There are mechanisms being rolled out for stocking microservices. There are software repositories for keeping up microservices. Now discovering microservices automatically in an unambiguous fashion to leverage to dynamically produce bigger and better applications is very vital.

Life Cycle Management: Containers are being pitched and positioned as the most optimal hosting and runtime environment for microservices. Containerized microservices acquire multiple benefits on their operational side. Now with the emergence of Kubernetes as the multifaceted container orchestration platform solution, the leverage of microservices as the unit of application design, development, and deployment gathers momentum. When upgrading an application, the container scheduler determines which individual services have been changed and deploys only the updated/upgraded services into the application. Because of the isolation property, a fully automated service upgrade and rollback of the containers go a long way in fulfilling the changing ideals of software engineering.

Stateful Applications: There are stateless and stateful applications. Stateless microservices and applications are quite easy to envisage, implement, and run. Stateless applications process users' request and subsequently deliver their responses. They need not store any of the session and application data anywhere. Or stateless applications store their session data in a separate stateful service, which physically stores the session details in memory or in disk. This allows for stateless application services to be self-contained, lightweight, independently upgradable, quickly recoverable, and highly scalable. With multiple instances of stateless services, the continuous availability is easily ascertained and attained.

On the other hand, stateful services and applications are quite challenging to develop and sustain because the service state has to be stored in a local file system, in memory or in a faraway cloud file system. Developers of stateful services therefore have to spend more time in addressing the availability, consistency, and portability of state. This requires replication across one or more containers while making sure that consistency of the state is maintained.

Stateful applications typically involve a database such as SQL, NoSQL, or distributed SQL database. Most of the enterprise-grade applications are stateful and use one or other persistent storage. Data analytics through traditional batch and real-time data processing is touted as an important activity for enterprises to march ahead in the uncertain world. Therefore, there are big, fast, and streaming data processing applications. With the faster maturity and stability of AI algorithms, frameworks, libraries, and accelerators, AI-based data processing is gaining prominence. All these clearly say that stateful applications are the future. Therefore, for profitable use of the proven and potential containerization concept, the IT industry is veering toward containerized stateful applications.

Availability and Resiliency: Cloud-native applications inherently guarantee for high availability and resiliency through service discovery and by load-balancing requests across stateless application containers. Containers are lightweight and hence the bootup time is insignificant and the much-celebrated real-time scalability is being achieved through containers. Responding to any slowdown or breakdown is very quick. For resiliency, incorporating a service mesh implementation ensures the application resiliency. Container orchestration platforms also contribute handsomely to fulfil these non-functional requirements (NFRs).

There are cloud-native purists and pundits, who believe that stateful applications are not suitable to be run in containers. As told earlier, stateful applications retain application state data across sessions in a persistent storage. One solution approach is that applications have to be refactored to move the responsibility of remembering the state to the client. For example, an e-commerce shopping cart service can use session cookies to store a shopper's purchase details.

However, the 12-factor framework states that any data that needs to persist has to be stored in a stateful backing service (typically a database). So, a shopping cart application that ought to verify inventory before proceeding, can pull that data from a database somewhere. Thus, state data persistence is essential for stateful applications. Containers started its long innings with stateless microservices. But, considering the trend and transition, it is inevitable for containers to handle stateful microservices. Therefore, databases and other stateful services are being increasingly hosted and run inside containers. The recent versions of Kubernetes have the appropriate mechanism incorporated to handle stateful microservices. The ultimate benefit is that all the distinct benefits of containers and stateless microservices are extended to stateful microservices. Stateful applications can run anywhere without any hitch or hurdle and get managed through Kubernetes. The immutability of containerized applications comes in handy in patching up and updating applications. Kubernetes supports the declarative model. Further on, Kubernetes is stuffed with built-in self-healing and API-driven interfaces. The common set of APIs across cloud environments (on-premise and off-premise) facilitate application portability.

Developers still need to spend time on efficient database designs and operations teams, on the other side, need simpler and swifter ways to update and rollback data processing applications. In order to simplify and smoothen these complicated tasks, there came a number of automated tools getting added into the Kubernetes tool ecosystem. Precisely speaking, building, deploying, and managing stateful applications are being given thrust these days. Stateful applications are adequately empowered with the power of containerization and Kubernetes.

For stateful applications, Kubernetes supported persistent volumes through the PersistentVolume (PV) and PersistentVolumeClaim (PVC) APIs. A PV is a storage volume that has a life cycle independent of any individual Pod that uses the PV. These volumes are created by an administrator of the system and can be backed by a variety of storage systems, including Amazon EBS or NFS or Ceph. A PVC is the request for storage from the user.

In Kubernetes, basic storage building blocks are known as volumes. A volume is attached to a pod. A volume is like local storage, and there is no persistence to it. A volume gets released when a pod is destroyed. As such, a regular volume lacks persistence, portability, and scalability. Persistent storage, however, stores the data generated by an application. This leads to stateful applications. A persistent volume is managed by clusters and it is not dependent on the life cycle of the pod. The volume plugins accentuated by Kubernetes in the beginning are not scalable enough for a fast-growing storage ecosystem. Therefore, in the recent past, Kubernetes is blessed with a Container Storage Interface (CSI). Such an interface allows new storage solutions from different vendors.

The CSI has opened up a common interface for storage solution and service providers to enter into Kubernetes. CSI gives third-party storage providers the ability to write plugins that interoperate with Kubernetes. In the case of stateless applications, Kubernetes will simply stop the application and restart it somewhere else. As there is no dependency, this does not arise any problem. Containerized applications emerge from immutable image files and declarative YAML files. These are typically stored in an artifact repository like Docker Hub, Artifactory (this sets up a secure private Docker registry in minutes to manage all your Docker images while exercising fine-grained access control), or Harbor (Harbor is an open-source registry that secures artifacts with policies and role-based access control, ensures images are scanned and free from vulnerabilities, and signs images as trusted).

However, when we consider stateful applications like databases or AI/ML applications, this becomes a complicated affair. Application data has to be stored and restored if something goes wrong. Thus, a number of advancements are being worked out in order to make stateful applications pervasive.

There are other improvements in the form of producing resilient microservices using service mesh solutions. API gateway functionalities and service mesh capabilities are being merged together to come out with a unified mechanism to enable service-to-service and user-to-service communications. DevOps tools are used to create automated continuous integration/delivery (CI/CD) pipeline to accelerate frequent service deployment. Service registry mechanism is in place in order to augment service discovery. Thus, a number of automation capabilities are being realized through MSA, containerization-enablement, and management platform solutions.

The cloud-native model not only eliminates the limitations and lacunae of the hardware virtualization but also has laid down a stimulating foundation for a series of innovations and disruptions for businesses and IT organizations. Through a host of deeper automation, IT infrastructure and resource utilization go up significantly. That is, the long-standing goal of more with less is being achieved through the cloud-native facility. Kubernetes plays an important role in shaping up the resiliency, versatility, and availability of business workloads and IT services. Service meshes contribute intrinsically to the resiliency of microservices. Through composition of resilient microservices, it is showcased to have reliable applications. Infrastructure elasticity is eventually leading to application scalability. Containerized applications are portable and hence employing multi-cloud environments for hosting and running enterprise-scale applications and data stores is made possible with the astounding developments in the cloud-native space.

With the general availability of lightweight versions of the Kubernetes platform solution, edge device clouds can be dynamically, quickly, and temporarily formed to service one or more emergency requirements in everyday environments such as homes, hotels, and hospitals. Further on, edge devices are typically heterogeneous and hence for bringing forth a kind of homogeneity, devices are being presented as services to the outside world through the incorporation of the proven and potential MSA. As we all know, the differing device functionalities are being exposed through APIs, which front-end device service implementations. Device services are meticulously containerized, and Kubernetes is leveraged to appropriately manage containerized device services. Multi-device computing is to result in process-aware and people-centric applications. Precisely speaking, cloud-native computing meets edge computing to visualize and realize a dazzling array of edge-native applications in plenty.

Thus, the concept of device clouds is flourishing with the availability of competent technologies and tools. The future belongs to and beckons edge, private, and public clouds. The cloud-native phenomenon is setting everything right and bright for the future of IT in succulently and sagaciously enabling intelligent enterprises. The business IT is all set to traverse and tend toward people IT with the smart application of cloud-native competencies.

Technical and Business Cases for Cloud-Native Computing [3, 4]

The cloud-native paradigm is seen as a game-changer not only for software engineering but also for IT operations. Cloud-native computing uses an open-source software stack to deploy applications as microservices, packaging each part into its own container, and dynamically orchestrating those containers to optimize resource utilization and to automate their operations.

- **Develop Cloud-Native Applications:** Having understood the importance of software engineering for the increasingly digitized and connected world, business houses and IT companies across the globe are keen to make use of the huge successes attained by the cloud-native idea. Developing sophisticated software solutions to complicated business sentiments is being accelerated through the cloud-native paradigm. This is a greenfield approach. It is all about designing, developing, and deploying cloud-native applications from the ground up. This is to capture new business opportunities to garner greater revenue through fresh avenues. Changes in business and customer sentiments open up opportunities for enterprises to visualize and realize new-generation products, solutions, and services. They can quickly evaluate their outcome in the new landscape and adapt accordingly. As articulated earlier, the cloud-native paradigm shrewdly facilitates the digital transformation, which every corporate yearns to achieve.
- **Modernize Applications:** We have a lot of monolithic applications, which turn out to be quite complicated to manage and maintain. Thus, application modernization has garnered a lot of attention. It is mandatory to increase the speed of change by modernizing applications to adapt to new realities. Legacy applications, which are massive and monolithic, are not a perfect fit for the digital era. So, it is mandatory to modernize them in order to be right and relevant for the digital world. However, a rip-and-replace approach is not always suitable. MSA is one sure way for application modernization and migration to cloud environments. The cloud-native paradigm is pronounced as the silver bullet to have modern and modular applications in plenty.
- Applications can be containerized and taken to a cloud environment to reap all the originally expressed benefits of cloud computing. Containerized applications are portable and hence moving from one environment to others is not a difficult affair. Applications can be refactored and redesigned as a collection of microservices to become cloud native. Container platforms in association with DevOps techniques and tools simplify the migration of applications.
- **Accelerate Application Delivery:** We have talked about software design and development. Now with the unprecedented adoption of DevOps concepts and tools, software delivery, deployment, management, and refinement are getting a strong boost. Containers with a life cycle management platform solution (Kubernetes) play an important role in shaping up the end-to-end DevOps process. The manual intervention and involvement in performing IT operations is bound to go down with tools-assisted automation of various aspects and activities associated with the setup and sustenance of IT environments with correct resources to host and run cloud-native applications.

- **Drive Business Innovation:** Without an iota of doubt, digitization, and digitalization, technologies have created an aura for producing many breakthrough innovations and disruptions, which collectively tend to bring up a slew of ground-breaking digital life applications. The cloud-native phenomenon cognitively energizes envisaging next-generation digital applications for making sense out of soaring digital data. Cloud-native digital infrastructural modules substantially empower building and releasing flexible and futuristic cloud-native digital applications for industrial establishments, service organizations, national governments, academic institutions, smart cities, etc. The remarkable advancements in the cloud-native space have laid down a scintillating foundation for catapulting cloud-native products and solutions across industry verticals. The new normal method (constructing cloud-native applications through configuration, customization, and composition) can blossom to unearth freshly brewed business-critical and people-centric applications.

Because of the convergence of multiple cutting technologies and state-of-the-art tools in sync up with sophisticated IT infrastructures, there is a huge uptake for the cloud-native phenomenon to flare up in the days to unfurl. This is the move from tightly coupled systems with many dependent components to loosely or lightly coupled systems made of tiny components that could run quasi-independently. In short, the cloud-native phenomenon is projected to be the key differentiator and game-changer for the future of computer science and IT domains.

Where Cloud Native is Heading Now? Rightfully the next destination for the phenomenal cloud-native concept is none other than envisaging intelligent and real-time edge-native applications. As we all know, edge devices emerge as the new and potential destination for next-generation computing. That is, edge computing promises real-time computing, which is explicitly needed for creating and sustaining real-time environments and enterprises. How this is made possible?

At the outset, it is not an exaggeration to state that the IoT paradigm has resulted in zillions of digitized entities and connected devices. The fast proliferation of digitization and edge technologies such as minuscule sensors, disappearing actuators, disposable barcodes and stickers, multifaceted microcontrollers, RFID tags, beacons and LED lights, and other nanoelectronics materials has laid down a scintillating foundation toward the much-expected digital world. That is, digital world is filled up with digital systems, which, when interacting purposefully, generate a massive amount of multi-structured data. On the other side, there are digital applications, platforms, and infrastructures to collect, cleanse, and crunch digital data to produce digital intelligence, which, when employed properly, can lead to the realization of intelligent devices, applications, systems, networks, and environments.

The process of digitization has picked up fast, and it penetrates everywhere, participates in everything, and has become a pervasive and persuasive instrument. All kinds of physical, mechanical, and electrical systems in our everyday locations (homes, hotels, hospitals, etc.) are methodically embedded with one or more digitization technologies to initiate the transition process. Such an empowerment goes a long way in bringing hitherto unheard or unknown innovations and disruptions for businesses and people at large. In other words, this is resulting in scores of powerful digital systems. All sorts of dumb systems become animated and ordinary items are all set to become extraordinary. In short, everything in and around us is becoming digitized. Such digitized systems join in the mainstream computing. Precisely speaking, with the unprecedented adoption of digital technologies, every concrete or tangible thing in our personal, social, and professional places contributes to real-world and real-time computing.

Further on, electronics devices are increasingly instrumented to be interconnected. Such local as well as remote connectivity enable electronics to readily gain extraordinary features. So, there are two main categories: digitized entities and connected devices. Digitized elements are also getting connected with nearby digital elements and with remotely held software applications and databases in an indirect manner through an intermediary. The Internet is the worldwide, affordable, open, extensible, and public communication infrastructure to enable digitized items to get connected. The cyber physical systems (CPS) domain illustrates this factor and facet. The IoT literally means connected things. To paraphrase everything in a nutshell, we have IoT sensors and devices in plenty capable of bringing in the dreamt digital era.

IoT edge sensors and devices are being situated where the real action or event happens. Devices emit out a lot of their operational, performance, health condition, and log data in real time. Edge devices are instrumented and interconnected to be self, surroundings, and situation-aware. Edge devices gather their environment data, aggregate, and transmit it to nearby edge device server(s). Analytics platforms deployed on edge servers then plunge into real action to extract hidden patterns, trends, and tips, which enable to take real-time decision and action.

Edge computing brings in business, technical, and user advantages. Edge device and environment data can be gathered and processed locally thereby data security and privacy are ensured fully. By not sending all the edge data to faraway cloud for storage and processing, a lot of prohibitive network bandwidth gets preserved. Above all, the problematic network latency gets avoided. These collectively facilitate the visualization and realization of real-world and real-time software applications. This has set in motion the process of moving away from the traditional cloud computing. The future beckons for the hybrid model of centralized cloud computing and distributed edge computing. Consider a manufacturer, who wants to process data from thousands of connected devices attached to various factory parts, and push that data to iPads used by employees on the factory floor. Right now, much of the data from connected devices is recorded manually. With edge computing in place, device data gets locally stored and subjected to a variety of investigations to create actionable insights in time.

The Emergence of Edge Computing

Computers are already networked. Now all kinds of edge devices such as smartphones, fridges, cars, watches, toasters, vehicles, and TVs are also getting integrated with the Internet. This transition brings in a series of delectable advancements for businesses and consumers. A variety of cloud-based software applications and services are being made available to connected edge devices. Such empowered devices are to disrupt, innovate, adapt, and deliver time-critical, people-centric, event-driven, insights-filled, and context-aware services to their owners and users. Edge computing is surely the new phenomenon on the planet Earth to create and sustain the bigger and beneficial Internet. The future Internet is to provide the strength and sagacity to envision and execute industry 4.0 and 5.0 use cases.

Edge computing has the intrinsic and indomitable power to guarantee real-time data capture from multiple edge sources, and store and process them immediately to extract actionable insights in time. Edge computing ensures a growing array of low-latency applications and services. While the centralized cloud computing model is continuously leveraged, there will be steady adoption of the edge computing idea in order to deliver. It is indicated that the hybrid model of centralized cloud and distributed edge paradigms will be supported and sustained for long.

Leading market watchers and analysts have forecast that there will be billions of edge devices, and hence unearthing competent and cool technologies and tools for enabling edge edges to deeply and decisively participate and provide compute, communication, sensing, perception, vision, data analytics, knowledge discovery and dissemination, and decision-making services are being given thrust these days. With the arrival of 5G communication, millions of IoT edge devices can be accommodated. Increasingly edge devices are being instrumented with more resources (higher memory, storage, processing, etc.). With the unprecedented stability of connectivity technologies, edge devices are interconnected with one another in the vicinity and with software applications and databases hosted and managed in centralized clouds. The much-dissertated 5G communication paradigm guarantees reliable communication. The multiplicity and heterogeneity of the future Internet comprising exponentially growing IoT edge devices is going to result in enhanced complexity. Not only the Internet complexity, but also the development, operational, and management complexities of edge computing are going to be on the higher side. Thus, the industry is seeking cutting-edge technologies and tools to moderate the rising complexity.

The number of edge environments is growing steadily across the world. All the mission-critical places such as hospital ICUs, manufacturing floors, retail stores, airports, railway stations, eating joints, entertainment plazas, smart cities (homes, hotels, etc.), auditoriums, stadiums, high-rise apartments, tunnels, expressways, nuclear establishments, product assembly lines, oil exploration facilities, educational campuses, telecommunication tower locations, and self-driving vehicles are being empowered with the edge capability. That is, edge computing is being provided in rough and remote environments with unmotorable roads. That is, edge cloud centers are being located in interior and harsh locations with unpredictable network connections with heightened security risks. There are edge appliances that can be quickly set up and remotely operated. However, their physical security is being questioned. Edge computing is to provide a dazzling array of real-time cognitive services to the humanity. Edge devices are to supply a bunch of unique edge services. Edge devices are capable of forming ad hoc, temporary, dynamic, and purpose-specific networks quickly to accomplish specific localized and low-latency applications.

Proximate data processing is being expected out of edge devices and their clusters. There are sensor fusion algorithms to fulfil complex operations through edge devices. An offshoot of edge computing is real-time edge data analytics through the quick formation of edge device clouds. Further on, with the splurge and surge of sophisticated processor architectures for resource-intensive edge devices, installing and running AI platforms, frameworks, libraries. and accelerators gain speed in the recent past. AI-inspired data processing at the edge becomes the new normal. AI models for computer vision and natural language processing are being deployed in edge devices to make real-time inferencing. Heavy AI models are pruned and quantized to make them easy to run on edge devices. Thus, for the edge world, AI model optimization techniques and tools are receiving widespread interest and inspiration among AI enthusiasts, experts, and exponents. Thus, there are many things happening concurrently in the edge space. The world can expect grandiose improvisations and transformations through edge computing in the days to unfurl.

Edge Device Communication Technologies: With the faster adoption of digitization and edge technologies, all kinds of ground-level assets are methodically transitioned into digitized entities. Now there are a few promising and potential connectivity technologies for beneficially networking digitized elements/edge devices.

Low Power Wide Area Networks (LPWANs) is a family of communication technologies empowering digital devices to interact with one another. These provide long-range communication for edge devices consuming negligible energy. These come in handy in producing connected devices for the connected era. LPWANs can literally connect all types of sensors. Such a connectivity goes a long way in laying a strong and sustainable foundation for next-generation software applications from asset tracking, environmental monitoring, and facility management to occupancy detection and consumables monitoring. LPWANs can only send small blocks of data at a low rate, and therefore are better suited for use cases that do not require high bandwidth. There exist technologies operating in both the licensed (NB-IoT and LTE-M) and unlicensed (e.g. MYTHINGS, LoRa, Sigfox, etc.) spectrum with varying degrees of performance in key network factors.

Cellular Communications: Currently it is 4G communication standards. The world is inching toward 5G communication. The research works of the 6G communication standard already initiated. The telecommunication forums and standard bodies are eyeing for the introduction of 6G services in the year 2030. The cellular networks offer reliable broadband communication supporting voice communication, data transmission, and video streaming applications. However, cellular networks entail high operational costs. The power requirement is also on the higher side.

Cellular communications fit well for specific use cases such as connected cars **or** fleet management in transportation and logistics. For example, in-car infotainment, traffic routing, advanced driver assistance systems (ADAS) alongside fleet telematics, and tracking services need the ubiquitous and high-bandwidth cellular connectivity. 5G communication networks are to facilitate reliable connectivity and accommodate a large number of edge devices supporting ultra-low latency. 5G is enabling next-generation personal and professional applications such as autonomous vehicles, augmented reality, real-time video surveillance for inland security, connected health, and time-sensitive industrial automation.

Mesh Protocols: Mesh protocols are being used for medium-range connected applications with an even distribution of nodes in close proximity. In mesh networks, all the devices connect directly, dynamically, and in a non-hierarchic way to cooperate according to a predefined protocol to route data across the network. The network will not fail if one or more devices fail.

Zigbee is a popular, short-range, and low-power wireless standard (IEEE 802.15.4). This is commonly deployed in mesh topology to extend coverage by relaying sensor data over multiple sensor nodes. Zigbee provides higher data rates but with lower power-efficiency. Zigbee mesh topology allows the relaying of data between the Zigbee devices to carry data over long distances. There are three types of nodes in a Zigbee mesh network. They are coordinators, routers, and end devices. Each Zigbee network requires one coordinator, which is a device responsible for forming the network and routing traffic. After a network is formed, the coordinator adopts the capabilities of a Zigbee router, which acts as an intermediate node relaying data from other devices. A router never goes into a sleep mode. Routers can also be a Zigbee end device. End devices can only communicate with parent nodes, i.e. the coordinator or routers. Zigbee end devices are very power-efficient devices and can enter sleep mode to save energy. Each parent node can serve up to 20 Zigbee end devices. Typically, Zigbee is a perfect complement to Wi-Fi for various home automation use cases like smart lighting, HVAC controls, and security and energy management.

Personal Area Networks (PANs): Bluetooth is a well-known short-range communication technology. Body area networks (BANs) and car area networks (CANs) are typical personal area networks (PANs). Optimized for power consumption, Bluetooth Low Energy (BLE) is introduced to address small-scale consumer IoT applications. BLE-enabled devices are mostly used in conjunction with electronic devices. Smartphones serve as a hub for transferring data from BLE devices to faraway clouds. Nowadays, BLE is widely integrated into fitness and medical wearables (e.g. smart watches, glucose meters, and pulse oximeters) and smart home devices such as door locks. BLE devices particularly shine in retail contexts. Providing versatile indoor localization features, BLE beacon networks have been used to unlock new service innovations like in-store navigation, personalized promotions, and content delivery.

Wi-Fi 6: In the IoT space, Wi-Fi's major limitations are in coverage, scalability, and power consumption. Wi-Fi is often not a feasible solution for large networks of battery-operated IoT sensors, which are prevalent in industrial and building environments. Instead, it is more pertaining to connecting devices that can be conveniently connected to a power outlet like smart home gadgets and appliances, digital signages, or security cameras. Wi-Fi 6 brings in greatly enhanced network bandwidth (i.e. <9.6 Gbps) to improve data throughput per user in congested environments. Wi-Fi 6 is poised to level up public Wi-Fi infrastructure and transform customer experience with new digital mobile services in retail and mass entertainment sectors. Also, in-car networks for infotainment and on-board diagnostics are expected to be the most game-changing use case for Wi-Fi 6.

Radio Frequency Identification (RFID): This uses radio waves to transmit small amounts of data from a radio frequency identification (RFID) tag to a reader within a very short distance. This technology has facilitated a major revolution in retail and logistics. By attaching an RFID tag to all sorts of products, parcels, and packages, businesses can track their inventory and assets in real time. This allows for better stock and production planning as well as optimized supply chain management.

With the faster proliferation of features-rich IoT devices, the edge computing phenomenon is gaining the overwhelming support across industry verticals. With more resources being stuffed in edge devices, the much-expected edge computing gains the momentum. Edge devices are getting digitized with the systematic usage of digitization and edge technologies. Then, the connectivity technologies enable edge devices to be the Internet enabled. Such connected edge devices (IoT devices) are being explored and experimented for performing real-time small-scale computation and storage. Further on, edge devices are being clubbed together to form edge device clouds, which can handle real-time edge data analytics. As indicated in the following text, AI algorithms are being made to run on edge devices to build and use intelligent edge applications and environments.

Cloud-Native Technologies for Edge Computing

Having deliberated the meteoric rise of edge computing, we now switch over to discuss the widely expressed and exposed challenges and concerns of having powerful yet pragmatic edge environments. Especially on the operational side, there are some serious limitations in setting up and sustaining edge compute environments. The rise of containers and container orchestration platforms along with a host of automated tools are seen as a blessing in disguise for the betterment and fast pickup of edge computing. Microservices empower any edge device to expose its unique and designated functionalities through microservice APIs. Such a wrapper helps to hide the internal differences of any electronic device. Service APIs bring in a kind of uniformity, universality, and stability. Any device can find, bind, and use with other devices in the vicinity and with remote devices in a formalized manner. Microservices natively support function calls thereby nearby as well as faraway devices can connect, communicate, collaborate, and correlate. Thus, device services will become the new normal in the ensuing digital era. Device integration and orchestration become a smooth affair. Device clusters and clouds can be a grand reality with the convergence of a bunch of proven technologies. Containerized microservices are being increasingly run inside single board computers (SBCs) such as Raspberry PI modules.

Precisely speaking, due to a few issues including the resource-constrained nature of edge devices, there is a craze toward competent technologies to surmount them. Device networking has to be natively facilitated in order to overcome the identified constraints of edge devices. To participate and provide compute services, devices have to coordinate and get things done. Heterogeneous devices get networked to form a kind of device cluster to perform bigger tasks. Operationalizing device clusters is beset with a number of practical difficulties. Thus, device management, orchestration, governance, security, task scheduling, resource allocation, etc. are being touted as the major challenges. In short, for realizing real-time, intelligent, and edge-native solutions, it is a widely accepted and adopted thing that cloud-native technologies are the best bet. By converging cloud-native and edge computing paradigms, one can help to overcome the other's limitations. Edge computing significantly extends and expands the scope of cloud-native computing.

As enunciated earlier, the ideals of cloud-native computing are being replicated across to bring in a host of delectable automations. By shrewdly using the cloud-native phenomenon, industry experts predict that the fast-emerging and evolving edge computing field will pass through a number of disruptions and innovations in the years ahead. As the world is earnestly looking for edge AI capabilities, the role and responsibility of cloud-native edge computing is bound to go up remarkably.

In terms of security, the cloud-native computing brings in the much-needed security and safety to business workloads and their operating environments such as containers. Throttling and network policies are incorporated to ensure the impenetrable and unbreakable security. Containers are being installed in edge devices in order to ensure device autonomy, which facilitates self-recovery. The cloud-native concept is becoming more applicable for IT environments with heterogeneous resources. The cloud-native technology supports a variety of processor architectures and communication protocols with low resource consumption.

For the emerging digital world, there is a need for powerful digital infrastructures and platforms. Real-time and intelligent digital applications are the need of the hour. Edge environments join the mainstream computing to prop up low-latency applications. With a large number of connected devices, edge infrastructures primely include edge device clusters. Additional devices can join with the cluster on demand to comfortably tackle spikes in traffic. Thus, edge computing opens up many possibilities for organizations looking to scale their infrastructure to handhold latency-sensitive applications. Edge compute infrastructures and platforms are being increasingly adopted by worldwide enterprises. As cloud-native infrastructures were created to improve flexibility, scalability, and reliability, companies are looking to replicate these benefits to edge devices. The cloud-native computing model can help organizations to fully leverage the edge computing capabilities by providing the same operational advantages and consistency at the edge. Cloud native offers interoperability, portability, and compatibility through the liberal usage of open standards. The cloud-native concepts serve as a launchpad for a series of innovation. Microservices, containers, container orchestration platforms, and DevOps combine well to ensure the highest flexibility for application development, delivery, deployment, and management.

Kubernetes for Edge Computing: As widely known, Kubernetes is one of the key technologies for the unprecedented success of cloud-native computing. Kubernetes started its innings as container orchestration platform solution. Now with a series of advancements, Kubernetes is being poised to be termed as the cloud orchestration platform solution with a declarative API and built-in reconciliation loops. These two features come in handy for surmounting the identified ills of edge computing. First, Kubernetes provides a standardized API to do the life cycle management of hardware and software across disparate and geographically distributed cloud centers. Here is the macro-level Kubernetes architecture taken from the site (https://sensu.io/).

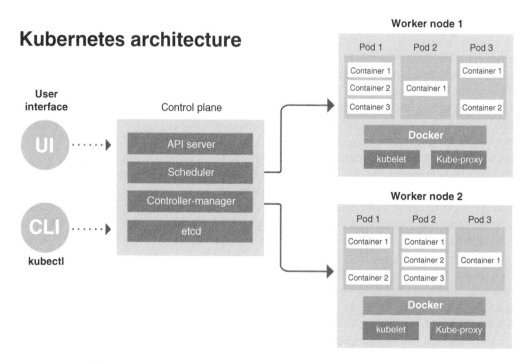

The macro-level Kubernetes architecture.
Source: Sensu.io.

The currently running cloud centers can be modernized with the leverage of Kubernetes thereby businesses can be useful to their royal and loyal customers in providing modern and premium software services and applications. Second, the reconciliation loops bring in the much-needed automation in realizing zero-touch environments with self-healing. Edge infrastructures are bound to be elastic and edge-native applications will thrive. Several non-functional attributes will be incorporated into edge applications with the power of Kubernetes. Methodically leveraging Kubernetes to provide standardization and automation of infrastructure and applications at the edge will allow companies to blossom through a bevy of next-generation software solutions.

5G, Edge Computing, and Kubernetes: Indisputably 5G communication is an indispensable tool for the anticipated and proclaimed success of edge computing. 5G promises faster speed (both downlink and uplink), reduced latency, higher device capacity (one million IoT edge devices per square kilometer), and efficient network slicing. Besides, 5G is more reliable compared to the earlier cellular communication standards. All these improvements and innovations are capable of establishing and sustaining hitherto unheard business, social, and consumer applications. Increasingly edge devices are stuffed with streaming data analytics platforms and AI algorithms. These help in realizing real-time analytics from exponentially growing IoT edge device and environment data. Now the next task is to systematically club together disparate devices together to form a kind of ad hoc, dynamic, and task-specific device clouds to accommodate and accomplish bigger assignments as individual devices may find it a bit difficult to perform complex tasks. The brewing trend is readily forming edge device clouds and running them successfully by the versatility and vitality of Kubernetes, empowering edge environments through the private and industry 5G paradigm, and unearthing real-world and real-time device services to offer premium offerings.

With edge clouds, edge analytics and edge AI are going to be a new normal thereby context-sensitive, real-time, people-centric, adaptive, insights-driven applications and services can be quickly designed, developed, and delivered. Self-driving cars, smart city services, factory automation, augmented and virtual reality (AR/VR) applications, video analytics, real-time games, etc. are being realized. Thus, 5G communication service providers (CSPs) ought to embrace the cloud-native capability fully to be distinctly beneficial. Such a technology integration goes a long way for CSPs to ensure best-in business growth. Customer experience will go up significantly. The operational efficiency gained through such technology collaborations remarkably props up CSPs.

Cloud-Native Network Functions (CNFs): We have been fiddling with physical network functions (PNFs) and then moved to virtual network functions (VNFs). The network virtualization idea has brought in a series of noteworthy savings for CSPs. Now, with the unprecedented adoption of the cloud-native concept across industry verticals, communication providers too jumped into the cloud-native bandwagon in order to avail all its originally expressed benefits. Thus, there is a rush to embrace cloud-native network functions (CNFs). Experts have articulated that there are simple ways and means to get the CNF capability.

1) **Host Containers in Virtual Machines (VMs):** By putting containers in VMs, CSPs can easily take advantage of the containerization features while enjoying the benefits of existing VM and hypervisor investments. The live migration, the load balancing, and scalability features of VMs come in handy here. Containers running inside VMs can be managed through Kubernetes. In the latest version of Kubernetes, it is indicated that it is possible to have a single monitoring and management system (Kubernetes) to manage both containers and VMs together.

   With containerization, edge devices are getting easily operationalized to serve bigger and better services. Telecom service providers are keenly strategizing to have edge cloud environments in large numbers in services jurisdiction in order to cater to their consumers' needs in real time. Small-scale edge servers (commodity) and appliances are being put up in telecom tower building/base stations to have edge clouds. Also, resource-intensive edge devices such as smartphones, drones, medical instruments, consumer electronics, information appliances, Wi-Fi gateways, and cameras are being clubbed together to form edge device clouds. Containerized device services are being installed and run inside edge devices to bring in a kind of stability and semblance to heavily heterogeneous devices. Making and managing device clouds using such disparate and dynamic set of edge devices tend to be a time-consuming and troublesome affair. As inscribed earlier, the shrunken versions of Kubernetes are being pronounced and presented as an enabling technological solution.

2) **Containers in Bare Metal Servers:** The widely reported benefits of BM servers include high performance because there is no system resource wastage for hardware emulation. It is easy for the admin because there are fewer hosts, network connections and storage disks to be meticulously managed. VMs offer the following advantages. Applications can be moved between hosts easily because VM images can be transferred from one server to another. Also, there is a clear-cut isolation between applications running on different VMs. Such isolated VM-hosted

applications enjoy security benefits. The management complexity correspondingly comes down. A consistent software environment across infrastructure can be realized when all applications are hosted and run on the same type of VM (homogeneous VMs). That is, the virtualization abstraction brings in a kind of homogeneity on the face of heterogeneous infrastructures.

But there are well-known drawbacks of VMs. Precious server resources are getting wasted. Every VM is stuffed with an instance of OS software. A hypervisor software is introduced in order to create and manage VMs inside a BM/physical server. Further on, every VM is allocated a separate storage space in the host physical server. But their full usage is not fully guaranteed. Other VMs in that same server also cannot access and use this storage allocated. Thus, various server resources are typically underutilized due to the virtualization concept.

Modern virtualization platforms can help a bit here in resolving the aforementioned- issues. That is, these platforms helps administrators to create a dynamic disk image as per the varying VM usage. Pass-through features ingrained in the latest platforms also provide VMs with direct access to physical hardware on a host. However, all these improvisations are not universal. Some work well in some systems but not on all.

Containers on BM servers get many of the advantages that are being offered by VMs. The advantage is that these benefits are availed without the drawbacks of virtualization. Containerized applications leverage the same OS kernel of the underlying server. There is no insistence for allocating server resources separately to each container. That is, a host can share its resources to multiple containers accordingly. There is a negligible performance degradation with running containers on physical servers. Containers do not provide the same level of isolation as VMs give. But there are viable mechanisms such as privileges and resource accessibility thresholds to enable admins to prevent applications from usurping and using other applications running in containers.

The Downsides of Containers on Bare Metal Servers: Physical server upgrades are difficult. To replace a BM server, you must recreate the container environment from scratch on the new server. If the container environment were part of a VM image, you could simply move the image to the new host. Container platforms do not support all hardware and software configurations. Containers are OS-dependent. Linux containers run on Linux hosts; Windows containers run on Windows hosts. A BM Windows server requires a Linux VM environment to host Docker containers for an application compiled for Linux.

BM servers do not offer built-in rollback features. Most virtualization platforms enable admins to take VM snapshots and rollback to that captured configuration status at a later time. Containers are ephemeral by nature. Container orchestrators such as Kubernetes can run on BM servers. Most container orchestrators are compatible with both BM- and VM-based environments. Some do not support BM deployments. On the other side, all the major orchestrators support VMs.

However, hosting a container orchestrator on BM can pose some risks. If you provision each BM server as a single node, if a node goes down, you will face more disruption to the cluster. Any fault will take away all the resources of the server. In contrast, a BM server can be logically segmented into multiple nodes. Each node runs a VM. In this case, if one VM goes down, it does not cascade into other VMs to knock them down. In other words, deploying an orchestrator on BM is akin to putting all of your eggs in one basket.

BM orchestrator nodes are also subject to the same portability and OS-dependency limitations as containers in BM servers. Moving an orchestrator to a new BM server is not an easy task. BM servers run only if the host OS supports the orchestrator. All Linux distributions support Kubernetes but running Kubernetes on Windows servers throws some challenges.

3) **Containers First with VM Support When Needed:** This architecture works by containerizing OpenStack services and running them in a container on top of a BM Kubernetes cluster. VMs and containers are managed equally and in the same way through Kubernetes. OpenStack can be run but only when needed to support legacy VMs. This solution is more lightweight with a thinner control plane, offers better performance, and enables CSPs to deploy OpenStack containers only when they have VMs that require OpenStack.

With the rapid adoption and adaptation of the Kubernetes platform solution, the concept of cloud-native computing is to flourish across. Software engineering gets hugely simplified through the smart leverage of the cloud-native design principles. Next-generation applications have to be intrinsically agile, interoperable, portable, highly available, and horizontally scalable. The cloud-native concepts comprehensively contribute for developing and providing such powerful applications. One of its core advantages is to provide a consistent experience across geographically distributed and disparate cloud environments (private, public, edge, and hybrid). There is special interest among product and tool vendors in unearthing a litany of cloud-native tools.

Benefits of Bringing the Cloud-Native Principles to the Edge

Without an iota of doubt, Kubernetes plays a vital role in digitally transforming enterprising businesses, government organizations, critical infrastructures, mission-critical establishments, and institutions. Kubernetes improves resource utilization and brings agility in software development cycle. Predominantly, Kubernetes can manage and orchestrate containerized applications along with legacy VMs in a distributed cloud environment. And not only containerized microservices, Kubernetes also contributes immensely in running advanced workloads such as AI models. There are majorly machine and deep learning (ML/DL) applications leveraging AI-specific processors.

In the recent past, Kubernetes has acquired the special status of efficiently running edge cloud environments. Edge device services ought to be combined to create business-critical, process-aware, edge-native, service-oriented, event-driven, real-time, and people-centric applications, which have to be centrally monitored, managed, and maintained. Here are a few of the key developments around how Kubernetes has evolved to become the important player in managing workloads at the edge.

- The project Akri (https://cloudblogs.microsoft.com/opensource/2020/10/20/announcing-akri-open-source-project-building-connected-edge-kubernetes/) is initiated and released by Microsoft to power the edge with advanced capabilities to connect to smaller "leaf devices," like microcontrollers, cameras, and sensors, making them all a part of the Kubernetes cluster.
- Microsoft has released another open-source project called Krustlet (https://krustlet.dev/) that runs WebAssembly (WASM) (https://webassembly.org/) modules to utilize the Kubernetes along with containers. Developers can compile code from their familiar languages (C, C++, C#, Rust, Go, etc.) using WASM. The same codebase can be executed on a wide range of devices.
- Baetyl (https://www.lfedge.org/projects/baetyl/) offers a general-purpose platform for edge computing that manipulates different types of hardware facilities and device capabilities into a standardized container runtime environment and API. This is enabling an efficient management of application, service, and data flow through a remote console both on cloud and on-premise.

- Linux Foundation Edge's Project EVE (https://www.lfedge.org/projects/eve/) enables life cycle management and remote orchestration of any application and hardware at the edge.
- The Open Infrastructure's StarlingX (https://www.starlingx.io/) project for edge and IoT use case deployments has evolved to run the containers to host infrastructure services at the edge. StarlingX basically combines OpenStack and Kubernetes to run the virtual machines and containers together. Also, it also makes possible to run only containers at the edge that utilize Kubernetes lightweight components.
- K3s (https://k3s.io/) is a highly available, certified Kubernetes distribution designed for production workloads in unattended, resource-constrained, and remote locations or inside IoT appliances.
- **High Availability K8s** (https://microk8s.io/): Low-ops, minimal production Kubernetes, for development environments, clouds, clusters, workstations, Edge, and IoT.
- **KubeEdge** (https://kubeedge.io/en/) is an open-source system for extending native containerized application orchestration capabilities to hosts at Edge.

As indicated elsewhere, worldwide enterprises and telecommunication service providers are checking how Kubernetes at the edge can be beneficial for them. Especially they are exploring and experimenting how they can gain a greater amount of flexibility, observability, and dynamic orchestration by deploying Kubernetes at the edge. Hyperscale cloud providers such as AWS, Microsoft Azure, Google Cloud, IBM Cloud, and Alibaba Cloud are integrating their edge solutions with their native Kubernetes services.

Edge Cloud Formation for Edge-Native Applications: The booming cloud-native concept can help organizations to fully benefit from edge environments. There are case studies and use cases illustrating how the promising cloud-native paradigm is doing wonders in the cloud space. Now it is expected that the cloud-native idea is to do the same in edge space. Edge-native applications will thrive. Edge cloud formation will be smoothened. Edge data analytics will blossom. The emerging domain of edge AI is to see remarkable growth with the contributions of cloud-native computing. It offers high levels of interoperability and compatibility through the use of open standards and serves as a launchpad for a series of innovations. Container orchestration platform solutions such as Kubernetes is to moderate the development and operational complexities of edge device clouds. DevOps engineers will find it easy to work on edge applications and infrastructures. The experts have articulated the following advantages.

Operationalizing Edge Cloud Environments: Cloud-native technologies and tools ensure the much-needed consistency and resiliency thereby the much-worried vendor lock-in problem gets eliminated. The cloud-native approach to edge fulfils the continuous integration/continuous deployment (CI/CD) requirement. This can simplify code changes, patching, update/upgrade, rollbacks, etc.

Visibility and Observability of Edge Environments: Edge clouds are extremely dynamic. Resource scheduling, task allocation, performance enhancement, productivity, and security are being addressed through Kubernetes. Minutely monitoring edge services and devices is getting fulfilled through the observability feature ingrained in Kubernetes. The health condition and performance metrics data of all the participating devices and their services ought to be continuously captured and subjected to a variety of investigations to extract actionable insights in time. Kubernetes intrinsically provides the full visibility into production workloads through its in-built monitoring system. The operational data collected goes a long way in sustaining edge device clouds. Monitoring tools in conjunction with knowledge visualization dashboards go a long way in safeguarding and shepherding edge devices and applications.

Kubernetes for the IoT Era: Kubernetes enables organizations to efficiently run containers at the edge. As elaborated, we are heading toward the IoT era. We will be succulently enabled through a host of multifaceted devices in and around us. Our personal, professional, and social environments are being decked with a host of diminutive, disappearing, and disposable yet dexterous sensors and actuators to understand and deliver our temporal, spatial, physical, informational, transactional, analytical, and operational needs.

Further on, everything in our midst gets Internet-enabled. That means we will be stuffed, sandwiched, and surrounded by scores of modern Internet-connected devices like smart watches, self-driving cars, intelligent instruments and equipment, cognitive appliances, sophisticated drones, humanoid robots, and networked embedded systems. The IoT devices need to operate in real time in order to be right and relevant to their owners and users. For achieving real-time data capture, processing, knowledge discovery, decision-making, and action, the roundtrip request going to a centralized cloud environment and returning with a response is not accepted. The way forward is to do proximate processing to extract actionable insights in real time.

Chik-fil-A (https://www.chick-fil-a.com/) is a technologically splurged service. The company uses GitOps to manage more than 2000 Kubernetes clusters at the edge. The "things" in their store such as kitchen equipment and trays connect with the Kubernetes clusters locally and are able to function in real time and sync data to the cloud as needed.

Through the leverage of the pioneering cloud-native principles, any IoT environment can be emphatically empowered with modern and modular device services that can ardently anticipate and respond to varied things and events in that environment. Containerization can fervently bring a kind of stability and solidity for IoT devices, Kubernetes takes care of device services to fulfil changing business requirements, DevOps and SRE needs are getting simplified and streamlined, etc. In short, currently running and future IoT environments will immensely benefit out of all these improvisations

Cloud-Native Edge Architectures: Containers turn out to be a popular lightweight runtime, which can be installed in edge devices. One or more container instances can be accommodated inside an edge device. Each container instance can host and run an instance of a microservice implementation. Because of the low footprint nature, edge devices gain much through containerization. As containers are ephemeral, scaling out containers is quite straightforward. To manage containers at the edge, it requires an architecture that is highly fault tolerant. There are other requirements for edge devices to contribute for the mainstream computing.

Kubernetes is introducing a layer of abstraction on physical infrastructure. Such an abstraction comes in handy in isolating software from the underlying hardware. Precisely speaking, Kubernetes makes any software to run on any hardware without any hitch or hurdle. Additionally, with its growing ecosystem of plug and play tools, Kubernetes elegantly equips edge computing administrators to facilitate monitoring, measurement, management, governance, security, enhancement, accessibility, etc. at the edge.

Forming Edge Cloud Centers: Edge computing resources need to be skillfully provisioned and managed. The goal here is how to enable edge services and infrastructures, which occupy the place of importance of digital infrastructure for the digital era. In other words, edge resources and applications have to exhibit unbreaking and impenetrable security, continuous availability, high reliability, etc. Workload consolidation and optimization have to be accomplished along with automated software deployment. Due to the multiplicity and heterogeneity of edge devices, the operational difficulties are on the rise. Kubernetes came as a solace for moderating the rising complexity. Kubernetes in association with GitOps accelerates and automates a number of operational activities. There are three layers in a standard edge infrastructure.

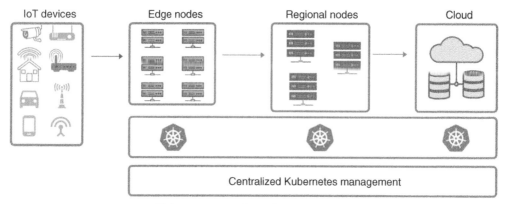

Kubernetes at the edge

There are edge servers in between a centralized cloud and a galaxy of IoT devices at the ground level. The intermediary (edge node/servers) does data aggregation, proximate processing, and temporary storage. Besides, the prominent middleware functionalities are being performed through these resource-intensive edge devices. As we all know, due to the on-demand availability of tremendous amount of compute, network, and storage resources at centralized cloud environments, long-term and persistent data storage is being done there. Also, historical and comprehensive data analytics is speeded up through centralized clouds. All types of data lakes, data warehouses, and databases are made available in centralized clouds. Big, fast, and streaming data analytics platforms are installed in centralized cloud environments.

For running containerized applications, Kubernetes is being used by hyperscale and small-scale cloud service providers. With the explosion of edge devices (resource constrained as well as resource intensive), Kubernetes is being finetuned and used in middle layer as well as ground-level edge device environments. Kubernetes is amenable and artistic enough to be run across all these environments (IoT device layer, IoT middleware layer, and general-purpose centralized cloud layer). Kubernetes unifies management of each layer and simplifies distributed and end-to-end complex systems. Multi-cloud strategy and planning get a strong boost with the stability of Kubernetes.

Empowering Kubernetes with GitOps: As Kubernetes is being considered for empowering edge clouds, the number of Kubernetes clusters is bound to go up significantly. That means an enterprise has to manage hundreds of Kubernetes clusters at the edge layer. This calls for centralized management of distributed Kubernetes clusters. GitOps is emerging as an option for centralized management.

Scalability: The Kubernetes control plane can handle tens of thousands of containers running across hundreds of nodes, which allows applications to scale as needed.

Efficiency Gains: At the edge, cost margins matter in making business models profitable. Dynamic scaling eliminates the need to consume resources that will not be utilized, and extra resources can be switched off once spikes subside. Cloud native enables an OpEx model, which inherently allows providers to leverage a demand-based approach, using flexible workflows and customized resource utilization to efficiently meet the needs of each application's unique requirements.

Thus, cloud-native capabilities bring in a series of technical benefits for edge computing. Especially Kubernetes takes away the complexities being associated with edge cloud setup and sustenance. The popular cloud-native paradigm contributes distinctively for the future of software engineering. Resilient and versatile microservices can be composed to construct highly scalable and reliable and continuously available applications that can be quickly taken to and run across different cloud environments. Similarly, when the cloud-native capabilities are taken to futuristic edge services, applications, and environments, there will be a slew of noteworthy innovations and disruptions, which will propel the movement toward digital transformed environments such as smart home, hotels, and hospitals.

The Deployment Scenarios at the Edge

The basic Kubernetes architecture is something like this

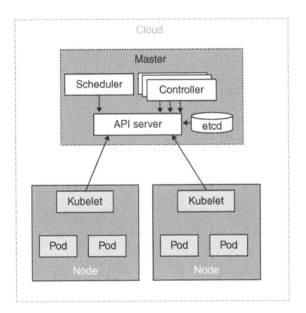

Running containerized services at edge devices.
Source: Container Journal, https://containerjournal.com/wp-content/uploads/2019/07/ Kubernetesedgepic2.png.

In this approach, the whole Kubernetes cluster is deployed within edge nodes. K3s suits well for this type of solution. K3s (https://k3s.io/) is wrapped into a simple package that reduces the dependencies and the steps needed to run a production Kubernetes cluster. The Kubernetes version is able to run on edge nodes.

K3s is highly available and is designed for production workloads in unattended, resource-constrained, remote locations, or inside IoT appliances. K3s is packaged as a single <40 MB binary that reduces the dependencies and steps needed to install, run, and auto-update a production Kubernetes cluster. Both ARM64 and ARMv7 are supported with binaries and multi-arch images available for both. K3s works great from something as small as a Raspberry Pi to an AWS a1.4xlarge 32GiB server.

The second approach of using Kubernetes for edge is referred from KubeEdge (https://kubeedge. io/en/). In this approach, the control plane resides in the cloud (either public cloud or private cloud) and manages the edge nodes containing containers and resources. This architecture allows support for different hardware resources at the edge and enables optimization in edge resource utilization. This helps to save setup and operational costs significantly for edge cloud deployment.

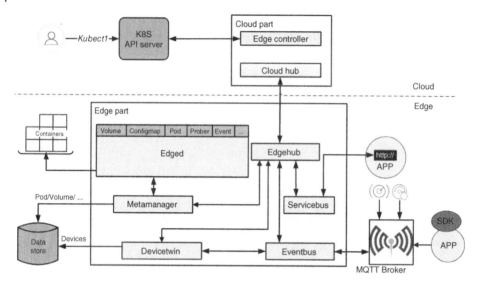

The KubeEdge architecture.
Source: Container Journal. https://containerjournal.com/wp-content/uploads/2019/07/Kubernetesedgepic4.png.

The third option is hierarchical cloud plus edge, in which a virtual kubelet (https://github.com/virtual-kubelet/virtual-kubelet) is used. Virtual kubelet is an open-source Kubernetes kubelet implementation that masquerades as a kubelet for the purposes of connecting Kubernetes to other APIs. This allows the nodes to be backed by other services like ACI, AWS Fargate, IoT Edge, and Tensile Kube. Virtual kubelet features a pluggable architecture and direct use of Kubernetes primitives, making it much easier to build on.

Virtual kubelets reside in the cloud and contain the abstract of nodes and pods deployed at the edge. Virtual kubelets get supervisory control for edge nodes containing containers. Using virtual kubelets enables flexibility in resource consumption for edge-based architecture.

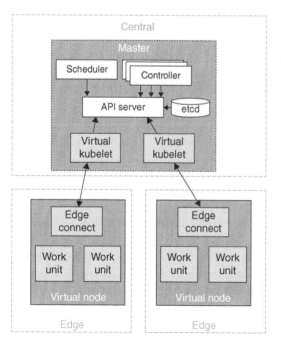

Using virtual kubelets for edge-based architecture.
Source: Container Journal. https://containerjournal.com/wp-content/uploads/2019/07/Kubernetesedgepic5.png.

Here is a list of considerations for choosing an edge platform. As indicated earlier, containers are the optimal runtime for microservices. Edge devices expose their unique services through well-defined APIs to the outside world. That is, edge devices connect, correspond, and collaborate with one another through well-intended service APIs. This paves the way for devices to find and bind not only with nearby devices but also with faraway devices and applications hosted in cloud environments. Device heterogeneity, a major worry for establishing and sustaining edge cloud environments, is being hidden through such APIs. In short, every edge device is presented as a device service. Containers can be installed inside edge devices. Such a setup provides the much-needed abstraction between device services from their underlying infrastructure modules.

- **Infrastructure Abstraction:** The edge-enablement platform has to facilitate the infrastructure abstraction as a way for lessening the multiplicity and heterogeneity-induced infrastructure complexity. That is, any competent edge platform has to enable hosting and running any edge workload on any edge infrastructure.
- **Ability to Leverage Distributed Compute Elements:** In an edge environment, there may be different and distributed edge devices. Therefore, any prospective edge platform has to be able to work with many differently enabled compute resources/devices and quickly ramp up infrastructure capacity and capability to meet up the traffic spike for edge-native applications.

The other characteristics of edge platforms are given below.

- **Device Discovery and Registration:** The edge platform solution has to be incorporated with additional tools to quickly and easily understand all the participating devices and their capabilities.
- **Robust Workload Placement Capability:** Task scheduling is always a tricky affair. There are methods postulated and popularized for making a mapping between the incoming application workloads and the available infrastructure modules. Besides, there are vital considerations such as latency and cost for taking the decision on workload placement on a particular resource. Such optimization-related works are being delegated to platform solutions. With serverless computing picking up, more operational tasks can get moved to cloud platforms. All these give additional time and leeway for application developers to shine in their core contributions.
- **Manageability Across Environments:** An edge platform ideally has to manage edge devices and their services across multiple cloud environments (edge, private, and public). Also, it has to interact with business workloads and databases running in public and private clouds. The way forward is to create a common interface in order to simplify and speed up seamless and spontaneous integration to arrive at composite, process-aware, and business-critical applications with less management overhead.

Fortunately, the Kubernetes platform solution has gained the stature to empower edge cloud environments. There are several ongoing open-source projects and scores of automated tools coming up to elegantly align the power of Kubernetes with the fast-growing edge requirements. The point here is that Kubernetes goes through a number of delectable transformations to adequately meet up new needs.

Not only establishing edge environments but also managing them efficiently is the key requirement for the edge era. To effectively manage edge processes, enterprises need a management layer that guarantees dynamic orchestration and automation. Typically, an edge architecture consists of disparate hardware and software resources. Kubernetes has the inherent wherewithal to meet these needs elegantly. Kubernetes provides an agnostic infrastructure capable of hosting and running diverse workloads. Additionally, Kubernetes can orchestrate and schedule resources. Kubernetes can use cloud configurations when managing and deploying edge devices.

Typically, control plane and analytics services are set up in the cloud. Data flows back and forth between cloud and edge locations. Kubernetes can provide a common platform for automating the processing and execution of instructions and apply this for all relevant network deployments. This way, policies and rules are applied uniformly across the entire infrastructure. Policies can be changed and refined to serve the unique needs of edge nodes ad their communication channels. Kubernetes intrinsically enable horizontal scaling of resources to meet up any traffic spike. This results in high availability, which ensures edge nodes to provide low-latency access to different and distributed IoT edge devices. Kubernetes also provides APIs for monitoring and tracking cluster nodes.

Kubernetes Deployment Options for Edge Computing

The Kubernetes platform is being primed to be run on edge devices. To run Kubernetes at the edge, you can use the public cloud or server facilities. There are different options as follows:

- **Public Cloud:** Edge processes, especially the edge management activities, are run in on-demand, online, and off-premise cloud environments. These processes, in turn, activate edge devices at the ground level to perform their services diligently. We have already written that low-latency and highly secure applications are increasingly deployed and executed in edge devices. The common capabilities for accomplishing edge-native applications are typically being made to run on public cloud servers, whereas specific tasks are being accomplished through edge devices. Thus, there is a sharing of workload between edge devices and cloud servers.

  AWS, a market-leading public cloud service provider, provides edge infrastructure and software to succulently move data processing and analysis to where data is created. This is to deliver intelligent, real-time responsiveness and streamline the amount of data transferred. The AWS Snow Family helps customers who need to run their operations in austere and non-data center environments and in locations where there is a lack of consistent network connectivity.

- **Server Facilities Outside the Data Center:** It is also possible to set up as many as edge environments outside public clouds. For example, for an industrial environment, it is possible to leverage such environments to provide edge capabilities. Predominantly the IoT paradigm is utilized by industry powerhouses to avail real-world real-time functionalities. Such an arrangement comes in handy for various industries to avail the compute facility affordably and artistically. Edge devices inside a manufacturing floor, warehouses, retail stores, etc., can get hooked to the nearby edge environments to get things down quickly.

- **Specialized Appliances:** Besides commodity servers and edge devices clusters, hyperconverged infrastructures are being preferred in some quarters. Some dedicated and expensive appliances are specifically designed for factories and process industries. Such appliances are quick to fulfil their ordained functionalities. They are being remotely monitored, patched, updated, governed, and managed. Such appliances are being overwhelmingly used in specific locations such as smart buildings, hospitals, and hotels. This is also a popular edge model. These appliances come with their own sensors, controllers, and other enablers. These appliances find and integrate with a wide range of edge devices including environment sensors, actuators, cameras, wearables, implantable, portables, handhelds, and portables.

There are plenty of benefits in using Kubernetes for edge computing. Most notable among these benefits is the ability to unify policies across edge devices and cloud environments while centralizing management and standardizing policies. There are three key ways to leverage Kubernetes for edge environments, from using public cloud components through setting up your own server facilities, to using specialized appliances.

Cloud-Native at the Edge: The Use Cases

We have quoted a number of reasons why cloud native is going to be a huge enabler of edge computing. We have also discussed different models and deployment scenarios for setting up edge environments to suit industry needs. It is found that enterprising business needs edge capability to provide real-time service delivery. Not only business houses, but also homes, office buildings, hospitals, malls, recreation facilities, nuclear establishments, space stations, oil exploration sites, border areas, defense areas, containment zones (as the world is battling the third wave of the corona virus and its variants), and other important junctions are also empowered through edge cloud environments. The edge infrastructure and architecture vary according to the size and hierarchy of businesses. Democratizing edge capability across industry verticals is the need of the hour. Besides manufacturing industry, telecommunication service providers are showing a keen interest in having edge facilities. In this section, we are to discuss a few transformations when cloud-native meets the edge.

The evolutions and revolutions in the Kubernetes space have set in motion a number of noteworthy transformations in the IT field. The application scope for Kubernetes has expanded rapidly in the recent past. Common interfaces have been incorporated in the recent versions of Kubernetes in order to ensure the much-needed consistency among Kubernetes-managed cloud environments. Today with the steady maturity of Kubernetes, fulfilling the multi-cloud strategy of many business behemoths is getting simpler. As cloud environments are following proprietary technologies and tools to ensure their operations, there is a need for viable mechanism to support inter-cloud interactions. Not only public and private clouds, but also edge clouds are getting beneficially integrated. Service composition (orchestration and choreography) are facilitated through Kubernetes. By combining the cloud-native technology with edge computing, edge devices individually and collectively become service execution and delivery points. Edge devices join in the mainstream computing.

- Edge environments provide secure workload operating environments. Containers are the prime runtime environment and they are reasonably isolated. It is possible to set throttling and network policies in order to ensure the tightest security for edge devices and their data.
- Edge clouds are self-contained and hence function in an autonomous manner. Even if the connectivity with remote clouds goes away, edge clouds can continuously deliver their designated functionalities without any compromise.
- With the faster proliferation of digitized entities (alternatively termed as IoT edge devices) in our everyday environments, edge clouds are being formed out of heterogeneous devices to tackle a variety of unique scenarios.

Cloud native has the inherent wherewithal to help organizations to gain much through edge computing. Edge gets the operational consistency through cloud-native computing. The faster adoption of open standards and an increasing level of automation being brought in through Kubernetes guarantee high levels of interoperability and compatibility for edge environments. Accessibility, portability, reliability, and productivity of edge devices go up significantly with the smart incorporation of the cloud-native concepts. Edge infrastructure elasticity is being fulfilled through Kubernetes for enabling edge-native scalability.

The simplified deployment of workloads in edge devices and observability of edge environments comprising edge devices and infrastructure modules including middleware solutions, data analytics platforms, and AI frameworks, databases, APIs, and containerized device services are being facilitated through Kubernetes. The observability feature brings in real-time edge data analytics to strengthen edge environments on all the performance indicators.

There are widespread innovations and disruptions in the edge landscape these days. Traffic management, fine-grained policy making and execution, governance and security, remote device management, the optimal usage of device resources, edge reliability, etc., are being fulfilled through a host of fresh Kubernetes-centric tools.

There are open-source initiatives for newer and advanced tools for running different applications in Kubernetes clusters. For example, through Kubeflow, it is possible for data scientists to deploy their AI models in Kubernetes environments. Knative is another popular framework to simplify running serverless workloads on Kubernetes clusters. These improvisations are meticulously replicated to edge cloud environments. Thus, the scope for edge computing is bound to escalate significantly with the seamless introduction of cloud-native and serverless computing paradigms.

For CSPs, the marriage of cloud-native and edge computing is to bring in a series of fresh competencies.

The promising multi-access edge computing will see the light. The much-touted CNFs will thrive in edge cloud environments to ponder and provide hitherto unheard services to their consumers. The emerging concept of virtualized radio access networks (vRAN) will revolutionize to create highly productive mobile networks by centralizing signal process and by distributing radio units at cell towers. Virtual customer premises equipment (vCPE) is to deliver managed services to enterprises in an affordable manner. The expensive hardware appliances and hyperconverged infrastructures will move away.

- **Virtualized Radio Access Network (vRAN):** This creates more flexible and efficient mobile networks by centralizing virtualized signal processing functions and distributing radio units at cell sites.
- **Multi-access Edge Computing (MEC):** This distributes compute resources into access networks to improve service experience and support new latency-sensitive applications.
- **Virtual Customer Premises Equipment (vCPE):** This virtualized platform delivers managed services to enterprises at lower cost and higher flexibility than hardware appliances.

The blend of cloud-native and edge computing models is to bring in several noteworthy business, technical, and user benefits in the long run.

Navigating Heterogeneous Environments at the Edge

Edge environments can be developed near to customers and users. For example, for telecommunication service providers, edge environments can be set up inside their base stations/towers. For businesses, their edge environments can be inside their factories. Similarly, inside retail malls, apartments, warehouses, stadiums, campuses, hospitals, entertainment plazas, eating joints, and other important junctions, edge centers can be built and maintained. The edge architecture varies depending on the situation and needs. It can be distributed and decentralized. The result is a heterogeneous architecture environment at the edge, whereas predominantly it is a centralized architecture for hyperscale cloud environments. The high-level edge computing architecture is given in the following diagram.

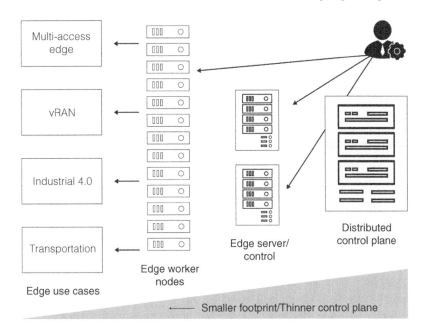

The next-generation edge architecture is going to be multitiered. A distributed control plane is an important component of the edge architecture. The control plane takes care of provisioning, life cycle management, logging, and security. There are resource-intensive edge servers and resource-constrained edge devices. The edge servers are like mini cloud centers with lightweight control planes that, in turn, manage the edge devices/worker nodes, which are located at edge locations such as retail stores, educational campuses, and manufacturing floors. In the case of telecommunication domain, worker nodes are put up at telecom towers/base stations. The worker nodes run the application workloads, including telecom applications, operational technology (OT)-based workloads such as factory automation, parking assistance system, and transit system management.

The decision regarding workload deployment fully depends on the latency needed. For fulfilling lower latency, worker nodes have to be very close to the edge. Then the requirement for lightweight control plane and smaller physical footprint crops up. Given the topology of distributed edge clouds, there are certain requirements needed to deploy edge clouds.

- **Workload Orchestration:** Enterprises and service providers (communication, cloud, etc.) have to make a decision on where an application workload should be processed in an n-tier architecture comprising compute, storage, and network resources being provided by edge clouds.
- **Zero-Touch Provisioning:** An automated system is essential for managing workload orchestration by taking the performance, time, and cost requirements of an application into account.
- **Centralized Management of Distributed Deployments:** With more edge locations, there is a need for gaining 360-degree view of all the participating edge systems through a single pane of glass. Therefore, a centralized control plane can easily provide services such as logging, storage, security, updates, and upgrades as well as life cycle management for all the contributing edge devices and servers.
- **Edge Cloud Autonomy:** If the connectivity between an edge cloud and centralized cloud is lost, the edge cloud has to continuously function and deliver its key services without any fail. In that case, the edge cloud has to have its own control plane.

Thus, edge environments are becoming complex and hence there is a need for sophisticated and state-of-the-art platform solutions to smoothen the rough road ahead.

Monitoring Kubernetes-Enabled Edge Environments

Networking edge devices to form real-world edge clouds is gaining the speed. Edge clouds are being presented as the competent infrastructure for producing and running next-generation edge-native applications. As the number of edge devices is going up significantly in any home or industrial environment, monitoring, measuring, and managing each and every participating edge device thoroughly remains a huge challenge for enterprises.

With the enabling technologies maturing and stabilizing fast, quickly forming and operationalizing edge clouds pick up fast. There are a slew of state-of-the-art tools for proactively and preemptively manning traditional cloud environments. Similarly edge clouds, in order to be a mainstream component, need path-breaking monitoring tools. The IT industry agrees that Kubernetes has the inherent wherewithal to be positioned as the futuristic and flexible OS for all kinds of clouds (public, private, hybrid, and edge). Even creating multi-cloud environments leveraging different and geographically distributed cloud environments is being facilitated through the growing power of Kubernetes. As discussed earlier, Kubernetes is being pitched and presented as the one-stop IT solution for running edge clouds, which are being touted as the best-in-class IT infrastructure for shrewdly running edge analytics and AI applications.

The open-source community has risen to the brewing challenge by embarking on a few noteworthy projects such as KubeEdge, K3s, and MicroK8s. These lightweight versions of enterprise-grade Kubernetes gain prominence and dominance for the edge era. Additional edge-specific libraries are being incorporated in order for these lightweight versions to shine in the edge world. The operational complexity of edge cloud centers, which are quite dynamic, purpose-specific, and ad hoc, is definitely on the higher side and hence there is a clarion call for additional automated tools to soothe edge cloud management activities. Hybrid edgeCloud platform empowered by edgeEngine (https://mimik.com/) enables all devices from smartphones to AI-based sensors to discover, connect, and communicate locally or through the cloud.

Monitoring Edge Devices and Their Cache: Edge devices are the new destination for real-time computing. Real-world use cases are being unearthed and marketed. Real-time applications, services, and data have laid down for real-time enterprises. Edge devices are being hooked into remotely held (cloud-based) software applications, platforms, and databases. Remote management of ground-level devices is being steadily enabled. Device monitoring and management software solutions are being installed and upgraded in traditional cloud environments. There are several mission-critical tasks such as self-driving cars, and remote surgery and they need constant and consistent monitoring. Even a small and short slip-up here complicates the whole system. Thus, edge device patching and care are expected for the edge idea to flourish in the days to unfurl.

Device monitoring has to be deeper. Device cache storage also has to be monitored with all the care and clarity. Any excel data in the cache has to be deleted, and this data should be stored in centralized cloud for enabling persistent storage. Due to the need for real-time decisions, all kinds of inhibitions ought to be identified and addressed through technological solutions.

Monitoring Edge Infrastructure: Besides edge devices, there are a few infrastructure modules contributing for edge cloud environments. Storage and networking are the other prime components to be monitored with all seriousness. With Kubernetes as the operating and management platform solution for edge clouds, there are additional ingredients to be minutely monitored. Containers, microservices running inside containers, pods with many containers, and clusters with many pods have to be taken care of. Additional tools such as service mesh for fulfilling reliable service communications need to be monitored. The status and health of each of these components need to be reported on.

Secure Monitoring at the Edge: With edges devices get integrated with one another in the vicinity and with remote ones through networking, securing edge devices and data emerges as one of the top requirements for security experts. Identity and access management (IAM) has been the centerpiece for cloud environments and their assets. With it, administrators can give users and applications the needed access to resources and can revoke the granted access periodically. KubeEdge and K3s have separate IAM modules to fully control access, authorization, and authentication of resources at the edge. Within IAM, a key component is secrets management. Secrets management refers to the tools and methods for managing digital authentication credentials (secrets), including passwords, keys, APIs, and tokens for use in applications, services, privileged accounts, and other sensitive parts of the IT ecosystem.

Monitoring edge environments is very critical for attaining the intended success. There are many moving parts in any edge environment. Monitoring each of them separately and collectively is essential for ensuring continuous availability and reliability of edge-native applications.

Edge Analytics for Real-Time Video Surveillance

Edge analytics turns out to be an excellent method for recognizing patterns, highlighting anomalies, and generating predictive insights. Video surveillance has become ubiquitous. But the real-time analytics of video data is lacking. Edge analytics has the potential to close in the gap.

Cameras are steadily becoming powerful. For example, when compared with analog cameras, IP cameras have more capacities and capabilities. Today's IoT edge devices are being stuffed with more resources. Data storage and processing power have gone up significantly. Therefore, edge devices have reached the state of doing data analytics locally. In other words, proximate processing has become the new normal. By deploying data analytics platform/framework/library in edge devices, it is possible to do real-time data capture and analytics. Today's edge devices especially cameras have gained the intrinsic competency to automatically detect objects, sounds, gestures, movements, signals, symptoms, etc. Facial and face recognition capabilities have become the core aspect of today's cameras. Cameras also contribute immensely for crowd management, people, and property safety.

At important locations, any untoward incident has to be proactively and pre-emptively perceived and stopped therein. Video cameras fit in these places generate a lot of video and audio footages, which have to be captured and crunched in order to extract actionable insights in time. Generally, data capture happens locally but data processing happens remotely. The network plays a very critical role in transmitting captured images, videos, and audios to faraway cloud environments for video processing and analytics. Such a scenario is not found favorable because of the high network latency.

Thereby, the idea of proximate processing is insisted to arrive at competent insights in time. Several technological innovations happen concurrently to make local analytics possible. Powerful and parallel processor architectures are emerging to boost edge devices to have the local processing power. Such a technological empowerment vastly reduces the amount of multi-structured data that needs to be relayed to cloud servers and storage appliances. In the following section, you can find more on running and leveraging machine and DL algorithms on edge devices to arrive at AI applications at the edge.

IoT edge devices are becoming slimmer, sleekier, and smarter. They are stuffed with more resources and hence their power has gone up sharply. For a security camera, this means less involvement and interpretation of humans. IoT edge devices such as compute, communication, vision, perception, sensing, and actuation systems are becoming more sharper than human beings in several everyday aspects. With empowered and edge cameras, there is a dramatic reduction in false positives. They have gained an improved ability to filter out "noise" in both video and audio recordings. Today's devices can process massive amount of information, generate the metadata needed to effectively categorize, and cross-reference data throughout the enterprise. With growing data volumes, the decision accuracy of analytics platforms embedded in edge devices goes up remarkably.

Cameras can be trained to differentiate between a human trespasser and a raccoon digging through a dumpster. It is also possible to train cameras to recognize specific noises, such as gunshots or breaking glass. In this third wave of the COVID-19 pandemic, cameras are empowered to do things like recognizing proper or improper personal protective equipment (PPE) use and to identify queues and gatherings of people as they formed. Thus, many industry verticals are exploring and experimenting edge devices to provide real-time and useful insights to automate repetitive tasks. Also, decision-makers and business executives can take tactically and strategically sound decisions and actions in time through the insights emitted by edge devices. With a series of commendable improvisations in the edge space, not only businesses but also commoners can benefit greatly.

Describing Edge AI

Lately AI has become the dominant domain of interest for business houses to become competitive and cognitive in their offerings, outputs, and operations. AI toolkits are being taken to edge devices. Such a transition empowers edge devices to acquire the much-celebrated AI capabilities. That is, AI-based data processing is being enabled at the edge. The typical capabilities of AI algorithms/ frameworks/libraries are classification, recognition, detection, segmentation, translation, etc. Now plentiful availability of edge devices stuffed with larger resources, the unique AI processing is being performed at the edge. The era of edge AI is therefore is all set to usher. Several things are happening concurrently in order to take the edge AI from ideation to implementation. Top companies are investing their talent, treasure, and time in bringing up highly competent edge AI products, platforms, solutions, and services. Here is an edge AI platform [5].

This is an era of continuous computing – where trillions of devices, sensors, and machines operate autonomously, running AI and enterprise applications in data centers, in the cloud, and at the edge. This vast network of the IoT will become 1000× the size of the Internet we know today. The NVIDIA EGX AI platform, with its end-to-end performance, manageability, and software-defined infrastructure, makes it possible.

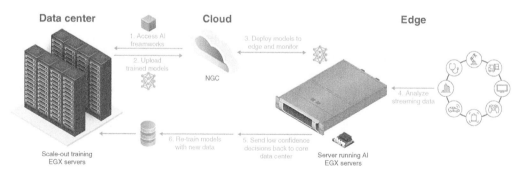

An AI platform for edge devices.
Source: Image courtesy of NVIDIA.

The NVIDIA EGX AI platform delivers the power of accelerated AI computing from data center to edge with a range of optimized hardware, an easy-to-deploy, cloud-native software stack and management service, and a vast ecosystem of partners who offer EGX through their products and services. The cloud-native phenomenon is contributing in simplifying and speeding up edge AI implementations. As discussed, cloud-native is facilitating deeper edge computing through simplified establishment and management of edge cloud environments. Edge AI is the next destination for edge computing. The role and responsibility of cloud-native computing are bound to escalate sharply as the world is painstakingly waiting for edge AI era. The cloud-native concepts are to extend the widespread adoption of edge AI.

Conclusion

The cloud-native technologies are enabling the realization of loosely coupled systems. Microservices emerge as the most optimal building block for cloud-native applications. Microservices has laid down a stellar foundation for producing highly scalable, reliable, available, and configurable applications. Kubernetes is a key ingredient in bolstering the cloud-native era. The steady growth of the features-rich Kubernetes platform solution is contributing immensely for the surging popularity of the cloud-native computing model. Now with the flourish of edge cloud environments, there is a tendency of leveraging the unique capabilities of the Kubernetes platform for empowering edge devices and environments. In this chapter, we have discussed about how Kubernetes and its shrunken versions such as KubeEdge [6] and K3s come in handy in surmounting the limitations being associated with edge devices and their clusters. Precisely speaking, the faster maturity of cloud-native technologies is turning out to be extremely beneficial for expanding the edge computing concept so that our everyday environments can deliver context-aware services to their owners and occupants.

References

1 Applying Cloud-Native Principles to Edge-First Development. https://www.section.io/blog/applying-cloud-native-principles-to-edge/

2 Unlock Opportunities with a Cloud-Native Ecosystem. https://www.arm.com/solutions/infrastructure/edge-computing/project-cassini

3 Latest developments in cloud-native edge computing infrastructure. https://techgenix.com/cloud-native-edge-computing-infrastructure/

4 Cloud-native Edge Computing – Web Resources. https://www.peterindia.net/CloudNativeEdgeComputing.html

5 The Future of Edge AI is Cloud-Native. https://developer.nvidia.com/blog/the-future-of-edge-ai-is-cloud-native/

6 KubeEdge: cloud native edge computing. https://www.cncf.io/blog/2021/07/05/kubeedge-cloud-native-edge-computing/

11

Setting up a Kubernetes Cluster using Azure Kubernetes Service

THE OBJECTIVES
By leveraging the various automation facilities being provided by Azure Kubernetes Service (AKS), a popular managed Kubernetes service, it is quite easy to embark on the much-celebrated cloud-native journey. This chapter is incorporated into this book in order to vividly illustrate the steps to be followed for setting up a Kubernetes cluster in the Microsoft Azure cloud using the AKS.

Introduction

Kubernetes is an insightful and integrated platform solution for efficiently and elegantly running and managing containerized applications. Kubernetes is dominating in the containerization era and there is no match for it. Even though Kubernetes includes a set of various impressive features, it requires significant manual configurations. However, manually establishing and sustaining Kubernetes environments is neither straightforward nor simple. Basically, Kubernetes is a sophisticated yet complicated platform. As articulated in other chapters, Kubernetes is being pitched as the uniform and standardized platform solution to deploy and manage containerized applications across varied cloud infrastructures such as public, private, hybrid, and edge clouds. Luckily the tool ecosystem of Kubernetes is large and growing rapidly. These automated tools come in handy in eliminating most of the manual activities associated with forming Kubernetes environments and proceeding with cloud-native application deployments. Hyperscale clouds have brought in managed Kubernetes services in order to lessen the workload of application developers and IT administrators. In this chapter, we are to discuss how to leverage the various features of Azure Kubernetes Service (AKS) in quickly setting up a Kubernetes environment.

Benefits of Azure Kubernetes Service

AKS is a managed Kubernetes service that lets you quickly create and manage clusters. With AKS, you can quickly create a production-ready Kubernetes cluster. It enables deploying and managing containerized applications. AKS offers serverless Kubernetes, an integrated continuous integration and continuous delivery (CI/CD) experience, and enterprise-grade security and governance. It also unites development and operations teams on a single platform to rapidly build, deliver, and scale applications with all the confidence. AKS has several features that are attractive for users of Microsoft Azure and provides the ability to easily create, maintain, scale, and monitor the AKS cluster.

- Elastic provisioning of capacity without the need to manage the infrastructure and with the ability to add event-driven autoscaling and triggering through Kubernetes Event-driven Autoscaling (https://keda.sh) (KEDA).
- Faster end-to-end development experience through Visual Studio Code Kubernetes tools, Azure DevOps, and Azure Monitor.
- Most comprehensive authentication and authorization capabilities using Azure Active Directory (AD), and dynamic rules enforcement across multiple clusters with Azure Policy.
- Availability in more regions than any other cloud provider.
- Easily define, deploy, debug, and upgrade even the most complex Kubernetes applications, and automatically containerize your applications.
- Add a full CI/CD pipeline to your AKS clusters with automated routine tasks and set up a canary deployment strategy in just a few clicks. Detect failures early and optimize your pipelines with deep traceability into your deployments.
- Gain visibility into your environment with the Kubernetes resources view, control-plane telemetry, log aggregation, and container health, accessible in the Azure portal and automatically configured for AKS clusters.
- Rely on built-in automated provisioning, repair, monitoring, and scaling. Get up and run quickly and minimize infrastructure maintenance.
- Get started easily with smart defaults and create scenario-specific cluster configurations in just a few clicks.
- Easily provision fully managed clusters with Prometheus-based monitoring capabilities.
- Use Azure Advisor to optimize your Kubernetes deployments with real-time, personalized recommendations.
- Save on costs by using deeply discounted capacity with Azure Spot.
- Elastically add compute capacity with serverless Kubernetes in seconds.
- Achieve higher availability and protect applications from data center failures using availability zones.

The common uses for AKS:

- Migrate your existing application to the cloud, build a complex application that uses machine learning, or take advantage of the agility offered by a microservices architecture (MSA).
- Easily migrate existing applications to containers and run them in the managed AKS.
- Use AKS to simplify the deployment and management of microservices-based architecture. AKS streamlines horizontal scaling, self-healing, load balancing, and secret management.
- DevOps and Kubernetes are better together. Achieve the balance between speed and security and deliver code faster at scale by implementing secure DevOps with Kubernetes on Azure.
- Use the AKS virtual node to provision pods inside Azure Container Instances (ACI) that start in seconds. This enables AKS to run with just enough capacity for your average workload.
- This reference architecture shows a recommended architecture for IoT applications on Azure using platform-as-a-service (PaaS) components.
- Training models using large datasets is a complex and resource-intensive task. Use familiar tools such as TensorFlow and Kubeflow to simplify the training of machine learning models.
- Use AKS to easily ingest and process a real-time data stream with millions of data points collected via sensors. Perform fast analysis and computations to develop insights into complex scenarios quickly.

You can find more details on the various competencies of AKS on the Microsoft AKS home page (https://azure.microsoft.com/en-us/services/kubernetes-service/).

Purpose

The purpose of this cookbook is to:

- Provide an introduction to AKS
- Provide a view of the architecture of the AKS Platform
- Provide step-by-step instructions on completing the AKS deployment pre-requirements
- Provide step-by-step instruction on how to implement AKS Platform on Azure Cloud.

Scope

The AKS Platform capabilities are listed as follows:

- AKS Platform v.1.20.5 installation on Azure Cloud
- Azure load balancing
- Dynamic persistent volumes provided by Azure Disk and Azure Volumes Files
- Support Calico plug-in
- Azure Container Registry to enable seamless deployments from a private image registry.
- Azure Monitor in addition to the CPU and memory metrics included in AKS by default
- AKS cluster with Azure AD
- Default Monitoring using Azure Monitoring tools
- Default Log management and visualization

An Introduction to Azure Kubernetes Service

AKS is a fully managed container orchestration service by Microsoft Azure cloud. This offering is being used to simplify the deployment, scalability, and management of Docker containers and container-based applications in a clustered environment. AKS offers automated provisioning, scaling, and upgrades of resources (compute, storage, and networking) on demand. This capability ensures the continuous availability of the Kubernetes cluster.

Features of Azure Kubernetes Services

AKS offers a variety of features such as creating, managing, scaling, and monitoring Azure Kubernetes clusters.

- **Efficient Resource Utilization:** The fully managed AKS offers easy and elegant deployment and management of containerized applications in a resource-efficient manner. The cloud resources get added and removed on a need basis automatically; thereby the much-needed resource allocation and utilization are done efficiently. AKS's inherent container-orchestration capability comes in handy in guaranteeing system efficiency.
- **Faster Application Development:** AKS reduces the time for software debugging while handling patching, auto-upgrades, and self-healing. This capability enables application developers to focus on their core activities while ensuring high productivity.
- **Security and Compliance:** The AKS offering gets integrated with AD for fulfilling the access control requirement. This substantially ensures cyber resilience. AKS is also completely compliant with the standards and regulatory requirements such as System and Organization Controls (SOC), HIPAA, ISO, and PCI DSS.

- **Quicker Development and Integration:** The AKS system takes care of infrastructure provisioning, sustenance, scaling, healing, governance, security, and management. This clearly speeds up the infrastructure setup and integration with other right and relevant services to bring up the system quickly. Further on, with serverless-enablement, provisioning of additional compute resources happens within seconds.

Precisely speaking, the AKS offers managed Kubernetes cluster deployment in the Azure cloud environment. The AKS manages the health of Kubernetes clusters well.

A template-based deployment uses Terraform and Resource Manager templates and can be used to deploy the AKS cluster that manages the auto-configuration of master and worker nodes of the Kubernetes cluster. Additional requirements such as advanced networking, monitoring, and Azure AD integration are also configured through templatization. It is possible to orchestrate any type of workload running in the AKS environment. It is also possible to move .NET apps to Windows Server containers, modernize Java apps in Linux containers, or run microservices in AKS.

Azure Kubernetes Service Use Cases

Here are a few use cases where AKS can be used:

- **Migration of Existing Applications:** It is quite easy to modernize and migrate existing applications to containers and run them with the help of the Microsoft AKS offering. Can gain tighter control on the access by leveraging Azure AD integration. Can easily leverage SLA-based Azure Services like Azure Database using Open Service Broker for Azure (OSBA) to have enterprise-grade and production-ready workloads.
- **Enable Cloud-Native Systems:** Firstly, build microservices-centric applications, containerize and deposit them in a public or private image registry, and operate them successfully through automated management of MSA applications by adding AKS-inspired load-balancing, horizontal scalability, self-healing, and secret management capabilities.
- **Bringing DevOps and Kubernetes Integration:** This clearly improves the security and speed of the development process with CI/CD with dynamic policy controls. It is made easy and faster to add a full CI/CD pipeline to AKS clusters with automated routine tasks and to set up a canary deployment strategy. AKS facilitates detecting failures early and optimizing pipelines with deep traceability into the deployed applications.

Common Uses for Azure Kubernetes Service

- Migrate your existing application to the cloud, build a complex application that uses machine learning, or take advantage of the agility offered by a MSA.
- Lift and shift to containers with AKS – Easily migrate existing applications to containers and run them in the managed AKS.
- AKS can also be used to ingest and process real-time data streams with data points via sensors and perform quick analysis.

Precisely speaking, the AKS offering is a robust and cost-effective container orchestration service that helps you deploy and manage containerized applications in seconds where additional resources are assigned automatically without the headache of managing additional servers. AKS nodes are scaled out automatically as the demand increases. All containerized resources can be accessed via the AKS management portal or AKS CLI. The observability feature comes in handy in visualizing additional capabilities for containerized applications. With deeper visibility into the Kubernetes cluster environment, control-plane telemetry, log aggregation, and container health can be made available and accessible in the Azure portal. All these can be automatically configured for AKS clusters.

High-Level Architecture

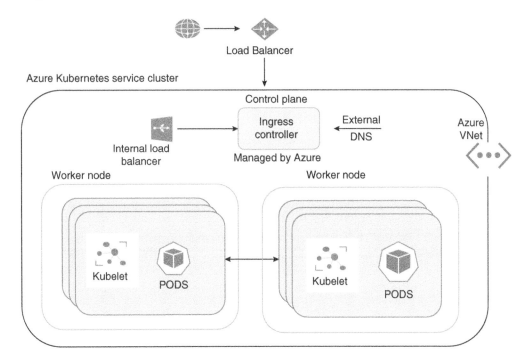

Architecture Design

This reference architecture will build a baseline infrastructure that deploys an AKS cluster.

Control Plane: While creating the AKS cluster on the Azure platform, a control plane is automatically created and configured. This control plane is provided as a managed Azure resource abstracted from the user. There is no cost for the control plane, only the nodes that are part of the AKS cluster.

Nodes and Node Pools (Worker Node): Node pools are used to run applications and supporting services and need a Kubernetes node. An AKS cluster has one or more nodes, which is an Azure virtual machine (VM) that runs the Kubernetes node components and container runtime.

Load Balancer: An Azure Load Balancer is created when the NGINX ingress controller is deployed. The load balancer routes the Internet traffic to the ingress.

Deployment Pre-Requisites

1) For Signup Azure portal https://portal.azure.com, follow the steps mentioned hereunder:
2) Open Azure Portal and click on "Create one"

3) Provide your email address and click on next

4) Provide the critical password and click on next
5) It will take the Azure Portal dashboard

6) Sign in to the Azure portal at https://portal.azure.com

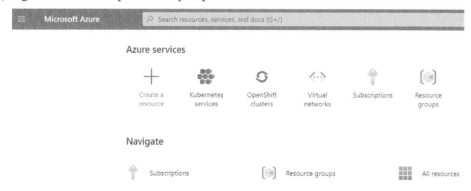

7) The user requirs a "Global administrator" access

   1) On the Azure portal menu or from the **Home** page, select **Create a resource**.

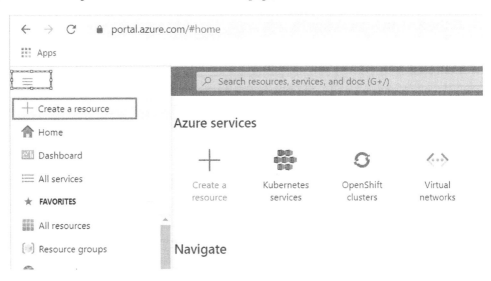

   2) Select **Containers** > **Kubernetes Service**.

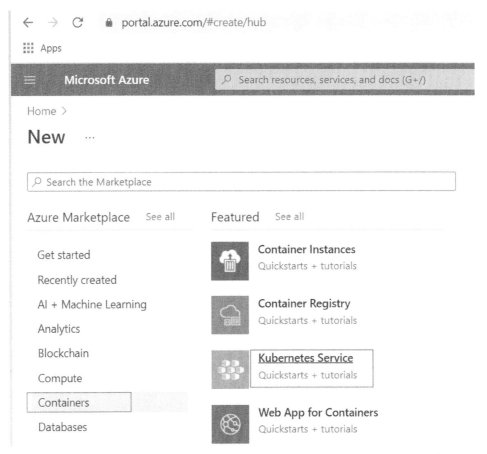

3) On the **Basics** page, configure the following options:

Project details:

a) Select an Azure **Subscription**.

b) Select or create an Azure **Resource group**, such as DemoResourceGroup.

Cluster details:

c) Enter a **Kubernetes cluster name**, such as DemoAKSCluster.

d) Select a **Region** and **Kubernetes version** for the AKS cluster.

Primary node pool:

e) Select a VM **Node size** for the AKS nodes. The VM size cannot be changed once an AKS cluster has been deployed.

f) Select the number of nodes to deploy into the cluster. For this quickstart, set **Node count** to 3. The node count can be adjusted after the cluster has been deployed.

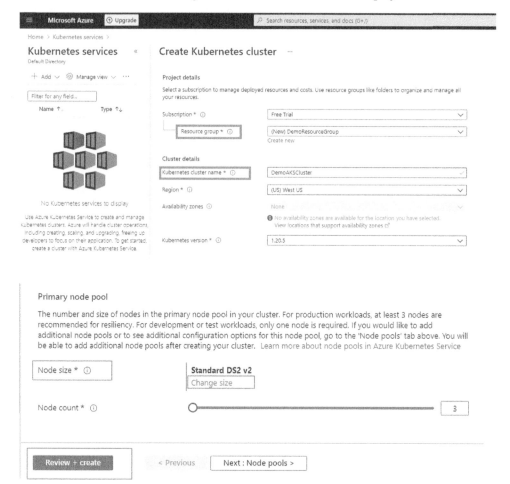

4) Select **Next: Node pools** when complete.

5) Keep the default **Node pools** options. At the bottom of the screen, click **Next: Authentication**.

Create Kubernetes cluster ···

Basics   **Node pools**   Authentication   Networking   Integrations   Tags   Review + create

Node pools

In addition to the required primary node pool configured on the Basics tab, you can also add optional node pools to handle a variety of workloads Learn more about multiple node pools ☐

+ Add node pool   🗑 Delete

	Name	Mode	OS type	Node count	Node size
☐	agentpool	System	Linux	3	Standard_DS2_v2

◀ ▶

Enable virtual nodes

Virtual nodes allow burstable scaling backed by serverless Azure Container Instances. Learn more about virtual nodes ☐

Enable virtual nodes ⓘ   ☐

Enable virtual machine scale sets

Enabling virtual machine scale sets will create a cluster that uses virtual machine scale sets instead of individual virtual machines for the cluster nodes. Virtual machine scale sets are required for scenarios including autoscaling, multiple node pools, and Windows support. Learn more about virtual machine scale sets in AKS ☐

Enable virtual machine scale sets ⓘ   ☑

Review + create		< Previous	Next : Authentication >

IMP: All node pools must have the same virtual network.

- User node pools serve the primary purpose of hosting your application pods.
- System node pools serve the primary purpose of hosting critical system pods such as CoreDNS and tunnelfront (CoreDNS and metrics-server).

SNO	Node pools	OS	Max number of node	Max number of pods
1	System node pools	Linux (Ubuntu)	1000	Min-10 and Max 250
2	User node pools	Linux and Windows	1000	Min-10 and Max 250

Enable virtual nodes	Network communication between pods that run in ACI and the AKS cluster. • Virtual nodes only work with AKS clusters created using advanced networking (Azure CNI) • Serverless Azure Container Instances

6) On the **Authentication** page, configure the following options:

- Create a new cluster identity by either:
  a) Leaving the **Authentication** field with **System-assigned managed identity**, or
  b) Choosing **Service Principal** to use a service principal.
    i) Select (new) default service principal to create a default service principal, or
    ii) Select Configure service principal to use an existing one. You will need to provide the existing principal's SPN client ID and secret.
- Enable the Kubernetes role-based access control (Kubernetes RBAC) option to provide more fine-grained control over access to the Kubernetes resources deployed in your AKS cluster. By default, Basic networking is used, and Azure Monitor for containers is enabled.

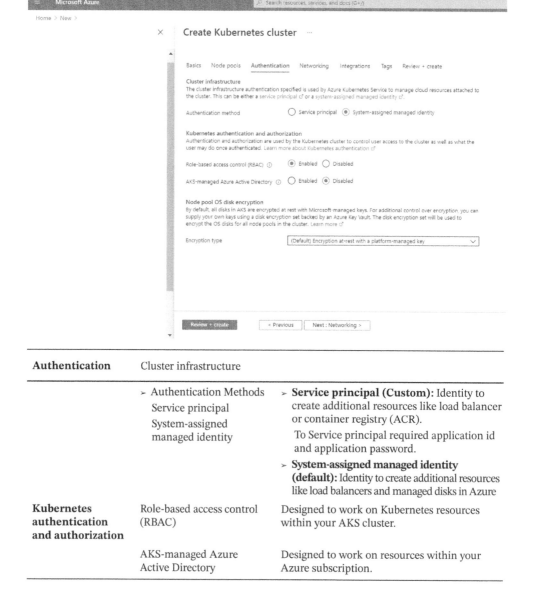

Authentication	Cluster infrastructure	
	➤ Authentication Methods Service principal System-assigned managed identity	➤ **Service principal (Custom):** Identity to create additional resources like load balancer or container registry (ACR). To Service principal required application id and application password. ➤ **System-assigned managed identity (default):** Identity to create additional resources like load balancers and managed disks in Azure
Kubernetes authentication and authorization	Role-based access control (RBAC)	Designed to work on Kubernetes resources within your AKS cluster.
	AKS-managed Azure Active Directory	Designed to work on resources within your Azure subscription.

7) Click on Networking

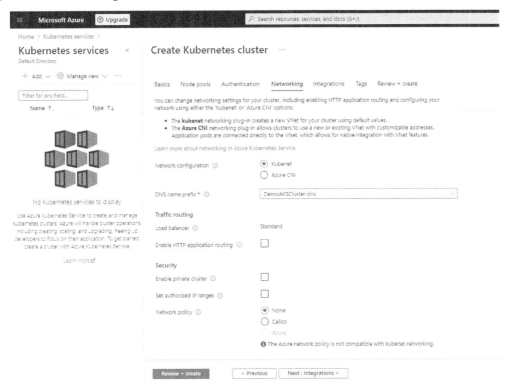

8) Click on Integrations, On Integration page configure the following options:
   a) Create a new "Container registry"
   b) Click on "Create New"

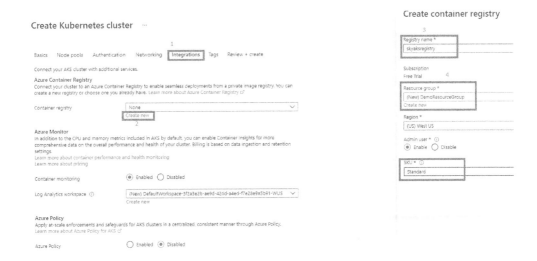

9) Click on OK on "Create container registry."

10) Click **Review + create** and then **Create** when validation completes.

11) It takes a few minutes to create the AKS cluster. When your deployment is complete, navigate to your resource by either:

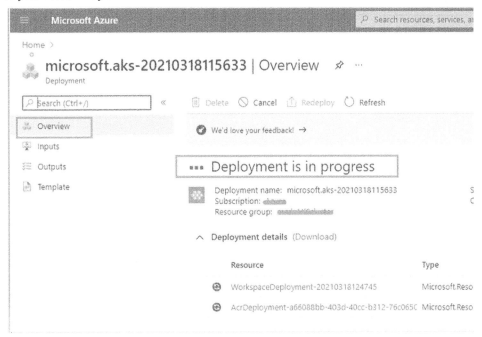

12) Clicking **Go to resource**, or
Browsing to the AKS cluster resource group and selecting the AKS resource.
a) Per example cluster dashboard below: browsing for demoaks and selecting DemoAK-Scluster resource.

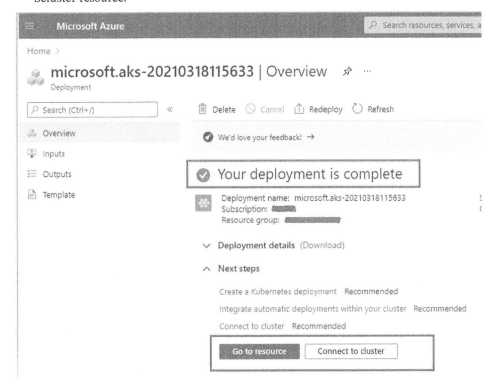

1) To follow below steps to Configure and Connect "kubectl" CLI.

   Connect to your cluster using command line tooling to interact directly with cluster using kubectl, the command line tool for Kubernetes. Kubectl is available within the Azure Cloud Shell by default and can also be installed locally.

   1) Click on "Connect."

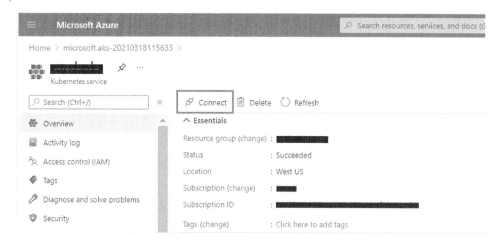

2) Connect to Demoaks window will be opened.

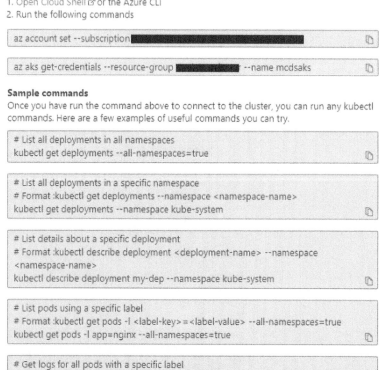

3) Click on "Open Cloud Shell."

4) Run the point number 2 commands.

az account set --subscription xxxxxxxxxxxxxxxxxxxxxxxxxxxxxxxxxxxxxxxxxxxxxxxxxx

```
skylab@Azure:~$ az account set --subscription ████████████████████████
skylab@Azure:~$ ▮
```

az aks get-credentials --resource-group xxxxxxxr --name DemoAKSCuster

5) List all deployments in all namespaces
   # kubectl get deployments --all-namespaces=true

```
skylab@Azure:~$ kubectl get deployments --all-namespaces=true
NAMESPACE     NAME                                                        READY  UP-TO-DATE  AVAILABLE  AGE
kube-system   addon-http-application-routing-default-http-backend         1/1    1           1          100m
kube-system   addon-http-application-routing-external-dns                 1/1    1           1          100m
kube-system   addon-http-application-routing-nginx-ingress-controller     1/1    1           1          100m
kube-system   calico-typha-deployment                                     1/1    1           1          100m
kube-system   calico-typha-horizontal-autoscaler                          1/1    1           1          100m
kube-system   coredns                                                     2/2    2           2          100m
kube-system   coredns-autoscaler                                          1/1    1           1          100m
kube-system   metrics-server                                              1/1    1           1          100m
kube-system   omsagent-rs                                                 1/1    1           1          100m
kube-system   tunnelfront                                                 1/1    1           1          100m
skylab@Azure:~$ ▮
```

2) List all node count.
   # kubectl get nodes

```
skylab@Azure:~$ kubectl get nodes
NAME                              STATUS   ROLES   AGE
aks-agentpool-18717502-vmss000000  Ready    agent   100m
aks-agentpool-18717502-vmss000001  Ready    agent   100m
aks-agentpool-18717502-vmss000002  Ready    agent   100m
skylab@Azure:~$ ▮
```

3) Create Application on Aks.
   1) kubectl create namespace dev
   2) kubectl config set-context $(kubectl config current-context) --namespace=dev

```
skylab@Azure:~$ kubectl create namespace dev
namespace/dev created
skylab@Azure:~$ kubectl config set-context $(kubectl config current-context) --namespace=dev
```

3) vi azure-vote.yaml

```
apiVersion: apps/v1
kind: Deployment
metadata:
  name: azure-vote-back
spec:
  replicas: 1
  selector:
    matchLabels:
      app: azure-vote-back
  template:
    metadata:
      labels:
        app: azure-vote-back
    spec:
      nodeSelector:
        "beta.kubernetes.io/os": linux
      containers:
      - name: azure-vote-back
        image: redis
        resources:
          requests:
            cpu: 100m
            memory: 128Mi
          limits:
            cpu: 250m
            memory: 256Mi
        ports:
        - containerPort: 6379
          name: redis
---
apiVersion: v1
kind: Service
metadata:
  name: azure-vote-back
spec:
  ports:
  - port: 6379
  selector:
    app: azure-vote-back
---
apiVersion: apps/v1
kind: Deployment
metadata:
  name: azure-vote-front
spec:
```

```
    replicas: 1
    selector:
      matchLabels:
        app: azure-vote-front
    template:
      metadata:
        labels:
          app: azure-vote-front
      spec:
        nodeSelector:
          "beta.kubernetes.io/os": linux
        containers:
        - name: azure-vote-front
          image: microsoft/azure-vote-front:v1
          resources:
            requests:
              cpu: 100m
              memory: 128Mi
            limits:
              cpu: 250m
              memory: 256Mi
          ports:
          - containerPort: 80
          env:
          - name: REDIS
            value: "azure-vote-back"
  ---
  apiVersion: v1
  kind: Service
  metadata:
    name: azure-vote-front
  spec:
    type: LoadBalancer
    ports:
    - port: 80
    selector:
      app: azure-vote-front
```

4) Save the file
5) kubectl apply -f azure-vote.yaml

```
skylab@Azure:~$ kubectl apply -f azure-vote.yaml
deployment.apps/azure-vote-back created
service/azure-vote-back created
deployment.apps/azure-vote-front created
service/azure-vote-front created
skylab@Azure:~$
```

4) kubectl get service azure-vote-front

```
skylab@Azure:~$ kubectl get service azure-vote-front
NAME               TYPE           CLUSTER-IP      EXTERNAL-IP    PORT(S)        AGE
azure-vote-front   LoadBalancer   10.0.254.157    104.42.142.9   80:31905/TCP   38s
skylab@Azure:~$
```

5) kubectl get pods -n dev

```
skylab@Azure:~$ kubectl get pods -n dev
NAME                                READY   STATUS    RESTARTS   AGE
azure-vote-back-554486c4c4-cqkhn    1/1     Running   0          93s
azure-vote-front-6f4bdd6c54-xkh6w   1/1     Running   0          92s
skylab@Azure:~$
```

6) Try browse with "external Ip" to access the app

Conclusion

Kubernetes is a powerful platform for artistically managing containerized applications. It insightfully takes care of the needed compute, storage, and networking components. It automates many things associated with IT infrastructure service management and hence developers and administrators could focus on business workloads, not infrastructure components.

However, Kubernetes is a complex platform because it automates a number of infrastructure operations. It is therefore cumbersome to install, configure, and maintain Kubernetes. In order to mitigate this burgeoning complexity, established cloud providers provide managed Kubernetes. AKS is one prominent managed Kubernetes service.

Further Reading

1 Azure Kubernetes Services
2 https://docs.microsoft.com/en-us/azure/aks/
3 https://azure.microsoft.com/en-in/services/kubernetes-service/

12

Reliable Cloud-Native Applications through Service Mesh

THE OBJECTIVES

With containerized services in large numbers even in reasonably sized cloud environments, service communication has to be specially taken care of in order to succulently enhance the service resiliency. Service mesh is a framework for ensuring service communication resiliency. In this chapter, we are to focus on how cloud-native applications are adroitly empowered by service mesh to be reliable in their offerings, operations, and outputs.

1) Describing the Service Mesh Concept
2) The Service Mesh Contributions
3) The leading Service Mesh Solutions
4) Why Service Mesh is Paramount?
5) Service Mesh Architectures
6) Monitoring the Service Mesh
7) Service Mesh Deployment Models

When resilient microservices get composed, reliable applications result. Cloud-based applications are being strengthened to be reliable through the smart leverage of a service mesh implementation.

Introduction

Containers emerge as the new-generation and highly optimized compute resource for efficiently hosting and running microservices. That is, containerized microservices are being pronounced as the next-generation building block and deployment unit for realizing and running enterprise-class, production-ready, service-oriented, event-driven, cloud-hosted, process-aware, business-critical, and insights-filled software packages, libraries, and tools. Microservices are highly configurable, customizable, and composable to produce and run sophisticated applications. Kubernetes is being pitched and positioned as the one-stop IT solution for operationalizing containerized services and applications in a greatly simplified manner. Containerized software, being insightfully managed by Kubernetes, has set the ball rolling to realize the much-needed business automation and acceleration. Kubernetes has laid down a stimulating foundation for creating multi-container composite applications, which are business-aware and process-centric.

However, it is found that there are some severe shortcomings as far as service-to-service communication is concerned. In other words, the salient features guaranteeing service resiliency are not being natively provided by Kubernetes. Experts and exponents, therefore, have

Cloud-native Computing: How to Design, Develop, and Secure Microservices and Event-Driven Applications, First Edition. Pethuru Raj, Skylab Vanga, and Akshita Chaudhary.
© 2023 The Institute of Electrical and Electronics Engineers, Inc. Published 2023 by John Wiley & Sons, Inc.

recommended that service mesh is the way forward to ensure service resiliency. How service mesh solutions come in handy in fulfilling the service resiliency requirements is vividly illustrated in this chapter.

Delineating the Containerization Paradigm

Containers emerge as the versatile application runtime for cloud applications (both cloud-enabled and native). Containers are the new computational unit for hosting and running microservices-centric applications. Containers are comparatively lightweight and hence hundreds of containers can be made to run in a physical or virtual machine (VM). There are other technical benefits such as horizontal scalability, portability, etc. Containers almost guarantee the same performance as physical machines. Near-time microservice/application scalability is made possible because their hosts (containers) achieve elasticity. Thus, the IT industry, especially the software engineering domain, is experiencing a variety of innovations with the faster maturity and stability of the enigmatic containerization paradigm. The tool ecosystem of the containerization movement is growing rapidly and hence containers are being positioned as the perfect way forward to attain the originally envisaged benefits of cloudification.

Containers are being positioned as the most appropriate resource and runtime to host and execute scores of microservices, their instances, and versions. The container monitoring, measurement, and management requirements are being speeded up with the availability of several open source as well as commercial-grade software solutions. The container networking and storage aspects are seeing a lot of tractions these days. Precisely speaking, there are a number of automated tools and viable approaches toward making containerization penetrative, participative and pervasive.

Why Containerization is Pampered? The old way to deploy applications was to install software applications on a bare metal (BM) server/physical machine (node/host) using the operating system (OS) package manager. This had led to the disadvantage of entangling the applications' executables, configuration, libraries, and other dependencies with each other and with the underlying host OS. With the faster maturity and stabilization of virtualization, the overwhelming practice these days is to build immutable VM images to achieve predictable rollouts and rollbacks. But the main challenges: VMs are heavyweight and non-portable.

The new way is to deploy containers, which implement OS-level virtualization rather than hardware virtualization. These containers are fully isolated from each other and also from the underlying host. The unique differentiation is that containers come with their own filesystems and cannot see other containers' processes. It is possible to bound the computational resource usage of each container. Containers are easier and faster to build than VMs. As containers are totally decoupled from the underlying infrastructure and from the host machine's filesystem, they are extremely portable across local and remote servers. Also, multiple OS distributions should not be a barrier to container portability.

Docker is the leading container-enablement platform solution. With Docker, you can pack your application with all the binaries and runtime libraries, back-end tools, OS tweaks, and even specific services your application needs for running. This makes it readily available for instant delivery and automatic deployment.

Containers are extremely lightweight. One application/process/service can be packed and hosted inside each container. This one-to-one application-to-container relationship brings up a bevy of benefits (business, technical, and user). That is, immutable container images can be created at build/release time itself rather than at deployment time. This enables generation of different images for the different versions/editions of the same application. Bringing in technical and business changes into application logic can be easily accomplished and accelerated. Each application need not be composed of the rest of the application stack. Also, the application is not tied up with the underlying infrastructure. Therefore, containers can run anywhere (development, testing, staging, and production servers). Containers are transparent and hence their monitoring, measurement, and management are easier to do. The key container benefits of containers are given hereunder:

Agile Application Creation and Running: The Dockerfile carries all the details for building a complete container image. A container image actually originates from a parent image. There are several child images for that parent image. When stacking up these images carefully, we arrive at a full-fledged container image. The image construction details are etched in the Dockerfile. Docker supplies a build command to build a container image from a Dockerfile. Once you have the image, the build command takes care of realizing a container instance.

Running an application means that you have to run the Docker Daemon with root privilege. Docker Daemon generally binds to a Unix socket instead of a TCP port. Users have to access the Unix socket using the Sudo command. The Sudo command is actually reserved for the root user. This is problematic. The alternatives are there.

Buildah (https://github.com/containers/buildah) is a tool that facilitates building Open Container Initiative (OCI) container images. Buildah provides a CLI tool that allows users to build OCI or traditional Docker images. Buildah can be used to create and run images from a Dockerfile. There is flexibility in building images without Dockerfiles and this allows for the integration of other scripting languages into the build process.

Podman (https://podman.io/) is a daemonless container engine for developing, managing, and running OCI containers and container images on your Linux System. Buildah and Podman are complementary tools to build and run containers. The main differentiation between the two tools is that Buildah focuses on building OCI container images while Podman specializes in the management of the entire container lifecycle.

kaniko (https://github.com/GoogleContainerTools/kaniko) is a tool to build container images from a Dockerfile, inside a container or Kubernetes cluster. kaniko does not depend on a Docker daemon and executes each command within a Dockerfile completely in user space. This enables building container images in environments that cannot easily or securely run a Docker daemon, such as a standard Kubernetes cluster.

There are automated tools to build container images. Creating container instances out of predefined images is another important task getting accelerated. Not only development but also packaging, shipping, and running containers are transparent, quicker, and simpler.

Continuous Integration (CI), Delivery, and Deployment: By the very nature of the containerization paradigm, developers can share their software and its dependencies easily with the IT operations team. Containerization has gained its name as it solves application conflicts between different environments. Indirectly, the much-celebrated containerization brings developers and IT operations professionals together. Such camaraderie is making it easier for them to collaborate effectively. Adopting the container workflow strengthens DevOps engineers to realize end-to-end build and release pipelines. In short, containers simplify the build/test/deploy pipelines. The given figure vividly illustrates the transitions being realized through the containerization paradigm.

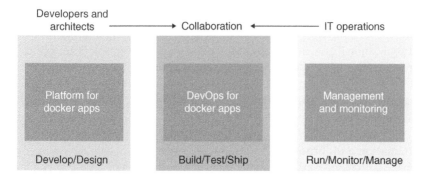

Developers own what is within the container (microservice and its software infrastructure components, and other dependencies). Developers decide how the containers and services team up to create and run composite applications. The interdependencies of the multiple containers are defined in a docker-compose.yml file (a deployment manifest). On the other side, IT operations teams can focus on server provisioning and configuration. They also have to worry about ensuring high application performance, scalability, security, observability, etc. There is a clear-cut demarcation between developers and deployers.

Developers write and run code locally in containers in their laptops or desktops. Now, they define the operating environment for the code by using a Dockerfile or any other alternative that specifies the base OS to run as well as the build steps for transitioning their application code into a container image. The developers define how one or more images will interoperate using the aforementioned docker-compose.yml file. Developers now push their application code plus the image configuration files to the code repository (Git).

The DevOps pillar defines the build–CI pipelines using the Dockerfile, which is made available along with the code. The CI system pulls the base container images from the selected Docker registry and builds the custom Docker images for the application. The images then are validated and pushed to the Docker registry used for the deployments to multiple environments.

Operations teams then manage deployed applications and infrastructure in production while monitoring the environment and applications so that they can provide feedback and insights into the development team about how the application might be improved. Container applications are run in production environments using container orchestration platforms such as Kubernetes. Helm charts are used to configure deployment units, instead of docker-compose files. The containerization concept has been hugely contributing to automating the DevOps tasks (CI, delivery, deployment, and improvement).

Separation of Concerns Between Development and Deployment: As indicated earlier, it is possible to create container images at the build/release time itself. The deployment is totally decoupled from the development and hence applications can run on any system infrastructure without any hitch or hurdle. That is, containerization fulfils the longstanding goal of software portability.

Observability: This is an important phenomenon for the container world. There are powerful tools and practices to aggregate, correlate, and analyze a steady stream of performance data, from a distributed application and the infrastructure on which the application runs, to effectively monitor, troubleshoot, and debug it to guarantee the agreed business objectives. Observability is an evolution of application performance management (APM) data collection methods to better address the mission-critical nature of cloud-native applications.

Observability platforms collect logs, metrics, traces, and dependencies data, and correlate them quickly to give the complete and contextual details to site reliability engineers (SREs), DevOps professionals, and the IT operations team to ponder about the next course of action with all the clarity and confidence.

Logs: These are time-stamped and granular records of application events. This is a file that contains information about events that have occurred within an application. These events are logged out by the application and written to the file. They can include errors and warnings as well as informational events. The developers can use log data for application troubleshooting purpose.

Metrics: There are important data about the health condition of the application and the underlying system. There are application performance metrics to be meticulously collected and stocked. A popular sample for metrics data is the memory being used by the application over a period of time.

Traces: This is all about the records of the end-to-end path of every user request from the UI through the entire distributed architecture and back to the user.

Dependencies: As applications are being built using a number of different and distributed microservices, the dependency factor of any enterprise-grade application has to be given utmost consideration. Besides microservices, there are other dependencies such as software infrastructures, resources, etc.

Once this telemetry data is collected, the platform then correlates it in real time to provide the SRE, DevOps, and IT teams with complete contextual information on application performance. With the containerization paradigm, not only OS-level information and metrics, but also application-level information such as the throughput, health condition, and other performance indicator details can be collected, cleansed, and crunched to extricate actionable and timely insights.

An Optimal Runtime for Microservices: As mentioned many a time, there is a cool convergence between containers and microservices. Containers are being positioned as the best-in-class environment for packaging and executing microservices. Both cloud-native as well as enabled applications are predominantly microservices-centric. Such a linkage results in a series of delectable innovations.

Improved Resource Efficiency and Developer Productivity: Containers are realized and strengthened by unique capabilities such as process isolation and virtualization capabilities, which are natively built into the Linux kernel. Especially, the two kernel features such as control groups (Cgroups), which are for allocating resources among processes, and namespaces, which are for restricting processes to peek into or usurp resources of other processes, enable the realization of multiple containers, which host microservices/application components/processes to share the various resources of a single instance of the host OS. This is almost similar to the VM monitors or hypervisors, which enable the creation of multiple VMs. Each VM shares the CPU, memory, and other resources of a single BM/physical server.

Thus, container technology offers all the functionality and benefits of VMs. Containers overcome some of the widely reported constraints of VMs. The lightweight nature of containers provides application isolation, real-time scalability, immutability, and disposability. Composing multi-container applications, which are composite in nature, is facilitated through additional platforms, such as Docker Swarm, Kubernetes, etc.

Unlike VMs, containers do not carry the payload of an entire OS instance and hypervisor. Containers include only the OS processes and dependencies necessary to execute the code. Therefore, the booting time of containers is negligible and hence quick provisioning of containers is made possible. Again, a greater number of container instances can be run on a single server. Hence, resource utilization goes up. In conjunction with the established DevOps solutions, containerized microservices can be quickly, easily, and frequently deployed, updated, upgraded, replaced, and restarted.

Resource Isolation: Due to the isolation capability being brought in through the application of the containerization concept, application performance can be deterministic and easily predicted.

Resource Utilization: Due to the lightweight nature of containers, accommodating many containers in a single machine is possible. Thus, containerization leads to dense environments. Because of the granular nature of containers, resource utilization is bound to go up significantly.

Containerization, without an iota of doubt, is being prescribed as the strategically sound tool for resolving most of the ills plaguing cloud environments. Docker is a hugely popular and widely used open-source containerization-enablement platform. Such platform solutions are to enable software developers to package applications into containers (these are actually the standardized executable components comprising application source code with the OS libraries and dependencies required to run that code in any environment). Docker platform helps in the automatic creation of container instances by stuffing application code into them. Docker can track versions of a container image, roll back to previous versions if necessary, and trace who built a version and how. It can even upload only the deltas between an existing version and a new one. There are publicly available registries and repositories to store container images. Developers can access and use thousands of user-contributed container images to produce mission-critical composite applications. Containers greatly simplify the delivery of distributed applications. Precisely speaking, containers contribute immensely for the ensuing era of cloud-native applications.

Demystifying Microservices Architecture

Lately, microservices architecture (MSA) is gaining a lot of mind and market shares. Monolithic and massive applications are being methodically dismantled into a pool of easily manageable and composable microservices. Application development and maintenance (ADM) service providers know the perpetual difficulties of building and sustaining legacy applications, which are closed, inflexible, and expensive. The low utilization and reuse are other major drawbacks. Enabling monolithic applications to be web, mobile, and cloud-ready is beset with a number of practical challenges. Modernizing and migrating legacy applications to embrace newer technologies and run them in optimized IT environments (alternatively termed as clouds) consume a lot of time, talent, and treasure. Software development teams take the agile and artistic route to bring forth business value for enterprise applications in the shortest possible time. Software delivery and deployment are getting equally speeded up through the DevOps concept, which is being facilitated through a host of powerful automation tools and techniques. Now the software solution design also has to be accelerated in a risk-free yet rewarding fashion. MSA is being pronounced as the way forward as it supports the proven "divide and conquer" approach, which has been deeply leveraged to sustain the software engineering field. Here come the MSA style and pattern.

Microservices is emerging as an excellent architecture style enabling the division of large and complex applications into many microscale services. Each service runs in its own process, has its own APIs, and communicates with one another using lightweight mechanisms such as HTTP. That is, software processes and procedures interact through in-process calls. Microservices communicate through network calls. Microservices primarily are built around business capabilities, loosely coupled and highly cohesive, horizontally scalable, independently deployable, technology-agnostic, etc. Each microservice is supposed to do one task well. On the other side, when these different and distributed microservices get systematically composed, the realization of enterprise-scale and business-critical applications is speeded up and simplified. Through composition (orchestration and choreography), innovations thrive in software engineering. That is, differently abled applications can see a grand reality. It is quite easy to package and deploy different versions of microservices frequently. That is, any kind of user recommendations, business sentiment changes, and technology updates can be deftly accommodated and delivered through microservices. Similarly, designing, developing, debugging, delivering, deploying, and decommissioning microservices can be swiftly done with the assistance of automated tools. There are enabling platforms and optimized IT infrastructures for the faster realization of microservices-centric applications.

Microservices are also innately facilitating horizontal scalability. Microservices are self-defined and contained and hence they could exhibit autonomous behavior. The dependency-imposed constrictions are elegantly eliminated, thereby faults are locally pinpointed and separated. That is, any error occurring in a microservice instance cannot cascade into other services so that the whole system does not go down. Faulty is proactively identified and tolerated through the isolation being achieved at the service and container levels. Microservices development teams can independently deliver on business requirements faster. However, there are some fresh operational challenges being associated with microservices-centric applications. Microservices ought to be dynamically discovered. There are service registries and API gateways to facilitate this need.

There has to be controlled and secured access to microservices, which need to be minutely monitored, measured, and managed in order to fulfill the designated business targets. All kinds of logging and operational data have to be consciously and consistently collected, cleansed, and crunched in order to extricate usable and useful operational insights in time. Microservices are increasingly containerized. In conjunction with powerful DevOps tools, the important tasks such as continuous building, integration, testing, delivery, and deployment are being neatly accelerated. Such a technologically empowered transformation empowers developers to quickly reach the market with their offerings.

In spite of all those top claims, MSA is simplistically an evolutionary one. It inherits some of the baggage of the previous incarnation, which is nonetheless the service-oriented architecture (SOA) pattern. Enterprise service bus (ESB) is the service bus/gateway/broker/messaging middleware in the SOA world. ESB comes with service discovery, mediation, enrichment, resiliency, security, and other concierge-like capabilities. However, in the ensuing microservices era, the ESB-like monolithic software gets expressed and exposed as a dynamic set of interactive microservices. The beauty lies in segregating business capabilities from all kinds of technical services. As illustrated here, the networking/communication functionalities are separated from the core activities of microservices. This segregation brings forth a number of business and technical advantages.

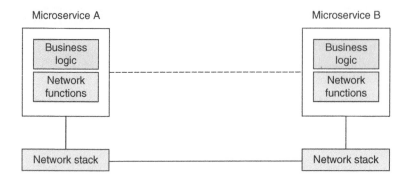

Combination of Microservices and Containers: We have discussed the containerization phenomenon and the faster proliferation of microservices. These two noteworthy developments are seen as a positive sign for the struggling software engineering field. They converge elegantly to fulfill numerous needs not only on the development side but also on the operational side. Microservices are a highly optimized application building block and deployment unit. Containers provide optimal packaging and runtime for applications. Now there is a greater interest in converging these two strategically sound concepts. The combination is going to be hugely disruptive, innovative, and transformative for business enterprises and start-ups as well. This fusion of these is to result in cloud-native applications, which are adaptive, cognitively capable of absorbing any business and technology changes, extensible, versatile, and resilient. Not only developers but also service providers, and the IT operations teams prefer cloud-native applications, which are portable across IT environments. Cloud-native applications are prescribed for IoT edge devices. Precisely speaking, cloud-native applications are constructive, competitive, and cognitive in their operations, outputs, and offerings. The blend of MSA and containerization is to open up hitherto unknown and unheard possibilities and fresh opportunities for business and IT domains.

Decoding the Growing Role of Kubernetes for the Container Era

Both enterprise and cloud IT environments are generally comprising clusters of nodes, pods, and containers for hosting and executing cloud-native applications. Therefore, cluster management solutions are acquiring special significance. Of late, Kubernetes has emerged as a promising cluster management solution. Having understood the strategic importance of Kubernetes for cluster management, the IT industry has embraced Kubernetes as the one-stop cluster management tool. Especially, for the container era, Kubernetes plays a very vital role in shaping container orchestration and lifecycle management tasks. The tool ecosystem of Kubernetes grows fast. In short, Kubernetes is emerging as a path-breaking platform for declaratively and decisively managing containerized workloads. Kubernetes automates the end-to-end container lifecycle management activities. Configuration requirements are aptly declared and a host of automation modules of the Kubernetes platform are working together in reaching and realizing the desired state.

As inscribed earlier, containers, being the favorite runtime to host and execute microservices, are turning out to be the most tuned resource for the cloud era. For automating the container creation, running, dismantling, stopping, replacing, replicating, etc., the contributions of Kubernetes are growing great. Kubernetes eliminates many of the manual activities for deploying and scaling containerized applications. Multi-container composite applications, which are business-centric, process-aware, mission-critical, flexible, event-driven, cloud-hosted, and service-oriented, are the new way of producing enterprise-scale applications. Kubernetes plays a very vital role in producing such kinds of versatile, resilient, adaptive, adept, and dynamic applications. Kubernetes is penetrating into every kind of cloud environment (private, public, hybrid, and edge).

As indicated earlier, futuristic applications are being derived out of multiple containers fusing together. Kubernetes orchestration enables building application services that span across multiple containers, schedules those containers across a cluster of nodes/hosts, scales those containers if necessary, and manages the health of those containers over time. The other important contributions of the Kubernetes include performing a seamless and spontaneous integration with networking, storage, telemetry, and other core services in order to give comprehensive yet compact container infrastructures for workloads. The idea is to bring as much automation as possible to empower applications and services to deliver their functions as per the service level agreements (SLAs) agreed between providers and users.

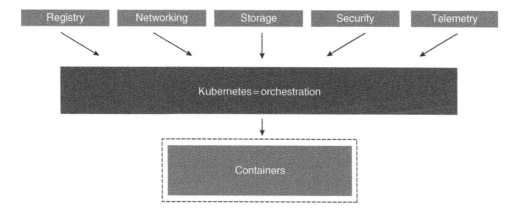

The Main Motivations for Kubernetes-like Cluster Management Solutions: Having realized the strategic contributions of containers for the flourishing cloud era, the container embarkation journey started with all the clarity and confidence. The lightweight nature along with high transparency makes containers more conducive for cloud applications and infrastructures. The direct fallout is that the number of containers in a cloud center go up significantly. Therefore, the operational and management complexities of containerized clouds have gone up sharply. The way forward is to bring in deeper and decisive automation through automated tools and platforms. It is all about complexity mitigation.

For the sake of simplicity, Kubernetes enables multiple containers to be clubbed together as a PoD. In a host/node/machine, there can be a few PoDs and each PoD comprises one or more containers. Docker networking capabilities can link multiple containers together. Kubernetes follow different mechanisms for container networking. Further on, Kubernetes schedule workloads onto container clusters. The load balancing feature of the Kubernetes platform can balance the dynamic loads across pods to ensure that the right number of containers are running all the time to facilitate the workloads to deliver without any hitch or hurdle.

Containers are efficient in the sense that more work can be performed with fewer resources. The expensive IT resources are being maximally utilized to guarantee the required affordability. Software deployments and upgrades are being taken care of. Kubernetes mounts and adds storage to run stateful applications. It scales containers and their instances to enhance the continuous availability of containerized applications. All the deployed software applications and their runtimes (containers) are being continuously monitored and managed to keep up their performance indicators. Various operational conditions including the application health condition are captured in order to do the activities such as auto-scaling, replication, etc., with all the clarity and confidence. There are a number of open-source tools emerging and evolving in order to make the beneficial leverage of Kubernetes and its unique competencies. There are several project initiatives and implementations to strengthen the Kubernetes platform, which is being overwhelmingly pitched as next-generation automation, acceleration, and augmentation platform for cloud-native applications. We have discussed Kubernetes extensively in other chapters in this book as Kubernetes is the cornerstone and centerpiece technology for the cloud-native era. The expected success of containerization is being enabled by Kubernetes. Container lifecycle management aspects are fully taken care of through the power of Kubernetes. Still there are some gaps and hence additional tools are gaining prominence and dominance. One such innovation is service mesh. In the subsequent sections, we are to detail the main motivations for the surging success of service mesh solutions.

Describing the Service Mesh Concept [1–3]

How microservices interact with one another (local as well as remote) determines their success. That is, ensuring resilient service communication is essential for availing of the widely articulated benefits of the MSA approach. For fulfilling the resiliency need, a kind of mesh network of microservices ought to be dynamically realized and used. The proven and potential mesh networking concept is gaining prominence in the microservices world. The mesh topology is resurfacing and rewarding for microservices to find, bind, and interact under strict governance. Messages flowing out of participating microservices have to be enriched accordingly to facilitate steady monitoring and management. Service discovery, routing, intermediation, security, etc., are to be strengthened adequately. Service communication logic has to be separated from the core business logic of microservices; thereby the communication logic can be reused for multiple microservices. The concept of "separation of cross-cutting concerns" is still at work. Thus, the idea of service mesh has drawn the attention of MSA experts and reliability engineers. There is a widespread acceptance that the methodical composition of resilient microservices leads to the realization of reliable applications.

Thus, besides fulfilling the functional requirements, microservices have to be versatile, robust, and resilient in their interactions in order to enhance service resiliency. Having understood these requirements, product and tool vendors have come together to bring forth the functional and non-functional requirements specification for realizing standards-based service mesh solutions, which are for guaranteeing resilient service communications. For the increasingly microservices world, the role and responsibility of service mesh solutions are being widely articulated and accentuated. Service mesh is a fresh concept for securing and shepherding microservices' interactions. There are several service mesh implementations in the IT industry today. Thus, there is a new service paradigm of "resiliency as a service."

With the participation and contribution of different and distributed microservices in visualizing and realizing enterprise-grade, digitally transformed, and mission-critical applications (e-business, e-commerce, etc.), the aspect of service meshes is being touted as one of the finest technical paradigms. There are a number of service mesh solutions that are becoming extremely critical for producing and sustaining both cloud-native and enabled applications.

Why Service Meshes? As discussed earlier, microservices are turning out to be the most competent building blocks and the standard units of deployment for enterprise-grade business applications. Because of the seamless convergence of containers and microservices, the activities of CI, delivery, and deployment get simplified and speeded up. As inscribed earlier, the Kubernetes platform comes in handy in automating the container lifecycle management tasks. Thereby, it is clear that the combination of microservices, containers, and Kubernetes, the market-leading container clustering, orchestration, and management platform, work well toward service operations automation and optimization. Not only infrastructure optimization but also the complicated nonfunctional requirements of applications are being easily enabled. This unique combination also activates and accentuates faster and more frequent software deployment in order to satisfy customer, user, business, and technology changes quickly.

However, there are still some gaps in ensuring the mandated service resiliency. It is widely insisted that the reliability of business applications and IT services (platform and infrastructure) has to be guaranteed in order to boost cloud adoption. The infrastructure elasticity and service resiliency together heighten the reliability of software applications. The underlying infrastructural modules also have to contribute immensely to guaranteeing application reliability. There are several techniques for enhancing the reliability of cloud infrastructures. The clustering of IT resources such as BM servers, VMs and containers is one widely accepted and accentuated approach toward cloud reliability.

With the faster proliferation of VMs and containers in our data centers, the aspect of auto-scaling is seeing the reality. Then there are these powerful techniques such as replication, partition, isolation, and sharding contributing immensely to the continuous availability of IT services and business applications. Distributed computing has come as a blessing to ensure high availability. However, the distributed nature of IT systems and business service components brings forth its own issues. Remote calls via fragile networks are troublesome. The predictability aspect is greatly lost when distributed and different systems and services are being leveraged to accomplish business goals. Thus, we need a fresh and flexible approach to solve the service resiliency problem for the ensuing service-oriented cloud era.

With the stability and maturity of DevOps toolsets and techniques, the IT industry could guarantee IT agility, which, in turn, fulfills business agility. Now the business world is insisting on business reliability, which can be provided through IT reliability. Thus, there is a renewed focus on unearthing cutting-edge technologies and state-of-the-art infrastructures toward IT reliability. With the cloud idea flourishing, the stagnating IT infrastructures are being tuned and turned into cloud infrastructures, which are highly optimized and organized to guarantee business agility and reliability. Thus came the phenomenon of service mesh.

A service mesh is an additional abstraction layer that manages the communication between microservices. In traditional applications, the networking and communication logic is also built and inserted into the application code. This gives the impression of monolithic code. Now, we are proceeding toward disaggregated mode. That is, applications are disintegrated into many purpose-specific and agnostic microservices. Business functionalities are being realized in business services. IT capabilities are being provided through IT services.

Now, there is another separation. That is, networking and communication capabilities are being abstracted out of business microservices. That is, we tend toward microservices, which focus on just business logic alone. All other associated actions are being separated and presented as horizontal and utility services. Such kinds of partitioning enterprise-class applications as a dynamic pool of fine-grained and single-responsibility services guarantees a number of benefits for service providers and consumers. In traditional applications, the resiliency logic is also built directly into the application logic itself. Now we are taking out the resiliency logic. There are several resiliency-enablement mechanisms such as circuit breaker, retries and timeouts, bulkhead, etc. These capabilities are being provided as resiliency logic on demand. Further on, service visibility, controllability, and observability are being enabled also through additional logic. Thus, for empowering business microservices, there is an array of common and utility services. Cross cutting concerns are being provided as support microservices to bolster microservices-centric applications. Precisely speaking, application architectures become increasingly segmented into refined, polyglot and microservices. For resiliency, it is paramount to move the communication logic out of the application and to present it as a module of any service mesh solution.

In short, a service mesh architecture uses a proxy called a sidecar container attached to every containerized microservice, or every Kubernetes pod or every node. This proxy can then attach to centralized control plane software, which is ceaselessly gathering all kinds of operations data such as fine-grained network telemetry data. The control plane applies network management policies, does proxy configuration changes, and then establishes and enforces network security policies. The other features are dynamic service discovery, load balancing, timeouts, fallbacks, retries, circuit-breaking, distributed tracing, and security policy enforcement between services.

A service mesh solution typically provides several critical features to multi-service applications running at scale. The resiliency patterns such as retry, timeout, circuit breaker, failure and latency-awareness, and distributed tracing are being optimally implemented and innately built in into the service mesh solutions. There are distributed tracing tools such as Zipkin (Zipkin is a distributed tracing system). It helps gather timing data needed to troubleshoot latency problems in the microservices environment) and OpenTracing, which is another popular tracing solution. The service mesh solutions also provide top-line service metrics such as success rates, request volumes and latencies. In addition to that, it performs fine-grained traffic management, failure and latency-aware load balancing in order to route around slow or broken service instances.

Kubernetes already has a very basic "service mesh" solution out-of-the-box. It is the "service" resource. This is for enabling the service discovery by targeting the needed pods. The famous round-robin method is leveraged for balancing service requests. A "service" works by keeping and managing the iptables on each host in the cluster. However, the "service" abstraction does not support the other key features of the standard service mesh solutions such as Istio, Linkerd, etc. There is a list of service mesh solutions on this page (https://www.peterindia.net/ServiceMeshes.html)

The full-fledged service mesh products carry the following capabilities:

Demystifying Service Mesh

As mentioned earlier, a monolithic application carries everything. But this is a disaggregation era. Microservices are typical disaggregated components of enterprise-grade applications. Increasingly, microservices are stuffed with only business capabilities. Technical features are abstracted out of microservices. Such a disaggregation has opened up a variety of fresh possibilities and opportunities for a software-driven world. For example, important nonfunctional capabilities are being provided to microservices-centric applications externally. A service mesh is a breakthrough disaggregation tool for adding observability, security, and reliability features to microservices-centric applications. There are distinct benefits if such features are supplied externally through a platform solution. These special features can be independently and individually enhanced and supplied to applications in a declarative fashion.

Service meshes consist of two components: the **data plane** consisting of a network of proxies that sit in between applications, and the **control plane** that tells the proxies what to do and provides an interface for the humans operating the mesh. Here's a diagram of a generic application running in a Kubernetes cluster. There are three application services A, B, and C. A talks to B and C is using http traffic, B and C talk to each other over gRPC, another recent and high-performing application protocol.

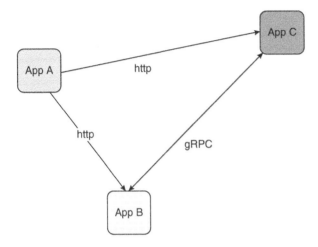

When adding a service mesh into this structure, these three application services do not communicate and correspond directly. Service mesh acts as an intermediary. Therefore, services interact with one another through a proxy of the service mesh solution. The proxy intercepts, minutely monitors, measures, and manages their interactions.

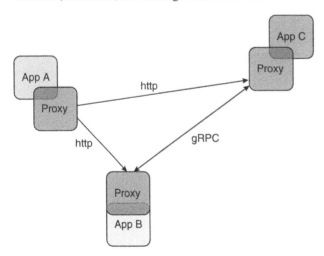

A proxy is now sitting between each component and intercepting all the messages between application services. The proxies are there to fulfill vital resiliency patterns. We have already mentioned the key resiliency patterns. Proxies add mTLS and perform request-level load balancing. Some service meshes are built on top of proven general-purpose proxies. For example, Istio (https://istio.io/), one of the widely used service meshes, uses Envoy as its proxy. Envoy is a matured and general-purpose proxy. Istio in conjunction simplifies observability, traffic management, security, and policy-making and management.

The Linkerd service mesh (https://linkerd.io/) is another popular service mesh and this uses the ultra-light "micro-proxy" Linkerd2-proxy. It is highly secure, lightweight, and consumes a lot fewer resources than a general-purpose proxy. The control plane provides a control point for mesh operators as well as for instructions to the data plane. It communicates directly with the proxies as shown here.

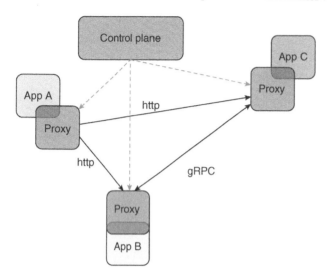

The Service Mesh Contributions

The primary goal of a service mesh is to establish service communication resiliency. Predominantly, service meshes guarantee key attributes such as security, reliability, and observability.

Protocol Translation: Service mesh does data transmission and communication protocol translation. Service meshes allow microservices to talk plain HTTP and there is nothing to bother about HTTPS on the application layer. Proxies can manage HTTPS encapsulation on the sender side and TLS termination on the receiver side. That is, application components can use plain HTTP, gRPC, or any other protocol without bothering about the encryption in transit.

Fulfilling Resiliency Patterns: As indicated earlier, the vital resilient patterns are being natively provided by service proxies. This is the key contribution of service meshes toward reliable cloud-native applications.

Adaptive Load Balancing: Service meshes are capable of performing different types of load balancing. That is, they can do latency-aware and queue-depth load balancing. Advanced parameters are being considered to ensure adaptive load balancing. Service mesh can route new requests based on the least busy target by understanding the processing amount of the current request. The service mesh knows the service request history. Service mesh can route particular requests marked by selected HTTP header to specific targets behind the load balancer. This makes it easy to do canary deployment testing.

Data-Driven Insights: Service mesh can do health checks and the instant eviction of any misbehaving targets. Service mesh can pinpoint a variety of decision-enabling operational, log, and performance metrics data. For example, the number of requests made per target, the latency metrics, the success and error rates, etc., can be minutely monitored, meticulously captured, and shared to data analytics and knowledge visualization platforms. Service monitoring is also activated and accomplished through service mesh solutions. If multiple services are chained together to fulfill a service request, then the issue/problem tracking and distributed tracing get greatly simplified through the end-to-end monitoring capability being offered by standardized service meshes. Such a setup can easily illustrate the outliers/anomalies and other vital parameters to take real-time countermeasures with all the clarity and confidence. Predictive and prescriptive insights can be obtained to guarantee business continuity.

Dynamic Service Discovery: Service mesh solutions can get integrated with service registry to identify services dynamically. This integration helps in discovering and involving/invoking appropriate services toward task fulfillment. Service mesh proxy knows which services are to be allowed to be accessed and used.

Strengthening Service Security: This requirement is also substantially enhanced as service meshes can authenticate services so that only the approved services can communicate with one another to implement business tasks.

The service mesh layer is for efficiently and effectively handling service-to-service communication. Typically, every service mesh is implemented as a series/mesh of interconnected network proxies and this arrangement is able to manage service traffic better. This service mesh idea has gained a lot of traction with the continued rise of microservice-based architecture (MSA). The communication traffic in the ensuring era of MSA is going to be distinctly different. That is, service-to-service communication becomes the vital factor for gaining a grip on the application behavior at run time. Traditionally, application functions occur locally as a part of the same runtime. However, in the case of microservices, application functions occur through remote procedure calls (RPCs).

In summary, microservice practitioners quickly realize the two operational problems – networking and observability – when embracing a distributed architecture. The real pain emerges when networking and debugging a set of intertwined distributed services. Another noteworthy consideration is the number of microservices participating and contributing to business workloads and IT applications, which is consistently on the rise. Thus, we need a competent solution to surmount these limitations. Standards-compliant service meshes are being pitched as a mission-critical infrastructure solution. Service mesh solutions have become an important ingredient in supporting and sustaining microservices-centric applications and their reliability considerably. The promising and strategic solution approach for enhancing resiliency in the ubiquitous service era (geographically distributed and disparate microservices communicate with one another) is to embrace the service mesh method. The service mesh relieves application service developers from that burden/drudgery by pushing that responsibility down into the infrastructure layer. There are a few open-source as well as commercial-grade service mesh solutions in the market. As it is an emerging concept, there will be substantial advancements in the days to come in order to strengthen service resiliency and robustness. The ingrained resiliency of services ultimately leads to reliable applications.

The Leading Service Mesh Solutions

There are a few popular service mesh-enablement solutions in the market. There are both open-source and commercial-grade solutions. Service meshes contribute immensely to cloud-native computing. Highly reliable cloud-native applications are demanded and service mesh solutions come in handy in elegantly fulfilling these ideals. In this section, we are to discuss some popular service meshes.

Linkerd (https://linkerd.io/): Linkerd is an open-source project and was the first product to popularize the term "service mesh." Linkerd is designed as a powerful, multi-platform, and features-rich service mesh that can run anywhere. This can instantly track success rates, latencies, and request volumes for every meshed workload. Linkerd comes with a Kubernetes-native design. This can transparently add mutual TLS to any on-cluster TCP communication without configuration. This has a self-contained control plane with an incrementally deployable data plane. It is blessed with a number of diagnostics and debugging tools.

This can instantly add latency-aware load balancing, request retries, timeouts, and blue-green deploys to keep your applications resilient. Finally, it is stuffed with an incredibly small and blazing fast Linkerd2-proxy micro-proxy written in Rust, which is famous for security and performance.

Envoy (https://www.envoyproxy.io/): This is another open-source project and is written as a high-performance C++ application proxy designed for modern cloud-native services architectures and applications. Envoy is designed to be used either as a standalone proxying layer or as a "universal data plane" for service mesh architectures. This provides the major capabilities of a typical service mesh solution. Envoy guarantees low latency at scale when running under load. It acts as an L3/L4 filter at its core with many L7 filters provided out of the box. Envoy has first-class support for HTTP/2 and gRPC for both incoming and outgoing connections. Envoy is API-driven and enables dynamic configuration and hot reloads. Envoy has a strong focus on metric collection, tracing, and observability. Built on the learnings of solutions such as NGINX, HAProxy, hardware load balancers, and cloud load balancers, Envoy runs alongside every application and abstracts the network by providing common features in a platform-agnostic manner.

Envoy fills the "data plane" portion of the service mesh architecture. This is a self-contained, high-performance server with a small memory footprint. This can support both the deployment models (shared-proxy and sidecar-proxy). Envoy can be easily embedded in security frameworks, gateways, or other service mesh solutions like Istio. When paired with the Istio control plane, Envoy can provide all the widely demanded service mesh features. Envoy supports advanced load-balancing features including automatic retries, circuit breaking, global rate limiting, request shadowing, zone local load balancing, etc. Envoy provides robust APIs for dynamically managing its configuration. It provides deep observability of L7 traffic, native support for distributed tracing, and wire-level observability of MongoDB, DynamoDB, and more.

Istio (https://istio.io/) extends Kubernetes to establish a programmable and application-aware network using the powerful Envoy service proxy. Working with both Kubernetes and traditional workloads, Istio brings standard, universal traffic management, telemetry, and security to complex deployments. Istio is an open-source service mesh that layers transparently onto existing distributed applications. Istio's powerful features provide a uniform and efficient way to secure, connect, and monitor services. Istio is the path to load balancing, service-to-service authentication, and monitoring with few or no service code changes. Its powerful control plane brings vital features, including:

- Secure service-to-service communication in a cluster with TLS encryption, strong identity-based authentication and authorization
- Automatic load balancing for HTTP, gRPC, WebSocket, and TCP traffic
- Fine-grained control of traffic behavior with rich routing rules, retries, failovers, and fault injection
- A pluggable policy layer and configuration API supporting access controls, rate limits, and quotas
- Automatic metrics, logs, and traces for all traffic within a cluster, including cluster ingress and egress

Istio is designed for extensibility and can handle a diverse range of deployment needs. Istio's control plane runs on Kubernetes, and you can add applications deployed in that cluster to your mesh, extend the mesh to other clusters, or even connect VMs or other endpoints running outside of Kubernetes. Istio has two components: the data plane and the control plane.

Service mesh uses a proxy (the data plane) to intercept all your network traffic, allowing a broad set of application-aware features based on the configuration you set. An Envoy proxy is deployed along with each service that you start in your cluster, or runs alongside services running on VMs. The control plane takes your desired configuration, and its view of the services, and dynamically programs the proxy servers, updating them as the rules or the environment changes.

Traffic Management: Routing traffic, both within a single cluster and across clusters, affects performance and enables a better deployment strategy. Istio's traffic routing rules let you easily control the flow of traffic and API calls between services. Istio simplifies the configuration of service-level properties like circuit breakers, timeouts, and retries, and makes it easy to set up important tasks like A/B testing, canary deployments, and staged rollouts with percentage-based traffic splits.

Observability: Istio generates detailed telemetry for all communications within a service mesh. This telemetry provides observability of service behavior, empowering operators to troubleshoot, maintain, and optimize their applications. Through Istio, operators gain a thorough understanding of how monitored services are interacting.

Security Capabilities: Microservices have particular security needs, including protection against man-in-the-middle attacks, flexible access controls, auditing tools, and mutual TLS. Istio includes a comprehensive security solution to give operators the ability to address all of these issues. It provides strong identity, powerful policy, transparent TLS encryption, and authentication, authorization, and audit (AAA) tools to protect your services and data. Istio's security model is based on security-by-default, aiming to provide an in-depth defense to allow you to deploy security-minded applications even across distrusted networks.

AWS App Mesh (https://aws.amazon.com/app-mesh) is a service mesh that provides application-level networking to make it easy for your services to communicate with each other across multiple types of compute infrastructure. App Mesh gives end-to-end visibility and high availability for your applications.

Modern applications are typically composed of multiple services. Each service may be built using multiple types of compute infrastructures such as Amazon EC2, Amazon ECS, Amazon EKS, and AWS Fargate. As the number of services grows within an application, it becomes difficult to pinpoint the exact location of errors, reroute traffic after failures, and safely deploy code changes. Previously, this has required you to build monitoring and control logic directly into your code and redeploy your service every time there are changes. AWS App Mesh makes it easy to run services by providing consistent visibility and network traffic controls, and helping you deliver secure services. App Mesh removes the need to update application code to change how monitoring data is collected or traffic is routed between services. App Mesh configures each service to export monitoring data and implements consistent communications control logic across your application.

Traefik Mesh (https://doc.traefik.io/traefik-mesh/) is a lightweight and simpler service mesh designed from the ground up to be straightforward, easy to install, and easy to use. Built on top of Traefik, Traefik Mesh fits as your de-facto service mesh in your Kubernetes cluster supporting the latest Service Mesh Interface (SMI) specification. Traefik Mesh is opt-in by default, which means that your existing services are unaffected until you decide to add them to the mesh.

Traefik Mesh does not use any sidecar container but handles routing through proxy endpoints running on each node. The mesh controller runs in a dedicated pod and handles all the configuration parsing and deployment to the proxy nodes. Traefik Mesh supports multiple configuration options: annotations on user service objects, and SMI objects. Not using sidecars means that Traefik Mesh does not modify your Kubernetes objects and does not modify your traffic without your knowledge. Using the Traefik Mesh endpoints is all that is required.

Kuma (https://kuma.io/): This is an open-source control plane for service mesh, delivering security, observability, routing, and more. Built on top of Envoy, Kuma is a modern control plane for microservices and service mesh for both Kubernetes and VMs, with support for multiple meshes in one cluster. Kuma provides out-of-the-box L4 + L7 policy architecture to enable zero trust security, observability, discovery, routing, and traffic reliability in one click. Built for the enterprise, Kuma ships with the most scalable multi-zone connectivity across multiple clouds and clusters on Kubernetes, VMs, or hybrid. Natively embedded with Envoy proxy, Kuma delivers easy-to-use policies that can secure, observe, connect, route, and enhance service connectivity for every application and services, databases included.

Kuma assists in building modern service and application connectivity across every platform, cloud, and architecture. Kuma supports modern Kubernetes environments and VM workloads in the same cluster, with native multi-cloud and multi-cluster connectivity to support the entire organization.

Consul (https://www.consul.io/) is a multi-platform service mesh. This can create a consistent platform for modern application networking and security with identity-based authorization, L7 traffic management, and service-to-service encryption.

One of the key features of Consul is its support for multiple data centers. The architecture of Consul is designed to promote a low coupling of data centers so that connectivity issues or failure of any data center does not impact the availability of Consul in other data centers. This means each data center runs independently, each having a dedicated group of servers and a private LAN gossip pool.

Consul service mesh secures service-to-service communication with authorization and encryption. Applications can use sidecar proxies in a service mesh configuration to automatically establish TLS connections for inbound and outbound connections without being aware of the network configuration and topology. Consul service mesh can also intercept data about service-to-service communications and surface it to monitoring tools.

Consul can run directly on Kubernetes, both in server or client mode. For pure-Kubernetes workloads, this enables Consul to also exist purely within Kubernetes. For heterogeneous workloads, Consul agents can join a server running inside or outside of Kubernetes.

There are standard-based, lightweight and lean service mesh implementations.

Service Mesh Interface provides:

- A standard interface for service meshes on Kubernetes
- A basic feature set for the most common service mesh use cases
- Flexibility to support new service mesh capabilities over time
- Space for the ecosystem to innovate with service mesh technology

Open Service Mesh (OSM) runs on Kubernetes. The control plane implements Envoy's xDS and is configured with SMI APIs. OSM injects an Envoy proxy as a sidecar container next to each instance of an application. The data plane (the set of Envoy proxies running as part of OSM) executes rules around access control policies, implements routing configuration, and captures metrics. The control plane continually programs the data plane to ensure policies and routing rules are up to date and ensures the data plane is healthy.

Why Service Mesh is Paramount?

There are a few compelling reasons and causes for the successful introduction and the runaway success of service mesh solutions. Microservices has emerged and evolved as the most appropriate building block for enterprise-grade applications and the optimal unit of application deployment. Further on, deploying a number of microservices rather than big monolith applications gives developers the much-needed flexibility to work in different programming languages, application development frameworks, rapid application development (RAD) tools, and release cadence across the system. This transition is resulting in higher productivity and agility especially for larger teams.

There are challenges as well. The problems that had to be solved once for a monolith, like security, load balancing, monitoring, and rate limiting need to be tackled for each microservice. Many companies run internal load balancers that take care of routing traffic between microservices. The fact of the matter is that these solutions were not designed to handle inter-application communication. The Kubernetes platform is certainly contributing to surmounting some of the container lifecycle management needs. Still, there are gaps between the supply and the demand.

As microservices are fine-grained, the number of microservices participating and contributing to any IT environment is on the higher side. It becomes very difficult to figure out which services are communicating with each other. Also, if there is any deviation, zeroing down on the root and the cause of the problem is a definite challenge for operational teams. The solution approach is "distributed deployment and central management." We need a central monitoring and management solution. Also, we need good visibility into metrics such as requests per second, response time, number of successes and failures, timeout, circuit breaker status, etc. in order to plan and manage resource capacities for microservices. Finally, we need a competent fault detection and isolation mechanism. It is not advisable to have separate solutions for these shortcomings. We need an integrated and standardized solution to address these issues. For attaining the originally expressed benefits of MSA, service mesh is the way forward. DNS provide some features such as service discovery but it does not provide fast retries, load balancing, distributed tracing and health monitoring. The old and failed approach is to cobble up several things together to achieve something bigger and better. The new approach is to go for an integrated suite. The service mesh solutions are able to offset the aforementioned problems sharply by substantially reducing management costs of services, improving observability and building a better fault identification and isolation mechanism.

Therefore, the focus gets shifted toward the service mesh approach. The service mesh solutions are capable of making Kubernetes more productive for bigger organizations trying to build a large number of microservices using different and distributed teams who own and operate their own microservices.

Forming and empowering service meshes by service mesh-enabling solutions, such as Istio, Conduit, etc., is the way forward. The reliability, security, and stability of microservices are being guaranteed through the formation of service meshes. A network proxy (data plane) is being fit in each container/PoD/host. Each proxy serves as a gateway to each interaction that occurs between microservices deployed in different containers. The proxy accepts the connection and spreads the load across the service mesh. A central controller (control plane) astutely orchestrates the connections. While the service traffic flows directly between proxies, the control plane knows about each interaction and transaction. The controller tells the proxies to implement access control and collects various metrics including performance, security, etc. The controller also integrates with various leading platforms like Kubernetes and Mesos, which are open-source systems for facilitating the automated deployment and management of containerized applications.

Service Mesh Architectures

There are a couple of choices for leveraging the service mesh solutions.

- In a **Library** that microservices-centric applications import and use.
- In a **Node Agent** or daemon that services all of the containers on a particular node/machine.
- In a **Sidecar** container that runs alongside the application container.

Library: In this case, each microservice application includes library code that implements service mesh features. The libraries like Hystrix and Ribbon are well-known examples of this approach. This works well for applications that are exclusively written in one language. There is limited adoption of this library approach as microservices-centric applications are being coded using different languages.

Node Agent: In this architecture, there is a separate agent running on every node. This setup can service a heterogeneous mix of workloads. It is just the opposite of the library model. Linkerd's recommended deployment in Kubernetes works like this. F5's Application Service Proxy (ASP) and the Kubernetes default Kube-proxy work the same. As there is one agent on every node, there is a need for some cooperation from the underlying infrastructure. Most applications can't just choose their own TCP stack, guess an ephemeral port number, and send or receive TCP packets directly. They simply delegate all these to the OS infrastructure.

This model emphasizes work resource sharing. If a node agent allocates some memory to buffer data for one microservice, it might use that buffer for data for another service in a few seconds. That is, the resources are shared in an efficient manner. However, managing shared resources is beset with challenges and hence there is an extra coding required for resource management. Another work resource that can be easily shared is configuration information. Instead of sharing configuration details to every pod, the node agent architecture facilitates the sharing per node.

Sidecar is the new model widely used by Istio with Envoy. Conduit also uses a sidecar approach. In Sidecar deployments, an application proxy in containerized format gets deployed for every application container. Multiple copies of the proxy may have to be deployed if there are redundant application containers. The load balancer typically would sit between the client and server. Advanced service mesh solutions attach a sidecar proxy to a client-side library and hence every client gets equal access to the load balancer. That means the single point of failure of any traditional load balancer gets eliminated. The traditional load balancer is a server-side load balancer but the sidecar proxy enables client-side load balancing.

The central responsibility of a service mesh solution is to efficiently handle the core networking tasks such as load balancing and service discovery. For ensuring the heightened service resiliency, a service mesh solution implements resiliency design patterns such as circuit breaking, retries, timeouts, and fault-tolerant. When services are resilient, the resulting application is reliable. The underlying infrastructural modules also have to be highly available and stable. IT systems and business workloads have to collectively contribute to business continuity.

Monitoring the Service Mesh

We need deeper visibility in order to have tighter control of any system performing its duties. In the ensuing microservices world, the number of moving parts and pieces is growing steadily and hence manning each one deeply and decisively is beset with a few challenges and concerns. Automated tools are the way forward to minutely monitor and activate the countermeasures in time with less intervention and interpretation from humans. Increasingly software applications are being presented as microservices-centric containerized applications. The increasingly inspiring and important ingredient in any microservice and containerized environments is service mesh solutions

Service meshes come with native monitoring capability. It provides a combination of network performance metrics like latency, bandwidth, and uptime monitoring. It does this for nodes/hosts/physical machines, pods, and containers. It also provides detailed logging for all kinds of events. The monitoring and logging capability ultimately helps find the root cause of any problem and to troubleshoot.

Distributed tracing turns out to be a key factor in achieving the goal of visibility. The idea here is that it gives each request an ID. As it passes through the network, it shows the path each request has taken. Using this, operators and troubleshooters can easily understand which parts of the network or which microservices instances are slow or unresponsive. The insights simplify and streamline the repair. Thus, monitoring tools are indispensable in microservices environments.

Security is another vital ingredient for achieving the intended success of microservices. Rather than relying on peripheral firewalls for the entire application, the new networking project (Calico) helps create micro-firewalls around each service within a microservices application. This enables fine-grained management and enforcement of security policies for guaranteeing unbreakable security for microservices. Bringing down one microservice does not have any serious impact on other services. Since service mesh operates on a data plane, it is possible to apply common security patches and policies across the mesh. A service mesh predominantly secures inter-service communications. A service mesh provides a panoramic view of what is happening when multiple services interact with each other.

Service Mesh Deployment Models

Service mesh can be deployed into two different patterns:

1) Per-host proxy deployment
2) Sidecar proxy deployment.

Per-Host Proxy Deployment Pattern: In this model, one proxy is deployed per host. A host can be a VM or a BM server or a Kubernetes worker node. Multiple instances of application services can run on the host. All application services on a given host route traffic through this one proxy instance. In the case of Kubernetes, the proxy instance can be deployed as daemonset.

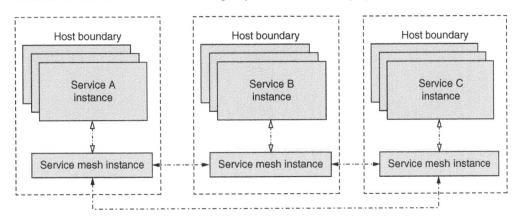

Services A, B, and C can communicate with each other via corresponding per-host service mesh proxy instances. Each host runs multiple instances of A, B, and C.

Sidecar Proxy Deployment Pattern: In this model, one sidecar proxy is deployed per instance of every service. This model is particularly useful for deployments that use containers or Kubernetes. In the case of Kubernetes, a service mesh sidecar container can be deployed along with an application service container as part of the Kubernetes Pod. The sidecar approach requires more instances of the sidecar; hence, a smaller resource profile for the sidecar is usually appropriate. If resource profile is an issue, as mentioned earlier, by deploying service mesh instance as a daemonset, we can reduce the number of service mesh containers to one per-host instead of one per pod.

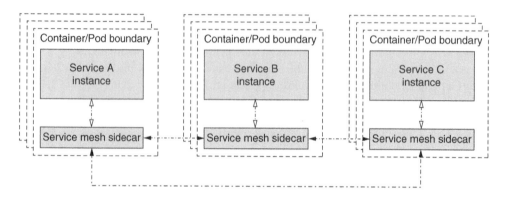

Services A, B, and C can communicate with each other via corresponding sidecar proxy instances. By default, proxies handle only intraservice mesh cluster traffic between the source (upstream) and the destination (downstream) services. To expose a service which is part of a service mesh to the outside world, you have to enable ingress traffic. Similarly, if a service depends on an external service, you may require enabling the egress traffic.

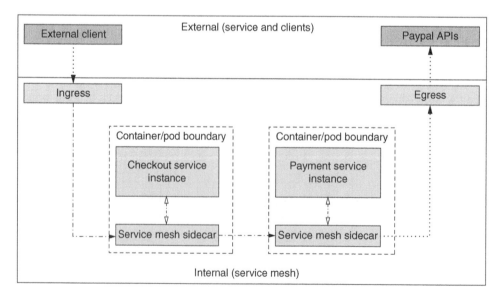

In this example, the external client requests to finalize the checkout process. This request reaches via ingress, which then invokes. depends on an external service to process the actual payment, which is routed through the egress.

Service-to-Service Communication: One of the core components of any mesh framework is service-to-service communication. To enable service-to-service communication, a service mesh framework offers the following key features:

- **Dynamic Request Routing:** In a service mesh implementation, dynamic request routing enables requests to be routed to a specific version of service (v1, v2, and v3) in the given environment (dev, stag, and prod) using routing rules. The actual implementation of dynamic request routing and routing rules may vary between different service mesh frameworks but basic mechanics remains the same – a source service requests a target service, and the exact version of the target service is determined by the service mesh instance by looking up routing rules. Dynamic request routing also helps with traffic shifting for common deployment scenarios such as blue-green deploys, Canary, A/B testing, etc.

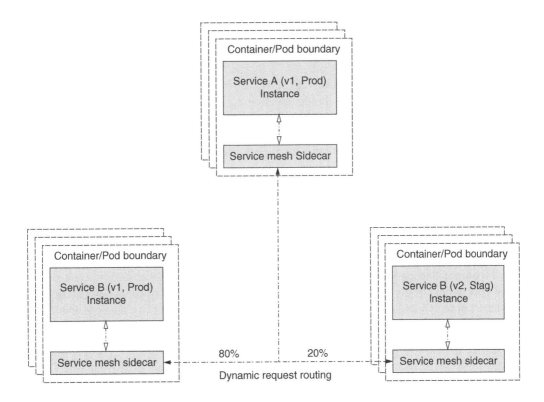

- **Dynamic Request Routing using Service Mesh:** In this case, service mesh determines the target service version dynamically based on the routing rules. It then controls the percentage of requests routed to two different versions of the target service enabling to shift traffic in an incremental and controlled manner.

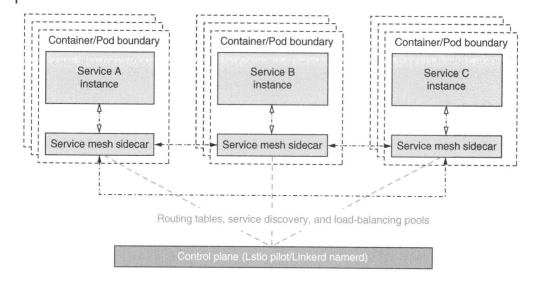

The control plane is responsible for managing the canonical representation of routing tables, service discovery, and load-balancing pools.

- **Service Discovery and Load Balancing:** Service discovery helps discover the pool of instances of a specific version of service in a particular environment and update the load-balancing pools accordingly. Linkerd provides failure and latency-aware load balancing that can route around slow or broken service instances. With Envoy, failure-aware load balancing is implemented differently, i.e. when health check failures for a given instance exceed a prespecified threshold, it will be ejected from the load-balancing pool.

In a sidecar pattern, the functionality of the main container is extended or enhanced by a sidecar container without strong coupling between the two. This pattern is particularly useful when using Kubernetes as a container orchestration platform. Kubernetes uses Pods. A Pod is composed of one or more application containers. A sidecar is a utility container in the Pod and its purpose is to support the main container. It is important to note that a standalone sidecar does not serve any purpose. It must be paired with one or more main containers. Generally, a sidecar container is reusable and can be paired with numerous types of main containers.

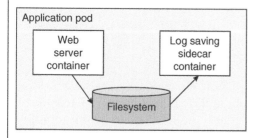

An Example of Sidecar Pattern: Here the main container is a web server which is paired with a log saver sidecar container that collects the web server's logs from the local disk and streams them to a centralized log collector.

Conclusion

Containers have definitely simplified how we build, deploy, and manage software applications by abstracting the underlying infrastructure. That is, developers just focus on and develop software applications. Then the developed applications get packaged in a standardized fashion, shipped and deployed on any system without any hitches or hurdles. They can run on local systems as well as remote systems. With clouds emerging as the one-stop IT infrastructure solution for running and managing all kinds of enterprise, web, cloud, mobile, and IoT applications, applications are containerized and deployed in cloud environments through a host of automated tools. However, there is a need for a number of automated tools in order to automate the end-to-end activities of application development, integration, delivery, and deployment. Further on, applications' availability, scalability, adaptivity, stability, maneuverability, and security have to be ensured through technologically inspired solutions. Service mesh solutions emerge as one of the important ingredients of containerized cloud environments and contribute immensely to elevating service resiliency.

Appendix

Service Mesh Configuration on OpenShift.

Follow these steps to configure "Service Mesh":

Step1: Steps to configure the Service Mesh Operator:

1) **Prerequisites**
   - Access to the cluster as a user with the `cluster-admin` role.
   - OpenShift Container Platform CLI (`oc`) installed.
2) **Red Hat OpenShift Service Mesh Installation Activities**
   Elasticsearch: Based on the open-source Elasticsearch project, enables you to configure and manage an Elasticsearch cluster for tracing and logging with Jaeger.
   Jaeger: Based on the open-source Jaeger project, lets you perform tracing to monitor and troubleshoot transactions in complex distributed systems.
   Kiali: Based on the open-source Kiali project, provides observability for your service mesh. By using Kiali, you can view configurations, monitor traffic, and view and analyze traces in a single console.
3) **Installing the Elasticsearch Operator**
   Prerequisites
   - Access to the OpenShift Container Platform web console.
   - An account with the `cluster-admin` role.

   Procedure

   1) Log in to the OpenShift Container Platform web console as a user with the `cluster-admin` role.
   2) Navigate to Operators → OperatorHub.
   3) Type Elasticsearch into the filter box to locate the Elasticsearch Operator.
   4) Click the Elasticsearch Operator provided by Red Hat to display information about the Operator.
   5) Click Install.
   6) On the Install Operator page, under Installation Mode, select All namespaces on the cluster (default). This makes the Operator available to all projects in the cluster.

7) Under Installed Namespaces, select openshift-operators-redhat from the menu.
8) Select the Update Channel that matches your OpenShift Container Platform installation. For example, if you are installing on OpenShift Container Platform version 4.6, select the 4.6 update channel.
9) Select the Automatic Approval Strategy.
   Note: The Manual approval strategy requires a user with appropriate credentials to approve the Operator install and subscription process.
10) Click Install.
11) On the Installed Operators page, select the openshift-operators-redhat project. Wait until you see that the Elasticsearch Operator shows a status of "InstallSucceeded" before continuing.

```
[root@installserver ~]# oc get operators | grep elasticsearch
elasticsearch-eck-operator-certified.openshift-operators     8d
elasticsearch-operator.openshift-operators-redhat           12d
[root@installserver ~]#
```

4) **Installing the Jaeger Operator**
Prerequisites

- Access to the OpenShift Container Platform web console.
- An account with the `cluster-admin` role.
- If you require persistent storage, you must also install the Elasticsearch Operator before installing the Jaeger Operator.

Procedure

1) Log in to the OpenShift Container Platform web console as a user with the cluster-admin role.
2) Navigate to Operators → OperatorHub.
3) Type Jaeger into the filter to locate the Jaeger Operator.
4) Click the Jaeger Operator provided by Red Hat to display information about the Operator.
5) Click Install.
6) On the Install Operator page, select the stable Update Channel. This will automatically update Jaeger as new versions are released. If you select a maintenance channel, for example, 1.17-stable, you will receive bug fixes and security patches for the length of the support cycle for that version.
7) Select All namespaces on the cluster (default). This installs the Operator in the default openshift-operators project and makes the Operator available to all projects in the cluster.
8) Click Install.
9) On the Subscription Overview page, select the openshift-operators project. Wait until you see that the Jaeger Operator shows a status of "InstallSucceeded" before continuing.

```
[root@installserver ~]# oc get operators | grep jaeger
jaeger-product.openshift-operators                          12d
[root@installserver ~]#
```

5) **Installing the Kiali Operator**
Prerequisites
- Access to the OpenShift Container Platform web console.

Procedure

1) Log in to the OpenShift Container Platform web console.
2) Navigate to Operators → OperatorHub.
3) Type Kiali into the filter box to find the Kiali Operator.
4) Click the Kiali Operator provided by Red Hat to display information about the Operator.
5) Click Install.
6) On the Operator Installation page, select the stable Update Channel.
7) Select All namespaces on the cluster (default). This installs the Operator in the default openshift-operators project and makes the Operator available to all projects in the cluster.
8) Select the Automatic Approval Strategy.
9) Click Install.
10) The Installed Operators page displays the Kiali Operator's installation progress.

```
[root@installserver ~]# oc get operators | grep kiali
kiali-ossm.openshift-operators                                12d
[root@installserver ~]# ▊
```

6) **Installing the Red Hat OpenShift Service Mesh Operator**
   Prerequisites

   - Access to the OpenShift Container Platform web console.
   - The Elasticsearch Operator must be installed.
   - The Jaeger Operator must be installed.
   - The Kiali Operator must be installed.

   Procedure

   1) Log in to the OpenShift Container Platform web console.
   2) Navigate to Operators → OperatorHub.
   3) Type Red Hat OpenShift Service Mesh into the filter box to find the Red Hat OpenShift Service Mesh Operator.
   4) Click the Red Hat OpenShift Service Mesh Operator to display information about the Operator.
   5) Click Install.
   6) On the Operator Installation page, select the stable Update Channel.
   7) In the Installation Mode section, select All namespaces on the cluster **(default)**. This installs the Operator in the default `openshift-operators` project and makes the Operator available to all projects in the cluster.
   8) Select the Automatic Approval Strategy.
   9) Click Install.

Deploying the Red Hat OpenShift Service Mesh Control Plane

Follow this procedure to deploy a basic Red Hat OpenShift Service Mesh control plane by using the web console.

   Prerequisites:

- The Red Hat OpenShift Service Mesh Operator must be installed.
- Review the instructions for how to customize the Red Hat OpenShift Service Mesh installation.
- An account with the `cluster-admin` role.

Procedure:

1) Log in to the OpenShift Container Platform web console as a user with the `cluster-admin` role.
2) Create a project named `istio-system`.
   a) Navigate to **Home → Projects**.
   b) Click **Create Project**.
   c) Enter `istio-system` in the **Name** field.
   d) Click **Create**.
3) Navigate to **Operators → Installed Operators**.
4) In the Project menu, select `istio-system`. You may have to wait a few moments for the Operators to be copied to the new project.
5) Click the Red Hat OpenShift Service Mesh Operator, then click **Istio Service Mesh Control Plane**.
6) On the **Istio Service Mesh Control Plane** page, click **Create ServiceMeshControlPlane**.
7) On the **Create ServiceMeshControlPlane** page, you can modify the default `Service MeshControlPlane` template with the form, or select the YAML view to customize your installation.
8) Click **Create** to create the control plane. The Operator creates pods, services, and Service Mesh control plane components based on your configuration parameters.
9) Click the **Istio Service Mesh Control Plane** tab.
10) Click the name of the new control plane.
11) Click the **Resources** tab to see the Red Hat OpenShift Service Mesh control plane resources the Operator created and configured.

```
[root@installserver ~]# oc get operators
NAME                                                            AGE
advanced-cluster-management.open-cluster-management             10d
cluster-logging.openshift-logging                               8d
compliance-operator.openshift-compliance                        4d2h
elasticsearch-eck-operator-certified.openshift-operators        8d
elasticsearch-operator.openshift-operators-redhat               12d
ibm-cp-data-operator.cpd-meta-ops                               12d
jaeger-product.openshift-operators                              12d
k10-kasten-operator-rhmp.openshift-operators                    10d
k10-kasten-operator.openshift-operators                         10d
kiali-ossm.openshift-operators                                  12d
local-storage-operator.local-storage                           12d
metering-ocp.openshift-metering                                 12d
ocs-operator.openshift-storage                                  12d
openshift-pipelines-operator-rh.openshift-operators             12d
servicemeshoperator.openshift-operators                         12d
[root@installserver ~]#
```

Try to open the istio Dashboard
oc get routes -n istio-system

```
[root@installserver ~]# oc get routes -n istio-system
NAME                              HOST/PORT
grafana                           grafana-istio-system.apps.ocpcluster.
istio-ingressgateway              istio-ingressgateway-istio-system.app
jaeger                            jaeger-istio-system.apps.ocpcluster.
jaeger-all-in-one-inmemory        jaeger-all-in-one-inmemory-istio-syst
kiali                             kiali-istio-system.apps.ocpcluster.i
prometheus                        prometheus-istio-system.apps.ocpclust
[root@installserver ~]#
```

Try to open host on a web browser

Click on Graph

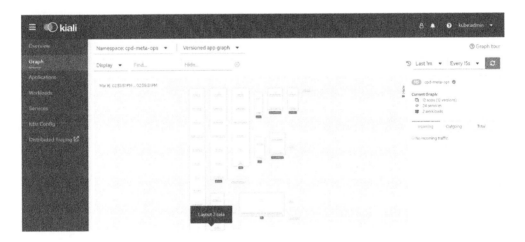

Try to click on Applications

Try to open services

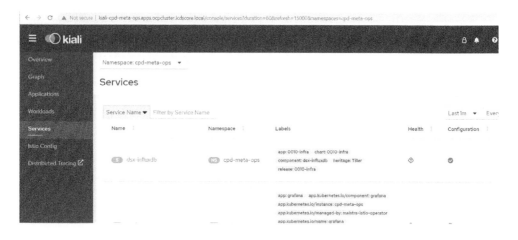

References

1 What is a service mesh? https://linkerd.io/what-is-a-service-mesh/

2 Service meshes in a microservices architecture. https://cloud.google.com/architecture/service-meshes-in-microservices-architecture

3 What is a service mesh? Service mesh benefits and how to overcome their challenges. https://www.dynatrace.com/news/blog/what-is-a-service-mesh/

13

Cloud-Native Computing: The Security Challenges and the Solution Approaches

---

THE OBJECTIVES

The new cloud-native paradigm is a growing collection of design principles and patterns, software building blocks, development platforms, best practices, and a host of automated tools for efficiently and resiliently building system architecture. CNAs, thus produced, are bound to be run on cloud platforms and infrastructures (public, private, hybrid, and edge). The overwhelming objective is to produce, host, run, and manage highly available, reliable, scalable, versatile, and easily manageable applications that can natively take the distinct advantages and capabilities of cloud environments. The CNA deployment becomes fast and frequent with the seamless integration of powerful DevOps toolkits. However, security is still persisting and hence pundits and pioneers are striving hard and stretching further to surmount security issues so that the cloud-native paradigm becomes penetrative, pervasive, and persuasive. This chapter is for articulating cloud-native security challenges and solution approaches along with security products and platforms.

Introduction to Cloud Capabilities

All kinds of enterprise-class, process-aware, service-oriented, event-driven, people-centric, and business-critical applications across the industry verticals are being increasingly run and delivered through cloud environments. Existing and monolithic applications are accordingly modernized and migrated to cloud environments (private, public, and hybrid). Fresh applications are being designed and developed accordingly to have them run across cloud environments without any hitch or hurdle. Thus, a majority of mission-critical applications are being deployed and managed in cloud environments to reap all the originally expressed benefits of cloud computing.

Precisely speaking, cloud-hosted applications are availing all the strategically sound benefits of cloud platforms and infrastructures. Cloud infrastructures (mainly commodity server machines getting segmented into virtual machines (VMs)and containers) are inherently elastic guaranteeing the much-needed application scalability. Cloud applications are made highly available through the proven method of redundancy. Promising and potential reliability engineering techniques and tools are vigorously leveraged to ensure cloud applications are resilient in their interactions, responses, and deliveries. A litany of trendsetting automation and orchestration tools are deployed in cloud environments in order to automate and accelerate a variety of error-prone and time-consuming cloud operations. Industrial standards are being strictly followed by cloud service providers (CSPs) in order to facilitate cloud interoperability and portability. Continuous integration, delivery, deployment, feedback, improvement, and security needs are being fulfilled through enterprise DevOps tools and principles. Monitoring, measurement, and management platforms are integrated with cloud applications and infrastructures to ensure continuous observability. Such a setup comes in handy in several ways. If there is any perceptible threshold break-in, it can be caught hold of immediately and such knowledge enables administrators and business executives to plunge into appropriate countermeasures in time with all the clarity, alacrity, and sagacity.

Further on, powerful data analytics capabilities are being provided in order to predict several important things. Such predictions and prescriptions go a long way in securing and strengthening cloud services and resources. With the distinct capabilities of operational, log, performance, and security analytics in real time maturing and stabilizing steadily, a number of noteworthy drawbacks of cloud environments can be identified and surmounted technologically. Thus, the cloud journey is continuously in the limelight and on the fast track. The cloud-induced benefits are realistically immense and futuristic. All kinds of software solutions and services for empowering personal, social, and professional needs are to reap greater benefits when developed and deployed in the cloud. The cloud-native approach, which has seen a meteoric rise in the recent past, for software development and deployment takes full advantage of the cloud environment (local as well as remote). CNAs leverage platforms, runtime environments, and a growing array of primary and secondary services being provided by cloud environments to be resilient, robust, nimble, and scalable solutions.

Delineating the Cloud-Native Paradigm

Due to the continued advancements in cloud technologies and tools, the much-celebrated cloud paradigm is all set to excitedly experience a series of newer capabilities. Let us understand the advancements and capabilities in this section.

Firstly, the evolution of microservices architecture (MSA) has set the ball rolling for envisaging the next-generation cloud paradigm (formally referred to as cloud-native computing). Microservices emerge as the most optimal software building block for constructing highly modular and modern applications. By establishing a seamless and spontaneous harmonization between the MSA and the event-driven architecture (EDA) styles, the software industry is flooded with event-driven microservices. As the software world is embracing the hybrid model, the role and responsibility of event-driven microservices are going up in realizing next-generation software solutions not only for enterprising businesses but also for citizen-centric governments, IT service providers, and people. Thus, the union of MSA and EDA is being applauded as the multifaceted foundation for building highly configurable, customizable and composable software. These architectural styles contribute to agile software design and development. They have laid down a stimulating foundation for the software-driven and defined world.

The second aspect of the surging popularity of cloud-native computing is none other than the emergence of containers as the best-in-class runtime for software services and applications. Containers are for compartmentalizing large-scale applications. The age-old phenomenon of divide and conquer is being replicated here too to simplify and speed up software engineering. Containers are typically lightweight VMs. Experts have pointed out several benefits of containerization and its enablement platforms. Microservices are beneficially associated with containers. Such synchronization has opened up fresh possibilities and opportunities. As mentioned earlier, applications are segmented into a collection of interoperable microservices. Now each microservice and its instances are being accommodated in containers. Microservices are combined to form service composites. At the infrastructure level, multiple containers are blended together to form multi-container applications, which are process-aware, mission-critical, and composite.

With containerization, any standard IT environment is stuffed with an increased number of containers. That is, container density is bound to go up significantly. There is a need for competent platform solutions to tackle the containerization-induced operational complexities. This has resulted in a bevy of container orchestration platforms. The market-leading container orchestration platform is none other than Kubernetes, which takes care of deployment, scaling, healing, management, and governance of containerized applications. The entire life cycle management activities of containerized applications are being accomplished by Kubernetes in an automatic and artistic manner. Practically speaking, Kubernetes is being positioned as the leading risk-free solution for faster and more frequent software deployment.

Thus, software design, development, and deployment get accelerated through microservices, containers, and Kubernetes. Now toward agile and end-to-end application deployment, there are DevOps principles and tools. DevOps comes in handy in formulating and sustaining data and workflow pipelines. Containers and Kubernetes contribute to setting up enterprise-wide and efficient DevOps capabilities for business houses. DevOps enabled by this unique combination of containers and orchestration platforms is the foremost requirement for agile software engineering.

There are additional technologies and tools such as service mesh implementations, API gateways, etc., to have next-generation CNAs. In the recent past, there are observability platforms for closely monitoring, measuring, and managing the key performance indicators (KPIs) of primary and secondary components of CNAs: middleware, databases, containers, orchestration platforms, infrastructure modules, and other internal and external solutions. In addition, real-time analytics of log, operational, health condition, performance, and security data is being activated through integrated data analytics platforms, cloud resources, data lakes, artificial intelligence (AI) algorithms, etc. Thus, the CNA ecosystem is steadily growing, and it is very clear that the future of the IT industry definitely and decisively belongs to cloud-native computing.

Why Cloud-Native Computing

There are a number of business, technical, and user advantages being associated with cloud-native computing. Firstly, the cloud-native paradigm has decisively impacted the enigmatic field of software engineering. As the whole world is increasingly software-defined and driven, the software engineering domain has to traverse through a host of innovations and disruptions. Clearly, the arrival of cloud-native computing has led to a delectable transformation in the way software solutions are being produced, run, managed, and secured. The software engineering paradigm is seeing a bevy of advancements and is journeying with the speed with which the world business is moving. Thus, the cloud-native idea has sharply catapulted the software engineering field. Breakthrough technologies and tools are being unearthed to simplify, streamline, and speed up software building. Software engineering methodologies are advancing fast. Software development is accomplished in an agile and adaptive manner. Further on, continuous integration, delivery, deployment, security, and improvement of software applications and services are being facilitated through DevOps toolsets. Agile software design is being enabled through the MSA pattern and style. This newly incorporated nimbleness brings a multitude of benefits, such as shorter time to market and faster accommodation of business sentiments.

The cloud-native capability makes the software highly available, scalable, reliable, easily observable, and manageable. CNAs are interoperable, portable, configurable, and composable. The cloud-induced benefits are readily being leveraged by cloud-native services to be distinct in their decisions, deals, and deeds. Cloud infrastructures carry some unique advantages through compartmentalization (virtualization and containerization). In other words, hardware programming is being enabled through cloudification. Also, microservices-centric applications running on cloud infrastructures are able to astutely aggregate the distinctions of cloud infrastructure capabilities to exhibit an agile and adaptive behavior.

Cloud-native innovations are being replicated across cloud environments (public, private, hybrid, and edge). Edge-native applications are flourishing with the voluminous production and deployment of slim and sleek, handy and trendy, resource-intensive and constrained, purpose-agnostic and specific IoT edge devices across our everyday environments such as homes, hotels, hospitals, etc.

CNAs are being empowered to be serverless in order to automate most of the time-consuming and tedious infrastructure management tasks to run applications. Thus, CNAs in conjunction with serverless computing are to be pervasive and persuasive. The term "cloud-native" refers to an approach to building and running applications that takes full advantage of a cloud computing delivery model. Clouds are popular for achieving some nonfunctional requirements (NFRs)/quality of service (QoS) attributes such as agility, scalability, availability, accessibility, fault-tolerance, data and disaster recovery, manageability, observability, affordability, etc. There are a number of automated tools for enabling a variety of things associated with cloud operations, brokerage, and management. There are algorithms for task/job scheduling, resource allocation, etc. Further on, there are infrastructure as code (IaC) and data (IaD) tools for resource provisioning, configuration management (CM) tools in plenty, scores of DevOps pipeline creation and implementation tools, monitoring and management platforms, security and governance systems, observability platforms, data fabrics and virtualization toolsets, visualization dashboards, etc. Thus, product, platform, and tool vendors are very active in simplifying and streamlining cloud-related processes. A variety of automation and orchestration solutions come in handy in making cloud IT an one-stop solution for all kinds of business requirements.

Now with the connivance and convergence of containerization, container and cloud orchestration platform solutions, microservices, EDA styles, DevOps toolkits, and other enabling tools, additional automation capabilities are being introduced in cloud operations. The much-needed portability and interoperability requirements are being easily accomplished through such improvisations in the cloud space. Multi-cloud environments see a grandiose reality with container orchestration platform solutions. The days of cloud-hosted, event-driven, service-oriented, process-aware, insights-filled, technology-agnostic, fault-tolerant, and people-centric applications and services are brighter.

About Cloud-Native Applications

The modern cloud-native architecture utilizes cutting-edge software technologies to provide worldwide enterprises with the means to develop and deploy their applications securely, speedily, and at scale. Cloud-native is a collection of design principles, software, and services that focus on building system architecture. Cloud is the application hosting and delivery platform. The overarching objective of a CNA is to be highly scalable, nimble, resilient, and secure by natively acquiring the special cloud capabilities. The cloud-native paradigm intrinsically carries out several automation and orchestration tasks. Enterprise DevOps concepts and toolkits automate continuous integration and build, delivery, deployment, feedback and improvement. The features-rich Kubernetes platform solution orchestrates application deployment, management, etc.

CNAs are software programs and services that are fully compliant with cloud-native architectures. CNA belongs to a next-generation application category encompassing advanced design principles, deployment paradigms, and operational processes. CNAs are modern, modular, portable, interoperable, configurable, composable, and extensible. CNAs are being built on MSA and EDA patterns. CNAs are apt for the hybrid IT era and can be meticulously leveraged for producing and running business workloads and IT services. CNAs empower tunable applications for devices (mobile phones, wearables, handhelds, embedded, and IoT devices). Further on, CNAs contribute immensely to applications across technologies such as blockchain and AI. With the emergence of different computing types including edge computing, serverless computing, mobile computing, etc., CNAs are bound to play a bigger role.

CNAs can be built in an accelerated and automated manner. CNAs are inherently scalable because the underlying resources are natively elastic. CNAs support and speed up application development through configuration, customization, and composition methods. Developing applications from the ground up is seeing the sunset and CNAs have laid down a stimulating foundation for faster and large-scale innovation in software engineering.

Cloud-native services and applications are designed, developed, and deployed with the connivance and compliance of cloud-native architectures. There are cloud-native design principles, patterns, platforms, deployment paradigms, and best practices in plenty in order to build and run highly interoperable, portable, scalable, available, and reliable cloud-agnostic applications. There are myriads of enabling technologies, tools, frameworks, libraries, and accelerators to simplify and speed up the application building and releasing tasks. When compared with traditional application development methodologies, CNA engineering is quite distinct. Through configuration, composition, and customization, newer CNAs can be realized quickly. Automation and orchestration prospects and possibilities are enormous in the cloud-native space.

Most CNAs rely heavily on automation. From automated testing and building of the core application code to automated deployment and scaling of the underlying infrastructure, the aspect of automation is prevalent and prudent too. Large-scale enterprises do hundreds of software deployments per day through highly matured and stabilized CI/CD toolsets in order to quickly meet up with technology and business changes. Through the highly elastic container infrastructure, CNAs are highly scalable. Through Kubernetes, automated deployment, management, healing, and scaling of containerized applications are achieved. As mentioned earlier, microservices, the hugely popular building block for independently developable, deployable, and manageable applications, collectively facilitate agile design and development of enterprise-class, production-ready, and cloud-hosted applications. Thus, a series of technological advancements and multiplicity of enabling toolkits along with the hardware programming capability being facilitated through compartmentalization (virtualization and containerization) have laid down a stimulating and scintillating foundation for envisaging and elegantly building state-of-the-art applications for the ensuing digital life era. Cloud-native services and applications support portability and interoperability. The openness of the cloud-native paradigm has set in motion a dazzling array of innovations and disruptions. CNAs are being recognized as the key ingredient for establishing digitally enabled organizations.

With a number of distinct advancements, CNAs throw fresh security challenges. Cloud-native security is therefore a pragmatic approach initiated to secure and deploy applications. Security products, platforms, processes, patterns, practices, and principles that were originally designed to handle the traditional and legacy software solutions are found to be inadequate due to the multiplicity and heterogeneity problems of CNAs. Borderless information flow and dynamism are important properties of CNAs. Thus, cloud-native security is a bigger challenge for software engineers in the days to unfold.

Beginning of Cloud-Native Application Security

Enterprise cloud environments are stuffed with hundreds of physical nodes, which, in turn, can host thousands of pods. Each pod can accommodate one or more containers. These pods are running business workloads with different security requirements. Nodes, pods, and containers are being removed and reconstructed very often. The challenge is how to secure these computational resources and their purposeful interactions to fulfill business processes in a reliable manner. Any security mishap can bring irreparable damage to productivity. Policy establishment and enforcement have to be accelerated and automated. Security controls have two broad categories: East-West (E-W) and North-South (N-S). Egress access control refers to the N-S security on egress. The following are typical use cases of egress access control:

- Configure default-deny without blocking access to essential services
- Permit access to the specific Internet APIs (Slack, Twilio, Watson, etc.)
- Permit access to internal resources in the corporate network (database, VMs, etc.)
- Automatic enforcement of egress policy on VMs as they come up (autoscaling, new node provisioning, etc.)

Enterprising businesses and national governments across the globe are revitalizing and readying for real business transformations through the smart leverage of digitization and digitalization technologies and tools. Cloud-native computing is being touted as one of the digital transformation technologies and key enablers for the desired and delectable transformation. As mentioned earlier, the MSA pattern, DevOps methods, and the containerization paradigm are being pronounced as the key ingredients for producing and running CNAs.

CNAs are generally composed of distributed microservices. Also, for a cloud-native system to be fruitful, there are many distinct participants in the form of application building blocks (microservices), middleware such as event stream processors, message brokers, etc., databases, API gateways, and service meshes. Microservices are dynamic and there may be multiple versions for a microservice. Each microservice and its different versions can run on multiple containers to guarantee high availability. DevOps is for bringing in automation and acceleration while the software is being developed, tested, debugged, delivered, deployed, and improved. That is, by establishing and sustaining a close collaboration between development and operations teams, the field of software engineering is readying for a paradigm shift. DevOps smoothens the rough edges so that features-rich and flexible software products, solutions, and services can reach the intended market quickly.

However, the core and critical aspect of any software package is none other than the security feature. Every facet of any software solution has to be subjected to a variety of deeper investigations in order to pinpoint any security vulnerability at the beginning stage itself. Any compromise or delay in security verification and validation may result in an irreparable situation. Therefore, security team members are being integrated with DevOps pipelines to guarantee the desired security. This is an extremely and deeply connected world. Cyberattacks are on the rise with venom, velocity, and vigorousness. So, security products, solutions, and services are gaining more importance as the IT industry is tending toward the proven, promising, and potential cloud-native paradigm. Let us start with the security threats and vulnerabilities of the Kubernetes platform.

Cloud-Native Security Challenges

There are a few critical security challenges for cloud-native infrastructures and applications. Let us start with the general security concerns of cloud-native systems. Then we move over to container security and from there, we can proceed with the security vulnerabilities of Kubernetes clusters.

Numerous Entities to Secure: In a cloud-native environment, there are multiple processes leveraging different and distributed microservices. In the past, software applications would run on one VM. Now, each process or business functionality (technically speaking, each microservice) is packaged and run in a separate container. For redundancy purposes, several instances of any microservice can be instantiated and run on multiple containers. Microservices communicate and collaborate through network calls. The age-old in-process calls are seeing the sunset. With the surging popularity of serverless computing, applications and services are being partitioned into a collection of functions. Each entity is vulnerable to compromise and needs to be protected throughout its entire life cycle.

The security must be built into the assets, which are to be secured and safe from any internal and external attacks. This has to be applied across layers from OS to the container to containerized application. To protect an application, it is important to understand the data flows and transactions to do an accurate assessment and to ensure its protection from any malicious threats.

The Growing Attack Surface: Some of the cross-cutting concerns and infrastructure services are being added to applications. For example, service mesh implementations take care of the communication and networking aspects of CNAs. Also, a number of common things are getting codified and containerized. Containerization-enablement and container orchestration platforms abstract away several tasks to be configured and automated. Hardware appliances make way for software appliances. Containers and VMs are easily pierced when compared with bare metal (BM) servers. Cloud-native systems may involve public, private, and edge clouds.

There are proprietary and standardized cloud management systems such as OpenStack and Kubernetes manning geographically distributed cloud centers. Cloud architectures are diversifying across local and remote cloud environments. Thus, brewing architectural differences, many moving parts, network accessibility, public discoverability, sharing, and dynamism being explicitly exhibited by CNAs have correspondingly increased the attack surface. Security advisors and experts are therefore required to understand this growing complicated attack surface and accordingly articulate the best-in-class solution approaches.

Dynamic Environments Require Dynamic Security: Software updates and upgrades happen fast and frequently. Thereby software services are deployed more often these days in order to cope up with the fast-changing business sentiments and to fulfill varying aspirations of clients and customers. CNAs are blessed with a new and distinct structure and hence they require an altogether different security approach. Legacy applications are closely tied up with a back-end database but generally each microservice is ordained to have its own database. That is, microservices are self-contained and isolated. And hence microservices can exhibit an autonomous behavior.

Also, cloud-native infrastructures are immutable and hence if there is any alternation initiated or needed, containerized applications are torn down and recreated. IaC and IaD tools are specifically used for modern and massive infrastructure provisioning. IaC tools automate infrastructure provisioning and software deployment and hence it is prudent to integrate security best practices into IaC. Such a thing ensures the protection of resources and reduces the attack surface. Deploying resources first and securing them later may affect application stability. IaC integration helps ensure security during dynamic scaling. You can deploy additional resources and they will have the security baseline integrated into them.

In short, the specific characteristics of CNAs compound the security scenario. Due to the fine-grained service-enablement of software products, solutions, and services, there is a need for multiple components to finding, binding, and leveraging one another for fulfilling complicated and long-running business processes. The added multiplicity and heterogeneity lead to heightened complexity. That is, service environments are becoming highly complex and a variety of security vulnerabilities may sneak in stealthily and cause irreparable damage.

Perimeter Security is Not Sufficient Anymore: Legacy security approaches erect and establishes a firewall around your IT infrastructure. Then it is all about observing and blocking any untoward access emanating from the outside. But with the faster adoption of cloud-native technologies such as containerized applications and serverless functions, perimeter-based security is bound to go away. A web application firewall (WAF) protects functions when they are API gateway-triggered. WAFs do not protect your functions if they are triggered from different event sources, such as cloud storage events, stream processing, and database changes.

Further on, the legacy security products and solutions do not take the much-needed context into consideration and hence their efficacy and accuracy are not to be appreciated much. Scans and perimeter defences lack understanding about the resources they are assessing and protecting. This gap may lead to costly mistakes and false positives.

Thus, the focus shifts from perimeter security to runtime security. While minimizing the attack surface is important, it is also crucial to ensure runtime security. When there is a large codebase to protect, methodically protecting all the code is beset with challenges. Therefore, the runtime protection is insisted as the last line of defence. That is, detecting and nullifying any attack that executes unauthorized code in real time is all about the runtime security.

Cloud-native Security Requires High Fidelity (Hi-Fi) Visibility Plus Context: Enterprise applications are accordingly modernized and migrated to cloud environments. With the uptake of cloud-native computing, software applications are being dissected into a collection of microservices. With containers joining as the most optimal runtime environment for microservices, any reasonably sized IT environments are stuffed with hundreds of microservices and their instances using many containers. Such a turnaround increases the operational and management complexities. Above all, the attack surface has gone up considerably and hence the traditional security methods are found to be inadequate. That is, any dynamic environment needs dynamic security capability. Also, there is a need for deeper visibility to have heightened controllability. Also, the aspect of observability of cloud-native environments is gaining the attention with the availability of observability platform solutions. In nutshell, a centralized administration of distributed resources is being mandated to detect any flawed configurations and conclusions. Such a setup can ensure tighter cloud-native security.

Container Security: Containers package all kinds of software services and applications and this is seen as a noteworthy contribution to the huge success of containers. Such a packaging enables software services to be isolated and this is being seen as the viable mechanism for abstracting applications from their underlying environments. This decoupling allows for easy and consistent deployment of containerized applications across cloud environments (private, public, and edge). Containerization allows development teams to compose enterprise-grade applications easily and quickly and the software deployment happens in an accelerated manner. However, there are a few security issues being associated with containers.

- **Using Insecure Images:** Containers are built either using a parent image or a base image. The issue here is the sanctity and purity of these images.
- **Containers with Privileged Flag:** Containers running with a privileged flag can run with all the capabilities and open up access to the container host. That means if a hacker breaches a container running with the privileged flag, the whole system is bound to collapse. Any

misconfiguration can be used by hackers to threaten the underlying host. Thus, containers have to be clearly isolated from their hosts.

- **Unrestricted Communication Among Containers:** Containers need to find and communicate with others to accomplish any business functionality. In a typical IT environment, the number of containers is on the higher side. Also, containers are generally ephemeral and hence it is quite challenging to implement networking/firewalling rules that adhere to the least privilege principle. The goal is to allow authorized containers to purposefully interact to minimize the attack surface.
- **Running Malicious and Rogue Processes in Containers:** It is imperative to minutely monitor running container processes. The ephemeral nature and frequent failure of containers make monitoring containers difficult. Thus identifying unwanted and malicious processes running in containers is quite tough to do.

The main concerns are enumerated as follows:

1) The security of the container host
2) Container network traffic
3) The security of containerized applications
4) The security of container management software
5) The foundation layers of your application
6) The integrity of the build pipeline

Securing containers is therefore assuming greater importance to having secure CNAs. As containers emerge as the most optimal runtime environment for microservices, any misdemeanor or misbehavior is definitely a thing to be concerned about.

Kubernetes security acquires special significance because any typical Kubernetes environment complies with the distributed architecture. Kubernetes environments are generally dynamic with several moving parts. A lot of automation capabilities are being provided by any implementation of Kubernetes platform standard specifications. The most prominent ones are:

- Automated rollouts and rollbacks
- Service discovery and load balancing
- Storage orchestration
- Secret and configuration management
- Automatic bin packing
- Horizontal scaling
- Self-healing
- Designed for extensibility

Kubernetes Security Threats: Kubernetes is emerging as a key platform for the container world. Containerized applications are being deployed and managed through the Kubernetes platform solution. Kubernetes, with a bevy of advanced and automation capabilities, is all set to play a very vital role in shaping up the vision of the cloud-native era. However, there are certain security challenges being associated with Kubernetes. Kubernetes-managed clusters of physical hosts and VMs are becoming a valuable target for data and/or compute power theft. Cyber actors seeking computational power for reasons such as cryptocurrency mining are drawn toward Kubernetes clusters. Further on, as Kubernetes is the core and central module for cloud environments, cyber actors also target Kubernetes to cause a denial of service (DoS). DoS vulnerabilities can also result from a lack of proper data validation, which would allow an attacker to send data larger than expected or send too many requests in a brief period

Precisely speaking, Kubernetes automates the deployment, monitoring, and maintenance (updates, etc.) of containerized applications. However, keeping Kubernetes secure is where things get trickier.

Supply Chain Risk: This is the risk that an adversary may subvert one or more components that makes up a system. Typically, a system comprises multiple internal and external services. This can include third-party software used to create and manage the Kubernetes cluster. Supply chain risks can affect Kubernetes at multiple levels including:

- **Container/Application Level:** Microservices-centric applications get containerized and made to run on Kubernetes clusters. The application dependencies, the trustworthiness of application developers, and the defence of the application infrastructure are important for ensuring security. A malicious container or application could provide cyber actors with a foothold in the cluster to proceed with their nefarious acts.
- **Infrastructure:** The dependencies of application and hardware infrastructures also matter for tightening the security aspect. Any compromise of systems used as worker nodes or as part of the control plane could provide cyber actors with a handle to decisively attack the cluster.

Malicious Threats: Any standard Kubernetes cluster has to have control and data planes. The control plane exposes APIs for its components to enable external interactions and for cluster management. Malicious actors can leverage these APIs to gain access from a remote location and take advantage of exposed control plane components that do not have appropriate access controls.

Worker nodes in the data plane host the kubelet and kube-proxy service, which are potentially and precariously exploitable by cyber actors. Additionally, worker nodes existing outside of the locked-down control plane can face the heat from cyber actors. Further on, containerized applications are the prime target for cyber actors. A cyber actor can remotely pivot from an already compromised container or Pod to escalate privileges within the cluster toward making irreparable damages to the cluster.

Insider Threats: Individuals from within the organization are given special knowledge and privileges. They can do some misuses and manipulations on Kubernetes clusters. Kubernetes administrators have full control over running containers, and they may execute arbitrary commands inside containerized environments. Containerized application users may have knowledge and credentials to access containerized services in the Kubernetes cluster.

The Emergence of New Attack Vectors: Each Kubernetes pod running one or more containers has a unique IP address for connectivity. This can become a doorway to launch attacks either from external networks or internally. A misconfigured container is another attack vector for attackers to explore weaknesses across. They can connect and check other pods.

Ephemeral Workloads: Containers are spun up and torn down as per the variation in capacity demands. This ephemeral nature of containers renders perimeter and IP address-based security controls less effective. Also, overlay networks and IP address reuse turn out to be a blockade for traceability. Logs and other evidence for forensic investigations get lost when containers are reset in response to a security incident.

Sandbox Limitations: Containers are not separated and saved through a true sandbox like a hypervisor is for VMs. Containers share the host OS that they run on. Thus container security needs a fresh approach. An orchestration layer can secure containerized applications and prevent any attack from spreading to other containers.

Pod-to-pod Communications: Kubernetes natively does not control communication between pods. If a pod is infected or inflicted with malware, there is a need for a competent solution to proactively and pre-emptively detect any deviation in time to curb any inter-pod communication.

Increased Attack Surface: Kubernetes can deploy containers across multiple physical machines and cloud environments. This traffic (east-west) across the pods can increase the attack surface.

Attack Sophistry: Cyberattackers keep increasing their sophistication to coolly evade detection by conventional security tools.

Native security features in Kubernetes are not designed to address these challenges. Even when correctly configured, Kubernetes native security is limited to RBAC to restrict containers' access to server resources. It does not have capabilities to audit and analyze container contents, and detect behavioral abnormalities (privilege escalation, malicious files, etc.) that could signal a threat.

Microservices Security: As widely articulated, microservices maintain a list of common characteristics. They are smart endpoints and dumb pipes, decentralized governance and data management, and infrastructure automation. This new type of highly distributed and dynamic system presents a new set of potential security risks. As with many emerging technologies, the security aspect has to be baked into architecture patterns and design. Further on, security ought to be integrated into the entire development life cycle, so that applications and data remain protected. Microservices contributing to composing CNAs have to be subjected to a variety of security-related verifications and validations in order to eliminate any visible and invisible security holes in code.

MSA is being adopted and adapted across industry verticals to bring agility in software design, development, and deployment. There are well-intended approaches and articulations on how microservices can be secure and safe while evolving at a rapid pace. Here are a few things for ensuring the tightest security for microservices. If individual microservices are safe, then the microservices-centric applications become safe and secure.

Defence in Depth: The days of leveraging a firewall to protect your monolithic application are over. Therefore, the valid and verified recommendation is to go for security enablement at multiple layers and levels. There are downstream and upstream microservices. Each microservice is blessed with its own database. Thus, security controls have to be incorporated in multiple places to guarantee unbreakable security for microservices-centric applications.

Isolation: Each microservice is programmed to be self-contained and hence capable of fulfilling the much-needed autonomic behavior. Microservices can be independently developed, deployed, managed, updated, upgraded, patched, governed, observed, replaced, and retired without impacting other microservices of the CNA. This isolation comes in handy for microservices to be safe and secure. That is, if a microservice is affected with a virus or phishing or malware, or any other cyberattack, it does not percolate or cascade into other microservices in order to bring down the entire system. That is, the loosely or lightly coupled nature of microservices is much appreciated.

Microservices Security Best Practices: Experts and architects have recommended several proven practices for ensuring microservice security. There are best practices for integrating microservices security patterns, and helping teams update their APIs, endpoints, and application data.

API Gateways: Microservices expose their service capabilities/contracts through application programming interfaces (APIs) to the outside world. APIs are primarily for enabling service requestors to leverage service implementations, which sit behind APIs. Microservices are typically distributed and are publicly discoverable and network-accessible. Microservices also find, bind, and collaborate with one another through network calls to produce composite services, which are typically process-aware and business-critical.

APIs are generally vulnerable and hence there is a need for API gateways, which act as a single point of contact to route external requests. API gateways curtail the access, do rate-limiting (throttling), and other middleware services. Potential attacks can be stopped by API gateways.

User Authentication and Authorization: For ensuring microservices security, securing endpoints is critical. User authentication and authorization turn out to be an important aspect of access control. Experts recommend OAuth/OAuth2 standard for user authorization. Authentication can be tightened through multifactor authentication.

Scan Dependencies: There are geographically distributed microservices participating toward CNAs. Microservices also rely upon a host of third-party services. Most of the third-party software are open source and hence if a dependency carries a security hole, then the microservice security is in danger. It is therefore important to track third-party software products including all of their dependencies. This dependency-scanning helps detect and destroy any security vulnerability as quickly as possible.

Cloud-native security must solve the context problem as well. An effective cloud-native security process has to gather the details about suspicious activity usage. There is a need to know decision-enabling details such as IP, destination, protocol, user and group, content and application function, etc. It is clear that the traditionally applied security practices, strategies, and technologies are no match for the sophisticated threats and the increasingly hybrid IT.

The aspect of cloud-native security is of particular concern because cloud-native workloads are being used by many businesses and individuals across the globe. Cloud-native systems are typically made out of multiple services (collocated and distributed). A security hole/vulnerability in one service (dependency) may cascade to other components to bring down the entire system. Further on, a CNA relies on scores of software libraries and dependencies. Many of these contributors are open-source software and are not generally subjected to a deeper and decisive verification and validation. Misconfigurations are the primary cause of cloud-native security issues. Thus, every participant of cloud-native systems has to be subjected to a variety of investigations in order to pinpoint not only security vulnerabilities but also performance bottlenecks in order to ensure the tightest security and safety for CNAs and data.

In a nutshell, CNAs have to be extremely fault-tolerant, adaptive, and accommodative in order to be found, bound, and used beneficially with all the confidence and clarity. The security issues have to be identified as early as possible so that appropriate fixes can be determined and deployed in order to ward off any security imperfections.

Capabilities of Cloud-Native Security Solutions

Any worthwhile cloud-native security strategy has to take several things into account. Security consultants point out the following cloud-native security considerations while forming and firming up cloud-native security strategies and implementations. All the key ingredients of any cloud-native system have to be individually and collectively security-strengthened to deliver highly secured and safe cloud-native systems.

1) **Continuous Security:** As articulated earlier, continuous delivery of software services is being fulfilled through DevOps toolsets. For the cloud-native era, technocrats recommend continuous security. Web-scale and customer-facing applications such as B2C e-commerce, social

media, professional networking, etc., are making hundreds of deployments every day in order to meet up with fast-changing business sentiments and customer expectations. In these types of complex environments, security-enablement activities have to be seamless, lightweight, and embedded into service deployment pipelines. Thus, the current DevOps model, which facilitates continuous integration, delivery, and deployment, has to be substantially enhanced in order to accommodate continuous security, which is very much demanded in the cloud-native era.

2) **Cloud Workload Protection:** Traditionally, enterprise security is ensured by securing the endpoints, segmenting the network, and protecting the perimeter. But in a cloud-native environment, it is not possible to rely upon fixed routes, gateways, network perimeters, etc. Cloud workloads are more exposed than ever and hence the quantity and quality of cyberattacks are on the rise. Therefore, shifting focus to securing cloud environments and their workloads is the way forward to keep attackers and hackers at bay.

3) **Run-time Detection at Speed and Scale:** Microservices are dynamic in actions and reactions. Also, service delivery, deployment, and upgrade are being performed continuously. Therefore, security monitoring has to be continuous and attack detection has to be completed proactively in order to plan correct countermeasures in time. Also, any fault or failure of a microservice has to be identified pre-emptively and isolated and should not be allowed to cascade into other microservices. Such a facility avoids downing the system. In short, fault detection has to happen at business speed.

Microservices are technology-agnostic and hence they can be implemented using any programming language as long as the APIs are kept intact. There are BM servers, VMs, and containers to host and run microservices. There is a myriad of enabling platforms, frameworks, and libraries for producing and running CNAs. Further on, there are cloud operating and management platforms. Simply speaking, public and private clouds are being activated through heterogeneous technologies and tools. In such divisive and diverse environments, it is not straightforward to establish and enforce security policies. Thus, securing CNAs and services needs breakthrough solutions and approaches leveraging cutting-edge technologies and tools. There are best practices being published by experienced hands. Cloud-native security platforms (CNSPs) are emerging and evolving fast in order to ensure unbreakable security for CNAs.

Cloud-Native Application Security Procedures

As articulated earlier, there is not an iota of doubt that the cloud-native idea brings up fresh approaches and novelties toward producing agile and adaptive software solutions and services. However, there are some significant challenges to be surmounted through advanced technological solutions. When massive-scale and monolithic applications become microservices-centric, the operational complexity attains a serious proposition because several different and distributed microservices are involved and invoked to accomplish business processes and goals. With heightened operational complexity, gaining end-to-end visibility of all the contributing and corresponding microservices is a difficult affair. Understanding which microservice talks to which another one at what point of time is definitely beset with challenges and concerns. Unauthorized service interactions may prove risky. Thus, deeper visibility, controllability, and observability of cloud-native systems are very vital for attaining the intended success of the cloud-native paradigm. Security is another widely deliberated challenge of CNAs.

As indicated previously, CNAs are typically made up of autonomous, dynamic, self-contained, and independently developable and deployable microservices. Also, microservice deployments are fast and frequent with the faster maturity and stability of enterprise-grade DevOps toolkits. A cloud-native system consists of man-moving parts. There are service meshes, API gateways, event stores and sources, message brokers and queues, event stream engines, etc. The decentralized and distributed nature of CNAs clearly indicates the existence and emergence of several known and unknown security drawbacks.

There may be many security vulnerabilities and holes. The current and classical security approaches are found to be inadequate in the cloud-native era. Security experts and researchers insist on fresh approaches and algorithms to ward off cloud-native security threats. Precisely speaking, cloud-native software engineering may be dexterous and strategic, but the security implications seem to be problematic. Security consultants and architects seriously contemplate breakthrough security solutions to mitigate cloud-specific cyberattacks. Therefore, the important aspects of cloud-native security strategy formation, implementation planning, approaches, algorithms, and tools are getting greater attention from the concerned. This chapter is fully dedicated to articulating and accentuating the key security cloud-native concerns and how they can be surmounted. There are CNPs, chaos engineering techniques and tools, cloud workload protection solutions, etc. Further on, based on the experience and expertise gained, security pioneers have come out with a list of cloud-native security best practices. All these are to be deliberated in detail in this chapter.

Enterprises are keenly leveraging cutting-edge technologies to compose and deploy CNAs securely at scale. Cloud-native security is very much indispensable for the cloud-native idea to flourish. Thus, there is a clarion call for proper nourishment from security organizations and standard agencies. Experts believe that cloud-native computing needs a fresh view and approach to security threats and solutions. Cloud-native security is, therefore, a modern and pragmatic approach that includes concepts like zero trust and defence in depth (DiD).

Due to microservices and containers, CNAs could be constructed and released to production environments quickly compared to previous application models. However, the cloud-native model opens up fresh security and operational challenges. Conventional security processes and tools are found to be insufficient for ensuring the tightest security for CNAs, which are inherently dynamic and enabling a borderless paradigm. Thus a major portion of cloud-native security is lying with CNA security. All kinds of application vulnerabilities and security holes have to be pinpointed and remedied during application development. The security checks have to be holistic and backed into every task associated with software development. In order to assist and augment software architects and engineers in designing and producing secured CNAs, a prominent aspect of any worthwhile cloud-security strategy is to employ competent security platforms. There are cloud-native security principles, patterns, practices, and processes.

Existing security tools are found to be inadequate to handle the speed, size, and dynamic network environment of CNAs. Previously, perimeter security methods are sufficient to secure IT infrastructure (data centers and server farms). These employ static network configurations to regulate control and traffic flow. This could prevent any unauthorized external traffic to penetrate internal server machines. There are firewalls, intrusion detection and prevention systems for safeguarding infrastructure modules. But in the case of cloud-native systems, the notion of perimeter security ceases to be a worthwhile effort. Because cloud-native services and applications are highly dynamic and publicly accessible through competent APIs. Multiple geographically distributed microservices have to interact to fulfill business processes. CNAs could potentially employ a bevy of computing, networking, and storage resources. There are highly optimized runtimes including VMs, containers, and serverless functions. Scanning artefacts and configuration files at runtime is critical to keeping up a strong security posture.

Securing Cloud-Native Applications

Cloud-native security necessitates a refocusing on security that operates in step with the overall cloud-native strategy of an organization. Cloud-native applications must be secured in an application context, and the approach needs to address the changes in the teams, processes, and infrastructure model that build and operate cloud-native applications. Thus, a key emphasis of cloud-native security needs to be cloud-native application security – ensuring that vulnerabilities are identified and remediated during development. The approach must be holistic, and security should be baked in throughout the software development life cycle (SDLC).

Developers should be empowered by a security platform to focus on delivering a design that meets the business goals and utilizes cloud-native principles, while at the same time recognizing that as more and more of our infrastructure is defined during application development, the development team acquires responsibility for ensuring that code is secure. If cloud architecture is not a first-class consideration in every discussion and design decision, then the goal of building a truly CNA may fall short.

Once the foundation of the design has been laid, application and infrastructure coding are likely to begin. At this stage, it is critical to begin testing the code as early as possible in the secure software development life cycle (SSDLC). As alluded to earlier in the article, the legacy, single-pronged approach of static analysis is no longer sufficient. Static application security testing (SAST), dynamic application security testing (DAST), interactive application security testing (IAST), and mobile application security testing (MAST) comprise just some of the array of tests that should be performed against cloud-native application code.

Securing the cloud-native infrastructure of an application presents unique challenges as well. IaC configurations result in live infrastructure being deployed, with developers often writing infrastructure and application code in tandem. Security tools that can address this unique challenge are needed, and should seamlessly integrate with existing workflows, providing insights and remediation advice directly to the developer. This typically means surfacing security information directly into IDEs and enabling local testing through CLI tools.

In addition to providing security insights into the local developer environment, cloud-native security tooling should also be integrated into each phase of the software life cycle. Automated scanning in source code management systems and scanning of derived artefacts such as container images through CI/CD systems should be a priority. The results of these integration scans should also provide remediation advice to enable developers to easily make prioritization decisions.

CNAs could potentially employ a bevy of different computing resources and runtimes, including VMs, containers, and serverless functions. Scanning artefacts and configuration at runtime is critical to maintaining a strong security posture when dealing with cloud-native environments.

Pillars of Cloud-Native Security

An effective cloud-native security model addresses threats across every level of a workflow. Typically, the security aspect is being focused on code, container, cluster, and cloud.

Code: Scanning, debugging, and clearing out all kinds of security vulnerabilities in source code are the first and foremost steps to building secure CNAs. There are several security holes creeping into source code knowingly or unknowingly during software development. SQL injection and cross-site scripting (XSS) are well-known security attacks. As indicated before, there are testing solutions such as source code analysis (static and dynamic) to clean up the code.

Container: This is a widely discussed topic. When the industry understood the huge benefits of containerization, container usage went up significantly. All kinds of software solutions are containerized and deposited in container image repositories (private and public). Some container images are unscrupulously created and added into image repositories to facilitate security attacks on container hosts. Therefore, it is made mandatory to fully scan container images before they get instantiated into containerized applications. Hackers could introduce malware into container images. There have been damaging security attacks on containers. Thereafter, there came a number of container security products and solutions in plenty. Experts also published a variety of best practices to have trustworthy containers. Without an iota of doubt, containerization is the key motivation for the huge success of the cloud-native paradigm. So, it is extremely critical to have highly secure applications and containers, which host the applications. There are suggestions such as minimizing the use of privileged containers, strengthening container isolation, continuous vulnerability scanning for container images, and certificate signing for images to substantially improve container security.

Cluster: In the Kubernetes world, one or more containers are being accommodated in a pod. Multiple pods are being utilized in a node (physical/virtual machine). Now many nodes are clustered to form clusters to run enterprise-scale containerized applications. Kubernetes is the container orchestration platform for deploying and managing containerized applications in an automated manner. Kubernetes has one or more master nodes on which the control plane runs on. And there are several worker nodes. The complete control of worker nodes rests with the control plane. The configuration files, policies, and other enablers are made to run on a control plane to flexibly and fruitfully monitor, measure, and manage applications hosted in worker nodes. The security best practices for Kubernetes clusters are as follows: (https://kubernetes.io/docs/concepts/security/overview/).

- All access to the Kubernetes control plane is not allowed publicly on the Internet and the control plane is controlled by network access control lists (NACLs) and restricted to the set of IP addresses needed to administer the cluster.
- Nodes should be configured to only accept connections (via NACL) from the control plane on the specified ports, and they accept connections for services in Kubernetes of type NodePort and LoadBalancer. These nodes should not be exposed on the public Internet entirely.
- Access to etcd, which is the datastore of Kubernetes, should be limited to the control plane only. It is recommended to use etcd over TLS and encrypt all storage at rest. And since etcd holds the state of the entire cluster (including Secrets), its disk should especially be encrypted at rest.

It is extremely critical for security teams to adopt security best practices and develop a threat model that focuses particularly on the Kubernetes layer and its components.

Clouds: Without any doubt, cloud security is the most prominent barrier for mission-critical businesses to embrace cloud technology comprehensively. Of course, besides enforcing physical security, ensuring the cloud infrastructure security lies with CSPs. Kubernetes is an advanced platform solution being deployed on physical machines or VMs. There is an API server, which is touted as the key module of the control plane of Kubernetes. This is the central and core layer for users and external services to communicate with any Kubernetes cluster. Any vulnerability in this layer ultimately affects Kubernetes-specific services and microservices-centric applications hosted in the Kubernetes cluster.

Cloud-Native Security: Best Practices

For facing cloud-native security issues with all the confidence, there are several solution approaches. Cloud-native security best practices are being popularized by security experts based on their project-based learning. In this section, we focus on container and Kubernetes-specific best practices and then look into the cloud-native best practices.

Kubernetes Security Best Practices

As reported earlier, the Kubernetes platform plays a very vital role in catapulting CNAs. However, security is important to reap all the originally expressed benefits of Kubernetes. Different security approaches ought to be applied for each of the three phases of an application life cycle: build, deploy, and runtime (https://www.vmware.com/topics/glossary/content/kubernetes-security).

Kubernetes natively comes in with a number of security-enablement facilities and features. Because of the immutability nature, application containers are typically not patched or updated. Instead, fresh container images are being created and deployed instantaneously. This enables strict version control and permits rapid rollbacks if a vulnerability is uncovered in new code. However, since individual pods are transient and ephemeral, the ever-changing runtime environment can present major challenges for Kubernetes security professionals. Applications and APIs to other applications and services are constantly in flux. This presents an opportunity for hackers to plan and execute their attack strategy. There are security tools specific to Kubernetes. These tools come in handy in accelerating the realization of error-free code. They provide digital signatures for a level of trust for code and facilitate visibility and transparency not only in code but also in configuration details. The tools also prevent ingress (incoming connection) or egress (outbound connection) of information to unsecure services.

The top Kubernetes security vulnerabilities during the build phase are using code from untrusted sources. As told earlier, container images may be corrupted. The second aspect is that during the container image formation for an enterprise-scale application, developers may not focus on optimization. That is, developers have to choose base images, which are not bloated. Otherwise, adding other application modules on bloated base images subsequently results in a bloated image for the final application. The point is that developers should carefully eliminate unnecessary packages, libraries, and shells that could be easily compromised.

As per Kubernetes experts, the well-known Kubernetes security best practices during deployment are as follows:

- **Granting Necessary Privileges Only:** It is prudent to keep privileges to a bare minimum and to mount only the secrets that a task requires at that point of time. This is to sharply shrink the attack surface.
- **Isolating Applications in the Cluster Through Namespaces:** Namespaces is the proven method to keep resources and teams separated from each other.
- **Preventing Lateral Motion Within The Cluster:** Use policies that segment the network to prevent any lateral movement of an attack within the cluster.
- **Stopping Unauthorized Access:** Ensure role-based access controls (RBACs) are properly configured to limit access.

The top Kubernetes security vulnerabilities during runtime are as follows:

- **Nullifying Any Infrastructure Attack:** During runtime, Kubernetes infrastructure elements including the API server, etcd, and controllers present their own attack surfaces. Thus, limiting access is the way forward.
- **Mitigating the Complexity:** The ongoing health of a Kubernetes cluster has many moving parts. Compromised containers must be quickly identified, isolated, stopped, and replaced with healthy ones while the source of the attack is located and remediated.

Strengthening Kubernetes Security: The first and foremost defence is to use Namespaces, enable SELinux, use least-privilege access control, regularly update system patches, verify configurations against Center for Internet Security (CIS) benchmarks, etc. However, without proper detection of threats, organizations could inadvertently be granting unauthorized access to Kubernetes clusters, applications, and customer data. The best practices are:

1) Ensure adequate monitoring to flag unauthorized access to Kubernetes cluster by processes and users
2) Provide adequate visibility into communication across containers and pods to detect suspicious traffic
3) Ensure file integrity at the service and application layers to defend against malicious software
4) Provide process-level visibility in containers and pods to identify a suspicious chain of events

Thus, securing Kubernetes components and clusters is essential for fulfilling the security requirements of cloud-native systems.

Securing IaC Scripts: DevOps engineers are heavily using IaC tools like Terraform in the cloud-native era for provisioning diverse IT infrastructure modules. That is, large-scale infrastructure provisioning is being automated through machine-readable code rather than cumbersome and time-consuming manual activities.

With IaC, configuration files are being created with all the details about the infrastructure. This is easy to edit and distribute these configuration specifications. With such a templatized approach, you can provision the same environment every time. By codifying and documenting configuration specifications, IaC clearly aids the hard task of CM and helps avoid any kind of misrepresentation of configurations. Automating the task of infrastructure provisioning by leveraging competent IaC tools means that developers do not need to manually provision and manage BM servers, VMs, operating systems, load balancers, firewalls, databases, and other infrastructure modules each time they develop or deploy an application. There are several benefits being accrued out of IaC tools.

1) **Faster Speed and Consistency:** A code-based approach makes infrastructure provisioning easier and faster. This standardization ensures infrastructure consistency.
2) **Efficient Software Development Life Cycle:** As infrastructure provisioning becomes more easy, automated, and consistent, developers can focus more on adding application capabilities. IaC tools help script code, which can be used multiple times to sharply reduce time and talent requirements while gaining complete control.
3) **Reduced Management Overhead:** Cloud center administrators have less load on governing and managing compute, storage, networking, and other resources such as software infrastructures. More details can be found on this page https://www.cloudbolt.io/blog.

Thus, IaC tools play a very vital role in provisioning large amounts of infrastructure with comparatively less effort. IaC configurations automatically result in live infrastructure being deployed. We have been fiddling with software programming these days, but hardware programming is seeing the grandiose reality these days. Thus, it is critically important that configuration scripts are fully secured. That is, the security of the cloud-native infrastructure of CNAs has to be secured. This greatly contributes to cloud-native security. The trend is that the security responsibility of IT operations is moved into the responsibility of application security. Therefore, developers have more responsibility in securing the aforementioned IT components besides securing business workloads.

Container Security Best Practices

Checking Container Images: Having understood the unique benefits being offered by containerization, all kinds of software products and solutions are methodically containerized and stocked in public or private image repositories. Software engineers can choose and use base images from these repositories to develop full-fledged applications. Container images ought to be scanned meticulously to eliminate any kind of security vulnerabilities in images. Especially the source of the images has to be verified. Any unwanted and unauthorized modification of images also has to be checked. It is prudent and paramount to scan images so that any kind of security holes, vulnerabilities, and threats can be found pre-emptively and addressed.

Further on, in the recent past, we are reading and hearing more about serverless computing. That is, IT infrastructure and resource management tasks are delegated to CSPs. With the faster maturity and stability of serverless computing platforms, cloud operations are seeing deeper automation. Serverless features further security woes. Cyber attackers look out for vulnerabilities in containers and serverless functions. Also they try to get misconfiguration details of cloud infrastructure so that they can easily access entities that contain sensitive information. Hackers can then use the stolen information to escalate privileges and compromise other entities.

Enterprise CI/CD toolkits are being increasingly used in conjunction with containerized microservices-centric applications and container orchestration platforms. Such an integration accelerates and automates application development, testing, and release activities. That is, continuous integration, delivery, and deployment of software services and applications are being simplified and speeded up substantially. The worrying point here is that the most important security aspect is not given its prominent place. But for the deeply connected world, security experts and pioneers mandate incorporating security checks at the beginning of the software life cycle. By scanning for image vulnerabilities, secrets, and malware early in the development process, developers can participate in enforcing the tightest security for containerized applications and infrastructures.

Applying Perimeter Security at the Function and Container Level: Large-scale software applications are partitioned into many microservices and serverless functions to reap the benefits of the longstanding mantra of "divide and conquer." Such a disintegration brings in a number of business and technical advantages. Massive applications are subdivided into a dynamic array of microservices, which are self-contained to be autonomous, independently developable and deployable, horizontally deployable, publicly discoverable, network-accessible, interoperable, and composable. Precisely speaking, microservices are the best-in-class and optimized software building block for creating enterprise-class software packages and programs. Lately, with serverless computing, applications are disaggregated into a collection of functions, which get triggered and activated by events emanating from different sources.

This gives attackers a larger space for initiating security attacks. As noted earlier, APIs are front-end microservices and serverless functions. There are API and application security tools for ensuring unbreakable and impenetrable security. Perimeter security is established and enforced at the functional level. These tools help in identifying functions that are triggered by a different source than usual and monitoring for anomalies in event triggers.

In containerized environments, it is important to activate security measures at multiple levels. There are container orchestration platforms (control and worker nodes), containers, pods, nodes, and clusters. Kubernetes is a declarative platform and is empowered with security features. Kubernetes is capable of isolating nodes, limiting and monitoring traffic between containers and using third-party authentication for the API server.

Minimal Roles and Privileges: There are access permissions and privileges. As there are many moving parts in a cloud-native environment, there are numerous and frequent interactions between cloud-native resources. The configurability facility to assign a unique set of permissions to each serverless function or container comes in handy in enforcing tighter security. If you are able to define granular permissions for serverless functions and containers, stricter access controls ensuring security. Thus, enacting controlled access to various CNA infrastructure modules is the way forward for cloud-native security.

Securing Application Dependencies: Microservices-centric applications comprise services with many upstream and downstream services. That is, CNAs carry several dependencies. Similarly, serverless functions too have many dependencies. Applications also depend upon software packages. To protect your application's dependencies, you need automated tools that include a comprehensive database of open-source software packages and their vulnerabilities. Cloud-native orchestration platforms have ingrained the capability to trigger application security activities during the development and composition process. By continuously running these tools, it is possible to prevent the inclusion of vulnerable packages in a function or container running in production environments.

Cloud-Native Security Best Practices

Security experts and professionals have come out with a series of best practices based on their education, expertise, and experience.

Gaining a Deeper Visibility: Visibility is very vital to have tighter control over anything. We generally have good visibility of our applications and services when they are run and delivered through our local cloud environments. But that is not the case when things are running in third-party, faraway, online, and on-demand clouds. The visibility of public cloud services is less and the control also goes to CSPs. That is the main reason why public cloud security is still being questioned by many. Not to be brought down by security vulnerabilities, mission-critical applications such as financial services are still being held back in private environments. Compliance is another problem when applications are deployed in public clouds. With the number of microservices and their instances going up significantly, tracking each one of them is a complicated activity. Thus, security monitoring has to be deeper and each worthwhile asset has to be consistently monitored and fully tracked from its inception till its retirement.

Gain Visibility into Context: Data alone does not fulfill the purpose. Context is vital for the accurate identification of error/fault/risk. By embedding context details into application security, it is possible to reduce both false negatives and false positives. For example, a given activity can be a suspicious act in one situation, whereas it is entirely innocuous in another. By combining context information, detecting malicious activities is quite easy and elegant.

Further on, cloud-native security must understand users' intent to detect malicious behavior with more accuracy. The recent advances in machine learning (ML) algorithms come in handy in building comprehensive and compact profiles of what constitutes normal use. Such profiles help to automatically find any deviant behavior.

Just having application visibility is not sufficient anymore. There is a need for deeper visibility of all the application requirements including software and hardware infrastructure modules, middleware solutions, and data management products. All kinds of operational, metrics, logs, and trace data of all these participants have to be aggregated and analyzed with a well-defined purpose. There are real-time and streaming data analytics platforms to extract actionable insights out of all kinds of application, platform, and infrastructure data. The details of performance bottlenecks, health conditions, security attacks, and vulnerabilities can be collected and crunched to emit true situational awareness, which, in turn, provides real-time insights into every data flow and audit trail.

Diverse Threats: With pervasive connectivity, more powerful attack types emerge and evolve. Newer attacks such as account takeover can be performed using a variety of tactics and techniques such as phishing, brute force botnet attacks, purchasing user credentials from the dark web, and even digging through discarded trash for confidential details.

Thus, the threat landscape expands fast and hence creative defensive approaches are needed to safeguard business-critical information. The famous cloud forensics become irrelevant when there is a massive amount of security-related data. Thus, security data analytics using big and real-time data analytics methods and ML algorithms is mandated to unearth all kinds of security threats in a proactive and pre-emptive manner. Besides data analytics, intrusion detection and prevention, threat modeling, and intelligence capabilities are needed to secure sensitive data falling into the hands of evildoers and hackers.

MITRE ATT&CK (https://attack.mitre.org/) is a globally accessible knowledge base of adversary tactics and techniques based on real-world observations. The ATT&CK knowledge base is used as a foundation for the development of specific threat models and methodologies in the private sector, in government, and in the cybersecurity product and service community. With the creation of ATT&CK, MITRE is fulfilling its mission to solve problems for a safer world – by bringing communities together to develop more effective cybersecurity. ATT&CK is open and available to any person or organization for use at no charge.

Detecting and mitigating the risks of cyberattacks is the prime challenge for security experts and architects. There are detection methods and enabling security frameworks. By smartly leveraging them, security professionals can fulfill their assignments with all the care, clarity, and confidence.

Misconfigurations: This happens when a cloud-hosted application or tool is not configured correctly. This opens up for data breaches and leaks and hence proper configuration has to be performed across the components (local and remote) of any cloud system. Cloud Posture Management (CPM) software provides rulesets and automatic remediation ensuring that all systems are configured properly and at all times.

Shared Responsibility for Security: Cloud-native systems involve software builders, DevOps professionals, site reliability engineers (SREs), and security experts. Developers have to embed the right and relevant security features in their code. Similarly, DevOps teams have to incorporate security checks and scanning into their activities. Security teams should know how software applications are being developed, tested, and deployed. They also should know the tools being used during software development and deployment. These details help them add security in a holistic and harmonized manner. It is all about identifying, assigning, and sharing ownership of maintaining security for individual components of a cloud-native system. This shared responsibility is to become complicated in multi-cloud environments.

It is clear that different teams have to team up in addressing security challenges and concerns with all the alacrity and astuteness to produce and run secured CNAs. In short, the cloud-native paradigm has all the ingredients and wherewithal to fulfill the real digital transformation goals for worldwide organizations. In nutshell, the cloud follows a shared responsibility model, where ownership of workload security is still with the customer. The different security options include implementation of RBAC, Pod security, network security, and application secrets management.

Multilayered Security – This is meticulously monitoring all layers of the network to identify and mitigate potential threats individually. There are enabling tools and best practices to initiate counterattacks alongside planning contingency in the event of a compromise.

Cloud-Agnostic Security: Increasingly enterprises across the world prefer multi-cloud capability to avoid the problem of vendor lock-in. This is done by leveraging a common CNSP for multiple CSPs. This facility gives a single pane of glass of security best practices to be followed by multiple parties and distributed teams to streamline monitoring, compliance, and disaster recovery.

DevSecOps: Once the CNA design is done precisely and perfectly, then application and infrastructure coding can start with a well-laid foundation. It is also critical to start testing coding early. Experts have pointed out that the legacy testing approach comprising static code analysis is no more adequate in the cloud-native era. Instead, SAST, DAST, IAST, and MAST are being recommended to strengthen application security. Other security measures include automated scanning of source code and scanning and curation of container images, which are the popular sources of CNAs. That means security testing is being incorporated in the early phases in order to pinpoint any error early. Thereby remediation actions can be taken by developers themselves.

In summary, CNAs lack fixed perimeters and hence the conventional static firewalls may find it difficult to secure CNAs. There are several ways to secure CNAs. These include shifting security left, applying perimeter security at the function and container level, enforcing minimal roles and privileges, securing application dependencies and leveraging shared responsibility for security. The cloud infrastructure's agility and elasticity, the service composability and configurability, and the application scalability make threat detection a difficult proposition. Establishing and enforcing security policies in any highly dynamic cloud environment is not an easy thing to do. Therefore, security experts and exponents recommend fresh approaches to secure cloud-native systems.

The Emergence of Cloud-Native Security Products and Platforms

Having understood the strategic significance of setting up and sustaining highly secure CNAs, there came a number of cloud-native security products (CNSPs). But these are generally point solutions. That is, they could solve one or other part of the security problem. They are not complete, comprehensive and compact. The point here is that they are not able to collect all the right information from all the participating components to take accurate decisions. This has led enterprise IT teams to explore and experiment with multiple security solutions. Employing different tools for guaranteeing cloud-native security is tedious, error-prone, and time-consuming.

Security pandits and purists hence insisted on unified CNSPs. CNSPs typically share context about infrastructure, platforms (development and deployment), users, data, and application workloads across cloud environments to provide heightened security. They also

- provide unified visibility for security, development, and operations teams
- offer advanced capabilities to proactively respond to threats and insightfully protect CNAs
- remediate vulnerabilities and misconfigurations consistently across the entire build-deploy-run life cycle.

In nutshell, CNSPs provide the tightest security for cloud-native workloads and platforms across cloud environments. CNSPs epitomize the benefits of a cloud-native strategy and ensures agility, adaptivity, and extensibility. CNSPs are being mandated to fulfill the goals of digital transformation initiatives.

Cloud-Native Security Platforms (CNSPs): The entire IT industry is highly optimistic about the flourishing idea of cloud-native computing. The deeper automation being brought in by the cloud-native phenomenon is being welcome across industry verticals. Besides IT professionals, business executives are showing keenness in embracing the cloud-native paradigm. However, as articulated earlier, security is the number one issue for cloud resources and assets. The security issues being widely reported for cloud environments are being further expanded to have additional security challenges in the ensuing cloud-native era. Having understood the varied implications of cloud-native security hitches and hurdles, worldwide product and tool vendors in conjunction with security researchers and experts have built and released CNSPs.

CNSPs share context about infrastructure modules, platforms, databases, and applications to substantially enhance cloud-native security. These security platforms are being ordained with a number of flexible and futuristic features.

- Provide unified visibility for developers, security, and IT operations teams
- Respond to a multitude of security threats to protect CNAs
- Remediate security vulnerabilities and misconfigurations insightfully during the end-to-end application life cycle

In the past, organizations had to buy and install several security products to ward off different attacks at different layers and resources. Stitching together disparate security solutions to give a unified posture and enforce consistent policies across is not an easy task anymore. However, CNSPs bring a kind of security, stability, and semblance across hybrid and multi-cloud environments. Organizations can choose the right configuration for optimally running any business workload without bothering about how to integrate the various cloud solutions with security features.

Security platforms come in handy in smoothly integrating these into CNAs. As inscribed earlier, ultimately CNAs are to land in cloud environments and hence any discussion on CNA development strategy, planning and implementation has to center around the enigmatic cloud architecture. CNSPs natively enable agility and flexibility.

Key Properties of Cloud-Native Security Platforms

Security products and tools are very important considering the serious security consequences of CNAs. When the cloud-native paradigm is picking up fast, CNSPs are emerging from security product vendors. The key features and functionalities are described later.

Automated detection and response are mandated for ensuring the tightest security for cloud-native services, applications, and infrastructures. In the recent past, chaos engineering principles and tools are fervently used to inject faults into software applications in order to understand and unearth hidden security vulnerabilities. This proactive security experimentation goes a long way in eliminating catastrophic errors. This process is primarily performed while software packages and libraries are run in production environments.

Observability and Analytics: This is emerging as the most important step in safeguarding cloud-native security. Software applications are upgraded every few seconds. Hence, the traditional application performance monitoring and management platform solutions are found to be insufficient. Thus, there came advanced observability platforms in order to guarantee high performance, scalability, and reliability for CNAs. By subjecting all kinds of observed data to a variety of deeper investigations, actionable insights can be derived in time in order to initiate safety and security measures with all seriousness and sagacity. Thus, the arrival of observability platforms and the solidity of data analytics methods are being seen as a positive signal toward the fulfilment of security goals. Deeper visibility is required for effective controllability of any system.

Security tools ought to be integrated with automation and orchestration tools. As articulated earlier, the Kubernetes solution contributes to a powerful cloud and container orchestration platform. There are several automated tools emerging to support Kubernetes in its complex assignment of shepherding and sustaining containerized workloads. There are managed services being provided by public CSPs. Thus, security has become an inseparable part of cloud-native architecture.

Modern Detection: Detection in a traditional security operations center (SOC) is based on the investigation and analysis of alerts and event logs. This becomes tedious and tough when there are several moving parts such as microservices and their instances running in redundant containers, message brokers and queues, etc. A typical SOC may see thousands of alerts and terabytes of logs per day. Manually managing such a humongous number of alerts, notifications, and outliers is a difficult proposition. Therefore, an automated detection process is being recommended in order to adroitly handle alerts and identify threats. Modern detection is about leveraging a system of tools, programs, and automated workflows to rapidly identify threats and act on them with all the alacrity and sagacity.

For instance, one component of a detection program is the automatic contextualization of alerts. This is made possible by pulling relevant information from various endpoints, network logs, Active Directory, threat intelligence feeds, etc. Another feature is to form a rule to automatically trigger a second-factor authentication workflow or force a password reset if a risky event is detected. Thus, establishing and enforcing threat detection rules are vital. Also, detection workflows are complex and may involve and impact multiple teams and infrastructure. You should employ integration testing principles to ensure the quality and reliability of detection workflows. As software developers encapsulate well-understood tasks into "subroutines," the frequently executed detection workflows can be codified into automated tools to improve the much-needed efficiency. These codified tools have to be centralized, deposited, and maintained. Efficacy metrics for rules and detectors should be tracked to allow continuous improvement.

The detection infrastructure needs continuous improvement. This is achieved by establishing feedback loops with infrastructure components, security devices, and even with different teams and users. Detection technology has to handle all kinds of cloud infrastructure components like BM servers/virtual machines/containers, serverless, and microservices. In the subsequent sections, we are to discuss the security platforms and products.

Cloud-native security tools have gradually evolved from rudimentary collections of multiple tools and dashboards to well-defined and integrated platforms that consider all layers of the ecosystem together. A CNSP focuses on the following elements of a technology stack.

- **Resource Inventory:** The security platform maintains all sorts of asset logs in the SDLC and keeps track of all the changes to facilitate automatic resource management.
- **Network Security:** This is accomplished by ingesting logs of traffic flow directly from the deployment platforms and by developing a deep understanding of cloud-native firewall rules to scan and monitor network threats. ML algorithms come in handy here.
- **Compliance Management:** This feature monitors security posture and compliance.
- **Data Security:** This utilizes out-of-the-box classification rules to scan for malware, monitor regulatory compliance, and ensure data compliance across deployment environments.

- **Workload Security:** This secures application workloads by proactively mitigating runtime threats.
- **Identity and Access Management (IAM)** administers robust access and authentication framework to secure user accounts as the first line of defence by leveraging multiple third-party tools.
- **Automatic Detection, Identification, and Remediation:** A robust threat model comes in handy in automatic threat detection, identifying the threat details and then doing the necessary remediation quickly. Forming a sophisticated threat model is essential.
- **Vulnerability Management:** This identifies and secures vulnerable points of the entire stack.

Modern CNSPs combine automation, intelligence, ML, and threat detection to mitigate security gaps. Security solutions for CNAs must satisfy the following functional requirements:

- Provide authentication and authorization for cloud administrators and developers, applications, and assets
- Provide network isolation, protection, and secure connectivity for cloud workloads and IT services.
- Protect against distributed denial-of-service (DDoS) attacks on cloud applications
- Ensure complete separation and isolation of microservices
- Protect data at rest, in transit, and in usage
- Automated scanning of infrastructure modules and applications for vulnerability identification
- Patching, updating, and upgrading of applications' resources
- Capture, store, and audit all cloud APIs and their invocations for audit and compliance purposes
- Ensure central monitoring and management of distributed applications to gain deeper visibility for effective controllability

Benefits of Cloud-Native Security Platforms: Modern CNSPs combine automation, orchestration, data analytics, and threat detection intelligence to pinpoint and mitigate security gaps and holes even in highly distributed cloud applications. Besides contributing to a robust security framework, some additional benefits of adopting a CNSP include:

- **Improved Visibility and Monitoring:** We have already discussed the importance of heightened visibility for better controllability. CNSPs enable early and continuous monitoring and testing across all phases including continuous integration, delivery, deployment, feedback, and improvement. Such enablement facilitates early detection and resolution.
- **Platform Flexibility:** CNSP supports transport layer security (TLS) across multi-cluster and cloud environments and hence CNSP is cloud-agnostic.
- **Enhanced Backup and Data Recovery:** CNSPs automatically enforce patch deployments and mitigate security threats to elongate the life of CNAs

CNAs need a new breed of security controls. Security should be implemented from the design phase.

Aqua Integrated Cloud-native Security Platform (CNAPP): Aqua secures your applications wherever you develop and run them across clouds, container, and serverless platforms, CI/CD pipelines, registries, DevOps tools and modes of deployment, and orchestrators. The key properties of this platform (https://www.aquasec.com/aqua-cloud-native-security-platform/) are given as follows:

Aqua scans artifacts for vulnerabilities, malware, secrets, and other risks during development and staging. It allows you to set flexible and dynamic policies to control deployment into your runtime environments. The much-discussed paradigm of "shifting security to left" comes in handy in nipping threats and vulnerabilities in the budding stage itself. That is, such a shift empowers DevOps professionals to detect issues early and fix them fast in a risk-free and rewarding manner.

Aqua checks your cloud services, Infrastructure-as-Code (IaC) templates, and Kubernetes setup against best practices and standards, to ensure the infrastructure you run your applications on is securely configured and in compliance. Aqua leverages modern microservices concepts to enforce the immutability of your applications in runtime, establishing zero-trust networking, and detecting and stopping suspicious activities, including zero-day attacks. It also protects VM, container, and serverless workloads using granular controls with instant visibility and real-time detection and response. The scale and velocity of CNAs mean an endless stream of code, potential risks, and security events. From testing to remediation, from detection to response, Aqua automates security to reduce that attack surface, block unwanted behavior, and keep threats at bay.

Cloud-Native Security Posture Management and Threat Intelligence Solutions: Cloud Security Posture Management (CSPM) tools can automate security management across diverse infrastructures including IaaS, SaaS, and PaaS. CSPM tools empower companies to identify and remediate risks through security assessments and automated compliance monitoring. CSPM can automate governance across multi-cloud assets and services including visualization and assessment of security posture, misconfiguration detection, and enforcement of security best practices and compliance frameworks.

Cloud-native security tools have gradually evolved from rudimentary collections of multiple tools and dashboards to well-defined platforms that consider all layers of the ecosystem. A CNSP focuses on the following elements of a tech stack to administer a comprehensive secure framework. The fundamental benefit of leveraging a CNSP to administer security is that it gives organizations the freedom to choose a security stack to suit the organization's specific use case.

Cloud Workload Protection Platforms

Cloud workload protection platforms (CWPPs) are workload-centric security-enablement products that protect business workloads in hybrid and multi-cloud environments. CWPPs provide consistent visibility and controllability for physical machines, VMs, containers, and serverless functions, regardless of their locations. CWPP offerings protect workloads using a combination of security techniques including system integrity protection, application control, behavioral monitoring, intrusion prevention, and anti-malware protection at runtime. CWPP offerings also include scanning for workload risk proactively in the development pipeline.

With digital life applications and services growing in stature and sagacity, the need and role of CWPPs go up steadily. As indicated earlier, the cloud-native paradigm is being touted as the primary contributor to easily and elegantly fulfilling the ideals of digital transformation. In the cloud-native era, software applications are composed of multiple workloads running on-premise and off-premise clouds. CWPP has evolved to be distinct from Endpoint Protection Platforms (EPPs). A well-architected CWPP solution will also work seamlessly with a CSPM solution. Mcafee has come out with a CWPP solution (https://www.mcafee.com/enterprise/en-in/security-awareness/cloud/what-is-a-cwpp.html).

There are valid reasons why CWPP is important:

1) Most of the enterprise applications are being meticulously modernized and migrated to cloud environments in order to reap all the originally expressed benefits of the cloud paradigm. Due to the distributed architecture being followed while cloud-enabled and cloud-first applications are being implemented, there is a need for CWPP solutions.

2) Worldwide business behemoths are increasingly leveraging many CSPs' infrastructures, platforms, and software to gain some special benefits. That is, the world is steadily tending toward the much-anticipated hybrid era. This transition makes it cumbersome and troublesome for security professionals to tightly secure applications and data across isolated environments. CWPPs come in handy here.

3) Today applications are being built by combining differently abled microservices. There are software repositories to grab source code and produce software solutions. Then, there are container image repositories to create and deploy containerized applications. Thus, software engineering is being speeded up in multiple ways. Architectural patterns, software code reuse, and containerization aid in software development. Thus, the automation and orchestration aspects become a new normal in the field of IT. Efficiently securing such new-generation applications requires a pragmatic approach.

The suppleness, versatility, and dynamism of business workloads make CWPP an indispensable security solution for the ensuing digital era.

CWPP: The Distinct Capabilities: A comprehensive CWPP solution gives you the ability to discover workloads that have been deployed in your private and public clouds. CWPP helps do a vulnerability assessment of the workload by comparing it to a relevant set of policies. Thereafter, you should be able to apply security practices such as integrity protection, immutability or whitelisting, memory protection, and host-based intrusion prevention. There are several other features such as:

- incorporating CWPP into the CI/CD pipeline,
- aligning CWPP with CSPM and
- linking CWPP solution to cloud infrastructure.

A CWPP solution has to seamlessly and spontaneously link with other security modules such as DLP and SoC. CWPP typically focuses on protecting workloads that run applications but data loss prevention (DLP) focuses on protecting the data that applications use and store. A SOC can significantly enrich its view of complex attacks if it is empowered with a competent CWPP. CWPP addresses the unique aspects of Zero Trust security for cloud workloads, which turn out to be critical for business transformation.

CWPP is important because it provides a scalable and low-friction solution for guaranteeing cloud workload protection. CWPP solutions can help mitigate the impacts of poor security practices during the rapid development cycles (https://www.checkpoint.com/cyber-hub/cloud-security/what-is-a-cloud-workload-protection-platform-cwpp/). A CWPP solution discovers workloads that exist within an organization's cloud-based deployments and on-premises infrastructure. Once these workloads are discovered, the CWPP solution will perform a vulnerability assessment to identify any potentially exploitable security issues with the workload based on defined security policies and known vulnerabilities.

Prisma Cloud (https://www.paloaltonetworks.com/prisma/cloud/cloud-workload-protection-platform): Prisma Cloud is a comprehensive cloud workload protection solution that delivers flexible protection to secure cloud VMs, containers, and Kubernetes apps, serverless functions, and containerized offerings like Fargate tasks. With Prisma Cloud, DevOps and cloud infrastructure teams can adopt the architecture that fits their needs without worrying about security keeping pace with release cycles or protecting multifaceted tech stacks. In nutshell, CWPPs are designed to protect your workloads regardless of their environment.

CWPP solutions like Intezer Protect (https://www.intezer.com/intezer-protect/) help prevent in-memory exploitation, which could otherwise go undetected in static disk-based vulnerability scanning. Alternatively, attackers can gain control over your resources by using legitimate software to inject malicious code. This would generally go unnoticed by security tools. Intezer Protect Runtime protection, Linux threat detection, end-to-end visibility, and prevention of breaches using specialized CWPP solutions. These have to be factored into your security strategy for comprehensive protection of your application stack.

Factors to Choose a CWPP: CWPPs primarily address the challenges of securing workloads. The following points have to be considered to choose the best-in-class CWPP:

Protection Strategies: Different vendors use different protection strategies. These typically include one or more of the following:

- **Antivirus:** Traditional signature-based malware detection
- **Microsegmentation:** Granular protection of network traffic at an individual workload level
- **Runtime Application Self-Protection (RASP):** Detection of suspicious behavior by monitoring the inputs, outputs, and internal state of each application
- **Anomaly-Based Threat Detection:** A benchmarking technique that detects unusual activity, which could be the sign of a potential attack
- **Allow List:** Threat mitigation by means of a list of approved applications or processes
- **Container Image Scanning:** A pre-runtime process that scans container images for compromises and unpatched vulnerabilities

Among the security competencies, runtime protection is the highest priority. Runtime security tools prevent code-targeted attacks while your applications are running. A more mature solution will also protect against other forms of stealth attacks, such fileless attacks, and Living-off-the-Land attacks. These evade traditional threat detection methods by concealing themselves in system memory.

Monitoring Mechanism: Many CWPP solutions are **agent-based**. That is, you need to install an agent on each of your target environments. You will also need to keep tabs on the health of your agents and patch them from time to time. Agentless solutions, on the other hand, access your resources over a network – usually via API. This generally makes them more lightweight and less intrusive than agent-based tools.

Deployment: The CWPP has to offer deployment flexibility by supporting a range of open-source tools and components, such as Chef, Puppet, and Ansible. Further on, a CWPP can be deployed through its container image.

Threat Response: It should be able to detect and terminate ransomware and other destructive attacks both automatically and at the touch of a button.

However, CWPPs also share a number of threat response features in common:

- Contextual alerts, providing useful information to help you identify the source of compromise and quickly fix the issue
- Native integration with security aggregation tools such as Security Information and Event Management (SIEM) and Security Orchestration, Automation, and Response (SOAR)
- Seamless integration with collaboration tools, such as Slack, and issue management systems, such as Jira

Without an iota of doubt, the cloud-native approach brings in a multitude of benefits for business and IT domains but it also introduces newer security challenges. As teams methodically embrace CNA development technologies and tools, security teams find themselves scrambling to keep up with the changes in software engineering. The lacunae such as limited prevention capabilities, poor visibility and hence less controllability, many moving parts, and paucity of automation tools yield incomplete security insights. These shortcomings correspondingly increase the bad security implications in the form of breaches and compromises in cloud environments.

As organizations started to gain immensely through the leverage of DevOps concepts and tools, the application development pipelines are accordingly getting updated and upgraded to speed up application development, delivery, deployment, and feedback. Security teams then quickly realized that their tools were ill-suited and insufficient for API-centric, service-oriented, and infrastructure-agnostic cloud-native systems.

Kubernetes Security Products

We have discussed the key differentiators of Kubernetes and also its basic security features. There are best practices for ensuring unbreakable and impenetrable security for Kubernetes clusters and components as widely articulated and accentuated by security experts. To simplify and streamline Kubernetes security, product vendors have come out with Kubernetes-specific security products. In this section, we are to discuss their unique features based on the content made available on their websites. An optimal Kubernetes security solution has to have the following features:

Multilayer Security: As organizations are expressing and exposing their presence through cloud-hosted applications, cyberattackers could target organizations at multiple levels and layers. Therefore, it is insisted that any worthwhile security solution has to have the wherewithal to identify the risks and threats across layers (compute, networking, platform, application, etc.). Especially, the physical hosts/nodes, Pods, containers, applications, and the Kubernetes-deployed infrastructure including publicly exposed and unsecured API servers, kubelets, and management consoles are targeted. File integrity monitoring helps identify malicious tampering with container configuration and management.

Deep and Persistent Visibility: Containers are ephemeral and hence it is quite difficult to trace back the origin of any attack. Therefore, process-level traces are essential to do the root-cause analysis. Once an event is logged at a process level, it cannot be deleted at any cost. This fine-grained and persistent visibility is insisted to prevent any threat from escaping in a containerized environment. In the recent past, we read about observability platforms that enable deeper monitoring. Also, the much-anticipated feature of real-time analytics of monitored/observed data is also embedded in security platforms in order to predict and nip any impending attack in the budding stage.

Automated Intrusion Detection: ML algorithms are adroit in identifying anomalous behavior. A robust and resilient threat detection system monitors and logs all sorts of inter-process activities, including those within the same file, process hierarchy, communications between processes, compute machines and clusters, changes in user privileges, and internal and external data transfers.

Precisely speaking, you need pioneering security solutions that can provide continuous and deep visibility into processes at various layers of the containerized cloud environment to artistically and accurately detect and alert potential threats to the security-monitoring team.

Alcide (https://www.alcide.io/) is a Kubernetes security leader empowering DevOps teams to drive frictionless security guardrails to their CI/CD pipelines, and security teams to continuously secure and protect their growing Kubernetes deployments. Alcide provides a single Kubernetes-native and AI-driven security platform for various Kubernetes aspects: configuration risks, visibility across clusters, runtime security events, and a single policy framework to enforce. Companies use Alcide to scale their Kubernetes deployments without compromising on security. This enables the smooth operation of business apps while protecting cloud deployments from malicious attacks.

- **kAdvisor** is an agentless pure API-based vulnerability scanner, providing a single-pane view for all Kubernetes-related aspects and is seamlessly integrated with your CI/CD pipeline. kAdvisor simplifies the security assessment for the entire Kubernetes environment while creating baseline profiles for each cluster, highlighting and scoring security risks, misconfigurations, and hygiene drifts.
- **kAudit** is a robust and ML-based tool, intelligently leveraging Kubernetes audit logs and summarizing detected anomalies and potential threats. kAudit highlights usage and performance trends across the Kubernetes clusters while providing user-friendly statistics for auditing and further investigation.
- **Alcide's kArt** network-based approach allows for the seamless collection of traffic information into centrally orchestrated cloud security policies and anomaly engines. This level of granular control combined with a hierarchical approach makes it easy to structure and enforce smart, application-aware, and label-based policies.

Containers continuously steady their position strongly in cloud environments. However, the container density has gone up remarkably and hence managing and orchestrating them in a cloud environment poses a bigger and bitter challenge. Kubernetes is a market leader in orchestrating CNAs but on the security front, Kubernetes lags behind. There are several product and tool vendors working in union with Kubernetes infrastructure and platform services providers in order to guarantee heightened security.

Lacework's Kubernetes security solution (https://www.lacework.com/) provides comprehensive threat detection for dashboards, pods, management nodes, and clusters, in addition to end-to-end security for their public cloud infrastructure workloads, accounts, and containers. This Kubernetes security platform identifies the risks and threats for Kubernetes-deployed infrastructures, including publicly exposed and unsecured API servers and management consoles.

Lacework provides deep visibility into your Kubernetes deployment. This includes high-level dashboards of your clusters, pods, nodes, and namespaces combined with application-level communication between all of these at the application, process, and network layers. This security solution for Kubernetes includes the detection of both risks and threats that may be specifically designed to breach vulnerability within Kubernetes, a possible misconfiguration, or a threat that can affect your infrastructure by installing malicious code onto one of your containers. The Lacework Polygraph is designed to detect both known and unknown threats that affect Kubernetes environments using behavioral analysis and ML capability.

Risks and threats, made visible within the Lacework dashboard, are ranked by risk severity and can be delivered through the most common modern methods such as a Slack channel or a Jira ticket. Whether you are triaging an alert or digging into deep details around the cause and effect of a change, this security solution has the information you need. The SaaS service allows you to go back in time and look at all related events across your Kubernetes infrastructure that may have caused a breach or exposed you to an unknown risk.

Lacework's Kubernetes security solution creates hourly Polygraphs that can demonstrate the change in relationships and events over time. This is a critical tool for understanding and triaging your events.

Portshift (https://www.portshift.io/product/kubernetes-security/) delivers rich context, declarative policy enforcement, improved risk profiling, vulnerability management, runtime detection, and remediation for CNAs. Portshift is a Kubernetes-native solution offering an agentless approach with a Kubernetes admission controller for seamless integration and native enforcement. It enables setting up Kubernetes-native guardrails on your deployed containers to prevent suspicious activities and dynamically microsegment them against runtime threats.

Portshift empowers DevOps and security teams to continuously protect their growing Kubernetes deployments and multi-clusters. This lightweight solution protects from threats and vulnerabilities across images, containers, runtime deployments, and Kubernetes infrastructure.

- **Greater Visibility:** Portshift platform delivers a comprehensive view of your Kubernetes deployments including images, pods, and namespaces. Gain visibility and control of your entire Kubernetes deployments. With Portshift, you can easily gain rich context data for every cloud-native workload with its associated CI/CD metadata, connections, and attributes.
- **Vulnerability Scanning:** Portshift's comprehensive scanning capabilities include the build, ship, and continuous integration and delivery (CI/CD) pipeline scanning. Portshift also offers vulnerability scanning during runtime with Kubei (https://www.portshift.io/blog/kubernetes-runtime-vulnerabilities-scanner-launch/). The idea behind Kubei is to offer the community a unique tool to help DevOps/SRE teams solve the pressing need for Kubernetes runtime scanning.

- **Policy Management:** Policies are important for enabling effective control. This security solution from Portshift helps in creating man and machine-readable security policies intuitively. Policies are not only established but also enforced to control which workloads run in your clusters, and block unknown workloads. Portshift also offers a "Policy Advisor" that suggests the right and relevant policies to accomplish things in an automated manner.
- **Kubernetes Network Encryption:** The Portshift product encrypts internal communication between services in the same cluster, and maintains the security level for communication between services across clusters.
- **Network Segmentation:** The Portshift platform offers a "zero-trust" security concept with segmentation and isolation based on Layer 7 application protocols.
- **Threat Detection and Prevention:** The Portshift solution has a threat detection engine that identifies anomalous behavior in your workloads. This also can pinpoint whether there is any malicious intent. Portshift prevents untrusted images or workloads from running. This also pinpoints and prevents making changes in running workloads.
- **Service Mesh Security:** The Portshift platform delivers service mesh security by leveraging Istio, an open-source service mesh implementation. This module protects network communications, multi-cluster communications, and communications with external resources.
- **Streamline DevOps:** Portshift delivers a simple and frictionless Kubernetes security platform. It has come out with a set of plugins enabling creating DevOps pipelines, and establishing "security as code" to enable robust, scalable, and portable controls.

Considering the strategic significance of secure cloud-native systems for the impending digital era, product and tool vendors are seriously bringing in highly competent security products and solutions. This section is dedicated to discussing some of the renowned security products to sufficiently boost the confidence of businesses as well as users in the fast emerging and evolving cloud-native paradigm.

The Check Point CloudGuard Platform (https://www.checkpoint.com/cloudguard/cloud-security-solutions/) provides you with cloud-native security, with advanced threat prevention for all your assets and workloads running in public and private cloud environments. This is touted as the one providing you unified security to automate full security. This security solution provides intelligent threat prevention across cloud environments (private and public). This securely protects and prevents threats across AWS, Azure, Google Cloud, and other hyperscale clouds. This also offers a centralized visualization for all of your cloud traffic, security alerts, and assets along with auto-remediation. The figure vividly illustrates the various features and functionalities of this security platform.

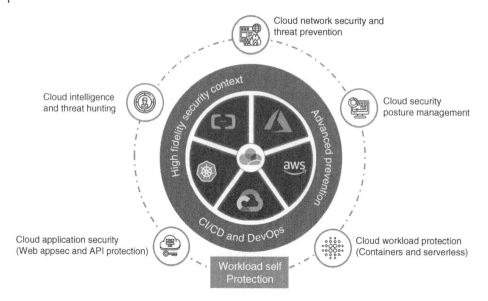

A Security Platform's Characteristics.
Source: Check Point [1].

The various modules of this great security product are as follows:

- **Security and Posture Management:** The CloudGuard platform delivers zero trust, multi-layer, and advanced threat prevention, leveraging enriched intelligence by combining the highest levels of intelligence inputs with the context information. In addition, with its comprehensive compliance and security engine, CloudGuard prevents critical security misconfigurations, and ensures compliance with more than 50 compliance frameworks and best practices.
- **Automated DevSecOps:** CloudGuard allows organizations to shift left for DevOps to seamlessly evaluate security posture, configuration, and governance during CI/CD. It seamlessly scales and deploys your security in real time through integration with tools like CloudFormation and Terraform, and evaluates posture pre-deployment to scale across thousands of assets. It automatically defines applications' security profiles and enforces zero trust boundaries between workloads.
- **Cloud Network Security:** This component guarantees network security to keep all sorts of assets and data protected while fully compliant with the dynamic needs of public and multi-cloud as well as on-premise environments.
- **Cloud Security Posture Management:** This module visualizes and assesses security posture, detects misconfigurations, models and actively enforces security best practices, and protects against identity theft and data loss in the cloud.
- **Cloud Intelligence and Threat Hunting:** Real-time analytics of security-related data captured from various system components supplies all the right and relevant insights into time in order to gain advanced security intelligence including cloud intrusion detection and network traffic visualization. Cloud security monitoring and continuous analysis of monitored data go a long way in establishing and sustaining unbreakable security for cloud-native systems.
- **Cloud Workload Protection:** Cloud-native security predominantly represents the security of CNAs. This module specifically provides seamless vulnerability assessment and delivers full

protection of modern cloud workloads. This takes care of containerized applications and serverless functions from code to runtime environment. In nutshell, it automates security with minimal overhead.

- **Cloud Web App and API Protection:** CloudGuard moves application security closer to the edge of the workload, giving more real-time granular protection than traditional WAFs. CloudGuard protects web applications and APIs from the most sophisticated types of threats, with an automated CNSP. CloudGuard transcends rule-based security by leveraging the power of AI.

Check Point cloud-native security solution provides automated security and advanced threat prevention to protect all kinds of cloud assets and workloads even from the most sophisticated cyberattacks. It secures cloud and workload environments with a unified security platform by automating security posture management. This controls workloads across cloud environments by gaining deeper visibility of threats. It guarantees multilayer cloud security across any cloud and workload. It detects activity anomalies leveraging ML algorithms and threat research.

Prisma Cloud from Palo Alto Networks: Prisma cloud secures infrastructure, applications, and data across hybrid and multi-cloud environments (https://www.paloaltonetworks.com/prisma/cloud). This is one of the popular CNSPs and is gaining a lot of market and mind shares. The important components of this product are given as follows:

- **Cloud Code Security:** This module primarily is for securing configurations, scanning code, and integrating security with developer tools.
- **Cloud Security Posture Management:** This module has become a regular one in any standardized CNSP. This monitors posture, detects and responds to threats, and maintains compliance across public clouds.
- **Cloud Workload Protection:** Securing cloud workloads gains more significance these days. This module is intended for securing cloud workloads including containerized applications and serverless functions.
- **Cloud Network Security:** This is for gaining network visibility, enforcing micro-segmentation, and securing trust boundaries.
- **Cloud Identity Security:** This is to enforce permissions and secure identities across workloads and cloud resources.

This product is being positioned as a single platform for all your cloud security needs. Prisma Cloud secures the infrastructure, applications, data, and entitlements across cloud environments, all from a single unified solution. With a combination of CSP APIs and a unified agent framework, users gain unmatched visibility and protection. Prisma Cloud natively integrates with any CI/CD workflow to secure cloud infrastructure and applications early in development. This also scans IaC templates, container images, and serverless functions while guaranteeing full-stack runtime protection.

AIOps for Cloud-Native Security

Building CNAs as a collection of self-contained and easily manageable microservices helps organizations to be agile, adaptive, and resilient. However, data volume and microservice complexity are only increasing as organizations embrace the cloud-inspired IT optimization and organization, refactor their monolithic and massive applications to create and run microservices-centric applications, embrace CI/CD-induced continuous integration, delivery and deployment, or extend and expand to offer new and premium services. Experts are in unison in stating that AI-inspired automation comes in handy in mitigating the rising complexity of CNAs. The new field of AIOps is to apply AI capabilities to operational data to extract actionable insights in time. As the cloud-native security requirement gains prominence and dominance, the faster maturity and stability of AIOps are seen as a positive development. In this section, we are to discuss one of the leading AIOps platforms for achieving service resiliency and security.

AIOps platforms are powered by ML algorithms that automate and simplify IT operations and application monitoring.

- **Data Collection:** AIOps tools collect application and infrastructure data in the form of logs, metrics, traces, and events. Then, the tool deeply analyzes and highlights data that has a hidden issue.
- **Pattern Discovery:** AIOps platforms correlate and find relationships between different data elements.
- **Root Cause Analysis:** AIOps determines the root cause of new and recurring issues through correlation.
- **Collaboration:** AIOps platforms simplify and streamline borderless information flow and frictionless collaboration across IT teams through unified dashboards and intelligent notification systems.

Thus, the distinct improvisations in the AI space are to empower the cloud-native era in realizing highly reliable and secure applications.

IBM Cloud Pak for Watson AIOps (https://www.ibm.com/cloud/cloud-pak-for-watson-aiops) enables organizations to predict, communicate, and resolve IT events before they become serious or impact the end user. This applies ML algorithms and models to structured and unstructured data from application logs and telemetry data generated by the disparate set of IT management tools. It can then analyze, prioritize, and provide insights into IT incidents. By pinpointing faulty components and root-cause of failures, it derives a likely impact assessment on related components. Finally, it recommends short-term remedies or long-term resolutions based on past incident history. Following is a brief explanation of each functional component:

1) **Data Ingestion:** IBM Cloud Pak for Watson AIOps is blessed with a number of connectors to facilitate connecting, observing, and ingesting right and relevant data from a variety of application and infrastructure components, in large volumes and at high velocity.
2) **Anomaly Detection:** IBM Cloud Pak for Watson AIOps provides unsupervised learning methods, such as clustering and principal component analysis to detect abnormal patterns in log and metric input streams.
3) **Correlation and Contextualization:** Context information is vital for enhancing the accuracy of any decision and conclusion. The correlation capability comes handy in capturing context details. This module ingests data from logs, metrics, external alerts, and events. It then constructs a holistic understanding of an ongoing incident. The extracted topology information then establishes point-in-time software-to-infrastructure mapping. Such a feature is hugely beneficial when dealing with ephemeral infrastructures such as containers.
4) **Visualization and Resolution:** Any perceptible deviation has to be identified and solved. This module specifically points out faulty components and all of their dependencies. This enables SREs to act accordingly.

There are a few more important modules. Thus, AIOps platforms acquire significance immensely as the cloud journey is on the fast track. We are heading toward hybrid and multi-cloud environments. AIOps delivers a great value for DevOps and SRE teams in the cloud-native era. AIOps tools establish resiliency and unbreakable security of CNAs.

AIOps and Observability for 360-Degree Visibility: As indicated earlier, observability is about 360-degree visibility through your applications. By combining business metrics with technical data, monitoring is a top view if things are working perfectly. AIOps is all about deriving insights from that complete visibility. DevOps teams collect and crunch observability data and emit insights, which, in turn, help predict and prevent any outages. Thus, the much-needed business continuity through the high availability of business workloads and IT services is fulfilled. So the convergence of AIOps and observability is being seen as a trendsetter for producing and sustaining highly reliable and secure software solutions.

The Benefits of AIOps: AIOps gives IT operations teams the much-needed speed and sagacity to ensure the uptime of mission-critical services. AIOps guarantees customer delight. The other advantages of AIOps are:

- **Removes Noise and Distractions:** This enables IT specialists to focus on their core works without any unnecessary disturbance. This speeds up the detection and resolution of service-impacting issues and prevents outages.
- **Correlates Information Across Multiple Data Sources:** AIOps eliminates silos and provides a holistic, contextualized vision, and version across cloud environments (infrastructure modules, platforms, middleware, databases, applications, etc.).
- **Facilitates Frictionless and Cross-Team Collaboration:** This accelerates diagnosis and resolution times. Consequently, there is minimal disruption to users.

ML algorithms and models empower AIOps tools to be accurate in their predictions and prescriptions.

Application Security Testing Tools: There are a variety of application security testing tools. There are SAST, DAST, software composition analysis (SCA) tools, etc., to subject applications for thorough checks. In the recent past, chaos engineering principles and practices are emerging to unearth any hidden and lateral security vulnerabilities. Thus, error-free microservices contribute immensely to secure CNAs.

Conclusion

CNAs deliver compelling benefits such as horizontal scalability, unmatched resiliency and versatility, and rapid development. However, they also raise some critical challenges. Security threats are on the rise and regulatory compliance requirements are increasing. MSA and highly distributed deployments introduce new security threats. Enterprises need the same level of control and visibility. Failure to provide an appropriate security architecture and protection for CNAs can result in higher costs and a potential loss of business. You must rethink your security architecture and the methods to secure CNAs. Therefore, it is mandated to follow the proven zero-trust model for cloud-native security. Every resource has to be assumed to be a potential target for security attacks.

The security planning has to cover each and every tangible asset. Microservices data also has to travel across logical and physical places to reach the desired destination. Authentication has to happen across all nodes or resources in a system, regardless of network location. To close security gaps caused by rapidly changing digital ecosystems, organizations must adopt an integrated CNSP that incorporates AI, automation, intelligence, threat detection, and data analytics capabilities.

Reference

1 Check Point, "Cloud Native Security." https://www.checkpoint.com/cloudguard/cloud-security-solutions/.

14

Microservices Security: The Concerns and the Solution Approaches

---

THE OBJECTIVES

This chapter will touch down the significant aspects of plugging the security layer into microservices applications. Without an iota of doubt, microservices architecture (MSA) is being recognized as the most pragmatic and paramount architectural style for producing enterprise-scale applications. However, security is being played as an antithesis. In monolithic applications, the implementation of a security layer to ensure their tight security is manageable. But securing microservices-centric applications presents a number of challenges and concerns. Incorporating and managing a security layer in any microservices application are not straightforward. Generally any MSA application typically comprises numerous distributed and disparate microservices. If a security capability is dedicatedly introduced in each of the participating microservices, the attack surface increases dramatically if a security capability is included in each microservice, as microservices are numerous and distributed. However, in the deeply connected world, securing microservices applications is very much needed. In this chapter, we discuss the various security challenges of microservices applications and how they can be surmounted through a host of security solutions and practices.

Microservice Security Challenges and Concerns

The use of (MSA to realize sophisticated software solutions is steadily growing. Microservices enable accelerated software design, development, and deployment. Microservices are being seen as the highly optimized software building block in producing business applications across industry verticals. Microservices are also leveraged to build applications across technologies. That is, Web 3.0 blockchain, mobile, the Internet of things (IoT), artificial intelligence (AI), scientific, database, middleware, cloud, Web, serverless, containerized, Graphical User Interface (GUI), and Virtual Reality (VR)/Augmented Reality (AR) applications are also being constructed through the proven and potential MSA. Further on, operational, transactional, and analytical applications are also being built using MSA. Any technology, tool, and programming language can be used to produce MSA applications. There are service composition (orchestration and choreography) platforms for realizing composite applications, which are business-relevant, mission-critical, and process-aware. In a nutshell, any software solution can be elegantly made through the power of the MSA pattern. Thus, the MSA scope is continuously expanding.

However, MSA comes with its own security challenges. MSA has a few noteworthy vulnerabilities due to its modular nature. MSA applications have larger attack surface when compared with traditional applications. Microservices communicate via application programming interfaces

(APIs) that are independent of machine architecture and even programming language. That is, microservices interact and transact through network calls. All these clearly tell that microservices expose more surface for any internal and external attack.

Thus, the security concerns of microservices applications are on the rise with the widespread leverage of microservices for accelerated software design, development, and deployment. MSA) in consonance with event-driven architecture (EDA) is being proclaimed as the most disruptive architectural pattern in implementing highly portable, scalable, available, and extensible applications.

Best Practices to Secure Microservices

An MSA typically represents distributed architecture of microservices encompassing the back-end services that provide data, the middleware code that talks to the data stores, and the UI that serves up the data in a user-friendly way. The data movement across has to be tightly secured. There are security-enablement tools and protocols in plenty. Besides, security experts through their vast practical experience have come out with a set of best practices to surmount the perplexing security issue.

Certainly, when it comes to securing microservices, there are abundant strategies and practices that you can follow. In this section, we are giving the important ones to help you understand the seriousness of security and to analyze the possible hotspots that can significantly help you in pondering about viable security mechanisms to MSA applications.

1) **Defense in Depth (DiD) Mechanism:** This is a technique through which you can apply layers of security countermeasures to protect sensitive services. To achieve it, first, identify the services with the most sensitive information and then apply multiple layers of security. This protects the services from potential attackers to crack down on the security in a single go.

2) **Configuring Tokens:** Tokens are used to easily identify and authenticate the user. They are stored in the form of cookies. The word "storage" is also associated with vulnerabilities as the stored data can be exploited by third-party resources. To protect this data, encrypting the tokens is the recommended move. JSON Web Token (JWT) is an example of storing encryption-based tokens.

3) **Configuring API Gateway:** Microservice applications comprise several service components that are widely distributed over a range of networks and accessible by a variety of clients. This poses a high security risk. To inhibit this, the highly recommended approach is to have a single entry point to all the client requests; API gateways are being positioned as the single point of contact for external users. Gateways efficiently hide the back-end microservices from any external client. This abstraction layer protects the microservice by not providing direct access to external clients. Any misadventure on microservices can be stopped by an API gateway, which is therefore considered one of the most powerful security-based mechanisms with other magnificent features.

   API gateways perform authentication and authorization, and a host of middleware features. The API gateway authenticates users and can provide additional security capabilities like SSL termination, protocol translation, intermediation, enrichment, monitoring, routing, and caching of requests.

4) **Distributed Tracing/ Monitoring of Services:** Distributed tracing is a method that detects the failures, bugs, and bottlenecks of microservices. Also, it identifies the reason behind the

errors. There are monitoring tools in plenty to minutely monitor microservices and their underlying platforms. Databases associated with microservices are also being monitored for their read and write performance. It is recommended to enable logging at the application layer by using tools like Splunk, Graphana, and ELK stack, that collect logs at the application, container, network, and infrastructure levels. Tools like Prometheus, Statsd, InfluxDB, and Logstash are used to collect the significant metrics of the system/services to be monitored.

5) **Secure Deployment at Container Level:** When it comes to the deployment of microservices, they rely strongly on containerization. Hence, providing security to the container is a crucial activity for ensuring microservice security. Container images being generated and deposited in image repositories have to be scanned fully to unearth any security hole. Second, it is advised not to store any secrets in the container.

As articulated in the previous chapters, there is a cool connection between microservices and containers. Microservices and their instances are being optimally packaged and run on redundant containers. Microservices are containerized and stocked in public or private repositories. The overwhelming suggestion is to perform regular scanning on those image files to ensure that no corrupt image gets instantiated and to be run inside containers, which are being managed by Kubernetes. Experts pitch that there is a great first step to protecting containers at runtime by adopting the principle of least privilege (POLP). It is recommended to limit permissions to the minimum required by users. It is advised not to keep secrets on the container because anyone with access to the container can get to know them. It is also important to define rules so that one process should not try to usurp the resources of any other process.

6) **Secure Service-to-Service Communication:** It is an effective practice to implement authorization and authentication mechanisms in order to have a deeper visibility and controllability over all kinds of service requests. Service-to-service communication and client-to-service communication have to be minutely monitored and observed in order to smell any kind of unauthorized and illegal transaction. One of the most popular approaches is to use mutual Transport Layer Security (TLS). That is, client microservice has to use key-pair to authenticate itself to other microservices. Each microservice generates a certificate during the authentication process. TLS is just one way hence is not secure. But mTLS provides authentication both ways.

TLS (HTTPS) ensures privacy and data integrity by encrypting communication over HTTP. HTTPS requires a certificate to authenticate your identity and provide access to encrypted communications via Public Key Infrastructure. Once you have acquired your certificates, you can continue enhancing your security posture by automating certificate generation and renewals – keeping bad actors that might want to compromise your architecture at bay.

7) **Rate Limit the Client Traffic:** To prevent DOS attacks, the rate-limiting (throttling) concept is found to be a winning method and hence it is widely recommended to secure microservice applications. Rate limiting is also helpful in saving the computational resources getting wasted. That is, besides preventing distributed denial of service (DDoS) attacks to make microservices inaccessible and unusable for other legitimate users, IT resource utilization can be rationed.

8) **Make Your MSA Secure by Design:** Security has to be given its due importance from the beginning. That is, from the design stage itself, security has to be incorporated in one or other ways in all the phases of software engineering. If necessary, security layers can be added to guarantee unbreakable security for microservices and their data. When a microservice gets coded, a form of stress testing has to be initiated and continued. This means the testing has to be continued into the continuous integration/delivery (CI/CD) pipelines. There are security

tests such as static analysis security testing (SAST) and dynamic analysis security testing (DAST). The new concept of DevSecOps is therefore gaining immense traction these days considering the importance of security. The Open Web Application Security Project (OWASP) also offers a series of resources and analysis tools to help your team implement best practices as they build out software.

9) **Scan for dependencies:** Microservices rely upon local as well as remote microservices to fulfil business processes. Microservices composition is critical for business success. The participating microservices are distributed and owned by different service providers. Hence to secure microservices applications, it is mandatory to scan all upstream and downstream microservices to weed out any security holes and vulnerabilities. The third-party applications, libraries, and other dependencies have to be subjected to scanning.

10) **Complete Isolation:** Microservices are independently developed and deployed, and hence there is a strong isolation between microservices. Further on, containers as the runtime for microservices bring in additional isolation. Such an isolation eliminates all kinds of dependency-induced errors and bottlenecks. Thereby microservices can be separately implemented, maintained, advanced, etc. Such isolation brings in numerous development, management, and operational benefits for microservices. It is recommended that isolation has to be practiced in all the layers of the microservice tech stack. Especially the isolation has to be ensured at the database level. By achieving this, data for any particular microservice is safe there.

11) **Don't Show Sensitive Data as Plain Text:** Plaintext can be easily read and copied by users and machines. So the way forward to protect personally identifiable information (PII) is to avoid displaying it in clear text. All passwords and usernames must be stripped or masked when saving logs or records.

As enterprises are keenly strategizing to be digitally transformed, the cloud movement has got accelerated. Monolithic and massive applications are being methodically modernized as a collection of microservices and the cloud migration is getting simplified and smoothened. With clouds emerging as the one-stop IT solution for all kinds of business automation requirements, securing cloud data, applications, and infrastructural components has gained an upper hand in the recent past. We have indicated the key security issues of microservices applications and how they can be overcome through a meticulous usage of all the best practices ingrained in this chapter.

Here is a detailed explanation of how to fulfil an authentication and authorization practice practically.

How to Implement Fundamental Authentication and Authorization Strategies

Authentication in microservices is a mechanism wherein the desired user with correct credentials is validated against the database to get access to the service. Authentication answers the question: Who are you? **Authorization** on other hand enables to verify whether the authenticated user is allowed to consume that information from the service or not. It answers the following question: Which permissions the user has? There are various ways to introduce the authentication logic into the microservices. Let us unveil the process of retrospecting the available possibilities and strategies.

There are two kinds of authentication mechanisms namely stateful and stateless. In stateful authentication, the server creates a session for the client after successful authentication. The session ID is then stored as a cookie in the user's browser and the user session is stored in the cache or database. When the client tries to access the server with a given session ID, the server attempts to load the user session context for the session store, checks whether the session is valid, and makes the decision that whether the client has the access to the desired resource.

Stateless authentication stores the user session on the client side. A cryptographic algorithm signs the user session to ensure the session data's integrity and authority. Each time the client requests a resource from the server, the server is responsible for verifying the token claims sent as a cookie.

Storing the user session on the client side makes this approach fairly easy and does not require additional effort when it comes to scaling.

1) Distributed Session Management
2) Client Token: JWT
3) Third-Party: API Token, OAuth

The most commonly used stateless authentication mechanism is JWT, a signed JSON object that contains a list of claims that allow the receiver to validate the sender's identity. The information in the token is digitally signed to avoid tampering.

Dive Deeper into API Gateway

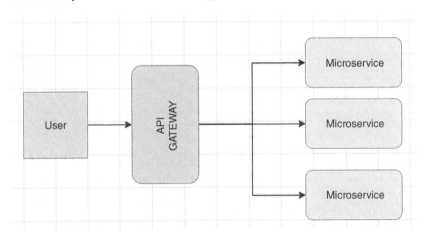

As discussed, the API gateway is a single entry point to the system. It is an excellent method to enforce a complete security layer (Authorization and Authentication). It reduces the latency (call to Authentication service) and ensures the authentication process is consistent across the application. API gateway has other key attributes such as service discovery, monitoring, load balancing, rate limiting, caching, request shaping and management, and static response handling. The client directly communicates with the API gateway rather than connecting with each service independently. Direct communication reduces the number of calls, this approach is also called API composition.

Implementing an API gateway enhances the performance and scalability of the entire MSA. Some of the most commonly used open-source API gateways include Kong Gateway, Apache APISIX, Tyk, Ocelot, Goku, Express Gateway, Gloo, KrakenD, and many more. Each API gateway provides plugins to support multiple features.

APACHE APISIX

It is time to kickstart the journey of API gateway configuration. Let us initiate by choosing the most effective API gateway named Apache APISIX. Apache APISIX is the latest in its features and capabilities. Before getting to the practical side of things, let us introduce you to Apache APISIX which was developed in June 2019 by ZhiLiu Technology. It was open-sourced and entered Apache incubator in October 2019.

The vice president of the APISIX project named Ming Wen stated that "Cloud-native architectures bring a whole new level of challenges, as does traffic from websites, mobile, and IoT applications. We investigated several popular open-source API gateway projects and found that none of them can solve these new challenges brought by cloud-native and microservices."

APISIX is designed to handle a large number of requests, unlike other API gateways which lack in certain areas of handling loads. It is lightweight, cloud-native, and easy to containerize. It supports multiple monitoring tools like Prometheus, Apache SkyWalking, and Zipkin. It supports a wide range of proxy protocols and has great adaptability. It can connect with the services of Auth0, Okta, and other identity authentication providers. The gateway node is stateless and can be expanded and flexible. APISIX consists of a data plane to dynamically control request traffic; a control plane to store and synchronize gateway data configuration, and an AI plane to orchestrate plugins, as well as real-time analysis and processing of request traffic. Apache APISIX replaces the Kubernetes-native ingress to handle all north-south container clusters and part of east-west traffic. APISIX's high-performance routing, flexible plugin mechanism, API management, and design concepts are just the needs of cloud-native architecture

Overall it has all the features like rate limiting, authentication plugins, traffic control, security-related numerous plugins. Hence, one should consider this API gateway to be part of their microservice-based ecosystem as it is the powerpack from a security perspective.

Configuring APISIX

There are numerous ways to install APISIX gateway but the easy one to get started is the Docker environment. The traditional approach can be implemented at the organizational level. For starters, it is always recommended to go ahead with the dockerized environment as it can be created and destroyed quickly and also is great for learning purposes.

Prerequisites:

1) You should have docker and docker-compose installed in your machine.
2) Curl Package should be installed for testing the API. Other tools like postman can also be used.

Step 1: Install APISIX

- APISIX supports multiple operating systems.
- Clone the repository, navigate to the folder, and start the APISIX server by running the docker-compose command.

- ```
  git clone https://github.com/apache/incubator-apisix-docker.git
  ```

- ```
  cd example
  ```

This folder consists of the following files:

```
apisix_conf                  docker-compose.yml  index.html.2  index.html.7
apisix_log                   etcd_conf           index.html.3  index.html.8
dashboard_conf               grafana_conf        index.html.4  mkcert
docker-compose-alpine.yml    index.html          index.html.5  prometheus_conf
docker-compose-arm64.yml     index.html.1        index.html.6  upstream
```

- Run the docker-compose.yml which will spin up all the containers for us in a few minutes.

```
docker-compose -p docker-apisix up -d
```

```
docker-apisix_web2_1 is up-to-date
docker-apisix_apisix-dashboard_1 is up-to-date
docker-apisix_etcd_1 is up-to-date
docker-apisix_web1_1 is up-to-date
docker-apisix_grafana_1 is up-to-date
docker-apisix_prometheus_1 is up-to-date
docker-apisix_apisix_1 is up-to-date
```

- Congratulations! Upon successful creation of the following containers, you have installed APISIX and can start working on it.
- You can use the docker command: < docker ps > to enlist the running containers. As mentioned in the docker-compose.yml file, all the containers will get started and run on the desired ports. In rare cases, some containers can fail to start. The most common reason is that the ports in your system are already in use. To resolve this issue you can modify the docker-compose.yml file accordingly based on your open and free ports.
- To check if your APISIX is running successfully, you can run the following command:

```
curl "http://<Your machine IP>:9080/apisix/admin/services/" -H
'X-API-KEY:
edd1c9f034335f136f87ad84b625c8f1'
```

It should return the following response:

```
{
    "node": {
        "createdIndex": 6,
        "modifiedIndex": 6,
        "key": "/apisix/services",
        "dir": true
        },
    "action": "get"
}
```

Step 2: Create a route and upstream in APISIX

- A microservice can be configured via APISIX through the relationship between several entities such as routes, services, upstream, and plugins. The route matches the client request and specifies how they are sent to the upstream (back-end API/service) after they reach APISIX. Services provide an abstraction to the upstream services. Therefore, you can create a single service and reference it in multiple routes.

- The route consists of the following three components:

1) Matching Rules

Matching rules contain URI, Host, remote-address, etc.

2) Upstream Information

Upstream is a virtual host abstraction that performs load balancing on a given set of service nodes according to configuration rules. Thus a single upstream configuration can comprise multiple servers which offer the same service. Each node will comprise a key (address/IP : port) and a value (weight of the node). The service can be load balanced through a round-robin or consistent hashing (cHash) mechanism.

When configuring a route, you can either set the upstream information or use service abstraction to refer to the upstream information.

3) Plugins

Plugins allow you to extend the capabilities of APISIX and to implement arbitrary logic which can interface with the HTTP request/response life cycle. Therefore, if you want to authenticate the API, then you can include the Key Auth plugin to enforce authentication for each request.

Step 3: Configure authentication for the service

- There are various Authentication plugins available with APISIX: key-auth, jwt-auth, basic-auth, authz-keycloak, and many more.
- Let us try to implement an authentication mechanism called key-auth.
- To enable key-auth, follow these two steps:

1) Create a consumer object and set the attributes of the plugin.

```
curl http://<your machine IP>:9080/apisix/admin/consumers -H 'X-API-KEY:
edd1c9f034335f136f87ad84b625c8f1' -X PUT -d '
{
    "username": "jack",
    "plugins": {
        "key-auth": {
            "key": "auth-one"
        }
    }
}'
```

2) Now create a route or service object and enable the plugin that you have created earlier.

```
curl http://< Your Machine IP>:9080/apisix/admin/routes/1 -H 'X-API-
KEY: edd1c9f034335f136f87ad84b625c8f1' -X PUT -d '
{
    "methods": ["GET"],
    "uri": "/index.html",
    "id": 1,
    "plugins": {
        "key-auth": {}
    },
    "upstream": {
        "type": "roundrobin",
        "nodes": {
            "<Node IP > :<Port>": 1
        }
    }
}'
```

- Validate the plugin to check whether the authentication plugin is working correctly.
  - **Scenario 1**: Without passing the key to the request, the desired result should be as follows:
    ```
    curl http://<your machine IP>:9080/index.html -i
    ```

```
HTTP/1.1 401 Unauthorized
Date: Fri, 21 Jan 2022 11:17:38 GMT
Content-Type: text/html; charset=utf-8
Server: APISIX/2.10.0
Age: 0
Proxy-Connection: keep-alive
Transfer-Encoding: chunked
Via: 1.1 JP3PRWSAPP01

{"message":"Missing API key found in request"}
```

  - **Scenario 2**: Passing the incorrect key to the request
    ```
    curl http://<your machine IP>:9080/index.html -H 'apikey:
    abcxyz' -i
    ```

```
HTTP/1.1 401 Unauthorized
Date: Fri, 21 Jan 2022 11:14:06 GMT
Content-Type: text/html; charset=utf-8
Server: APISIX/2.10.0
Age: 0
Proxy-Connection: keep-alive
Transfer-Encoding: chunked
Via: 1.1 JP3PRWSAPP02

{"message":"Invalid API key in request"}
```

  - Scenario 3: Passing the correct key to the request
    ```
    curl http://<your machine IP>:9080/index.html -H 'apikey:
    auth-one' -i
    ```

```
HTTP/1.1 200 OK
```

- This is how you can implement any authentication plugin at your convenience.

Step 4: Access dashboard
- Creation of routes, services, etc., can be done using the dashboard as well.
- The dashboard container is up running and to access the UI navigate to the <IP of your machine>:<port> in the browser and you will be able to see your APISIX dashboard.

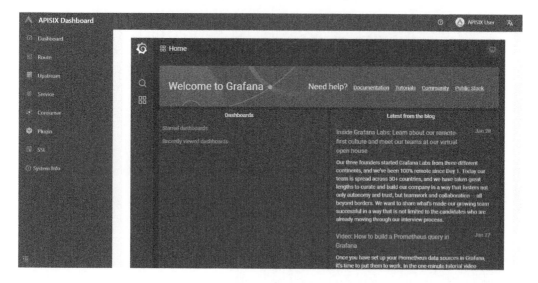

- The dashboard makes it easy to create routes, services, etc., and can enable all the plugins upon configuration. The thing that we followed above was the manual way of doing things, the same can be achieved using the dashboard in a few clicks.

Conclusion

We have briefly discussed various ways on how, why, and where should we integrate the security layer in the microservice-based architecture. We have discussed a few drops of security principles in the ocean of microservice-based vulnerabilities. Following the best practices, implementing the latest cutting-edge tools, automating the process of securing the microservices will save your cost, time, and most importantly your microservice-based application from any kind of vulnerability.

Further Reading

1 Apache APISIX. The Apache Software Foundation. (2019–2022) https://apisix.apache.org/docs/apisix/getting-started; https://blogs.apache.org/
2 Books: Microservices Security in Action By Morgan Bruce, Paulo A Pereira (3 October 2018).

15

Setting Up Apache Kafka Clusters in a Cloud Environment and Secure Monitoring

---

THE OBJECTIVES

Apache Kafka is a high-throughput distributed messaging system that you can use to facilitate scalable data collection. In this chapter, we detail how to set up an Apache Kafka cluster in a cloud environment and how to monitor the cluster minutely to keep up its performance.

Introduction

Hello Readers, Warm welcome to another enticing topic none other than Apache Kafka! The talk of the tech town!

Kafka is an open-source distributed event/message streaming platform. It has been developed with the intent to maneuver real-time message processing and successfully manifest asynchronous communication between publisher and subscriber. In simpler terms, Kafka is a resilient messaging queue that can accommodate trillions of data events in a day. It works as a message broker between two parties. This chapter is going to provide you a glimpse of Kafka in a practical manner. Let us divide and conquer Apache Kafka into four phases.

Introspecting Kafka

To understand Kafka, we must understand whys ? and whats? associated with it.

WHAT? An easy-peasy way to describe it could be: Kafka is a message queue.

WHY do we need a message queue?

When we build distributed services, we have multiple running process instances that communicate with each other over the network to exchange messages. For example, we have two process networks where a sender process communicates but the receiver process exchanges data. In this case, the sender needs to know the address of the receiver. In addition, both the sender and the receiver need to agree upon a common data protocol. This creates a strong static binding between the two processes. Now suppose we have three receivers each responsible for a different type of processing based on the data received from the sender. In this case, the sender needs to know about all three receivers. The addition of new receivers requires changes on the sender side to configure the new receiver. Again, this creates a strong coupling between the senders and receivers.

Cloud-native Computing: How to Design, Develop, and Secure Microservices and Event-Driven Applications, First Edition. Pethuru Raj, Skylab Vanga, and Akshita Chaudhary.
© 2023 The Institute of Electrical and Electronics Engineers, Inc. Published 2023 by John Wiley & Sons, Inc.

The management becomes a lot more cumbersome when there is the involvement of multiple senders or receivers. Add fault tolerance into the picture and it will get more complex.

A clean and scalable solution here is to use a message queue. Each sender needs to only know about the message queue and simply publish the messages to the queue. A receiver becomes a subscriber and subscribes to the message queue. When a new message appears in the queue, the subscriber is notified, who then proceeds to pull the message and use it. In this case, each of the publishers and subscribers only need to know about the message queue. They are unaware of other publishers and subscribers using the same queue. This is the publish-subscribe pattern also called the pub-sub model. The message queue enables the persistence of data. Therefore, it is beneficial to enhance the fault-tolerant capacity.

We have answered our questions conceptually. Thereby, we can conclude that the idea to capture and transport the messages in real time is called event processing. From a technical perspective, the event can be generated from any point (a database, software application, service, etc.). The goal of this activity can be achieved when an event processing platform is in place. Hence, choosing Kafka is the best choice one can make.

Attributes of Kafka, in brief, are as follows:

- **High throughput** can be achieved with Kafka as it can support multiple publishers and subscribers. As mentioned earlier, it can handle large volumes of data.
- **Low latency** because the communication in a pub-sub model of Kafka can be accomplished within milliseconds.
- **Fault tolerance** ensures the reliable delivery of the messages despite issues with the individual process.
- **Decoupling** is possible in Kafka, as producer and consumer are independent and they need not know about each other which in turn ameliorates the management and the configuration.
- **Backpressure handling** is another advantageous trait of Kafka enabling it to provide a buffer mechanism in the middle to hold data until it is consumed.
- **Horizontal scalability** is also attainable as Kafka can have multiple brokers in the Kafka cluster to deal with the traffic.

Kafka Component Overview

- **Messages**: Kafka's message is a unit of data that is collected, stored, and distributed by Kafka. A Kafka message is also called an event. It can be any piece of data. A message can be equivalent to a row or record in a database. Kafka treats all the messages as a byte array. Messages in Kafka contain a key, this key is used for partitioning the data. Keys are not mandatory and they also need not be unique. The message contains another attribute called value which contains the actual message.
- **Topics**: A topic in Kafka is an entity that holds messages. Messages are stored in topics, which is similar to the file that contains documents. A topic can contain all kinds of messages with different formats. Typically, the topics can be considered as a queue for similar messages. Each topic supports multiple producers to publish data to the topic concurrently. Similarly, multiple consumers can consume data from a single topic. Each topic has multiple partitions. The messages in the topics are distributed across multiple partitions.
- **Kafka Brokers**: A Kafka broker is nothing but a running Kafka instance. It is a physical process that runs on the base operating system and executes all the Kafka functions. The Kafka broker receives

messages from producers and stores them locally in logs. Consumer subscribes to specific topics within the Kafka broker. Kafka broker keeps a heartbeat with every consumer. When a consumer dies, it keeps track and resets. Multiple Kafka brokers form a cluster to achieve load balancing thereby making it resilient. Brokers use Zookeeper to manage and coordinate the cluster. Each broker instance has the capability of handling read and write quantities reaching hundreds of thousands each second (and terabytes of messages) without hampering the performance. Each broker has a unique broker ID. Within a Kafka cluster, there is one Kafka broker instance that will act as the active controller for that cluster. Each partition has a corresponding Kafka broker as its leader. The leader manages that specific partition. A broker also takes care of replicating topic partitions across multiple brokers. Even if one broker goes down, the others can take over the corresponding topic partitions.

- **Kafka Producers and Consumers**: A producer is a client that publishes the messages(data) to Kafka. To build a producer, a developer needs to use a Kafka client library within their code and publish data. These client libraries are compatible with multiple programming languages. The producers need to serialize the message data to bytes. The consumer should make sure to deserialize the same to recreate the data. There are synchronous and asynchronous options available for publishing to Kafka. There can be multiple concurrent consumers per topic and each consumer will get a complete set of messages from the topic. Consumers can also be grouped and share the load. Consumers can manage the offset for the message that they would consume. They can consume from the start of the topic or a specific offset. Consumers also provide acknowledgment to the brokers once they have successfully consumed the message.
- **Kafka Zookeeper**: Zookeeper manages the Kafka brokers. It is a centralized service for storing configuration information. It acts as a central information store for Kafka. Each Kafka broker registers themselves with Zookeeper. The Zookeeper also manages the topics. All the topics and their partitions are registered with Zookeeper. All the components are synchronized with Zookeeper. It provides fault tolerance.

Kafka consists of Records, Topics, Consumers, Producers, Brokers, Logs, Partitions, and Clusters. Records can have key (optional), value, and timestamp. Kafka Records are immutable. A Kafka topic is a stream of records ("/orders", "/user-signups"). You can think of a Topic as a feed name. A Topic has a Log which is the Topic's storage on disk. A Topic Log is broken up into partitions and segments. The Kafka Producer API is used to produce streams of data records. The Kafka Consumer API is used to consume a stream of records from Kafka.

How can Kafka scale if multiple producers and consumers read and write to same Kafka topic log at the same time? First Kafka is fast, Kafka writes to filesystem sequentially which is fast. On a modern fast drive, Kafka can easily write up to 700 MB or more bytes of data a second. Kafka scales write and read by sharing topic logs into partitions. As indicated earlier, topic logs can be split into multiple partitions which can be stored on multiple different servers, and those servers can use multiple disks. Multiple producers can write to different partitions of the same topic. Multiple consumers from multiple consumer groups can read from different partitions efficiently.

Guide to Set Up a Kafka Cluster

After exploring the concepts, it is time to get pragmatic and build our cluster.

Use Case: This guide empowers you to install Apache Kafka on two different Virtual Machines, i.e. two nodes. The following steps will not cover Kafka clients as those are independent applications written in Java or another language plugged in with the Kafka client libraries.

Prerequisites

Specifications of the virtual machines used in this scenario are as follows:

- Cloud: Private cloud is being used in this case. One can choose any public cloud provider such as AWS, Microsoft Azure, or Google Cloud Engine
- Two virtual machines named
  1) Dev-Kafka1
  2) Dev-Kafka2
- Operating system: CentOS Linux 7 (Core)
- RAM: 8 GB
- VCPUs: 4 VCPU
- Volume: 50 GB

Steps to Install

Note: Same steps shall be followed on both the virtual machines based on the desired cluster architecture.

Step 1: Setup virtual machines for Kafka

- Install Java
  sudo yum -y install java-1.8.0-openjdk
- Download and install Kafka Binaries from the latest available mirror link
  sudo yum -y install wget
  sudo wget "<Latest HTTP mirror link>"
  Latest mirror link used in this installation scenario:
  https://mirrors.estointernet.in/apache/kafka/2.8.0/kafka_2.132.8.0.tgz

```
kafka_2.13-2.8.0.tgz
```

- Uncompress the binaries using this command
  tar -xvzf kafka_2.13-2.8.0

There are two main directories in the Kafka installed folder:

1) Bin Directory: The bin folder includes all executables such as various Kafka and Zookeeper tools.
2) Config Directory: The config folder holds two main configuration files.

```
[centos@dev-kafka1 config]$ ls
connect-console-sink.properties      connect-mirror-maker.properties    server.properties
connect-console-source.properties    connect-standalone.properties      tools-log4j.properties
connect-distributed.properties       consumer.properties                trogdor.conf
connect-file-sink.properties         kraft                              zookeeper.properties
connect-file-source.properties       log4j.properties
connect-log4j.properties             producer.properties
```

I) zookeeper.properties
   All the zookeeper configurations are defined in the zookeeper.properties.

II) server.properties
   All the Kafka configurations are defined in the server.properties file.

Add the bin directory in your environment variable. Edit the bash_profile and add the Kafka bin directory path as follows

PATH=$PATH:$HOME/.local/bin:$HOME/bin:$HOME/Kafka/kafka_2.13-2.8.0/bin

Step 2: Configure Zookeeper and Kafka on both the machines

- The Kafka installation directory always contains a copy of the zookeeper. Zookeeper can be configured on any machine.

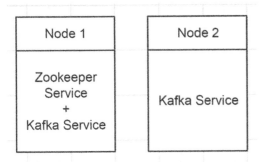

- In this use case, the process of setting up a cluster involves a zookeeper service running on one machine and Kafka running on both machines. In the case of development scenarios when you have multiple machines involved, a zookeeper can be set up on a single instance as well. As we have considered a two-node scenario, we have not dedicated one entire instance for the zookeeper alone. This diagram implies that we have two Kafka brokers with one zookeeper who will manage the cluster. Hence, the zookeeper will be enabled only on Dev-Kafka-1. Rest all the steps will be followed on both the machines.
- To configure both the essential components, we must create a systemd service that always runs as a background process.
- Both Zookeeper and Kafka generate logs and store them in the log directory. This property is configurable in their respective properties file as per user needs. One can change the location of the log directory and store the logs in their folder of choice.

Kafka:

```
# A comma separated list of directories under which to store log files
log.dirs=/home/centos/kafka_logs
```

```
# the directory where the snapshot is stored.
dataDir=/tmp/zookeeper
```

Zookeeper:

- Steps to configure zookeeper and Kafka service

```
[centos@dev-kafka1 ~]$ cd /etc/systemd/system/
```

1) Navigate to the system folder path.
2) Create a new file with ".service" extension. Here, we can create zookeeper.service and kafka.service which contain a list of commands that define the service configurations.

zookeeper.service

```
[UNIT]
Description=zookeeper
Requires=network.target remote-fs.target
After=network.target remote-fs.target

[Service]
Type=simple
User=centos
Group=centos
ExecStart=/home/centos/kafka/kafka_2.13-2.8.0/bin/zookeeper-server-start.sh /home/centos/kafka/kafka_2.13-2.
8.0/config/zookeeper.properties
ExecStop=/home/centos/kafka/kafka_2.13-2.8.0/bin/zookeeper-server-stop.sh
Restart=on-abnormal
SuccessExitStatus=143

[Install]
WantedBy=multi-user.target
~
```

kafka.service

```
[UNIT]
Description=Apache kafka
Requires=zookeeper.service
After=zookeeper.service

[Service]
Type=simple
User=root
Group=root
Environment="/home/centos/scripts/env.sh"
Environment="KAFKA_OPTS=-javaagent:/home/centos/prometheus/jmx_prometheus_javaagent-0.15.0.jar=8081:/home/ce
ntos/prometheus/kafka-2_0_0.yml"
ExecStart=/home/centos/kafka/kafka_2.13-2.8.0/bin/kafka-server-start.sh /home/centos/kafka/kafka_2.13-2.8.0/
config/server.properties
ExecStop=/home/centos/kafka/kafka_2.13-2.8.0/bin/kafka-server-stop.sh
Restart=on-abnormal
SuccessExitStatus=143

[Install]
WantedBy=multi-user.target
```

3) Systemd is a system service manager for Linux-based operating systems. **ExecStart** is the main process of the service. Such units are executed when the script command is to be executed and **ExecStop** script is to be executed when the unit is stopped.

4) To start a zookeeper and Kafka service, the bash script of server-start.sh present in the bin directory is passed in the command along with the zookeeper/Kafka properties configuration file as a parameter. The entire location path needs to be present while execution. This command can be run independently on the command line, however in this case we are configuring it within a service file as systemd daemons can make it easier to supervise and control processes, making it possible to start, stop, and restart services running in the background

5) The service file has been prepared. Now before starting the systemd services, the user must tweak some parameters present in the server.properties file of the Kafka brokers present on both the machines.

   a) In the dev-kafka-2 machine server properties file, edit the zookeeper connection property. Point the connection to the dev-kafka-1, i.e. broker 1 machine's zookeeper.
      zookeeper.connect= <dev-kafka-1-IP>:<2181>

   b) There are other parameters like
      o broker.id
        It is a unique ID property for every broker instance.

o broker.rack

This is a paragon feature that ensures fault tolerance. Kafka distributes replicas of partition over different racks.

o offsets.topic.num.partitions

The default value of this property is 50 which is quite high and can be lowered in the case of a development environment.

o offsets.topic.replication.factor

The default value of the replication factor is 3, but the number of alive brokers has to be equal to at least the replication factor, else the offset topic creation will fail.

o min.insync.replicas

This property is a setting for a topic. It enables to set the minimum number of replicas that is required to exist for the producer to successfully send all records.

6) Run the following commands to reload, start, and stop the created systemd services.

```
# Reload Systemd Manager Configuration
sudo systemctl daemon-reload
```

```
# Start-up Linux Services
sudo systemctl enable zookeeper.service
sudo systemctl enable kafka.service
sudo systemctl start zookeeper.service
sudo systemctl start kafka.service
```

```
# Stop Linux Services
sudo systemctl stop zookeeper.service
sudo systemctl stop kafka.service
```

7) Once you start up the Kafka and zookeeper services, you can check the status of whether the services are running in the background by triggering the following commands on both machines:

```
[centos@dev-kafka1 system]$ sudo systemctl is-active zookeeper.service
active
```

```
[centos@dev-kafka2 ~]$ sudo systemctl is-active kafka.service
active
```

8) If the services are inactive, then the user can check the logs by using this command and troubleshoot the problem.

```
# Check the logs for your services
sudo journalctl -u zookeeper.service
sudo journalctl -u kafka.service
```

Step 3: Test Zookeeper and Kafka installation

- Execute the zookeeper shell and list all the broker IDs associated with it.

```
[centos@dev-kafka1 ~]$ zookeeper-shell.sh localhost:2181 ls /brokers/ids
Connecting to localhost:2181

WATCHER::

WatchedEvent state:SyncConnected type:None path:null
[]
```

Kafka Command Line Features

- Create a topic

```
kafka-topics.sh --create --zookeeper localhost:2181 --partitions 1 --replication-factor 2 --topic test
```

- List all the topics

```
kafka-topics.sh --list --zookeeper localhost:2181
```

- Describe a topic

```
kafka-topics.sh --describe --topic test --zookeeper localhost:2181
```

- Publishing messages to the topic and consuming messages from the topic. This action can be performed through the command line as well as through an independent producer application that acts as a Kafka client.

```
kafka-console-producer.sh --broker-list localhost:9092 --topic test
```

```
kafka-console-consumer.sh \
 --bootstrap-server localhost:9092 \
 --topic test \
 --from-beginning
```

Set Up Your Monitoring Tools for Your Cluster: Prometheus and Grafana

Now it is time to monitor the cluster that we have built. Monitoring is incomplete without the visualization which involves graphical or chart representation based on the desired data source. To visualize Kafka cluster, the significant step is to gather the Kafka Metrics. Prometheus helps us to record real-time metrics of the cluster. Based on the metrics collected by Prometheus, the dashboard is built by the Grafana tool. Grafana and Prometheus are integrated wherein data from Prometheus is used by Grafana to show graphs and charts.

Both Prometheus and Grafana can be run as services in the background. Let us look at the setup steps for the same.

Fetch Metrics Using Prometheus

Install JMX Exporter Agent on Kafka broker

1) To fetch the Kafka Metrics from the cluster, we use Java Management Extensions (JMX) Exporter. As Kafka is built using Java, it extensively uses JMX technology to expose its internal metrics over the JMX platform. JMX exporter is a collector that can run as a part of an existing java application and expose the JMX metrics over an HTTP endpoint which is thereby consumed by Prometheus. To understand this in a better way, let us initiate by creating a folder for Prometheus.

2) Ensure that the following three components are included in this folder: Java agent for Prometheus, YAML Ain't Markup Language (YML) samples for Kafka, and Zookeeper containing the metrics of Kafka and Zookeeper that must be retrieved. These files and java agent are available on the world wide web and can be easily accommodated in the folder. Once we have these three components, we are just required to run this as a java agent.

```
[centos@dev-kafka1 prometheus]$ ls
jmx_prometheus_javaagent-0.15.0.jar   kafka-2_0_0.yml   zookeeper.yml
```

3) As we have a Kafka service running in the background, we also want to fetch the metrics in real time. Hence, instead of running the java agent independently, we will make it run with the service that will enable to fetch all the metrics.

4) Edit the "kafka.service" file and add the following command

```
Environment="KAFKA_OPTS=-javaagent:/home/centos/prometheus/jmx_prometheus_javaagent-0.15.0.jar=8081:/home/centos/prometheus/kafka-2_0_0.yml"
```

Now, your "kafka.service" will look like

```
[UNIT]
Description=Apache kafka
Requires=zookeeper.service
After=zookeeper.service

[Service]
Type=simple
User=root
Group=root
Environment="KAFKA_OPTS=-javaagent:/home/centos/prometheus/jmx_prometheus_javaagent-0.15.0.jar=8081:/home/centos/prometheus/kafka-2_0_0.yml"
ExecStart=/home/centos/kafka/kafka_2.13-2.8.0/bin/kafka-server-start.sh /home/centos/kafka/kafka_2.13-2.8.0/config/server.properties
ExecStop=/home/centos/kafka/kafka_2.13-2.8.0/bin/kafka-server-stop.sh
Restart=on-abnormal
SuccessExitStatus=143

[Install]
WantedBy=multi-user.target
```

5) Repeat the same step to run the java agent in the Zookeeper service using the zookeeper.yml file

```
[UNIT]
Description=zookeeper
Requires=network.target remote-fs.target
After=network.target remote-fs.target

[Service]
Type=simple
User=centos
Group=centos
Environment="KAFKA_OPTS=-javaagent:/home/centos/prometheus/jmx_prometheus_javaagent-0.15.0.jar=8080:/home/centos/prometheus/zookeeper.yml"
ExecStart=/home/centos/kafka/kafka_2.13-2.8.0/bin/zookeeper-server-start.sh /home/centos/kafka/kafka_2.13-2.8.0/config/zookeeper.properties
ExecStop=/home/centos/kafka/kafka_2.13-2.8.0/bin/zookeeper-server-stop.sh
Restart=on-abnormal
SuccessExitStatus=143

[Install]
WantedBy=multi-user.target
```

6) Restart both the services after making changes and check whether metrics are being fetched on the mentioned port of 8080 and 8081. Running the following commands will list all the metrics fetched by the agent.

```
[centos@dev-kafka1 system]$ curl 8080
```

```
[centos@dev-kafka1 system]$ curl 8081
```

Create Prometheus as a service on the Admin machine

1) Download the setup file for Prometheus from the official website to the Admin machine from where you would like to manage your Prometheus.

```
prometheus-2.28.0.linux-amd64.tar.gz
```

2) Unzip the setup file and change the name of the folder to Prometheus.

```
[centos@dev-app1 prometheus]$ ls
console_libraries  consoles  data  LICENSE  NOTICE  prometheus  prometheus.yml  promtool
```

3) Edit "prometheus.yml," if the file does not exist, create a new one. Add the following information about the broker machines. There are two jobs defined in this Prometheus configuration file. Kafka's job includes information on both the Kafka brokers. Zookeeper job includes the broker machine where zookeeper service is running, i.e. dev-Kafka1.

```
global:
  scrape_interval: 10s
  evaluation_interval: 10s
scrape_configs:
  - job_name: 'kafka'
    scrape_interval: 5s
    static_configs:
      - targets: ['10.157.251.104:8081','10.157.250.190:8080']
  - job_name: 'zookeeper'
    scrape_interval: 5s
    static_configs:
      - targets: ['10.157.251.104:8080']
```

4) To check whether your YML file is configured appropriately, run the following command

```
./promtool check config prometheus.yml
```

5) Now Prometheus will scrape out the metrics from all the Kafka brokers. Let us run the Prometheus server using the following command

```
[centos@dev-app1 prometheus]$ ./prometheus
```

6) As the Prometheus server starts, we can check the URL through the web browser on port 9090. If the Prometheus portal is reachable and all the metrics are visible in the query section, this implies that we have configured the Prometheus server successfully.

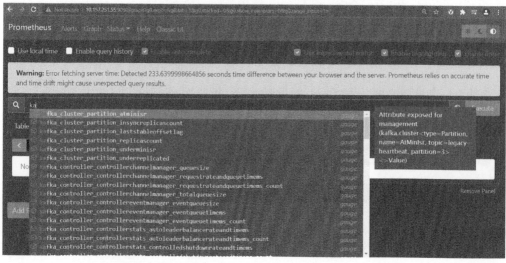

7) Create Prometheus as a systemd service so that it can run successfully in the background.

```
[Unit]
Description:Prometheus Server
After=network-online.target

[Service]
Type=simple
User=centos
ExecStart=/home/centos/prom-grafana/prometheus/prometheus --
config.file=/home/centos/prom-grafana/prometheus/prometheus.yml
--storage.tsdb.path=/home/centos/prom-grafana/prometheus/data

[Install]
WantedBy=multi-user.target
```

Visualize using Grafana

Install Grafana on the Admin machine

1) Download the setup file from the official website of Grafana.

```
[centos@dev-app1 grafana-setup]$ ls
grafana-8.0.3.linux-amd64.tar.gz
```

2) Unzip the file and navigate to the folder to check the contents.

```
[centos@dev-app1 grafana-8.0.3]$ ls
bin    data    nohup.out    plugins-bundled    README.md    VERSION
```

3) Start the Grafana server by executing the nohup command.

```
nohup ./bin/grafana-server &
```

4) Setting up Grafana is quite convenient. As soon as you run the Grafana server as a background service using nohup command. You can check it through the browser with <Machine Ip> : <port 3000>. Enter "admin" for username and password as a default login for the first time. Create new credentials to secure your Grafana portal.

5) In Grafana, the next step is to upload the data from the data source and create dashboards for the same. The data source is Prometheus in this case.

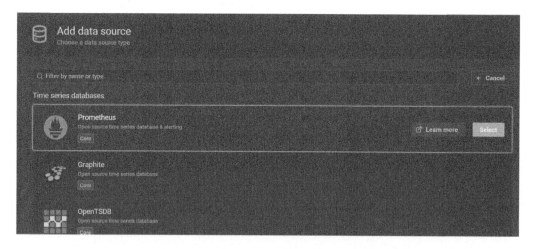

6) Configure the details of the Prometheus server which include the URL and the Port. In this case, Prometheus is running on the same admin machine and the port is 9090.

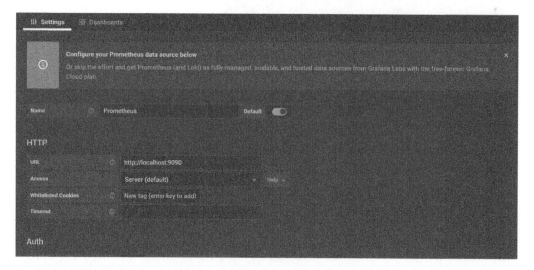

7) After configuration, click on save and test. If the data source details are correct, then the following notification will pop up confirming the same.

8) After updating the data source, create a new dashboard.

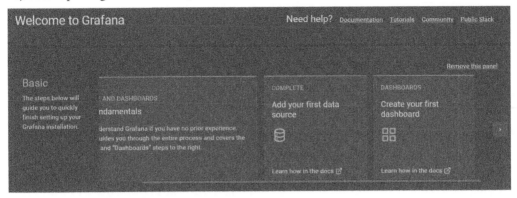

9) On selection of a new dashboard, click on create a new panel that will navigate you to this page. This is the area where the user can select the updated data sources from the dropdown menu. In this case, we have only one imported data source which needs to be used for monitoring purposes.

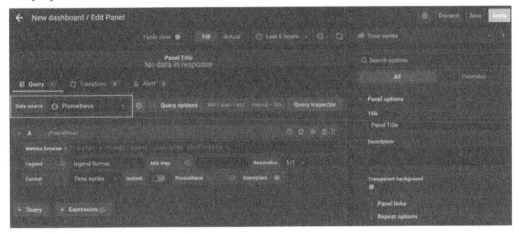

10) Integration of Prometheus enables us to write a Prometheus query to load the specific metric which needs to be monitored. The metric browser consists of all the available metrics.

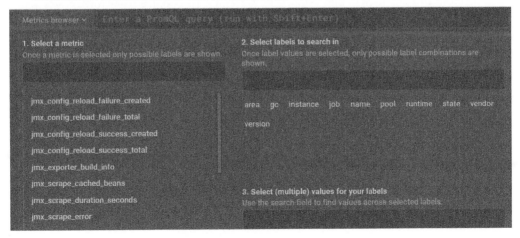

11) An example of some important metrics could be
    - Number of active controllers – should always be 1
    - Number of under replicated partitions – should always be 0
    - Number of offline partitions- should always be 0
12) Finally, all the necessary and required metrics can be considered while creating a dashboard. In Grafana, there are multiple configurable options to make your dashboard look appealing and your monitoring hassle-free. We have finally unveiled the way to integrate your Kafka cluster with Prometheus and Grafana. Thereby kickstarting the journey toward monitoring the notable variables within Kafka.

Secure your cluster

The last phase of this chapter describes the security of the cluster. We have discussed varied aspects in Kafka. Discussing and implementing security is a paramount dimension. Security features and their usage are extremely flexible in Kafka. This can avoid data breaches and attacks at many levels.
We can divide Kafka security into three levels:

1) Encryption
2) Authentication
3) Authorization

These features need to be implemented wherever the communication takes place in the Kafka cluster because the security is hampered at the time of data communication within the cluster. Understanding communication makes our job fairly easy.
Major types of communication within Kafka cluster are

- Zookeeper <-> brokers
- Brokers <-> Producer/Consumers
- Broker <-> Broker

Encryption

- Encryption is a method in which original information that is being sent or received is converted into secret code that hides the real information making it almost impossible for the hacker to decode it. Hence, the process of encoding the data is possible in Kafka cluster.
- Default Protocol that is used in Encryption is PLAINTEXT. This implies when there is no explicit encryption protocol configured, the data is transferred as is.
- The encryption mechanism can be configured: Secure Socket Layer (SSL)/ TLS v1.2

Authentication

- This is the most crucial security layer wherein the identity of the Kafka components communicating with each other is recognized and validated.
- Two major protocols that can be used during Authentication:
  1) Two-way SSL
  2) Simple authentication security layer (SASL)
- Let us implement the SASL authentication mechanism. SASL is a framework that is used to implement authentication in Internet protocols. There are many kinds of SASL mechanisms. It can be implemented using Java Authentication Authorization Service (JAAS), Kerberos, OAUTHBEARER, SCRAM, PLAIN, Delegation tokens.

SCRAM

We are going to implement SCRAM-based SASL mechanism. SCRAM stands for Salted Challenge Response Authentication Mechanism. This type of authentication is done by securely transmitting computed hash value which is based on the secret/password used between two communicating parties.

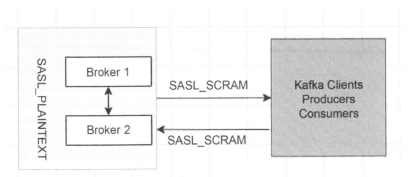

- Kafka supports the use of two hash functions: sha-256 and sha-512.
- Steps to configure SCRAM are as follows:

1) We are going to implement the above-mentioned design for the security layer where the broker-to-client application will use the SASL_SCRAM sha-512 protocol and the inter-broker communication will use SASL_PLAINTEXT

2) In case, if there is a cluster already configured with two-way SSL authentication mechanism, then it can be reconfigured to one-way SSL and two way as SASL_SCRAM

3) Create SCRAM credentials
   - For Kafka broker,

   ```
   kafka-configs.sh --zookeeper localhost:2181 --entity-type users --
   entity-name broker-admin --alter --add-config 'SCRAM-SHA-512=
   [password=TEST@123]'
   ```

   - For Kafka producer, these credentials will be used by Kafka producer while communicating with Kafka.

   ```
   kafka-configs.sh --zookeeper localhost:2181 --entity-type users --
   entity-name sasl-producer --alter --add-config 'SCRAM-SHA-512=
   [password=TEST@123]'
   ```

   - For Kafka consumer,

   ```
   kafka-configs.sh --zookeeper localhost:2181 --entity-type users --
   entity-name sasl-consumer --alter --add-config 'SCRAM-SHA-512=
   [password=TEST@123]'
   ```

   Note: The password can be kept differently unlike demonstrated in this scenario. It can be fairly complicated with the usage of a combination of special characters and digits as well.

4) Edit the server.properties of both the Kafka brokers to add the following configurations for SASL_SCRAM authentication.

   ```
   ######################### SASL Properties between a broker and its client ###################
   security.inter.broker.protocol=SASL_PLAINTEXT

   sasl.enabled.mechanisms=SCRAM-SHA-512
   sasl.mechanism.inter.broker.protocol=SCRAM-SHA-512
   listener.name.sasl_plaintext.scram-sha-512.sasl.jaas.config=org.apache.kafka.common.security.scram.ScramLogi
   nModule required username="broker-admin" password="TEST@123";
   super.users=User:broker-admin
   ```

5) Uncomment the listeners and advertised listener property present in the server.properties file

```
#    EXAMPLE:
#     listeners = PLAINTEXT://your.host.name:9092
listeners=SASL_PLAINTEXT://:9092

# Hostname and port the broker will advertise to producers and consumers. If not set,
# it uses the value for "listeners" if configured.  Otherwise, it will use the value
# returned from java.net.InetAddress.getCanonicalHostName().
advertised.listeners=SASL_PLAINTEXT://:9092
```

6) Finally, these credentials will be used while configuring the producer and consumer applications

Authorization

- Authorization decides the scope of the Kafka client. This security layer permits whether the desired action can be performed or not.
- Authorization is implemented through Access Control List.
- To provide authorization to the above-created user credentials, run the following command. Here we are permitting the Kafka client (Producer) to write to a specific topic named "test."

```
kafka-acls.sh --authorizer-properties
zookeeper.connect=localhost:2181   --add --allow-principal User:sasl-
producer --operation WRITE --operation DESCRIBE --operation
DESCRIBECONFIGS --topic test
```

- Similarly, we can provide permission to read and write the topics and also to a specific consumer group.
- Add the following configuration in both Kafka brokers to implement authorization.

```
#Properties for Authorization
authorizer.class.name=kafka.security.authorizer.AclAuthorizer
```

We have tapped various aspects of Kafka where we got to introduce ourselves to the power of the message queue. This demo has made us realize that it is not strenuous to set up, monitor, and secure your Kafka cluster.

Conclusion

Apache Kafka is an open-source and widely used distributed event streaming platform. This is hugely famous for establishing and sustaining high-performance data pipelines, streaming analytics, and data integration.

Increasingly mission-critical applications are being realized through the Kafka platform. As events (business, personal, social, industry, etc.) abound in scale and complexity, it is essential to meticulously grasp all kinds of events in order and process them with the prime aim of event-driven activation and integration of different and distributed applications and services. Cloud-native applications are going to be predominantly event driven, the role and responsibility of Kafka are well-known. This chapter is prepared with the notion of conveying how to set up and support Kafka to envisage and elegantly implement next-generation cloud-native systems.

Further Reading

1 Apache Software Foundation (2017). Kafka official documentation. https://kafka.apache.org/documentation/

2 Vinod Chelladurai. Kafka security configuration demo guide. https://github.com/vinclv/data-engineering-minds-kafka/tree/main/config/sasl_ssl

3 Abhishek Walia (2021). Monitoring Kafka with Prometheus and Grafana.Blog (29 March). https://www.confluent.io/blog/monitor-kafka-clusters-with-prometheus-grafana-and-confluent/

16

Installing Knative Serving On EKS

THE OBJECTIVES

This document will walk through how to install Knative Serving on Elastic Kubernetes Service (EKS) cluster, along with how to install EKS cluster on AWS and what are the prerequisites for EKS installation.
Amazon Elastic Kubernetes Service (Amazon EKS) is a managed service that you can use to run Kubernetes on Amazon Web Services (AWS) without needing to install, operate, and maintain your own Kubernetes control plane or nodes. Kubernetes is an open-source system for automating the deployment, scaling, and management of containerized applications.

Prerequisites

For installation of EKS cluster, user requires administrator access to create IAM roles and virtual private cloud (VPC) for EKS installation.

EKS Installation Procedure

1) Login to AWS cluster
2) Filter with EKS Services

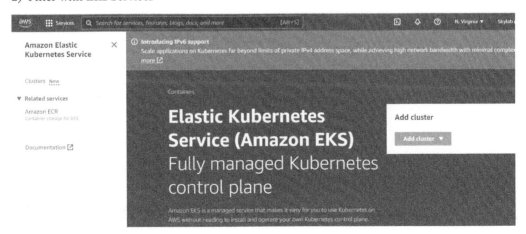

EKS Installation Procedure.

Cloud-native Computing: How to Design, Develop, and Secure Microservices and Event-Driven Applications,
First Edition. Pethuru Raj, Skylab Vanga, and Akshita Chaudhary.
© 2023 The Institute of Electrical and Electronics Engineers, Inc. Published 2023 by John Wiley & Sons, Inc.

3) Click on Add Cluster >> Create cluster

4) Provide Cluster name, Kubernetes version, and role

5) Click on Next and specify networking

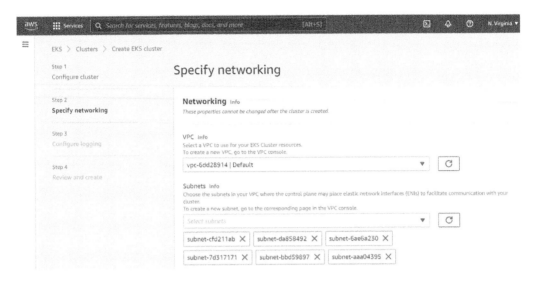

6) Based on Proof of Concept (POC), select the "Cluster endpoint access," that is if the cluster wants access to public or private. The cluster endpoint is accessible from outside of your VPC. Worker node traffic will leave your VPC to connect to the endpoint.

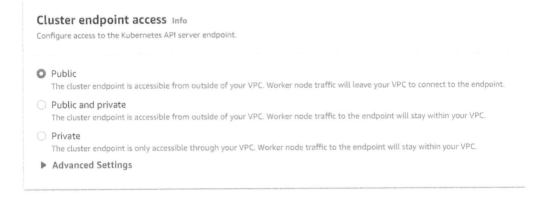

7) Select networking add-ons

Networking add-ons

Configure add-ons that provide advanced networking functionalities on the cluster.

Amazon VPC CNI Info

Enable pod networking within your cluster.

Version
Select the version for this add-on.

v1.10.1-eksbuild.1	▼

> ⓘ This add-on will use the IAM role of the node where it runs. You can change this add-on to use IAM Roles for Service Accounts after cluster creation.

CoreDNS Info

Enable service discovery within your cluster.

Version
Select the version for this add-on.

v1.8.4-eksbuild.1	▼

kube-proxy Info

8) Click on Next

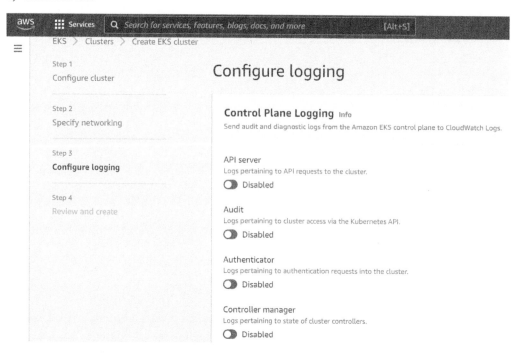

9) Configure logging

Amazon EKS control plane logging provides audit and diagnostic logs directly from the Amazon EKS control plane to CloudWatch Logs in your account.

The following cluster control plane log types are available. Each log type corresponds to a component of the Kubernetes control plane.

Select API server, Audit and Controller manager

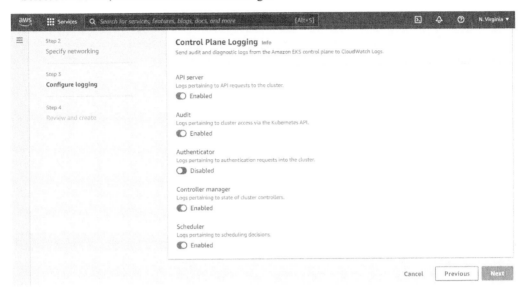

10) Review and create cluster

11) Click on Create

12) Check the status of EKS cluster under EKS >> Cluster

13) Click on cluster check the status

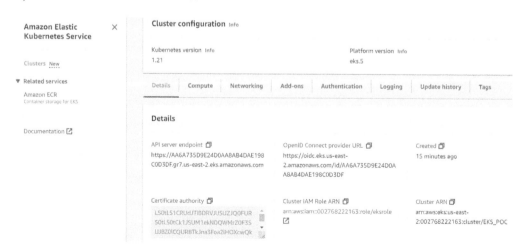

Installing Knative Serving Using YAML Files

Prerequisites

System Requirements

For prototyping purposes, Knative will work on most local deployments of Kubernetes. For example, you can use a local, one-node cluster that has 2 CPU and 4 GB of memory.

For production purposes, it is recommended that:

- If you have only one node in your cluster, you will need at least 6 CPUs, 6 GB of memory, and 30 GB of disk storage.
- If you have multiple nodes in your cluster, for each node you will need at least 2 CPUs, 4 GB of memory, and 20 GB of disk storage.

Before installation, you must meet the following prerequisites:

- You have a cluster that uses Kubernetes v1.18 or newer.
- You have installed the kubectl <u>CLI</u>.
- Your Kubernetes cluster must have access to the Internet, since Kubernetes needs to be able to fetch images.

Install the Serving component

To install the serving component,

1) Install the required custom resources:
   # kubectl apply -f
   https://github.com/knative/serving/releases/download/v0.22.0/serving-crds.yaml

2) Install the core components of Serving:
   # kubectl apply -f
   https://github.com/knative/serving/releases/download/v0.22.0/serving-core.yaml

3) Install a networking layer

   Will following commands install Kourier and enable its Knative integration.

1) Install the Knative Kourier controller:
   # kubectl apply -f https://github.com/knative/net-kourier/releases/download/v0.22.0/
   kourier.yaml

2) To configure Knative Serving to use Kourier by default:

```
kubectl patch configmap/config-network \
  --namespace knative-serving \
  --type merge \
  --patch
  '{"data":{"ingress.class":"kourier.ingress.networking.
  knative.dev"}}'
```

3) Fetch the External IP or CNAME:

 # kubectl --namespace kourier-system get service courier

```
[root@bastion8 skylab]# kubectl --namespace kourier-system get service kourier
NAME      TYPE           CLUSTER-IP      EXTERNAL-IP   PORT(S)                      AGE
kourier   LoadBalancer   172.30.234.146  <pending>     80:32446/TCP,443:31489/TCP   2m18s
[root@bastion8 skylab]#
```

Verify the Installation

Monitor the Knative components until all of the components show a STATUS of Running or Completed:

 # kubectl get pods --namespace knative-serving

```
[root@bastion8 skylab]# kubectl get pods --namespace knative-serving
NAME                                    READY   STATUS    RESTARTS   AGE
3scale-kourier-control-67c86f4f69-5q7j6 1/1     Running   0          3m44s
activator-799bbf59dc-gkmp6              1/1     Running   0          29m
autoscaler-75895c6c95-2qzvw             1/1     Running   0          29m
controller-57956677cf-frq8b             1/1     Running   0          29m
webhook-ff79fddb7-5bfg5                 1/1     Running   0          29m
[root@bastion8 skylab]#
```

Configure DNS

You can configure DNS to prevent the need to run curl commands with a host header.

Install kn Using a Binary

You can install kn by downloading the executable binary in your system and placing it in the system path.

Install kn Using Go

1) Check out the kn client repository:

 # git clone https://github.com/knative/client.git

```
[root@bastion8 skylab]# git clone https://github.com/knative/client.git
Cloning into 'client'...
remote: Enumerating objects: 731, done.
remote: Counting objects: 100% (731/731), done.
remote: Compressing objects: 100% (623/623), done.
remote: Total 26562 (delta 173), reused 297 (delta 77), pack-reused 25831
Receiving objects: 100% (26562/26562), 19.29 MiB | 20.90 MiB/s, done.
Resolving deltas: 100% (16346/16346), done.
[root@bastion8 skylab]#
```

2) Build an executable binary:
   ./build.sh -f

```
[root@bastion8 go_projects]# cd /usr/skylab/client/hack/
[root@bastion8 hack]# ./build.sh -f
⊬ Compile
[root@bastion8 hack]# █
```

3) Move kn into your system path and verify that kn commands are working properly. For example:
   # mv kn /usr/local/bin

```
[root@bastion8 client]# cp kn /usr/local/bin
[root@bastion8 client]# kn version
Version:       v20210409-local-33deb82a
Build Date:    2021-04-09 12:26:38
Git Revision: 33deb82a
Supported APIs:
* Serving
  - serving.knative.dev/v1 (knative-serving v0.22.0)
* Eventing
  - sources.knative.dev/v1alpha2 (knative-eventing v0.22.0)
  - eventing.knative.dev/v1 (knative-eventing v0.22.0)
[root@bastion8 client]# █
```

Sample Application

Creating Your Deployment with the Knative CLI

To create a Service directly at the cluster, use:

   # kn service create helloworld-go --image gcr.io/knative-samples/helloworld-go --env TARGET="Go Sample v1"

```
[root@bastion8 skylab]# kn service create helloworld-go --image gcr.io/knative-samples/helloworld-go --env TARGET="Go Sample v1"
Creating service 'helloworld-go' in namespace 'default':

0.090s The Route is still working to reflect the latest desired specification.
0.109s ...
0.129s Configuration "helloworld-go" is waiting for a Revision to become ready.
23.202s ...
23.307s Ingress has not yet been reconciled.
23.384s Waiting for load balancer to be ready
23.588s Ready to serve.

Service 'helloworld-go' created to latest revision 'helloworld-go-00001' is available at URL:
http://helloworld-go.default.example.com
[root@bastion8 skylab]# █
```

Interacting with Your App

To see if your app has been deployed successfully, you need the URL created by Knative.

1) To find the URL for your service, use either `kn` or `kubectl`
    # kn service describe helloworld-go

```
[root@bastion8 skylab]# kubectl apply --filename config-domain.yaml
error: the path "config-domain.yaml" does not exist
[root@bastion8 skylab]# kn service describe helloworld-go
Name:       helloworld-go
Namespace:  default
Age:        2d
URL:        http://helloworld-go.default.okdcluster.icdscore.local

Revisions:
  100%  @latest (helloworld-go-00001) [1] (2d)
        Image:  gcr.io/knative-samples/helloworld-go (pinned to 5ea96b)

Conditions:
  OK TYPE                   AGE REASON
  ++ Ready                  22s
  ++ ConfigurationsReady     2d
  ++ RoutesReady            22s
[root@bastion8 skylab]#
```

Index

Cloud-native Computing: How to Design, Develop, and Secure Microservices and Event-Driven Applications,
First Edition. Pethuru Raj, Skylab Vanga, and Akshita Chaudhary.
© 2023 The Institute of Electrical and Electronics Engineers, Inc. Published 2023 by John Wiley & Sons, Inc.